INTRODUCTION TO MISSIOLOGY

Introduction to Missiology

Alan R. Tippett

William Carey Library

P.O. Box 40129 • Pasadena, California 91104

William Carey Library
P.O. Box 40129
1705 N. Sierra Bonita Avenue
Pasadena, California 91104

ISBN 0-87808-206-9

Cover Design by Mary Lou Totten

Library of Congress Cataloging-in-Publication Data

Tippett, Alan Richard.
    Introduction to missiology.

    Includes bibliographies and indexes.
    1. Missions—Theory. I. Title.
BV2063.T49   1987   266'.001   86-9605
ISBN 0-87808-206-9

Printed in the United States of America

95   90   89   88   87
 6   5   4   3   2   1

CONTENTS

PART III
THE HISTORICAL DIMENSION

PART IV
THE PRACTICAL DIMENSION: A CLUSTER OF
MISSIOLOGICAL PROBLEMS

PART V
RETROSPECT AND PROSPECT

FIGURES

FOREWORD

It is with great joy that we, backed by our institutions—the Fuller Seminary School of World Mission and the Biola University School of Intercultural Studies—have been able to arrange for the publication of this volume.

Alan R. Tippett possesses one of the keenest missiological minds of this century. When he retired from the Fuller faculty in 1977 to return to his beloved Australia, it was his (and our) hope that he would be able to work over, improve and prepare for publication several of the 30 plus manuscripts filled with a mixture of published and unpublished writing that he took with him into retirement.

For various reasons, such publication has been delayed until now. The present volume is, we hope, but the first of several of these manuscripts to be formally published. It is accompanied by an effort to get photocopies of the whole series into the libraries of our two institutions and, perhaps, into those of other missiological centers as well.

This volume portrays a dynamic discipline in process. Missionaries have served faithfully and courageously for years. The study of what they do, how they do it and how their ministries can be improved is, however, just coming into its own. Furthermore, it is coming into its own at a time when the plethora of problems raised by the present Post-colonial Era need to be dealt with. It is, therefore, not at all adequate for missiologists to simply study what has gone on in the past. We are faced with a whole set of new problems that demand attention, in addition to all of the old ones.

It is in this kind of a context that Tippett taught and wrote. It is the search for principles to enable us to deal effectively with the post-colonial situation that underlies the selections from his writing collected here. As he himself points out in his preface to the book, an "introduction" written in a dynamic context can hardly be expected to provide the "last word." All of us who continue to struggle with the problems Tippett deals with will, however, find his insights and guidelines invaluable.

We want to thank Alan R. Tippett, first of all, for allowing and encouraging us to bring this book to publication. Colleague, mentor and special friend, we thank God continually for bringing you into our lives and into the lives of thousands of His choicest servants around the world.

Secondly, we thank Mr. Larry Caldwell, presently a Ph.D. candidate at the Fuller School of World Mission, for his dedicated labor in getting the manuscript into publishable shape. Without him this book would still be but a dream.

Our thanks also to faithful and hard working secretaries, Sineina Gela and Betty Ann Klebe, to graduate assistants Ian Grant and Nickolay Mak, and to Fuller for providing support for all of these and for Larry Caldwell as well. Finally, we thank the staff of William Carey Library, David Shaver, manager, for their commitment to this project.

May God use this book as He has for many years used its faithful author to bring further glory to His name.

Charles H. Kraft
Marguerite G. Kraft

From "Adventures" to "Introduction"

My friends, Dr. Kraft and his editorial assistant Larry Caldwell, have changed effectively a "Pilgrimage," my "Adventures," into an "Introduction," thereby transforming a personal record for preservation into a functional work for publication. I appreciate their literary operation, whereby the book has been given a more even structure.

An Adventure or Pilgrimage is normally too specific in its contents, too exploratory or experimental in its approach, too dated by its location at fixed points in time and too tentative in its findings, to be an Introduction. Had I originally envisaged this as an "Introduction" no doubt I would have attempted a more systematic approach to the discipline. Missiology, however, came to me out of the raw material of life itself, thus perhaps it is appropriate that this *Introduction to Missiology* reflect the results of my life journey. Maybe a better title would have been an "Introduction *Protem,*" since the discipline has and is developing so rapidly. The contents of this book reflect my contribution to that development.

In their sifting they have dropped out specific items,[1] and selected items from other works for inclusion, to give the *Introduction* more body and balance. This was necessary because the whole was not written at one point in time and this is implicit in the chapters.

However, as the chapters are all mine, this lengthy Preface is called for to safeguard an aspect I most certainly would have included had the *Introduction* been planned as a whole work.

GETTING FROM "ANALYSIS" TO "SYNTHESIS"

The coordinate parts of this *Introduction* are categorized in terms of "Dimensions" — theological, anthropological, historical and practical — Note and this is itself a tool of convenience, a survival of the historical process of our developing the components of a post-colonial missiology at Fuller Seminary's School of World Mission over the 1960s and early 1970s. These were formative years in missiology (if they were not indeed years of fighting for survival) and it seems good to retain this terminological trace of those times in the structure of this *Introduction:* its emerging analysis.[2]

However, an analysis of the parts is never the whole. That presupposition was the error of my generation and led to the compartmentalization of life into segments for specialized consideration as if they were independent isolates. While I fully recognize the importance of specialization, its danger is that we lose our perception of the whole. Worse still, the specialist loses that perception of wholeness. In no area of thought was this more apparent than in theology, unless it was anthropology. These two avoided each other like plagues. Each composed its own lifestyle and set of values as if the other did not exist.

My school life was wrecked by my being forced into certain areas of study at the complete expense of others. The greatest event in my educational life came in my middle years of academic experience when I signed up for my first course designated as "interdisciplinary." I moved from ethnolinguistics, to ethnopsychology, to ethnohistory. They were my academic "highs." They took me into liminal areas to discover the linkages between the disciplines. These discoveries, far from downcrying my old specializations, rather increased their value by seeing how they fitted into each other. I was discovering that life is not analysis, but synthesis.

What then did this mean for missiology? If missiology was to be worth anything in the new age — a Post-colonial Age which was just round the corner — what had to be discovered? What lay between "theology, theory and history of mission" and anthropology (social, theory and history of mission) and anthropology (social, theoretical and applied)? What were the hidden linkages? What were the dynamics (multirelational, cross-cultural and methodological) that would have to be mastered to shape an adequate post-colonial missiology? In the 1950s we were confronted by numerous new, post-war guidebooks and programs for mission, but they offered no answer to these questions. They were utterly colonial. They presumed the survival of colonialism and had bypassed the progressive trends of the 1930s.[3] They heralded no hope, but rather a state of missionary anomie. The missionary world was headed for extinction — at least as far as the Western world was concerned.

Inspiration came from the interdisciplinary courses in American universities which were shouting aloud that analysis and isolation and compartmentalism would get us nowhere. We were challenged to explore the linkages between them, the dynamics of synthesis.

I recall an advertisement which used to appear regularly in *Time* magazine. It comprised a display of the component parts of a telephone system, and had the caption: "Put them all together and dial anywhere!" I knew, of course, that if I put them together I would not be able to get any sound at all on that telephone. That advertisement implied too many unspecified things: that I had the specialist knowledge to know what I was doing, to put the parts together in the correct relationships, that I understood the theory behind their assembly, also that I had the manual skill to do it and knew the safety rules to be observed. Even if I could recognize all the component parts illustrated, and knew their respective functions,

Missiology, itself a communication system like that telephone, activates a whole network of forces — some reaching out beyond itself, others linking up relationship within, systems within systems, variable structures, linkages, synapses, material and immaterial aspects which may be sensed or felt, but not necessarily observed, measured or documented. They interact on each other binding the whole together in a synthesis. It is easy enough to define missiology in terms of its purposes, but there is no living person who can adequately define it as a complex of interacting impulses. It is easy enough to describe missiology in terms of the theological, anthropological, historical and practical dimensions as in this book, but it is quite another matter to present those dimensions as a synthesis or a cohesive entity. There yet remains a great deal of research to be done on the networks which give missiology its cohesion as a discipline.

In light of all this, how should missiology be defined? The simplest definition of missiology is "the study of individuals being brought to God in history," but perhaps for the clear understanding of what lies before us in these pages one should attempt a more formal definition showing the component parts of the discipline. Such a working definition is badly needed. When I wrote the introduction to *Solomon Islands Christianity* (1967a), which was a missiological study, I struggled with a paragraph which had to say that this was "historical but not a history," and with another that had to say it was "anthropological but not an anthropology" and I might well have added a third saying it was "theological but not a theology." It was, in point of fact, missiology, belonging to an interdisciplinary realm, with a vocabulary of its own that somehow needs to be related to the theory and research of each of the related disciplines. Here then is an attempt which I have shared for criticism with my colleagues:

Missiology is defined as the academic discipline or science which researches, records and applies data relating to the biblical origin, the history (including the use of documentary materials), the anthropological principles and techniques and the theological base of the Christian mission. The theory, methodology and data bank are particularly directed towards:

1. the processes by which the Christian message is communicated,

2. the encounters brought about by its proclamation to non-Christians,

3. the planting of the Church and organization of congregations, the incorporation of converts into those congregations, and the growth and relevance of their structures and fellowship, internally to maturity, externally in outreach as the Body of Christ in local situations and beyond, in a variety of culture patterns.

Immediately it will be apparent that such research requires some familiarity with the tools and techniques of anthropology, theology and history. Yet even this is not all. The missiologist may call on the resources of, say, linguistics or psychology. Nevertheless, missiology is a discipline in its own rights.[4] It is not a mere borrower from other fields, for these dimensions are related to each other in a unique manner. They interact, influence and modify each other. Missiology is dynamic not static.

In the 1930's, scholars like Aldous Huxley complained of the imbalance in academic life (its research, personnel involved and funding), its heavy weighting towards analysis and neglect of synthesis. About the same time Alexis Carrel in *Man The Unknown* (1938) warned us that some branches of science had gone far ahead of others and the world would face serious strife if the imbalance was not corrected. The sad history of the world since that time reveals how prophetically he was speaking. When McGavran established his Institute at Eugene, one of the firm tenets of his platform of principles was Research. He urged for its inclusion in the budget of every new mission project. As a result of that program we have been able to analyse the dimensions and components of missiology. Now it is even more urgent that we learn how to synthesise the results of our analytical research. The missiological value of ethnolinguistics, ethnotheology, ethnohistory, ethnopsychology, etc., etc., now lies open before us as we search out linkages and integrating relationships which can hardly be measured or documented, although they give both mission and missiology their cohesive synthesis.

RESEARCHING SYNTHESIS: A COOPERATIVE ACTIVITY

Once we have established the need for researching the character of the process of synthesis, and the manner in which a network of forces gives both mission operations and missiology their cohesion, and have determined to start our research with elements already identified in ethnotheology, ethnolinguistics, ethnohistory, ethnopsychology, ethnomusicology, etc., etc., we must recognize that all these methodologies (they are not really disciplines or subdisciplines, but methods that emerge when two disciplines interact) are cooperative exercises. Missiology likewise requires the interaction of more than one mind, more than one system, more than one methodology. There is no such person as a solitary missiologist. He or she is always involved in some kind of cooperative action, always drawing from someone else and always giving something as well.

Always when two methodologies come together in interaction something new is born. It is not the conjunction of two methods with the option of using either or both. Something quite new is born. In my writing I have called this *Syngenesis,* a new birth, something new created in the interplay. I venture to suggest that one of the great experiences awaiting missiologists of the new day, after my demise, will be the exploration of new insights born in yet-to-be-discovered interrelationships of this kind. But being cooperative achievements, they cannot be discovered until interdisciplinary fields are properly explored.

We had a man come to us to do his Ph.D. He was a superb scholar and researcher but had "fallen between two stools" at the best English universities, because the Professor of Theology and the Professor of Anthropology could not interact academically, and neither could come to terms with such a notion as "ethnotheology."

There was a period in my own struggles as a missionary doing anthropology, when I found anthropologists drawing on historical data in a quite uncritical manner; and top historians using cultural specifics as generalities regardless of their contexts. In each case their findings were manifestly wrong. Each needed the other. They saw ethnohistory as the sum of the two, and each treated their own field critically and was simplistic with the other's. This kind of "ethnohistory" was an impediment to each. Each needed a methodology born of interaction.[5] Missiology draws from all the social and human sciences and if the interaction is genuine something methodologically new will be born and missiology will expand.

COHESIVE COMPLEXES WITHIN THE GREATER WHOLE

Just as the community (meaning people) is composed of smaller communities within the community, and these provide the sociological base of people movements, and group dynamics, so too social structures have smaller structures within them, and these smaller components may be held together with significant cohesion. They hang together, and resist change. One element will not change unless the whole cluster is socially ready for change, and then all the elements will change together.

This has been well demonstrated in anthropology.[6] Sapir demonstrated it in the study of linguistic drift.[7] It features in the breakdown of the reservoir of tension in tribal conversion from animism,[8] and explains the survival of clusters of animism in Christopaganism.[9] It is a key to the interpretation of the significance of the small group in modern evangelism, of house churches, of the old fashioned Wesleyan class meeting in the larger whole, and indeed of the Wesleyan movement itself within Anglicanism while John Wesley was still living.[10] In urban church growth studies it explains why, when a congregation becomes too large statistically for the pastor to know all his flock, the operation of small groups is so fundamental. The principle is of equal importance and application to either the African or urban jungle.

This aspect of the social cohesion of cultural clusters and small groups within the larger whole is so widespread in its relevance at both the discipling and the perfecting levels of church growth that it is certain to be the subject of many theses and dissertations still to come, both the interpretation of case studies and the advocacy of methods of evangelism.

In the history and dynamics of missiology itself this principle may be seen positively in the cohesion of the church growth movement in spite of denominational differences (e.g. at Eugene) and negatively in the resistances to church growth by the fundamentalist literalists.

AN "INTRODUCTION TO MISSIOLOGY" MUST BE OPEN-ENDED

This book has to be left open-ended. Missiology is not a static thing. It grows. It adapts. It relates to the ever changing world. Yet in every new situation it must also retain its own internal integration.

Every new aspect of learning, new technologies, new research methods, new modes of communication, new revelations of truth, will influence its form, and require a new synthesis. Synthesis is not a "once-and-for-all" fact. That would make it static. It responds to new environments, interacts with new contexts, speaks to new situations, and meets new felt needs. It never rests.

No person can ever know all there is to know about missiology, because it is always an ongoing entity, relating afresh to new forms of social, cultural and other kinds of change. This will continue until the end of the age.

Even so, although we can never fully understand missiology, it must always be integrated by cooperative endeavor at every given point in time and place. The nature of communication may change but the Gospel itself must be continually communicated. The structure of the church may change through time, and place, and culture, but there must always be a church. In time, place and culture again, research methods will change, but research itself must never stop. New subdisciplines may emerge but they must not remain untapped isolates. Missiology must relate to all continuing systems and speak to all felt needs everywhere in time, place and culture until He comes again.

Missiology will be continually expanding by syngenesis, and continually discarding elements that are outmoded. With each change in its character it will need to reestablish itself as a cohesive whole. With each new situation the expansions and reductions of missiology will require critical appraisal by missiologists. In other words, all missiological theory must be tested and all missiologists are to be held responsible, in terms of the theology of stewardship.[11]

If missiology is to be a valid construct it must have an inbuilt system of self-examination. Missiologists must interact, not only with scholars from other disciplines, but among themselves. From the very start of McGavran's Institute at Eugene he demanded this of his research fellows, and at Fuller Seminary's School of World Mission, of the faculty. We knew that although our theology was fairly conservative our methodology was radical, so much so that new terminology was continually required. So much of what is now accepted post-colonial missiology was thrashed out there by debate and self-exposure. The basic principle laid down there was an interrelationship of three factors: credible theoretical analysis and models; models tested and applied in field situations; and their critical exposure among missiological peers.

New missiological theory comes out of the mission field situation, and eventually returns to the field for practical testing after academic testing by experienced missiologists as a team. These are essential validity tests for the formulation of new missiological theory. This is a major change for the old colonial missiology which was largely determined by home church theologians who set Board policy and determined strategy on a basis of "absolutes" without regard for cultural contexts. This led to much discord between Board officials and field missionaries, although the critical world has held the latter responsible for the colonial mission errors.

Having attempted to interact with Continental missiologists at many of the vital points of mission field growth I have often found them academically sophisticated and theoretical, but unable to cross a cultural barrier. Moreover, quite often their graduates are normally devoted to a type of institutional mission that has no cultural relevance and plants a small foreign church—if it plants one at all. I knew one such mission station which announced in a sign over the front gate: "Tradition is the Enemy of Progress." Missiological theory has to come from the field, not from the West. And it has to demonstrate its fruit in the field.

Missiology is important in Western theological and missionary training institutions to assist missionary candidates to forget themselves and to get immersed into cross-cultural situations, to appreciate the other culture's values and felt needs and to help candidates in these new worlds to achieve their own Christian selfhood there. The justification for missiology's existence as a discipline is just that very thing. If it produces advocates of a foreign church it has failed. That is why missiological theory should both originate and be applied on the mission field itself.

As an academic "go between" the missiologist has not only to prepare the missionary candidate for the cross-cultural experience but to do it in a manner which also validates the missiologist's procedures in the academic world of the West from which the missionary candidates come. A doctoral degree in missiology has to be a valid doctoral degree. That means missiology has to be validated as a discipline in a Western educational system. That requires a continuing validation year after year, a continuing updating, a continual retesting by reference to other disciplines. There has to be a professional forum of some kind among qualified missiologists with the regular widening of the personnel. This is why missiology and the post-colonial approach was so long delayed in emerging.

The offering of a degree in missiology really requires a faculty with a number of trained missiologists so that this interaction is possible and so that its degrees can be widely assessed. In the case of an institution with a solitary professor of mission, that person is so greatly handicapped by the deprival of peer interaction that the institution is duty bound to demand and provide for regular attendance at seminars and conferences, not only in missiology but also in other interdiscipinary societies like ethnohistory, say. Furthermore, that same person should arrange for some field contact that may be made regularly, say, in-term vacations: something cross-cultural either urban or rural, so that he or she never forgets the existence of other worldviews. Over my own twelve years in the School of World Mission as a missiologist I made thirteen visits to the Navaho reservation and off reservation towns. They varied from a long weekend to a month or so. I saw the social change in process. They kept alive my cross-cultural awareness. I observed various missions at work with different methods of communication. I established rapport with a number of Navaho friends with whom I could share. I found this essential to my missiological awareness.

I was making the point that missiology has to be open-ended; always exposed to new ideas, drawing from outside itself, and reexamining within, always seeking relevance in its theoretical and practical acceptances.

With such an approach we will also be confronted with some ideas and structures that may need to be discarded rather than accepted. A situation has changed and something is no longer relevant. Some battle has been won and an item is no longer needed. A better way of achieving an old purpose has been found. Something has just been outmoded. Sometimes the missiologist is faced with the task of disposal and the decision of when and how to dispose of an item, policy, strategy, or procedure when there is some sentimental attachment to it.

Sometimes things are discarded unintentionally, dropped because they are difficult, or nobody wants to do them, or by plain neglect. Or perhaps an emphasis on one feature is at the expense of another. Missiology has to see that balance is maintained and things are not discarded if the need for them is still there and no better functional substitute has been found to meet it.

That is true both on the field and within missiology itself as a methodology. Examples are not hard to find. A technique is dropped because it is time consuming or difficult, and a faster but less accurate substitute is used.[12] A basic aspect of the essential whole is dropped because nobody wants to teach it, say.[13] These can be serious losses, and leave a dimensional void in the total missiology itself which must affect the validity of the training.

Finally a word to the missiologist and missionary as persons. I found when I explored a new interdisciplinary area, however far the content seemed to be from missiology I always got something worth while out of the phenomenon of the interdisciplinary interaction itself. It always said something to me in missiology. I have continually found new approaches, methods of testing and useful models, that have been applicable to the Lord's work with good effect. I reiterate that missiology is never complete. There is always something out there awaiting discovery and application.

I cannot give you a complete and final outline of missiology in my *Introduction.* Neither is your work as a missiologist ever complete. As long as there is change going on in the world both missiology and the missiologist must change, too.

And to the missionary: You must distinguish the eternal from the changing, and allow for both. You serve an eternal Lord, and communicate an eternal Gospel. You translate the written Word, and form converts into fellowship groups. These are eternal tasks in an everchanging world. You fix your sights on the Eternal, but everything you do has to be relevant and meaningful in the terms of the culture and situations wherein you minister until He comes. That you may be effective in this ministry or stewardship, missiology has come into being to help you. That is its goal, that the Great Commission of Jesus to His Church may continue in our day and generation, and the Gospel may be heard, the lives of people transformed, and they may be incorporated into His Church and have fellowship with Him and with each other. The existence of missiology as a field of study is justifiable only if it expedites this purpose.

Notes:

1. Items eliminated because of their specificity may be found still in the original bound *Adventures in Missiology* (1972) at St. Mark's Library, Canberra, or at Fuller Seminary's School of World Mission in Pasadena.

2. McGavran was known by *Bridges of God* (1955), and *How Churches Grow* (1959). His major missiological work, *Understanding Church Growth* (1970) had not yet appeared. Our instrument of literary exchange at the time was the *Church Growth Bulletin.* We were still in the period of analysis.

3. Roland Allen: *Missionary Methods* (1930), *Spontaneous Expansion of the Church* (1927); S.J.W. Clark: *Indigenous Church* (1928), *Indigenous Fruit* (1933); A.S. McNairn: *Native Church: Exotic or Indigenous* (1934); A. McLeish: *Jesus Christ & World Evangelization* (1934); Peill & Rowlands: *Church Planting* (1924), etc.

4. Some critics have objected to the term *missiology* because of its derivation, being half Latin and half Greek. The English word *mission* came into common use in a number of ways in the 16th and 17th centuries—theological, ecclesiastical and political. The common element was the act of sending forth with authority. Although the word itself is not biblical the concept is. Whether we see the Christian mission as "in the world" (Jn. 17:18) or "to the nations of the world" (Mt. 28:19) both are sendings forth under the authority of Christ and thus the modern word *mission* would seem appropriate.

The suffix *ology* from the Greek logia, is regularly used in modern lexical *formations,* especially as referring to "science and departments of science." Since the beginning of the last century this procedure has been used in English to define new areas of scientific study, regardless of the character of the root to which the suffix is affixed: i.e. in modern usage it makes no real difference that a Latin root may have a Greek suffix. Many such words came into English scientific writing in the last century via the European languages, and the process is still active. Sociology, terminology, numerology, methodology, scientology and culturology are examples.

For further discussion on the term "missiology" see Myklebust: *The Study of Missions in Theological Education,* (1955; 1:26-31), and Webster: "Should Our Image of Missions Go?"

5. For numerous examples of this, see my *Aspects of Pacific Ethnohistory* (1973c).

6. See Kroeber: *Anthropology* (1948) for an example of the rejection of an advocated idea because the time was not ripe, then its acceptance a few years later. Relate to my *Church Growth and the Word of God* (1970a).

7. See Chapters on "Phonetic Law" & "Linguistic Drift" in *Language* (1949a) where "p.t. & k" are discussed as a cohesive cluster.

8. See *People Movements in Southern Polynesia* (1971:281), and *Verdict Theology in Missionary Theory* (1973a:117, 122-124, 133-147).

9. See Taber and Yamamori (eds.) *Christopaganism or Indigenous Christianity?* (1975).

10. *Ecclesiola in ecclesia:* "a little church within a church."

11. If there is to be a human side in the program of Christian mission there has to be a strong doctrine of responsible stewardship under God in it. This theology is strong in church growth writing. See *Church Growth and the Word of God* (1970a:17, 18, 41, 56, 68, 72), for example.

12. Thus I deeply regret the loss of logarithmic graphs for percentage growth charting. They validated our techniques with many sociologists and made our case studies more quotable. Furthermore, they were more accurate graphics.

13. For example, what a tragedy it would be for the teaching of ethnohistory to be dropped in this way. Some of our very best case studies have come from its methodology.

INTRODUCTION

The Dimensions of Missiological Theory

The two basic dimensions of missiological theory and action may be designated as (1) *theological* and (2) *anthropological* — theological, because the message is a word from God concerning His purpose for, and promise to mankind; anthropological because it has to be communicated within the structure and organization of human societies. This message is theological because it concerns not only the inner life of an individual, one's spiritual experience, but also one's eternal state. It is anthropological because this takes place in an earthly environment on which humans depend for their physical life and where these spiritual experiences have to be worked out in a series of human relationships that are culturally conditioned. When Jesus spoke of the disciples as being *not of this world,* and yet in the same utterance as being also *in the world,* he was demonstrating a basic dichotomy in the Christian mission. Both in missionary policy making and in missionary action in the world these two dimensions must be kept in *equilibrium.*

While it is true that we cannot say the Church will certainly grow because of this balance, for in the last analysis the growth is of God, nevertheless we can safely affirm the opposite, namely, that growth will be obstructed when these dimensions are in a state of imbalance. This obstruction of church growth due to human missionary policy and action that develops one dimension at the expense of the other, may be called in

The original shortened version of this chapter was published in *Church Growth Bulletin,* September 1969, Vol. VI, No. 1, pp. 1-3, under the title, "The Components of Missionary Theory." Gratitude is hereby expressed to the publisher to include it here.

biblical phrase, "limiting the Holy One of Israel" or "quenching the Spirit." Both the Old and New Testament thus speak of human attitudes that hinder the work of God. If we are to be engaged in carrying out the Great Commission, the terminology of which suggests it is to be operative until the end and is therefore applicable to us today, we ought to ask the question: Do our attitudes as reflected in either our missionary policy or action help or hinder the purpose of God in the world and for the world?

We can also affirm that if we are to create (as far as is humanly possible) a "climate" which is propitious for church planting and church growth we should pay attention to the balance of these two dimensions in our missionary policy and action. In both my reading of church history from the dynamic position and in church growth research I observe some undefined but nevertheless definite relationship between balanced policy and action on the one hand, and the manifest blessing of God in the form of quantitative or qualitative growth on the other.

THE THEOLOGICAL DIMENSION

When I speak of the theological dimension in missiological theory and action I am not thinking in denominational terms. Church growth cross-denominational studies show clearly that this can be discounted as a factor in growth. Those critics who imagine church growth as denominational church extension have not read much about church growth. The theological dimension concerns the nature and content of the message. The idea of mission, if not the word, is scriptural. If this is to be our norm we have a message to proclaim, an experience to share through witness, a goal of bringing individuals to Christ and then into a fellowship of believers, and thence into the world again to participate in service and witness. The whole we call the *ministry* of the Church. That part which communicates the good news in one way or another we call the *mission*. Both this salvation theme and the idea of its communication to mankind run through the Scriptures. Whether you accept my semantics or not you must accept this basic theological dimension—that is, if you accept the Bible on its own terms.

When mission policy and/or action is theologically defective in its basic concept of mission we frequently find one of two effects—either the subsequent growth is warped in some way, or the church that was planted has become static. The New Testament struggles with syncretism show that warped growth was a real problem from the start. I have seen some tragic cases of syncretism in supposedly Christian churches that can be traced back to defective theological nurture in the planting days. Sometimes a church is planted by means of a service project, but the theological dimension is not developed. It is planted in a time of some crisis and gains some initial growth. Then it is static for a century. The problem of Christian/pagan coexistence, especially where a church comprises half a tribe and has resigned itself to a coexistence without a missionary sense of responsibility to the other half, is another example of a defective theological dimension. It may have been defective advocacy or defective follow up—but it is theological.

THE ANTHROPOLOGICAL DIMENSION

The anthropological dimension of missiological theory and action reminds us that "our conversation is in this world." We deal with human beings in human situations, with felt needs that have to be met, and personal relationships that have to be preserved. They live in formal or customary structures and communicate in the language that suits their condition. In many diverse cultural situations the Church at large is represented by a local fellowship which must be relevant in that cultural situation. An *enclosed* or *sealed off* church, a church which contributes to social projects but never participates, which has no concern for social justice, is defective in the anthropological dimension of mission. It also tends to become static.

Faith and function have to be kept in equilibrium, belief and action, the theological and the anthropological, the hope beyond and the situation in this world. My categories are abstractions for the purpose of analysis. In reality they integrate into each other, but it was our Lord who made the distinction in the first place. Although we have to aspire to things not of this world, we must witness in the world and win the world for Christ. To be faithful in this and to pay attention to it in our theory and practice so that neither dimension is neglected seems to me to be, at least, a serious attempt to bring our programs into line with what Jesus revealed of his will in mission. One is therefore not surprised that research does suggest a frequent relationship between such a policy and effective church growth. Although the harvest is of God, He certainly allows the farmer's part to count for something in the harvesting.

As ethnography is the basis of anthropological theory, so research into the planting and growth of churches provides the data and repetitive patterns, the missiological ethnography, on which a theory of mission can be based. This research is in harmony with the experiences of both the New Testament Church and the history of the expansion of Christianity, and time after time we find ourselves saying that the Bible still speaks to us today. Despite the changing environment due to technological advance and acculturation the basic issues the Church has to face in mission are not new. The theoretical principles of church planting and cultivation are abiding. Of course the environment, the cultural forms and historical factors will differ from field to field and from generation to generation, but the basic principles remain. Thus there are two dimensions—one theological, biblical, abiding; the other anthropological, which applies and relates that which is abiding to each precise situation where individuals need to be won for Christ.

All this takes place in history. The equilibrium of theology and anthropology must be maintained in human history. The Creator God initiated the dimension of history when He determined a time span for human activity on this earth. In history He revealed His way of salvation. History is the arena for mission. The written record from which we have our commission is an historical document, recording historical events quite as much as philosophical and symbolic concepts. That commission is valid, by the word of Jesus, to the end of the age. Thus is the Christian mission set firmly in time. Elsewhere (1970a:73) I have developed the notion that "this Christian mission was commissioned in history, is continuous through history, and finds finality only when history itself comes to an end."

Figure 1 illustrates, in a simplified way, the relationship between theology, anthropology and history, and how missiology combines and expands upon all three dimensions. Figure 2 is a more detailed refinement of these interacting elements.

FIGURE 1
A Breakdown of the Dimensions of Missiology

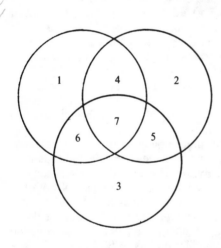

1. Theology
2. Anthropology
3. History
4. Ethnotheology
5. Ethnohistory
6. Expansion of the Church
7. Theory and Theology of Mission

What follows in Parts I, II and III of this *Introduction to Missiology* is an analysis of some of the different aspects of these three overarching dimensions of missiology: the theological, the anthropological and the historical. Part IV will address the practical dimension of missiology which incorporates all three of these other dimensions to one degree or another.

FIGURE 2
The Interacting Elements of Missiology

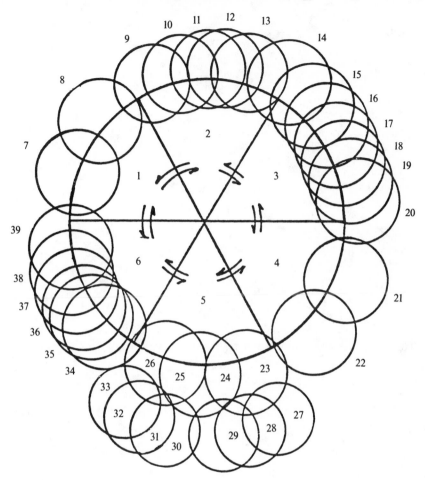

1. Theology of Mission
2. History of Missions
3. Research
4. Encounter with Other Religions
5. Mission Methods and Techniques
6. Missions Across Cultures
7. Historical
8. Biblical
9. Biblical History
10. Church History
11. Modern Missions
12. Ecumenical Studies

13. Current Problems
14. Ethnohistory
15. Data Collecting
16. Evaluation
17. Comparison
18. Reporting
19. Data Bank
20. Dissemination
21. Comparative Religion
22. Theory Communication
23. Communication Techniques
24. Missionary Training
25. Church Growth
26. Church Planting
27. Leadership Training
28. Christian Education
29. Church Renewal
30. Extension Education
31. Conversion
32. Consummating
33. Organization
34. Cross-Cultural Communication
35. Ethnolinguistics
36. Culture & Personality
37. Primitive Religion
38. Applied Anthropology
39. Social Anthropology

PART I

The Theological Dimension

PART I

The Theological Dimension

No amount of proficiency in the other component disciplines of missiology and their methods of research will compensate for shortcomings in the theological dimension. Much so-called theory of mission today stands on the false assumption of noncommitment and the mere notion of Christian presence being Christian mission. This is not to challenge the value of the notion of Christian presence *per se,* but it certainly is to deny that just "being there" as a Christian is an adequate conception of mission, for our definition of Christian mission is to strive to bring individuals out of paganism so that they may confess that Jesus is Lord.

It seems to me that the theological dimension of missiology should have the following structure:

1. It begins with an act of *faith* and *acceptance* on the part of the missiologist. The missiologist is personally involved in some way. This is not an objective philosophy from a distance. Missiologists should have *convictions* in their discipline.

2. It must have some firm base with *authority* and a set of *criteria* as mechanisms for evaluating policies and techniques of mission.

3. It must operate within or with respect to some definite *frame(s) of reference* or *context(s).* For the time being these may be specified as (1) the fellowship group (the Church) and (2) the world.

4. It must formulate a *theology of mission, church planting and growth,* which is concretely defined and located within the total system of Christian theology. It must be competent to come to grips with any inadequate theology which threatens the biblical base of the missiology.

Not all "missiologists" will accept this final sentence. Some may regard it as apologetic rather than descriptive. Nevertheless it comes within the orbit of my *Introduction to Missiology* in which I have defined Christian mission in the terms of Matthew 28:18-20 and John 17:14-18. To me any idea of mission or missiology which fails to line up with these words of our Lord is ruled out "by definition."

In this section, therefore, I have selected studies which fall within the above structure. These are not presented as a polemic for disputation with theologians with some nonbiblical view of mission. I merely narrate my spiritual adventures for any reader who will to share my experience. I do not feel disposed to argue the *pro* and *con* of the semantics of missionary theory.

The missiologist's personal theology tends to condition his or her definitions and goals. This brings the evangelical into conflict with the universalist and demythologizer, who are more common among mission policymakers at home than on the field. But the missiologist and the field missionary must both have confidence in their missiology and its methodology. They must have personal conviction in their faith, confidence in their message and reliance in their approved criteria. They must be aware of the precise nature of the contexts within which their specialization has to be applied.

In any interdisciplinary area of theory and research the component parts must demonstrate a certain harmony. Either they must fuse together as one or they must operate in symbiotic relationship. In this book I have argued that missiology is itself a *new* discipline, more than just the *sum* of the components, because they exist in new relationships and interact creatively upon each other. The interplay of theology must not injure the techniques of history and anthropology. One's research must remain adequately historical and anthropological on the one hand and adequately undergirded with valid theology on the other. In this section I have tried to show that this condition can be met by a simple biblical faith. On the level of personal experience we have Christ as Lord. On the level of the fellowship group we have an organism (the Church) with both an inner life and an outreaching field of activity—both being part of what we might call "church growth." At both levels the Holy Spirit is at work actively using Christians, individually and in fellowship, to win responses for Jesus Christ.

The theology of church growth, on which an adequate missiology may be based, is only part of Christian theology, and indeed, only part of the theology of the ministry of the Church. It is that part especially concerned with the conversion of individuals and their incorporation into the fellowship, that they may go forth to witness and serve. This is not to deny the other aspects of Christian theology, which are recognized as essential to the totality of our religious experience and operation.

This theological section ends with some current trends which have had, and are continuing to have, tremendous effect on the theological dimension of missiology. Such trends as power encounter, contextualization and indigeneity, to name but a few, cause us as missiologists to rethink our sometimes rather staid theological presuppositions.

As the chapters in this section were prepared originally for different purposes, some repetition of these basic ideas may be found, but I leave the studies essentially as they were first given in the hope that any repetition will impress the reader that this *Introduction to Missiology* has a theological constant.

CHAPTER 1

The Faith of a
Social Anthropologist

The emphasis in this first chapter lies more on that word, *FAITH*, than on the discipline in which I am at work. This is not a scientific analysis of collected data such as one would use to test some hypothesis. It is simply a statement of faith—a testimony, if you like. At the same time I hope to put before you a set of beliefs which *do* form a practical frame of reference which I find adequate for my life. I do not intend probing the theological dimensions or implications of this faith. My purpose is rather to present a structure, a pattern of faith, which does not compartmentalize science here and religion there, but accepts the psalmist's claim that "The earth is the Lord's and the fullness thereof" (Ps. 24:1).

I BELIEVE IN GOD

Either the creation (i.e. the physical universe, including this world and what is on it) has come into being by accident or it was the result of design and purpose. I see no other alternatives. This applies also to the human race and each individual in it. When I consider these two options in the light of all the scientific data available to me (which I must admit is small compared with that which the next generation will have at its disposal) I must confess that I am much more disposed to believe in some design and purpose than to believe all this came into being by accident. Even if I argue that life begets life and culture begets culture, or even if phenomena is found to operate because of some inherent power or life or law, I have still to account for the original emergence of that power, life or law. How did it come to be there in the first place? The more I delve into this problem, the more I am convinced that the only tenable position is that "Someone" capable of design and purpose set it there.

6

Rom 12: 1-2

My training as a social anthropologist gives me a particular interest in patterns—social structure, patterns of culture. I do not believe these structures ever come into being by accident. In our social studies we ask why this or that pattern exists and quite frequently, especially when we engage in careful diachronic studies, we are able to isolate the forces responsible, and sometimes the persons behind the forces.

As I look at the patterns of life, I find a life force from outside myself which influences me. To a certain extent I can develop myself. I can also recognize factors about me in my environment which bear upon me. But beyond *all* that I can see and measure, there is still a purposive force which I have not accounted for.

Passing from my individual introspection to the human community at large, once more, as I examine societies and cultures, I am aware of this same "force" greater than humanity itself, wider than the observable and measureable environment of mankind. I see it also in the inanimate creation and in space.

Now I must admit that I see all this differently from some people. An atheistic spaceman returns to earth and says he found "Nobody" out there. A theistic spaceman returns and says "I found God with me everywhere." This only shows how differently we view our data and what we bring of our own orientation to our interpretations. As with the computer we get back what we first feed in. We pride ourselves in our objectivity, but in the last analysis our science stands on what we believe.

Some say that science is closing up the gaps in knowledge and some day we shall know everything about the physical universe and mankind will have no further need for religious belief. As I look at science, this is not the impression I get. Each new discovery rather opens up whole realms of mystery for further exploration. If it shows us anything—it reveals further design or patterning, which only strengthens my conviction of a "Mind" behind it all.

So this is the first thing I believe—the existence of a life force outside myself, a force greater than humanity and bigger than the created world. This Force I shall call *God.* If we allow the poet licence for poetic symbolism or anthropomorphism, I have no trouble in singing the song: "Somebody bigger than you or I."

② *I BELIEVE IN A LIVING GOD*

Can we go further and discover something more about this God in whom I believe? I eliminate first a number of popular beliefs which, to me, are untenable.

Having accepted the idea of God as Creator, I reject the idea of a Creator who has completed his work and "retired" as it were. This is a common idea among some people with whom I have worked. It requires the conceptualization of new contemporary deities to account for the unmeasured forces currently at work in human life. There is some primitive logic in this view, but I see no reason for believing that the current creation processes do not stem from the same "Force" that has operated from the beginning. There has been no change in their scientific or spiritual character to suggest a change of Cause.

Another animistic belief is found in the supposed existence of a supply of *mana* or power which can be built up quantitatively and stored for good or evil intent, and that this may be acquired by reciting certain magical formulae to a fetish. I do not deny the existence of powers for good and evil and I may find myself in encounter with these powers, but I reject this kind of fetish god although statistically it may well be the most widely worshipped kind of deity in the world today. With this I place the *idol* (however we define that term). I cannot accept a dumb god of stone or wood, whether a natural formation or the creation of mankind. Nor can I put my trust in any supposed spirit which is thought to possess such a stone or piece of wood. The arguments against this kind of belief are presented in the prophetic books of the Old Testament and in such early Christian writings as *The Letter to Diognetus.*

Nor can I find any satisfaction in the idea that God might be an abstraction in the mind of mankind and presented in the form of a poem, or a myth, or in philosophy. Such a view, to me, has no authority. The view of one poet or philosopher may be no better than that of his neighbor, or of my own. There is nothing here on which to build a faith, no real frame of reference in which life can operate.

But there is one common reason why I reject all these concepts of God. My God is a *Living God,* a title which I have from the Bible. A Creator who has ceased to work, a fetish, an idol, a mythical or philosophical abstraction: none of these will account for the forces I find at work in my life. The only explanation I can offer, facts which I experience day by day, is that my God is a Living God.

Furthermore, it is a Living God that I need. As an anthropologist I am deeply concerned with the needs of mankind and how mankind (both as individuals and as societies) meet their needs with satisfactions. I ask myself what are my needs as I face life and what kind of a God do I need to provide those satisfactions. My analysis brings to me the belief that no God can meet my needs but a Living God. I need guidance, correction, motives and attitudes that are higher than those I seem physically capable of. I need Someone who will help me overcome being *what I am,* and make me *what I long to be.*

Turning to God for these satisfactions was, of course, an act of faith. There was, at first, no scientific proof that He would do all this for me. My needs led me to cry out to Him. The proof, for me, is that He heard my cry and satisfies my needs.

I BELIEVE IN A SAVING GOD

I believe I can strengthen that anthropological concept of needs and satisfactions by using a theological term—salvation. There are many ways in which an individual may be saved—from trouble, from danger, from fear, from sorcery, from the enemy and so forth. Anthropology makes an allowance for all these in its discussions, but for some reason or other it has very little to say about salvation from sin. Yet this is a matter for which scientific data can be collected and which anthropology cannot sidestep indefinitely. This is specially true when we remember that this is not confined to the individual, but in many societies the salvation experience has come to whole cultural units, families and tribes.

Here is an amazing fact which can be observed—a broken life is restored, a lifelong dread of evil spirits is overcome, an enslavement by some disgusting habit is terminated, and all this perhaps in a moment of time. In place of fear or deceit or crime one is confronted by a new radiance, a new peace and freedom, and a completely changed life. Old motivations and attitudes have changed overnight and the change has been permanent. I have seen this happen so often and under so many different conditions, but always leaving the convert a "new creature" with a devotion to God from whom salvation has come. Anthropologically we are confronted with a limited number of regular patterns, which cry aloud for interpretation. Now, it seems to me that the most obvious explanation is that this is the work of God, though such a hypothesis would be difficult to test. Yet saved lives are observable facts. I personally recall such transformations—a slum youth who became a marketplace evangelist, a prostitute who began life again and made a success of it, a Fijian converted in jail who became a preacher and Sunday school teacher.

My second discipline is history. I have worked through thousands of documents in the archives of Pacific Island missions—letters, reports, journals. They are literally saturated with accounts of individuals changed from ferocious cannibals to teachable and helpful human beings—and changed overnight. Lest you think these are only missionary reports, they include secular observers also—sea captains, doctors and others of science. In all my reading in science and anthropology, I have never found any adequate explanation of these life transformations. I do not believe they can be explained in terms of psychology, although there are psychological factors present. Obviously, our present knowledge of the nature of mankind is inadequate to interpret these events. We know the presence of a Force by its observable results. The best explanation I can put forward is that God saves individuals when they honestly turn to Him in faith and take Him at His word.

I believe in a saving God. I can tell you now of the night over forty years ago when He came into my life and when everything was changed. I can recall every detail of the occasion. It was about 9:30 on Friday night and I could take you to the very street corner in North Melbourne near the old Victoria Market—it was the watershed of my life. I have never gone back on that decision. I've never found Him to fail me in the forty years since. My motives, my desires, my direction, my orientation to life, all changed that night. Something came into my life I had not met before. Yes, I believe in a saving God.

④ *I BELIEVE IN A COMMUNICATING GOD*
by which I mean
I BELIEVE IN A GOD WHO KNOWS AND CAN BE KNOWN

I reason in the following manner:

1. If God could bring me into being—a reasonable creature, who can know and communicate with other reasoning beings—it seems to me that such a Creator should know me and should be able to communicate with me. My Fijian friends call this *na veikilai kei na Kalou*—"Knowing God and being known by Him." The grammatical construction implies mutuality.

2. My capacity to know God is partly dependent on His capacity to reveal Himself in terms of my experience—*i.e.* in humanity. This is met, in my case, by two Christian doctrines—the Incarnation and the Witness of the Spirit. Thus in history and in experience, God becomes to me more than a mere notion or philosophical concept.

3. When I explore this *veikilai* in faith I find that my knowledge of Him grows. In the Christian Church we have numerous institutions (using that word anthropologically) for assisting the growth of this experience—prayer and corporate worship (not peculiar to Christianity), but also Bible study by means of which prayer and worship are made more meaningful.

4. The relationship is one of mutual acceptance. "Can two walk together except they be agreed?" asked the prophet. This is why John got more out of meeting with Jesus than Pilate did. This applies both in making contact and in maintaining contact.

5. There is one way in which this mutuality of knowing between God and man differs from that between two persons. Two persons meet and make a covenant on equal terms as human beings. In a covenant with God the initiative comes from the divine side by an act of grace, just as there are some liberties servants cannot take with their lord unless the lord invites them to do so, or it used to be for a student with the teacher, or an employee with an employer. The Greeks had words for differentiating between these types of agreement.

Coming back then to my belief—I find that God reaches out to me and opens the way for this fellowship relationship. It is necessary for me to accept the invitation. In point of fact many do reject it, but I can testify that acceptance brings a whole realm of new and desirable experience. Seeing that God has revealed Himself to humanity in human terms—*i.e.* in Christ—this acceptance is what evangelicals mean when they say "I accepted Christ," and this makes him or her a "new creature" because of this new relationship with, and understanding of, the Creator. It means a changed attitude and orientation for me. I cannot *enjoy* this experience unless I *respond* to the divine initiative, and this is why we sometimes speak of making the *"decision."* I made the decision myself and have seen thousands of others do it. It is also spoken of as *conversion,* but I want to make this clear, conversion is not the goal of Christian life, it is the entry into it.

I am not speaking here of the theology of conversion, but of its dynamics. Conversions take place. Individuals respond to Christ. They discover the joy of sin forgiven and some of them are quite unschooled. But having made the decision and having established the relationship, thereafter they "grow in grace."

(5) *I BELIEVE IN A PROVIDING GOD*
and this means He is
A GOD WHO MAKES LIFE MEANINGFUL

I do not expect God to make life an easy way for me. As far as I know He never promised this to any person. But even so He does give me a strength beyond my own and I believe He does guide me and adds meaning to life. I think there are three things that need to be said at this point.

1. God does not promise that I have no burden to bear. In fact the Bible, which I accept as my rule for faith and practice, says that every one shall carry their burden. I am therefore committed to some effort myself, and while it is true that He helps me grow, it is also true that growth requires something from me. I remember how Wallace, the naturalist, saw a struggling moth trying to break forth from its cocoon. Taking his penknife he sought to aid the creature by making the way easy. The moth came forth, struggled forward a little and then died. It needed that struggle for its own development and Wallace had done the moth no service at all.

2. Let me say a little more about the Bible. I believe this is God's word to mankind, but this written word cannot be understood unless it is put to the test. One has to go forward in the venture of faith. If one is prepared to live by the Bible, it will be found to be filled with exciting disclosures. It is the frame of reference for my life action patterns. By its values I measure success and failure. I find it a truly valuable criterion which has never once let me down. But the study of the Bible as a book is not adequate. One does not really appreciate the latent depth of the Bible until he or she is prepared to act upon it, to put it to the test in one's life. The true meaning of the Bible has to be experienced to be understood.

3. I know that sometimes in life we run into dark hours. There seems to be no light at all. Even the Bible seems to offer no direct light for the moment, just a faint glimmer perhaps. But I have found

that when one acts on that glimmer, continuing in faith, going forward into the darkness believing that God is there, that such spiritual quest is never unrewarded. It is good for us to be tested by hours of darkness. It helps us to remember the inadequacy of human resources. Then, when we have come through and look back we discover that there was a pattern there all the time, and the faint glimmer we followed was sure and true.

I remember walking home with a Fijian companion one dark night. I walked 32 miles that day and we came out on the coast and made our way through the heavy sand. The way led across a swamp and a creek and we searched for the narrow gauge railway for carrying sugar across the swamp. No stars were visible. It was utter darkness. Yet somehow from nowhere the rail track picked up some light and I followed it through the darkness. It led me across the swamp and home. My Fijian friend, following the other rail, did not see my ray of light, but he had one of his own and it came from the same source, and we went through the darkness side by side.

I believe in a God who makes life meaningful, who can bring me through the darkest night. All He asks is that I follow the gleam. So my God will place a burden on my shoulder and expect me to bear it, but He gives me the strength for the task by providing a frame of reference within which I can operate, namely the Bible, and by Himself being beside me when I am prepared to step forth on His word in faith. This makes life meaningful.

There are many other things I could tell you about my faith, but this is all I need say:

1. I believe in God.
2. I believe in a living God.
3. I believe in a saving God.
4. I believe in a communicating God.
5. I believe in a providing God.

And I find nothing in my discipline of social anthropology that denies me the right to this belief.

CHAPTER 2

The Bible as a
Frame of Reference

I began with a statement of faith presented in a single, developing theme: God, a living God, a saving God, a communicating God and a providing God. It had to be in a form something like this in order for a study in missiology to be seen against the background of other faiths. Consciously or unconsciously, the missiologist, like the scientist, starts his or her research with an act of faith. In spite of Durkheim's first corollary that "all preconceptions must be eradicated" (1962:31), there is no other way to begin research but by an act of faith. In point of fact Durkheim himself does exactly this. Saltman, the biochemist, has pointed out that "science is a religious experience" (1970). The scientific researcher believes that, first, there is order in the universe; second, mankind, by investigations, is capable of understanding this order; and third, that it is a good thing for mankind to achieve this understanding.

All missiologists may not begin with precisely the same form of faith, and I do not hold others to my presentation; but nevertheless it has seemed good to me that if my *Introduction to Missiology* is to be meaningful to the reader I should share my presuppositions of faith.

Not only does a researcher begin with a personal faith, but what also is needed is some kind of a *frame of reference* for the arranging, testing and interpreting of his or her experiences. It may be a map or chart, worked out by someone else on a basis of previous research and tested over the years by a developing series of scientific inventions. It may be a system of calculation, with formulae and trigonometrical methods that have been proved mathematically. It may be an approved method of collecting, classifying and comparing quantitative data and recording it on graphs so that certain conditions and trends may be detected. The number of frame-of-reference options available for one form of research or another is almost unlimited. Every academic discipline has one or more according to its purposes.

The frame of reference for missiology has to meet the following requirements:

1. It must be adequate with respect to the discipline itself; i.e., it must be workable within the idea of the Christian mission and its goals.
2. It must provide an adequate means for classifying and testing the observed and collected data; i.e., it must have religious morals and values.
3. It must be a testing tool in which the missiologist has personal confidence and which he or she finds reliable.

Now it follows that when a researcher selects a frame of reference and has confidence in it, he or she will use it honestly and consistently, and will not manipulate it, like some crafty diviner, for self-serving purposes. A frame of reference is something from outside the researcher, which is adopted for the purpose of testing, to get a result that is not just one's own value judgment. It is to the researcher not only the structure for the classification of data, but also the source of the researcher's criteria and the authority by which that data is to be tested. It reduces the subjectivity of the findings and helps the researcher to arrive at a conclusion scientifically. Some subjectivity and value judgments will always be there to be sure, but the researcher will "play the game according to the rules."

In missiology we find our frame of reference in the Bible. We accept this book *as it is,* as a tool for classifying and evaluating our material. This material comes from historical and archival sources and anthropological research, collected by the approved techniques of history and anthropology and placed on the biblical grid for interpretation.

The world agenda, comparative religion and philosophy provide no adequate scale for testing missiology. But the Bible does for many reasons. It is a written record which preserves the words of our Lord, by which He commissioned His followers to mission, in the world and to the world, in the first place. It reveals the precise context of that commission. It records the basic information about the *Person* who is central in Christian mission, the nature of His own mission to mankind and the authority in which He commissioned His followers. It tells of the purpose and scope of the world mission. It is natural that we should go back to these things for testing the mission as we practice it ourselves. The Old Testament tells of God's dealing with humanity through Israel. Two ideas develop: that of *the nations,* and that of the *responsibility* of the *people of God* towards the nations. The Old Testament shows how Israel failed in that responsibility. All this is the context in which the life of Jesus was lived on earth and against which the Great Commission was given. The New Israel inherits the promises. Furthermore, the Bible is an account of the early out-workings of the Christian mission in the Roman Empire, with a clear statement of the various kinds of growth patterns and the problems—both of which are remarkably similar to what we meet in our own day. Furthermore, the Bible contains a corpus of material, which though scattered, can be sought out by study to provide an adequate theoretical and theological base for such an enterprise as the Christian mission. Some of these dimensions of theology I have put together in *Church Growth and the Word of God* (1970a). For these and other reasons it seems to me that no other frame of reference is more suitable for testing the Christian mission than the Bible itself. So I take this as my frame of reference, and as I have found it quite adequate over the years, I do not feel disposed to reject it for something within myself (philosophical) or some other ideology based on the world's agenda, which makes it the authority of mankind instead of God.

I take this tool as a *whole thing*. There is no reason to tamper with this tool, to eliminate this part or that for some imagined critical reason. It stands as it has always stood for me as God's word to mankind and with His authority. As an anthropologist a credible word of God to mankind, assembled over maybe two thousand years of history, has to reflect the different literary forms and structures of patriarchal nomads, oriental kingdoms and Graeco-Roman rural and urban communities. I have no problem here with the Bible. The form is quite multicultural and God speaks in time and place through many forms. If I read the Bible allowing for the cultural context of the particular passage, I always find myself being taken beyond the form to some eternal truth which speaks right to me in my own cultural situation. To me it is a perfect tool for evaluating the cross-cultural situations of world mission.

At no point in this study does the problem of biblical criticism arise. This does not mean I am ignorant of it. I have studied it in my day and have come to regard it as purely academic and theoretical, and not a relevant missiological problem. If I clip the Great Commission off the end of the gospels (it is a post-resurrection pronouncement) then with no Great Commission there is no need for missiology at all. If I remove the resurrection, either as a later addition or as a myth, then the preaching of the resurrection becomes an idle thing—a mere idea. The Scriptures are made false, our faith is in vain and we are yet in our sins; furthermore the Christian mission is made a phony concept and there is no need for missiology. The Bible hangs together as a *total thing*. I want no measuring tool with a major cog removed. Either you take it as it is or you give it up as a frame of reference. If you give it up, you give up Christian mission and missiology with it. So it seems to me that any *Introduction to Missiology* must presuppose the acceptance of a total Bible.

Without such things as a total Bible, the risen Lord, the encounter which brings the verdict of accepting Christ as only Savior, or the commission to go to the nations and make disciples, what is left of the

Christian mission? Of course, there could still be many Christian projects, serving those in need, training the undertrained, fighting for social justice and so on. This is all part of the Christian duty, but it is an accompaniment of mission and not a substitute for it. They are scripturally conceptualized as two different ministries of the one Church. The ministry of the Church in the world is thereby a *partial thing* and this idea clashes with the Scripture presentation of the Church. We could indeed perform this half-service and be Universalist or even Hindu. What we would have is a humanitarian ministry (and a noble one as far as it goes) but there would be nothing distinctively Christian at all—and certainly no mission. So whatever way we come at this we find that either the Bible has to be taken as a whole thing or our claim to engage in Christian mission, and therefore the idea of missiology, is phony. Obviously there is no other frame of reference for the Christian mission, in which I believe, but the whole Bible, and that is certainly presupposed in this *Introduction to Missiology*.

CHAPTER 3

Mankind in Context

I am a social anthropologist. I am also an evangelical Christian. ✯
Sometimes I am asked how I reconcile the two. Not only can they be
reconciled but each has much it can contribute to the other. Anthropology,
for instance, can help Christian missionaries to improve their missioning,
for missionaries are not inanimate instruments in the hand of God, but
active agents of their Lord. Paul saw Christian workers as God's fellow
workers or *sunergoi* (1 Cor. 3:10-13; 2 Cor. 6:1). The role is one which
implies responsible action by the worker and knowledge of the relevant
techniques. Anthropology has so much to say about the patterns in which
people live in societies, how they should and should not be approached
and how best to communicate with them, that missionaries are unwise to
ignore the new techniques that are at their disposal. When this available
knowledge and method is deliberately passed by, how can we expect to
earn the commendation "good and faithful servant"? Are we not burying
the available "talent" in the earth? I believe that the parable (Mt. 25:14-
30) has a current meaning for the Christian mission, that commits us to
the good use of all the wonderful resources science has provided in our
day.

Anthropology is the study of *mankind in context.* The theologian ✯
may speak of an "existential situation," but as a social anthropologist I
prefer to write in terms of my own discipline using the concept of context.
Context determines meaning. Most of the trouble in our world can be
traced to somebody getting out of their context, individuals seeing themselves as isolates rather than in context. All selfishness comes from the
exaltation of the individual and the refusal to recognize the social context.

In this chapter we shall consider first the matter of context and
meaning and then pass on to the human context itself. Having delineated

this, we shall discuss its bearing first on anthropology, then on theology
and finally on the Christian mission. The argument is important in our day
because of the increasing resources and numerous techniques that anthropology places at our disposal. Yet some missionaries are manifestly
hostile to the discipline because they consider it agnostic. It was the same
with sociology. However in the cooperative task of the Lord and His
sunergoi, anthropology provides an abundance of tools and techniques
which assist mankind. So often we pass them by. It seems therefore that,
in order to press the claim that anthropology has something significant to
offer missionaries in their work, that one must first establish that an
evangelical can be also an anthropologist. As we turn to the argument it
should be noted that within the limits of this article "anthropology" shall
be taken to mean "social anthropology."

CONTEXT AND MEANING

All things have contexts. It is the context that makes the thing what it
is functionally. The meaning will change according to the context. It
makes a difference to the accountant whether the ten dollar entry is in the
context of the left or right column in the account book. It makes all the
difference in the world to a community of people if an atomic process is in
the context of destructive warfare or of the provision of power to light a
city.

Words have contexts. A commission was enquiring into the workings
of the young Church in Fiji. An interpreter's translation was disputed. He
used the word *beka,* which usually means "perhaps." But the translator
had used it in another way, as a respectful softener to give a polite
warning. His translation was perfectly correct idiom and clearly understood by the nationals, but not by all the missionaries, one or two of whom
thought the translator was party to the debate. It is not enough to know the
vocabulary. One also has to understand the context to understand the
meaning.

Scripture also has context, as every preacher knows. What can be
done with a text out of context! What heresy can be based on isolated
texts! As was said of Shakespeare's Shylock: "The devil can cite Scripture
for his purpose."

As things and words and texts all have contexts, the social anthropologist presses that so too mankind has a context. The missionary needs
to learn that bringing people to Christ may be a different thing in some
communal society from what it is in ours. Let us then examine more
carefully the human context.

THE HUMAN CONTEXT

As an anthropologist I find fault with the person, evangelist, psychologist or any other, who extracts humans from their context. Humans

are individuals, but always *individuals in a context*. The lives of all other people who cluster around an individual's own existence are part of his or her environment, as that individual is part of theirs. Humans are ever *involved* with other people. They ever live in so many *sets of relationships*. Although each person is a unique individual, who must make separate decisions, no person is ever in isolation. Neither can we consider humans in the abstract. We cannot understand people without recognizing the human context which is their world.

This fact has significance for the Christian mission, either to the evangelist in an urban community at home or to the missionary overseas. It makes anthropology relevant in their training. It requires deep understanding to communicate in a world other than one's own.

Anthropologically speaking, mankind's context is *confined* by a number of limitations, any of which may be considered for purposes of research of classification. There are, for instance, geographical limitations which are shared with one's neighbors. We speak of Southerners, mountaineers, swamp dwellers and so on. There are political limitations, by which we differentiate nationalists from conservatives or democrats from republicans; or national limitations by which we classify the French from the Germans; or racial limitations which permit the grouping of Melanesians, Polynesians and Micronesians. We may break mankind up into language groups—Nilotic or Bantu—or into the subdivisions of, say, the scores of Bantu languages. Or we may associate a language or dialect with some occupational group—the southern cotton pickers, the underworld, the boomers of Canada or the Mexican Braceros. All these limitations have their influence on the individual in the context. It is even claimed by many that they condition one's personality.

The historians reconstruct the human context at different periods of history: of Pericles' Athens, of Elizabethan England, of the New Bedford whalers. This is important because it recognizes a time depth. The decrease of distance in our day has brought the so-called primitive closer to home, and we see the human groups whom we contemplate in the light of the Great Commission are distributed through what seems to be a range of different time depths. Extant societies are not all at the same point of time, as it were; or to change the figure, they are widely scattered along the axis that lies between the poles of simplicity and sophistication. Thus we have learned that besides the context of a personal daily life each person has a wider context, a community larger than one's family or occupational unit.

Take the case of a young Church with great opportunities in the urban industrial centers and universities, but it draws its national ministry from rural communities that belong in a period of history the city has long forgotten. What does it mean for these young workers to be transplanted to a context strange to them—geographically, culturally and in a different period of history? Even if we bring them to America for urban training that urban situation to which they return is never American, however

Americanized it may be. How wrong are we to assume that the missionary trained for the home pastorate is also trained for an overseas role as if the training could be achieved in isolation. We cannot understand humans cross-culturally until we grapple with the whole configuration which is their existential situation.

If mankind has a domestic and occupational context, and also a communal context, we may extend this to an even wider scale in our day, when communications and speed have confronted us with the idea of one world. We think of mankind as a whole in this larger context. With the possibility of annihilation before us the need for each group to understand its neighbor is obvious. We are suddenly and dramatically aware of the fact that not only has each individual a context but *each context has a context.*

Can we assume in this desperate situation that humans will suddenly change their nature and learn to live together in love? Only two possible positions are before us. Either the biblical view is correct and mankind is the object of God's love, both mankind and each context being the "work of His fingers," and mankind has meaning in the purpose of God; or our coming this far has been entirely fortuitous. Terrific sources of power are now in mankind's control, but mankind has manifestly not the spiritual maturity to control them for its own good. The possibility exists but, in point of fact, there is no real evidence of an intention to use atomic and other resources for world "salvation." Humans use them rather to national glorification.

However, science has by no means disposed of the biblical view. That many persons have rejected it is no proof of its error. Some say that every new discovery of science closes up some gap in knowledge and God becomes more dispensable. On the contrary, each new discovery opens up a new world of mystery. Rather than closing gaps we are discovering the infinite and always there are laws at work which could hardly be by accident. If the biblical view of the Creator has not been disposed of, then the world is not the last of mankind's concentric contexts, and we are face to face with the *eschatological context of mankind.*

Our problem here is to conceive this context, so limited are we by physical, temporal and spacial dimensions. At present we can only see ourselves in a period of time which commenced with the first coming of our Lord and ends with His return. It is here that we make our decisions and live our lives and are held responsible for our actions. The eschatological context has deep significance for mankind as a whole, for humans in groups and for humans as individuals. It is the one universal context for all people everywhere of every race. The physical world, where people live, has suddenly shrunk in our day, bringing us closer together. Greater physical resources, increased reservoirs of power, more highly developed tools and techniques for communication and service than we have had before, are at our disposal. Furthermore we face the grim vulnerability of the human race with its capacity for self-destruction.

Each of these factors gives a new meaning and urgency to the Great Commission in our day.

Because the biblical view of mankind in context has not been scientifically disposed of and no better hypothesis has been posited as a basis for our thinking, I propose to leave the matter there. While it is true that there have been numerous interpretations of the Scriptures, the basic biblical position is clear. God created the world and brought forth humans as the object of His love and providence and made them beings capable of spiritual fellowship. He made them to live together in communities and it is His will that they should love each other. This love of creature for creature becomes real when the creature knows and loves the Creator. This is possible because the Creator revealed Himself in the form of the creature. For scientific purposes this is the biblical claim. We are not concerned here with literary forms or imagery which were the cultural features of the times when the Bible was written.

ANTHROPOLOGY AND THE HUMAN CONTEXT

On the practical level anthropology, as the study of mankind in context, has much to give the pastor and missionary confronted with the communication of the Gospel to men and women in their context. Anthropology itself has no salvation to offer. It is a discipline which seeks to understand people, why they think, feel and act as they do, how they make their decisions and why, what their felt needs are, and how individuals strive to meet them, and many other things. If the missionary and pastor can come to know what people feel their needs to be and how they think, act and make decisions, this deeper understanding of human thinking and acting within a context is bound to deepen sympathy, pastoral effectiveness and methods of presenting the message of salvation. But this can never be done by isolating humans from their context.

Of course, mankind is saved by grace alone, but the Lord has chosen to work through human servants and it behooves them to be as practical and wise as possible in their appointed roles. The biblical imagery of God's fellow workers — vine-dressers, servants, farmers, fishermen, shepherds — is that of responsible agents, who know their trade or craft and are responsible for diligence and good workmanship. Irresponsible service is open to judgment (Mt. 25:26-27). Thus, disciplines like anthropology are available in our day and should be employed to improve the human aspect of the *Master-agent* program. If we ignore the facilities available for improving our missionary techniques we are surely guilty of neglect.

Every anthropologist, like every theologian, brings something of his or her personal philosophy and faith (even if negative) to the discipline. Every scientist does this—no matter how vehemently it may be denied. Complete objectivity is impossible—and undesirable. Identification, subjective involvement of the researcher in the context of those studied increases the researcher's insights, sympathy and influence. The anthropologist goes as far as possible without losing scientific "objectivity." The anthropologist seeks "participant observation" but is always alert lest one goes too far.

A missionary, on the other hand, must become subjectively involved. This is why the missionary has deeper insights than the anthropologist at certain points. But the missionary also has deeper biases, and because of this he or she would do well to learn from some of the things the anthropologist can show of the context in which the missionary is involved.

I have served as an involved missionary in one country and an objective anthropologist in another. The two groups were culturally similar, but my experiences were dramatically different. There is much the missionary and anthropologist can learn from each other about humans in their context.

The anthropologist has developed methods of classification, data collection, analysis and the testing information. Social patterns of mankind's cultural context have been reconstructed. There are many points of reference for interpretation. The anthropologist has explored the relationships of human with human, and written many useful monographs. All these have value for the missionary and pastor confronting the problems of cross-cultural communication. The more the *sunergoi* learns of the human context the more effective should be his or her workmanship as God's fellow worker.

THEOLOGY AND THE HUMAN CONTEXT

If we are to borrow from the methodology of anthropology the theological question may arise: What is the relationship between anthropology and theology and how does this bear on a study of mankind in context? Is there any place for God in the picture? If anthropology is a subject for inclusion in courses for the training of missionaries then this question must be asked and answered.

Anthropologists range from agnostic, deterministic culturologists to philosophical theorists, who reduce the writings of the former to a bunch of fallacies. As I have already suggested, all scientists bring their personal beliefs into their work, whether they admit it or not. Is there then a place for an evangelical anthropologist, and if so, how is this matter of humans in their context interpreted?

I believe we have before us four relevant theological fundamentals, which are the distinctive emphasis of the *Christian* anthropologist.

In the first place both mankind and the environment are concrete and observable facts. The traditional Christian belief is that they owe their existence to God, whom we speak of as the Creator. Whether we reason this by rational argument or accept it on a basis of faith, or however we may otherwise try to explain the process, is not the point here. *If we accept the position that God created mankind and gave them a context, we have a practical working hypothesis on which to organize our life and behavior. We understand the relationship of God to humans and humans to God.* The hypothesis holds together and does not betray us. It makes our existence and motivation meaningful. I therefore submit that it is up to the agnostic to disprove the traditional position. The onus of proving one's position does not fall on the traditionalist. The fact that the Christian can live meaningfully and effectively on the basis of this faith validates it at least until it is disproved. If disproved, then the Christian has to restructure his or her frame of reference, but as long as the "machine" functions effectively there is no reason why it should be discarded.

The second fundamental arises from the first. *If God is the Creator of the creation it would seem logical that He has also the capacity to reveal Himself in terms of the limitations of His creation.* This He does in the Incarnation. To be a true incarnation, the Word had to be truly made flesh. It is not enough for incarnation to be conceptualized abstractly in poetry or myth. The Man had to be set in the human context— physically, geographically, culturally, historically, linguistically. Thus He was born within the Hebrew tradition, in the land of Palestine in the days of Herod the King, a speaker presumably of Galilean Aramaic within the social complex of the village carpenter's shop. Here is a man within the limitations of his context, as Charles Welsey expressed it:

> Our God contracted to a span
> Incomprehensibly made man.

The Incarnation, as the evangelical conceptualizes it, implies even more than this. The record reports the wonderful life and ministry of One "tempted in all points like as we are." We are told of the convergence of hostile forces against him, the trial and cruel death on the cross. There is the triumph and glory of the resurrection. All of these things are set in history: in the political context of the period of Pontius Pilate, in the cultural context of the interplay of Jewish and Roman legal procedure, in the geographical context that can be indicated on the map of Palestine and which tourists visit today. Whether we speak of the act of incarnation or the demonstration of redeeming work on the cross, we are in each case studying mankind in historic context.

Again I say, that for centuries Christians have accepted this record in faith and have found it valid. To believers throughout history the proof has always been in personal experience; the onus is on the agnostic to disprove it.

The third fundamental arises from the second. *If anthropology is to be regarded as the science of mankind, and this science is to be applied to improving the condition of humans within their context, the way should also be open by means of which humans can rise spiritually above the limitations of their context and become what we describe as the "new people in Christ."*

In applied anthropology we bring the discipline to bear on elevating the life of humans: in agriculture, education, health and other dimensions. We speak of the social improvements brought about by applied anthropology in terms of "the new day." We conceptualize this task of making things new as a role in *directed change*.

Yet anthropology has insisted on seeing life as a whole, in preserving the concept of integrated and interacting totality. Part of that totality is the religious configuration. If there is to be a new day for mankind in terms of religion, there has to be "a way for humans to rise" and know their eternal inheritance—"to inherit the kingdom prepared for (you)."

Much evidence exists for the claim that religion is the *integrator* of society and that when it ceases to be so the society concerned may be regarded as decadent and ready to break up, unless it finds a new religion adequate for the characteristics and atmosphere of the day of change. Many societies have changed religion under political, military or economic stress, yet have survived by the introduction of new religious rites and by modifying religious and moral values. Even an agnostic anthropologist cannot bypass this data and must allow for the functional role of religion in society. Religion is part of the context.

Religion is *in the data* and this is a problem to some observers. There are four ways of looking at the "problem of religion":

1. Individuals can compartmentalize religion and treat it in isolation (as many Christians who treat their worship purely as a Sunday exercise). This is either compromise or an indication of social decay. In any case it is to dichotomize human existence.

2. Individuals can deny religion (including God) as mere superstition, a primitive belief from which one must evolve. In point of fact, when the functional substitute for religion is merely another ideology it is still functionally religious, be it at the negative pole.

3. Individuals may try to dispense with God, regarding Him as no longer of consequence in modern life, science having disposed of Him. This is merely the deification of mankind.

4. Individuals may recognize a power beyond themselves, on whose resources they may draw, and who is active in the human situation. As long as this general principle is accepted a person may change to a particular religion if it suits one to do so, but he or she remains religious.

The first three are all unsatisfactory as they injure the totality of the human context, and do not account for all the data. The fourth is found in the data of most integrated societies and must be allowed for in the interpretation. The Christian communities are not alone in recognizing that humans have a context (environmental and social) and that context seems to imply the existence of a Creator.

It is therefore a valid investigation for the anthropologist to probe the relationships of *humans, their contexts,* and the *Creator*. Although many anthropologists prefer to list data objectively and leave the matter there, there is no reason why, if an anthropologist has a body of satisfactory data an interpretation should not be attempted.

Once we justify applied anthropology as a discipline and approve
directed change in principle, we automatically validate the study of
conversion to Christianity. We have seen the function of applied
anthropology—to raise the level of a society in education, agriculture,
health and so forth. Directed change is approved if it leads people to a
higher state of living. If religion is a configuration of the pattern, like
health, education and agriculture, as a scientific analysis of data suggests,
then surely the techniques of applied anthropology may justly be directed
to this configuration also. What criteria have we for directed change in
agriculture and health that we do not have in religion?

Therefore, it is open for the Christian apologist to argue that the
"chief end of man is to glorify God and enjoy Him forever" and also that,
if this be so, God must be able to enter the human context to save
individuals from themselves and thus the Christian mission itself is both
justified and essential as directed change if unregenerate mankind is to
become *new mankind.* What is good for the physical and mental renewal
is good for the spiritual renewal also.

Finally, out of the concept of mankind in context the Christian
anthropologist finds the doctrine of the Church.

The anthropologist locates the "happiness" of mankind in the awareness of, the entity and solidarity of the group which satisfies felt needs and
gives confidence, security and a sense of belonging. A human in isolation
is a social irritant. Even the Western youth, cut off from home and with no
other alternative, may join a street gang to win thereby some sense of
belonging. *The only group which will really meet the human needs is the
Christian fellowship, because it is the only social context where humans
meet with both their fellow humans and with God* (1 Jn. 3:4).

This opens the way for a doctrine of the Church, but it demands that
the Church be conceptualized in specific terms of fellowship, and of
belonging. The moment the Church becomes a mere organization or a
discordant community it ceases to be the Church.

Anthropology reveals specific processes by which people are incorporated into the group, institutions for preparing them for reception into
membership and celebrations for rejoicing on their incorporation. I do not
use this as an allegory, but as the statement of a principle—humans
always belong, in context. We cannot escape the significance of an
individual belonging to the group. Of all the possible interpretations of
mankind's belongingness, the highest is that of the Christian communion.

Samuel Johnson was conceptualizing the Christian Church in terms of
an integrated structural configuration in its defense, its goals, its work
program and authority when he wrote:

> One holy Church, one army strong,
>   One steadfast high intent,
> One working band, one harvest song,
>   One King Omnipotent.

As an anthropologist I feel quite at home in this type of thinking. As a *participant observer* I share the experience of belonging and derive personal satisfaction thereby. It is good to belong to a fellowship where people know each other and together they commune with God.

THE HUMAN CONTEXT AND THE CHRISTIAN MISSION

Throughout this study we have kept in the background the consideration of the relationship of the anthropologist and the missionary. It would seem necessary to conclude this essay by reaching the point where the two most frequently come into encounter; viz., the rightness or wrongness of missioning, *per se.*

One frequently meets with anthropology undergraduates, who ask how one can possibly be both an anthropologist and a missionary together. It is true that among the teachers of anthropology the missionary "image" is often an unhappy one and this impression is transmitted in lectures. Examples of missionary error in cross-cultural approach have provided some instructors with many of their lecture examples and opportunities for barbed wit. Even so, much of the criticism behind this is often justified. This is the very reason why missionary training should take anthropology seriously.

However, I believe that the best critical analyses of missionary failings have come from among the anthropologically-minded missionaries, not from outside—best, because it has been directed most to the correction of error. Anthropologists, especially in their days of Ph.D. research, are themselves not free from error and have themselves created an "image" which needs correction. I have observed them at work for twenty years and speak with knowledge on this matter. Nevertheless there are a great many places where each can and should help the other. We have reached the day for positive rather than negative interaction. With this in mind, then, I return to the question: what has anthropology to say about the *idea of mission?*

Philosophically, as I have already suggested, the would-be critic gives the case away if the *idea of applied anthropology* is accepted. Once this is accepted as a legitimate discipline, and admits *directed change,* the Christian mission is anthropologically legitimate also. Some anthropologists refuse to admit the idea of applied anthropology and prefer to keep their science as purely objective study. To these I should have to argue that their position is unrealistic and untenable because they are placing themselves in isolation. They do, in point of fact, belong to the human context itself and their very data-collecting *involves* them in the situations they investigate.

From the other side, the evangelical Christians want to know what anthropology has to say to them as believers and supporters of Christian mission.

Anthropology would perhaps say first that change is going on all the time. Most anthropologists would then admit that it would seem good that change should be *directed to desirable ends,* although they might disagree on their definition of what are desirable ends. However, there would be a second thing to say. They would stress the importance of the *responsibility* of those involved in the *role of directing change.* In doing so, they would emphasize, not only the definition of desirable goals, but the *processes* by which those goals are to be reached. In other words anthropology has a great deal to say with respect to the techniques of missioning.

This area of thinking has been explored by the anthropologist, F.E. Williams, in a monograph entitled, *The Blending of Cultures,* which deals with the role of missions and governments and stresses responsibility.

Administrators justify their policy of planning and directing change on a basis of progress, law and order, and are responsible for their concepts and decisions. Missionaries insist they are acting on a basis of the Great Commission to go to all nations, but again they are responsible for their interpretation. This commission requires preaching, teaching the things which the Lord commanded, and if we link this with the other commands of Jesus, healing and casting out demons. But I am unaware of any commission to break up social structure, family entities and cultural organization—unless His reference to "bringing a sword" be so interpreted. In any case, this would only explain how at some points there will be division, it is not a commission to divide. On the contrary, Jesus had much to say about the unity of the flock, and when he won the woman of Samaria he did so in the context of winning the Samaritan group to which she was the key. Above all, there is no commission to impose foreign patterns, and no scripture passage I know can justify our denominationalization of the Christian mission. Anthropology has much to say to all this. It says that if we direct change in this or that way, we are responsible. It would never support the undirected and irresponsible forms of evangelism that leave the convert isolated and not incorporated into some active body. It demands a context for converts. It demands for every person a right to know a sense of *belongingness.* It says that if we destroy institutions, we must find adequate functional substitutes at the time of change. These must meet the old needs in a better way so that the change is acceptable to the converts. They themselves then become the innovators. When no functional substitutes are provided the resultant cultural voids will become apparent within a few years, and may be neopagan resurgences. The directors of change are to be held responsible for these delayed disturbances.

For these and many other reasons it behooves us to study the cultural contexts within which we perform our missioning and to know what we are about when we advocate or direct change. We tend to justify ourselves under the broad terms of the Great Commission. I do not question this at all, but I do point out that the commission is a general directive only. As we respond to it we are involved in many cultural factors not provided for in its general terms of reference. At these points not enumerated, anthropology can serve as a useful guide.

Finally, therefore, anthropology does not deny Christians the right to their Christian missioning, but very forcefully it does say that if cultural changes are advocated, the advocate is responsible. The responsibility lies in the degree of knowledge and resources that are available and the techniques that go with them, at the point of time of the advocacy. This means that missionaries of today stand in a very different position from their predecessors of a century ago. The early missionaries had no anthropology—indeed anthropology itself built on their experiences—but the missionaries of today have abundant resources at their disposal. There is here a well-known biblical principle. We have in anthropology a valuable "talent" presented to us for our use in the Lord's service (Mt. 25:14-30). Will we some day reply to the Lord:

> I was afraid and went and hid thy
> talent in the earth?

If so, we may expect the answer in which we are classified as "wicked and slothful servants" and held responsible for our failure to use the "talent" which we hid. Responsibility leads to judgment when the "unprofitable servant" is "cast out." In providing the tools and resources by which the missionary can direct change without ignoring the human context, anthropology helps to show us how we can better perform our role in a responsible manner. Anthropology does not bring individuals to Christ, but it shows missionaries how they may be more effective and less of a hindrance in doing so.

CHAPTER 4

The Church
Communicates with Mankind

How and where does the Church communicate with mankind? It does so both *internally* and *externally*. In other words the ministry of the Church has both an inward and an outward dimension. The Church is a complex organism. In the Scriptures it is described as the *Body* of Christ. It performs the ministry of Christ *in the world*. It speaks his mind, it performs his healing and comfort, it demonstrates his love in the world. Yet at the same time, under another figure, it is described as a fellowship of men and women *called out of the world*. These two ideas of being called out of the world and being commissioned to a ministry in the world are not in conflict. Rather they remind us that the Church has two areas of communication with mankind and that for the Church to be the Church it must take care of both its inner life and its outward ministry.

This is a *cyclical process* for there is an element of perpetuity in the idea of the Church. At least the Scripture would have us understand that the functional ministry and mission of the Church should continue "until he comes." So we are not dealing with a linear process which runs its course with each individual and perishes at his or her death. Witness is testifying to what we know to be true so as to bring people thereby into the fellowship (I John 1:1-3). But it does not end there with incorporation into the group, which becomes more and more like a salty inland sea because it has no outlet. Converts themselves have to go forth again and tell among those who knew them as unregenerate persons "what the Lord has done." This is a cyclical and not a linear process, as Figure 3 illustrates.

This ought to be a *corporate process*. The fellowship should be a complex of persons living in right relationships with Christ and with each other, attending the ministry of the Word and building each other up in

FIGURE 3
The Cyclical Process of Christianity

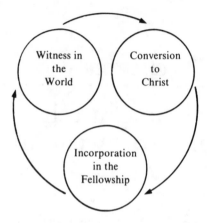

faith. If this is not so in any given congregation then that congregation is
not fully the Church, because the fellowship of believers is defective. On
the other hand, if a congregation is not making a corporate impact on the
world, it is defective at the level of the ministry of the Body of Christ in the
world. Our communication can break down at either level. I shall address
each in turn.

THE FELLOWSHIP OF BELIEVERS

If a new convert to Christ from out of the world seeks to share in the
fellowship of believers, but finds loneliness or drifts out again after a few
weeks, then this faulty incorporation indicates something defective in the
congregation. It may be structural, operational or spiritual, but in some
way or other it is functionally ineffective.

So a fellowship is essential. The idea of a ministry of Christ in the
world without the existence of the Church, which is His Body, is not
biblical. It was the Lord's specific intention to found a fellowship to leave
in the world after his departure. This fellowship is not a loose collection of
unrelated individuals, although it is multiindividual. All individuals enjoy
a set of relationships, both stimuli and responses. They relate to both
individuals and things, like the worship service itself and the written word,
to which they give something of themselves and receive something of
themselves.

The Church is a total complex: a living organism, where the process of maturation is going on, where individuals are growing in grace, aided by teaching, praying, worshipping, participating and interacting. In every relationship there should be a warm two-way flow of energy. Not until all the believers share this two-way flow of experience can we call a congregation a *fellowship of believers*. It is precisely at this point that we find one congregation with lonely and unincorporated individuals, and another a vibrant multi-individual fellowship (cf. Figure 4). In the latter, the Church communicates internally with its own members, building them up in peace, strength, direction and joy. In the former, what witnesses the Church may produce will be defective because they do not themselves know the full potential of their own message and because they have no true fellowship into which to incorporate converts and make them feel at home.

FIGURE 4
Isolated Believers Vs. Incorporated Fellowshippers

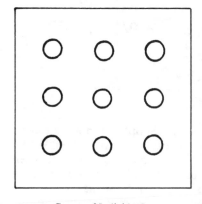
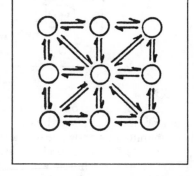

Group of Individuals   Multi-individual Fellowship

One serious problem of many evangelical churches is the way in which so many converted from the world enter the fellowship by the front door only to go out through the back door after a few weeks, having discovered that they were not adequately received into the life of the group. This is a problem that I hope you will all think about: what is the value of winning people out of the world and introducing them to the new life in Christ if you cannot provide them with a home in Christ where they can feel they belong? As an anthropologist I cannot adequately stress this craving of the heart of mankind to *belong*. One of the biggest problems we face in winning individuals for Christ is the structure and spirit and

operation of the fellowship into which we have to incorporate them. So
often our churches are a complex of substructures or in-groups, with lots
of lonely individuals drifting about in isolation until they drop out
altogether. When an evangelical church is known to win scores of
converts every year but never grows in membership I can only see one
reason, as illustrated in Figure 5.

FIGURE 5

**The Church as a Complex of Enclosed In-Groups and Isolated
Individuals Who Do Not Belong**

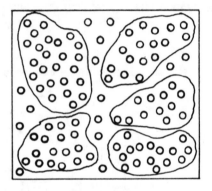

We cannot do without the Church as the Scriptures show us clearly.
We have no liberty to discard the Church because of malfunction. We are
rather committed to recognize its shortcomings and to correct them. There
is no substitute for the Church. In the biblical symbolism of the ultimate
consummation, the Church will stand as the Bride of the Lamb (Rev.
22:17). However, the Church may need to change in *form, through time*
and *across cultures,* but she must go on to the end. We cannot therefore
think of Christianity in terms of a *Post-church Age.*

Of course there is a deep relationship between the inner life of the
Church and her outward ministry. The Christian witness in the world,
whether from individual Christians or the corporate group is inadequate
and less than whole if it fails to draw from the fellowship. The functioning
Church is like a library and a data bank where the resources are found.
The researchers have to return to these regularly in order to be able to
interpret their outside opportunities and plan their ministry in the world. If
the Church fails to provide these resources, or fails to provide facilities to
make them available, then this malfunction certainly needs correction. I
attended a large church for three years and not once in that time was the
word of truth dispensed to me. This *freezing of the resources* explains why
this church has no converts from the world. It also explains why so many

members who migrate into the area and transfer into the fellowship soon pass out the back door and go to another church. Now, as we leave the fellowship and turn to the ministry in the world, let me reiterate that half of our failure in the world is due to prior failures within the fellowship itself. I cannot stress too much in this conference that all these wonderful technical devices and plans for communicating the Gospel to the needy world will be of little value if your home base and data bank are defective and you cannot incorporate your converts when you win them.

THE BODY OF CHRIST

Biblically speaking, the Church is the *Body of Christ,* which ministers the mind and word of Christ and demonstrates His concern and love for mankind in the world. Anthropologically speaking, the Church is a structured institution, a multi-individual corporate group living in the world in a complex series of relationships with both isolated individuals and other corporate groups. When I speak of the Church, I do not mean a set of buildings, even though a body of believers must have some physical form and must provide a functional fellowship wherein its members build up one another in prayer and sharing and mutual comfort and where the Scriptures are expounded for their spiritual growth. But this does not become the Body of Christ until all the parts acting under the Head (Eph. 4:15-16; Col. 1:18) begin doing the work of Christ in the world. This total complex we may call the ministry of Christ.

The ministry of Christ, *the thrust into the world* by the Church which is His Body (Eph. 1:22-23) comprises the following aspects:

1. the ministry of *mission*—the proclamation of the good news for the salvation of a person's soul;
2. the ministry of *service*—the work of Christ meeting the physical and material needs of people;
3. the ministry of *reconciliation*—the restoration of broken human relationships that people may live in peace together.

These are not exclusive or discrete categories but are merely abstractions so that we may see that in our Christian activity none of these aspects of the ministry of the Body of Christ in the world is neglected. Any act of ministry may involve one or all of them, but any Christian congregation should be doing all these things through some of its members corporately as well as individually in the world outside. An individual may be called to one specific form of ministry, but the Church as a corporate Body should see that the ministry is total. The peril of our ministry in the world today is that we become so taken up with one aspect of it that the others are neglected. This is surely one reason why in the providence of God we are asked to do things as a whole Church. We have this *corporate responsibility in the world.*

✗   The Church must continually have before it this threefold ministry of
Christ in the world: the ministry of mission, the ministry of service and the
ministry of reconciliation. This ministry must be total. The Lord's introduction of his program at Nazareth (Lk. 4:18-19) has a certain wholeness
about it, and if the Church is His Body doing His work in the world, the
various thrusts of ministry should be *in equilibrium.*

Perhaps with Christian literature stressing the things it is today I
hardly need to point out what is involved by the phrase *"in the world."*
We should not allow our emphasis on the fellowship of believers to be so
one-sided that the Church is allowed to become *an enclosure without
outreach.* The fellowship exists in order to equip it for outreach. To fail to
have outreach in the threefold ministry is to deny its "churchness." We
have that corpus of material in the Gospel of John where the Lord tells his
followers that they are in the world but not of the world. They are taught
to come out of the world and to go back into the world. Thus, though the
fellowship is a necessity, the fellowship must never become a dead end. If
the Church is winning individuals from the world, it must be that these
individual converts are never left as isolates in the world but are
incorporated into the fellowship, and that there they grow in grace that
they may go forth as a corporate witness into the world again. Individual
witness without *the Church idea* is largely futile because it ends with the
death of the individual Christian. To be incorporated into the Body, which
is the Church, is like the growth of a tree in which the multiplication of
fibers over the years causes the tree to grow in bulk and strength. There is
continuity in the world about the Church idea that we do not see in the
conversion of individuals if they are left isolated in the world.

Those of us who have studied intensively the planting and growth of
churches on the mission field have found that the churches that grow best
and vibrate with indigenous life have paid attention to three things—a
concern for winning large numbers of people from the world, a concern for
effective nurture within the fellowship, and a concern for the development
of functional roles and opportunities for service. Each of these stimulates
a form of church growth, which we may call *quantitative, qualitative* and
organic. However, two doctrines must accompany these forms of development: first the doctrine of *equilibrium,* for the growth must be whole, and
one dimension should not outstrip the others; and second the doctrine of
continuity for the process has to go on from generation to generation.
Each generation must experience the new birth and make the church
growth discovery for itself. It does not have to live on the experience of
the older generation but is involved in current happenings.

In conclusion, then, I hope that I have outlined an adequate frame of
reference, theoretical and theological, within which we can operate as the
Church communicating with mankind. I hope it fixes the key points of
reference so that we will not be evangelical individualists in the world,
winning individuals and not incorporating them into a congregation or
fellowship of believers. I hope we will not bypass the Church as an

archaic institution that does not belong to the space age. I hope that we, realizing first what it means to be a fellowship of believers, will see this same fellowship as also the Body of Christ ministering His word and mind and demonstrating His love in the world and bringing men and women face to face with Christ. This *church idea* came from Jesus and to lose sight of it is to lose part of His word to mankind.

In the final analysis, however, the work of Christ grows or does not grow on the level of the thousands of small local fellowships of believers, operating as the Body of Christ in every local situation. If the plans to win the world are not brought to focus on the idea of *planting small churches in every local scene* so that converts can be incorporated into something warm and personal and there become responsible for winning their own little world around them, then the *church idea,* which springs from the teaching of Jesus himself, has not been learned. This, it seems to me, should be the criterion by which we test the effectiveness of our communication.

CHAPTER 5

Glowing

The Florescence
of the Fellowship:
Missiological Ecclesiology

A missionary, whose witness was in the university circles of a large foreign city, told me of his confronting students with the challenge of decision for Christ, but of his refusal to introduce converts to the pastors of any local congregation because he thought his converts would be misfits there. He could not see that his view of Christian mission was internally self-contradictory. If there is any validity at all in bringing men and women in conversion to Christ, the corollary must also be valid that converts must be incorporated into congregations or fellowships. As P.T. Forsyth is said to have put it, the "same act which sets us in Christ, set us also in the society of Christ" (cited in Miller 1966:18).

It may be that the forms of our congregations need reform, but we have no mandate to dispense with them altogether. On the contrary, the notion of a *koinonia* is scripturally essential, both at home and abroad. We confront this missionary problem situation in many forms. Let me cite a few examples.

The original version of this chapter was published in *Missiology,* April 1975, Vol. III, No. 2, pp. 131-141, under the title, "The Florescence of the Fellowship." Gratitude is hereby expressed to the publisher for permission to include it here.

CHRISTIAN ISOLATES OR KOINONIA?

Example 1:
   One day I received an unsolicited appeal from a missionary who claimed to have just returned from a tour of rural Mexico. Everywhere he had "called men and women to Christ." Everywhere there was response— he recorded a precise figure over twenty thousand. As far as I could tell they were only figures. The Church had certainly not grown by that number. He appears to have made no provision for them to be incorporated into Christian fellowship groups or any effort to see the responses were followed up and nurtured. Apart from the objectionable promotional character of his literature, theologically it showed a defective doctrine of the nature of conversion. Twenty thousand "halfbaked" Christians are no more than so many lonely individuals if no practicing corporate group emerges to carry on after the departure of the evangelist.

Example 2:
   The green light turned red in front of the Broadway department store and I had to stop. Two huge women descended on me like eagles on a rabbit. They told me the danger of hell-fire and the "shortness of my time" before the light turned green again. They had a supply of "hell-fire" tracts to inflict on their victims: there must have been hundreds like myself that day! Their "gospel of escape" led nowhere and left me feeling alone. It came from nowhere and was gone, leaving the bewildered passer-by with a troublesome tract, which, even if it had influenced him, would never have led him into a Christian fellowship group.

Example 3:
   One Sunday I decided to sit at the television set and watch the various religious programs. Partly I wanted to see what kind of programs were supplied for the aged, the shut-ins, and Christians in remote places. Partly I wanted to see how the matter of evangelism and follow up were handled by the media. And, of course, I hoped I would find it a worship experience. My impressions were otherwise: I was engaged in a spectator, not a worship experience. Some of the programs were topical and only remotely religious. Others offered me salvation in very narrow individualist terms, which would have left me a Christian isolate, although as a compensation I should have received a free medal, or a key ring, or an autographed photograph or a book (any of which would have put my name on their mailling list). One by one I turned off the programs. They left me feeling that I "did not belong."[1]

Example 4:

Years ago, during my missionary days in the Fiji Islands, I spoke at the worship service of the Suva Medical School students. One of them asked me afterwards, "If I read my Bible and say my prayers daily, is there really any need for me to attend church worship?" We chatted for some time. The young fellow was about to "turn off" the familiar worship service, yet the very fact that he asked the question showed that he felt the need of the corporate group.

What brought these four unrelated incidents to my mind at one point of time I cannot say, except perhaps that they are part of a nagging feeling I have about our failure to appreciate the basic dynamics and functions of the Christian fellowship—the *koinonia*—and this is basic missiology. For a young university student to be stranded as a lone Christian in a hostile environment and separated from the protection of his lineage must be a heartbreaking experience. For one to be lost in a huge city with a frightening "hell-fire" tract, which misconstrues the faith, and have no one with whom to talk about it; or to find "salvation" through the enticement of a free medal or book and to be plagued with the "envelope within the envelope" thereafter, but to enjoy no face-to-face relationships with other pilgrims on the way (the spectator experience of a TV "show" is a poor substitute for this); or to live a genuinely devotional individual Christian life that stops short of the experience of corporate worship—these are all the same basic problem of loneliness and isolation.

Christians are not isolates. They are never whole (even as individuals) until they assume their roles as *koinonoi* in the fellowship. This group is far more than a sum of so many individuals. There is a network of spiritual interaction and relationships that gives a totally new value and quality to the whole, like the florescence of flowering shrubs in spring. When Carl Linnaeus fell on his knees and praised God for the glory of the English heath of blossoming gorse, he was not stimulated by the beauty of a single flower (although he was never unaware of this). It was the florescence of the whole countryside which overwhelmed him.

Anthropology has tried to grapple with the notion that a true community is more than a sum of individuals, and more even than a multi-individual entity. A new quality comes from the interacting dynamics of the totality. As yet we have no tool for measuring this quality but its reality cannot be doubted. To describe it, Anthropology has borrowed its analogies from Botany and Chemistry. I want to apply them missiologically to the biblical concept of *koinonia,* the multi-individual community of *koinonoi,* since the goal of evangelism at home is to incorporate converts into the Christian group, and abroad to establish an indigenous fellowship group or church. The act of bringing individuals to Christ has to be consummated by their acceptance of the new status and role of *koinonoi* in the *koinonia.* Let us now explore the structure of the *koinonia* and the functional roles of *koinonoi,* using the analogy of florescence.

THE STRUCTURE OF FLORESCENCE

1. Inflorescence

Inflorescence is the process of coming into flower, including such things as the arrangement of flowers in the cluster on the branch. On the wastelands of Australia, I have seen shrubs whose flowers are tiny and inconspicuous but so arranged by the good Lord of Nature that hundreds of these tiny forms are bunched together so that from a short distance they look like large and beautiful blooms, which again collectively leave the landscape a blaze of color. The botanical analogy can be used of human society. Those anthropologists who try to deal with "national character-istics" are, in point of fact, observing their own impression of collectivity or cultural florescence. We do the same thing in missiology when we feel or declare that some particular church congregation is static, or that some other is active. The congregational inflorescence, in one case, may display a social emphasis, or in another its evangelical outreach, for example, but it represents a total quality by which that particular group may be recognized.

I remember years ago, just after my conversion, when I was beginning my first serious explorations of Christian literature, how I came upon a description of the Church Universal. (I think the writer was W. L. Watkinson.) He described the Church as a mighty tree growing in bulk and strength by adding millions of seemingly insignificant fibers year by year. It was my first diachronic picture of the Church. Years later it helped me to understand why Christians in a traditional society set such a high value on the diachronics of the *Te Deum,* for example. But the analogy of florescence is a synchronic one. It helps me consider the fellowship group *across* time rather than *through* it, the church as it floresces today.

2. Efflorescence

Efflorescence (if we shift from Botany to Chemistry) is a process of crystallization, the production of "crystal flowers" due to slow evapora-tion. In my boyhood days I used to spend my Saturdays playing at adventure among the saltbush between the shallow pans of the Geelong Salt Works. From my secret lair in the shrubbery I observed the marsh wildlife, the sea birds, an occasional hunter shooting snipe, and I ate my lunch in the imagined surroundings of Robinson Crusoe. One day I pulled up a wooden peg, which had a huge head of rock salt with inch-cube crystals, the biggest I had ever seen. The abundance of salt and the slow evaporation by the sun had given this cluster of crystals an efflorescence of great beauty. I took it home for my schoolboy museum and was the envy of all my playmates.

The cube of crystal salt was not merely a material object. It was the outcome of *an ongoing process,* as the salt pans were filled time and time again and evaporated by the heat of the sun. It is here that the analogy is appropriate for the *social group*—we have a beauty and perfection of form that comes as the result of an ongoing process. So Chemistry provides an analogy for Anthropology—and my conviction is that Anthropology, having "humanized" the figure of speech, speaks to Missiology.

Anthropologist Raymond Firth articulated the idea in *We, the Tikopia,* as in his research he sought the meaning of the "aesthetic elaboration of the society's basic forms":

> The vital things in society are the forces which keep it in action, which draw and hold groups together, and allow of the functioning of institutions, of sets of human relationships. These forces come to expression in different ways in different societies, and once having taken one form of expression, a kind of institutional efflorescence sometimes takes place. . . (1963:211).

The area of aesthetic elaboration in any society is always reflected in its vocabulary—kinship structure in one case, war in another, the life of the herd in another. The same elaboration or diversification has been discussed by many anthropologists under different terms. Herskovits, for example, called it "the cultural focus" (1951:Ch. 32). Whatever term be used, the theoretical concept may well be applied to the Christian *koinonia,* which we shall now proceed to do.

THE KOINONIA AND THE KOINONOI

We meet the concept of *koinonia* in the Acts of the Apostles at the very beginning of Christian history. The participants *(koinonoi)* are reported as "continuing steadfastly in the fellowship" and practicing certain specific religious exercises, including an apostolic teaching program, the breaking of bread and the prayers "in the fellowship" (Acts 2:42). This brief passage suggests that the Christian *koinonia* had already established certain forms and values, the direction of the process was already apparent, the "crystals were efflorescing."

The biblical writer who developed the concept of *koinonia* more than any other was the apostle Paul. He tied the whole Christian faith and practice, including the missionary outreach, into the life of the Church. John's view of the *koinonia* as a two-dimensional fellowship is located in only one Scripture passage (1 Jn. 1).[2] Paul's concept ramifies through his writing, and is implied in places where the word is not actually used. He used it most frequently in writing to the Corinthians, where significantly the nature and function of the fellowship needed the strongest articulation.

After defining the aesthetic elaboration of basic forms in terms of efflorescence, Firth schematized the ramifications of the Tikopian dual kinship system (1963:212). In a certain Solomon Island society, I myself have described the "most central element for determining the life of the community, the most specialized feature of life" in terms of the "minting of custom money" (Tippett 1967a:173-177). Such a schematization requires, first, the identification of the basic elements that set the values of a group and hold it together, and then their arrangement in proper relationship. I think this can be done for the Christian fellowship group as conceptualized by Paul, by working from the Greek New Testament and pondering the ways Paul used the *koinon*-group of words in his letters. The seven elements of the following reconstruction have been assembled in that manner.

1. A Spiritual Experience

Participation in the *koinonia* is a highly spiritual experience. It is not an intellectual matter (although the Lord does claim the intellect); it is an experience. The *koinonoi* are "called to the fellowship of His Son" (1 Cor. 1:9) and to "fellowship in the Spirit" (Phil. 2:1). They are to share the "fellowship in the gospel" (Phil. 1:5). Individuals are not "new creatures" because they understand theology, but because the grace of Christ has transformed them and thus each person can say with assurance, "I know whom I have believed . . . " (2 Tim. 1:12).

2. Focused in Worship

This fellowship in the Lord, this spiritual experience, comes to a physical focus in the Christian worship pattern (Phil. 3:3; 1 Cor. 14:25-26), especially in the central rite of Holy Communion, which Paul speaks of as "the fellowship of the blood" and "the fellowship of the body" (1 Cor. 10:16). This is both an individual and a corporate act, and it cannot be fully meaningful without each dimension, when we gather to partake of "the full benefits of his passion" ("The Invocation" in "The Order for Holy Communion").

3. A Rigorous Commitment

Participation in the koinonia demands a rigorous commitment to the Lord. This refers to faith and loyalty. The Corinthian Christians were sorely tested at this point. They had a tendency to incorporate aspects of Corinthian cults into their Christianity, making it syncretistic. Paul was quite definite: there was to be no religious coexistence or syncretism. "Ye cannot be partakers of the Lord's table, and the table of devils"—what Paul calls *koinonous ton daimonion,* "the fellowship of devils" (1 Cor. 10:19-21). This significant phrase indicates Paul's mind on the subject of commitment and loyalty. There were two quite distinct and opposite *koinonia,* and there could be no divided loyalty.[3] The passage is direct and refers to the precise temptations in Corinth—the issues of idolatry, sacrifice and religious ritual. In cross-cultural mission this is still a real confrontation. In mission on the home front it is just as real, although the forms of idolatry may be different.

4. A High Moral Life

For the *koinonoi,* a high moral life is essential. In the "fellowship of light" it is impossible for one to walk in darkness (1 Jn. 1:5-7). The righteous must not have traffic with the unrighteous (2 Cor. 6:14). To be identified with the wrong *koinonoi* will lead the *koinonia* to destruction. This dimension of Christian holiness has its roots in the Old Testament, in which the people of God were called to be holy, because God himself is holy (Lev. 19:2; cf. Mt. 5:48). The *koinonos* is Christ's person—and this is a holy relationship. The word group comes from the Greek classics— where the sharing might be a business partnership, a citizenship or a marriage, and in some of the later cults a mystical union with deity, but the use of *koinonos* with the "genitive of person" is confined to the Judeo-Christian tradition (Hauch 1965:799). The relationship between Christ and the Christian is unique and holy, and this conditions the life of the *koinonoi* with respect to the expectation of Christian holiness.

In his short epistle to Philemon, Paul's appeal for Christian charity is not based on the mere bond of friendship, but on the spiritual oneness in the faith in and through Christ—the "communication" (AV) and "sharing" (RSV) in Philemon 6 is *koinonia.* The "characteristic of the Church," Cranfield says, "was a *togetherness* far deeper than camaraderie" (1957:82). Only in the fellowship of grace can mankind aspire to holiness.

5. Fellowship in Suffering

Those who are called to the Christ life may also expect to discover something of "the fellowship of his sufferings" (Phil. 3:10) which is related in the same passage to the resurrection. The Christian becomes involved in the life, death, and resurrection of his Lord. Participation in the sufferings of Christ foreshadow participation with Him in glory (2 Cor. 1:5-7). In verse 7 the clause, "ye are partakers of the suffering," has *koinonoi* for "partakers." This has been called the "fulfilment of the law of fellowship" (Hauch 1965:806).

It is appropriate that Paul's last word to the Corinthians should be a benediction, praying for them the "communion of the Holy Spirit' — communion again is *koinonia.* Nothing but the power of the Holy Spirit can maintain the holy life and the relations between *koinonoi* that are required for the florescence of the fellowship in the world where it is growing (2 Cor. 13:14).

6. Fellowship in Service

The phrase "the fellowship of the ministry to the saints" (2 Cor. 8:4) is interesting, not only for the type of service ministry Paul is discussing, but because it *relates the koinonia and the diakonia.* The root, *koinon-* means "to share with others," not merely to share by giving, but to share in their needs and sufferings, and to give empathetically in the Lord. It is a relationship between *koinonoi* within the *koinonia.* "Its foundation," says Cranfield (1957:81), "is the sharing together by Christians in his benefits." Or as Barclay says, that in the "sharing between Christ and man, and man and man, there is that sympathy of those who have passed through the common experience" (1956:74). The new relationship between the *koinonoi* stems from their relations with Christ. The *diakonia* is part of the *koinonia,* and because of this it obtains a deeper meaning. We should not separate the service idea from that of the entity of the fellowship.

7. An Obligation for World Mission

But this is not all that Paul has to say to the *koinonoi* of the various congregations to which he wrote letters. *The koinonia is tied by obligations to a program of world mission.* With the sending forth of Paul and Barnabas with the symbolic "right hand of fellowship" (Gal. 2:9), we have the congregational act which validated Paul, not only as a *koinonos,* but also as a missionary sent forth. Two missions are here identified in the ministry of the Church—"to the circumcision" (within their own culture), and the other "unto the heathen" (*eis ta ethne*). The mission is to communicate "the unsearchable riches of Christ," revealing to the Gentiles "the fellowship of the mystery," which is tied up with the purpose of God from creation (Eph. 3:8-9) in terms of the Church (v. 10) to the glorification of our Lord (v. 14) among all mankind (vv. 14-15). This is Paul's *cosmic koinonia,* of which the local congregation, the *koinonia* at any given place, is a microcosm, partaking in the divine purpose in the task of bringing all mankind under the challenge of the Lordship of the Cosmic Christ. In this configuration of the *koinonia* we have a concentration of forces: the service ministry (*diakonia*), the loyalty of the *koinonoi,* the spiritual resources (the fellowship of the Son, the Holy Spirit, and the Gospel), the ritual of worship (especially the fellowship of the body and blood), the life of holiness and the missionary program of the outreaching Church.

"In the Pentecost story," as Williams points out in his discussion of the *koinonia* from its origin to its consummation,

> . . . the Spirit created a community that broke through the barriers of language, culture, race. . . . Here is the promise of new life for the nations. . . . The church is called to be the moving sign on the front wave of history, revealing to the nations the promise of their destiny (1968:63).

This is not a simple single cell fellowship group, but a highly developed organism with direction and with purpose, with resources and with a patterned way of life (cf. Figure 6). This is no dream or embryo. This is a *koinonia* which is mature, developed, florescent—having burst into flower—demonstrating the life force pulsating within it, the ongoing spiritual process and its capacity to reach from Jew to Gentile and open their spiritual resources to be shared by the nations (Rom. 15:27).

FIGURE 6
The Florescence of the *Koinonia*

According to Paul

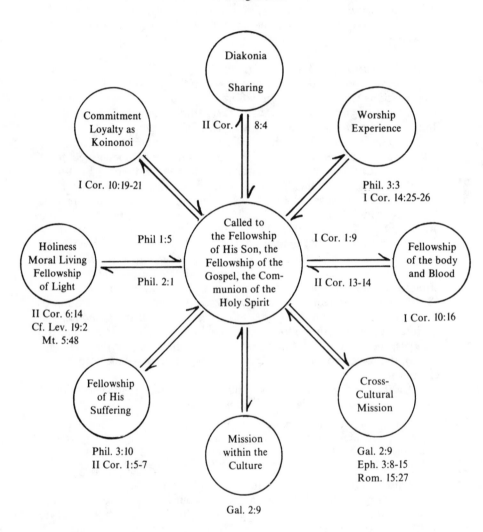

Notes:

1. I do not mean to imply that the media cannot be used for the glory of God and the communication of the Gospel. I mean that when I took a random sample of what was being actually communicated, I came up with a negative result.

2. See my "Editorial" in *Missiology* (1974b) for a further discussion of this passage.

3. The rival "table of devils" and the "cup of devils" were not mere oratorical figures of speech, but a highly realistic sacrificial rite in which the worship comprised the eating of the sacrifice by the celebrants (Hauch 1965:80f.n.) and a cup of wine consecrated to the pagan divinity first by libation (Massie n.d.:208). This coexistence was a moral impossibility, though unfortunately a physical reality which threatened to destroy the *koinonia* at the point of loyalty.

The Readiness of the World.

CHAPTER 6

The Holy Spirit
and Responsive Populations

The business of Christian mission is to seek conversion responses, and certainly in the final analysis this is the work of the Holy Spirit.[1] However, on deeper reflection, the title brings together two much debated issues in current missionary theory and theology, both with serious consequences in the existential missionary situation. I shall discuss first the *fact* of responsive populations so that we may understand the conversion phenomena to which the theology of the Holy Spirit is to be applied.

RESPONSIVE POPULATIONS

(1)

Why *populations,* one may ask, why populations and not *persons*? In this context the word *populations* directs one to the non-Western world of extended families, clans, tribes, castes and age grades, where whole villages may represent precise ethnic entities, and where such groups may elect to turn from animism to Christianity as total units at one precise point of time. This kind of religious movement may be positively drawn *toward* Christianity or negatively pushed *away* from it. For purposes of differentiation we may describe the former as a *people movement* and the latter as a *nativistic movement.* Spiritually they are direct opposites, but psychologically they comprise almost identical dynamics. When we speak of "responsive populations" we are thinking of large homogeneous units of people who, once they have made their decision, act in unison. Many

The original version of this chapter was published in *Crucial Issues in Missions Tomorrow,* Donald A. McGavran (ed.), (Chicago: Moody Press, 1972), pp. 77-101. Gratitude is hereby expressed to the publisher for permission to include it here.

46

peoples have become Christian in this manner; indeed, most parts of the world where Christianity is solidly entrenched were originally won from paganism in the first place by people movements. A decade ago the debate on the validity of this kind of conversion complex was quite heated. Today the people movement idea is more widely accepted by evangelical missionaries and strategists because it is better understood. Many of its critics still speak of it wrongly as *mass movement*. Church growth writers, however, have been working on people movements for years and have resolved the basic problem by means of the term *multi-individual* to describe the phenomenon. This came into use about 1962 and has been written up at length in statements which demonstrate its anthropological and theological validity (Tippett 1971:251-256, 338; 1967; and McGavran 1970:296-315).

ⓐ CHURCH GROWTH AND PEOPLE MOVEMENTS

Church growth writers have also engaged in considerable research with respect to the use of group structures in "the transition from animistic to Christian forms" in the process of church planting (Tippett 1967a:269-285). Generally this has been well received by both anthropologists and nationals. Side by side with this, some new dimensions, and warnings, have been developed about the *indigenous church concept* to make it more theological and more realistic on the practical level (Tippett 1973a:126-141; McGavran 1970:335-353). Likewise, Bavinck's idea of *possessio* (1964:179-190) has been appropriated and given a little more depth (Tippett 1973a:105-106) by tying it in with the notion of the *functional substitute*. The concept relates to the *permanence of culture change* when the social group accepts it, and speaks especially to *directed* change and therefore is significant both in anthropology and mission. The cultural ramifications of functional substitution in church planting has been discussed by this writer on the theoretical level (1963), on the existential level with respect to data from Fiji (1958) and the Solomon Islands (1967a) and as a principle to be allowed for in planning church planting (1970a). These ideas bear on the handling of people movements and have been well received by Christian nationals who have known this type of experience. The development of this concept permits the preservation of many cultural features in the church being planted — thus a more indigenous church emerges from the beginning because it allows for the congregation acting as a multi-individual group. At the same time it is a safeguard against syncretism — a long standing criticism against some group movements. The people movement idea is thus culturally acceptable and Christian mission can be undertaken with a minimum of cultural disruption and a maximum of indigenity.

The character of missionary role has changed, but there must be a *continuing* missionary role. Now that the era of the old mission station approach (McGavran 1955:ch. 5; Bradshaw 1968:27) has virtually given way to a new era of partnership with, or fraternal worker service in, indigenous churches, there is no other feasible option before the Christian mission in communal and tribal societies but that which is commonly called "the church growth approach." The church growth viewpoint is anthropologically based, indigenously focused and biblically orientated. It is certainly not, as some superficial critics have maintained, mere statistical "denominational extension," although the church planting may be denominationally serviced.

THE THEOLOGY OF PESSIMISM AND PEOPLE MOVEMENT

The missionary strategists who nonchalantly reject church growth as an adequate approach to mission are usually conditioned by a *theology of pessimism*. This may be labelled universalist, liberal or even conservative and still be pessimistic. This pessimism may spring from any one of three causes:

1. The wartime experiences of Christianity driven underground in Europe and the philosophical adjustments demanded by existence in the oppressive situation.

2. The current frustration and despair because of the encroaching secularity, the scientific agnosticism, the selfish individualism and permissiveness, the multi-individual rejection of the establishment, including institutional religion, and the frequently articulated idea that the church is fighting for its survival.

3. The experience of nongrowth in the resistant mission fields, where after a century or more of our foreign missioning, there has been created only a small, foreign church, worshipping in English, French or German instead of the vernacular, with our own foreign denominational structure, content to remain dependent on foreign funds and leadership, and who (if they have produced any leaders of their own) will be so foreignized as to be seen as foreigners by their fellow countrymen.

Many of the vocal theologians of today, and likewise many makers of mission policy, are victims of one or more of these factors, so that we do not wonder at the cloud of gloom and pessimism over everything;[2] and the futile attempts at reevaluating missionary philosophy to meet these conditions. The error here lies in the assumption that the *whole* world is resistant: that there are no ripe fields waiting for harvest anywhere. This error is tragic.

It is tragic because it accepts a wrong criterion. The idea of mission (i.e. bringing peoples to discipleship in terms of accepting the name of Father, Son and Holy Spirit) is not determined by the physical and social conditions that cast the gloom about us, but by the word of the Lord. He said that all power was now given him, that his followers were to make disciples of all nations, and that he would be with them to the end of the world. If you accept that word, the implication is that mission in these terms goes on to the end. The idea that "the world sets the agenda" is true only in one sense. There is another sense in which it is false. That the needs of the world should not claim our attention is not argued; what is argued is that the Great Commission has not been withdrawn.

→ *It is tragic because it is a wrong evaluation of the world situation.* This view presupposes there are no responsive populations and no doors wide open. It overlooks hundreds of communities in Africa, in Latin America, in Indonesia and New Guinea, and bypasses what has really been happening in these post-war years. Winter, a provocative church growth historian, realist and yet an optimist, pointed out in *The Twenty-Five Unbelievable Years: 1945-1969:*

> The church in Korea grew more in the years 1953-60 than it had in the previous sixty years. The church in Sub-Sahara Africa more than tripled from thirty to ninety-seven million. In Indonesia at least fifty thousand Moslems became Christians. . . . The South India Conference of the Methodist Church in the face of persecution grew from 95,000 to 190,000 members. The Presbyterian Church in Taiwan between 1955 and 1965 engaged in a "Double the Church Campaign" concluded it successfully. In Latin America, largely due to ceaseless and effective personal evangelism on the part of the Pentecostal family of Churches, Protestants grew from about 1,900,000 in 1945 to at least 19,000,000 in 1970. In Brazil alone, by 1970, new congregations of the evangelical variety were being founded at the rate of three thousand per year (1970:67).

The battle is by no means lost. If the Church has her back to the wall in some places it is certainly not so in others—even if it means that the responsibility of the Church is being taken away from the West.

→ *It is tragic because a theology of pessimism can never handle these responsive population opportunities.* The great majority of these people movements have been husbanded by Christians with a simple, biblical faith of a conservative type and a spirit of optimism. Another factor which frequently comes to notice in church growth case studies is the way missionaries explain nongrowth as due to their "being in resistant fields" and being quite convinced that this is so; while comparative analysis reveals that the Pentecostals or some neo-pagan religious movement is going ahead by leaps and bounds. We find the growth may be Baptist here, Methodist there, Presbyterian over yonder, but I have never found growth in a church or society clouded with a theology of pessimism. There have always been a vibrant missionary drive, a clear goal and a simple clear-cut faith.

Those pagan movements which are bounding forward in our day are frequently using the techniques of evangelical Christianity, and they indicate that people are open for religious change and probably looking for it. For a century or more Christians have been striving to win the American Indians. Some are Christian, usually where they got caught up in revivals or people movements. Now, before our eyes, 45 percent of the Navahos are reported to be involved in the Peyote Cult. It may be that missionaries have used the wrong methods. It may be that few have learned the Navaho language. It may be that they have offered a foreign church. It may be that the white man's poor relations with the Indians through history was too great an obstacle. But we can never say Indians are now resistant to religious change. No one who has investigated the spread of peyote among them can say that. We are surrounded by winnable peoples in locations we call resistant.

→ *It is tragic because it is satisfied with something less than the best.* As long as we are in the world as Christians, being there and finding God's presence there, merely "witnessing" by our presence, or "being faithful" and engaging in dialogue with people of other faiths — the theology of pessimism leaves it there. To strive to bring the pagan to a decision for Christ, what church growth theory calls *verdict theology,* is to create a *dialogical crisis,* and this is frowned on. This attitude of "if you cannot bring individuals to decision, then come to terms with them and coexist" is certainly not scriptural. It eliminates the existential cross of the disciple of Christ from his or her ministry in the world. We turn to a missionary theologian who came from people movement experiences in New Guinea, whose opinion was that:

> Today we have a Christianity that shies away from suffering, which still goes on dreaming of a Christianized world, appeals to the rights of man and the freedom of conscience and wants to put them into operation; all this in order to escape suffering and to make that suffering impossible instead of recognizing her call to suffer. Suffering does not fit into the Church's need for security nor into the modern philosophy of men (Vicedom: 1965:139).

Vicedom's book throughout is one which realistically faces up to the confrontations of the Christian with the world, and sees the mission of the Church in the world and "the congregation as the point of breakthrough for the Holy Ghost in the world" with a responsibility to lead men and women in the world to commitment (1965:93). In a smaller book he described down-to-earth events which showed converts being formed into congregations by people movement patterns (1962). Here is the Holy Spirit at work on a responsive population, and here is a book which fits in with the church growth case studies. His *Mission of God* reacts against the theology of pessimism because the defeatism of the latter has no way of dealing with people movement responses and therefore ignores them.

To recapitulate to this point, I have claimed that the fields open for mission are not as resistant as often imagined, that the people who await the Gospel should be seen as large groups—tribes, peoples, population—

that they may be expected to turn Christian as social groups, that from these multi-individual people movements we may expect indigenous churches—formally cultural, rather than denominational extension. I have also pointed out the current theology of pessimism that controls much missionary policymaking, and I find it a wrong criterion, a wrong evaluation of the world situation, unable to handle the responsive situations, and less than scripturally prescribed in that it avoids responsibility to which we have been called. Against all this the Bible calls us to a theology of encounter and does not promise any escape from a way of the cross. Nevertheless, we are encouraged to go forward with expectation and optimism, knowing that ultimately victory will be with the Lord. It is important that we *recognize the existence of responsive populations.* Anthropology has taught us much about how to handle them, but this is not enough, we have to bring ourselves into tune with the Spirit of God and put ourselves under His direction.

THE HOLY SPIRIT

The other dimension of our title is the Holy Spirit. Some Evangelicals still relate cross-cultural missions to their own Western conversion requirements. They cannot see a people movement as "under God." I have known some Western missionaries to refuse to harvest a field "ripe unto harvest," and even in one case to hold off people at gunpoint when they came as a tribe to burn their fetishes and thus demonstrate their change of heart. These missionaries wanted them to come one by one, against their tribal cohesion. Church growth literature has not bypassed this problem; it is one of the most recurring themes. The multi-individual conversion pattern has been examined on a basis of its New Testament precedents and prototypes, and usually Evangelicals who take the trouble to follow through the relevant passages are soon convinced that multi-individual people movements are quite biblical.

In my earlier writing I have been mostly concerned with simply demonstrating that many types of people movement are found in Scripture, and that these may therefore be presumed to have been "under God." But one can go further. These movements, which followed social structure, were under the specific direction of the Holy Spirit and the biblical writers have said so. It was only when I began following them as a theme through the book of Acts that this recurring feature struck me. I had studied the Holy Spirit as a doctrine. I had been instructed in His role in conversion, in the life of faith, in the church and its ministry and so on. When I thought of the Holy Spirit I tended to recall certain specific passages of Scripture, but the Spirit as a recurring feature of the episodes of church expansion was a belated realization. I had read about this in Roland Allen (1927) but it had not registered until I discovered it for myself:

Missionary work as an expression of the Holy Spirit has received such slight and casual attention that it might almost escape the notice of a hasty reader . . . it is in the revelation of the Holy Spirit as a missionary Spirit that the Acts stands alone in the New Testament. The nature of the Spirit as missionary can indeed be observed in the teaching of the gospels and the epistles; but there it is hinted rather than asserted. In Acts it is the one prominent feature. . . . Directly and indirectly it is made all important. To treat it as secondary destroys the whole character and purpose of the book (1962:21).

In this chapter I am concentrating on a single aspect of the work of the Holy Spirit, namely *His relationship with responsive populations, with the winning of human communities to Christ.*

The mission to the world to which our Lord called his followers was built on *the prototype of his own mission to the world.*[3] This is clearly stated in John 17. His coming to this world, as the nativity stories in Luke show, was charged with the power of the Spirit (Lk. 1:35; Mt. 1:18, 20). Even those persons associated with the nativity complex received the Spirit—Elizabeth, Zacharias and Simeon (Lk. 1:41, 67; 2:25-26). The Spirit was at the Lord's baptism (Mt. 3:16; Jn. 1:33), his temptation (Lk. 4:1) and with him throughout his ministry (Acts 10:38). Jesus himself lived in the power of the Spirit and accomplished his mission to the world in that power. It was in the same power that he commissioned the apostles both before (Mt. 10:20; Jn. 17:18) and after the resurrection (Mt. 28:19), promising them the resources of the Spirit, a promise he had made on other occasions for other purposes also (Jn. 15:26; 16:13). Not only are we sent as he was sent into the world, but we are to teach what he taught (Mt. 28:20) and love as he loved (Jn. 15:12, 13:15). The Spirit was clearly with Jesus during his lifetime (Mt. 3:16; Mk. 1:10; Lk. 3:22; 4:1; 10:21; Jn. 1:32; 3:34; Acts 1:2), and in this power he achieved his mission on earth (Mt. 12:28; Lk. 4:14-15, 18 ff.; Jn. 3:34, etc.). Furthermore, he took his stand on a basis of prophecy related to the Gentile world mission (Mt. 12:18 ff. and Lk. 4:18; cf. Isa. 42:1-4; 61:1-2).

So Jesus taught his followers to interpret his own mission to the world as a prototype for, and a prelude to, their own. Quoting the Scriptures, he claimed the Spirit (Lk. 4:18), and the gospel writers who reported what they remembered of him certainly declared that the Spirit was with him. *Thus for their mission to be built on the prototype he had provided, there had to be an event something like Pentecost.* The mission of the apostles presupposes the *availability* of the Spirit as a source of power. An intellectual or social Christian "mission" without the power of the Holy Spirit is invalid because an essential ingredient is missing. When Jesus gave his own model for mission it implied the power and activity of the Spirit.

There is one other thing to be noted about this prototype of our Lord—one other implication besides the availability of the Spirit: he also implied the *importance of the social group.* If we are to relate the Holy Spirit to responsive groups, as distinct from individuals, we must pause here for a moment. We have emphasized Jesus' dealings with individuals and, of course, he was deeply concerned with individuals. But our Western individualism has closed our eyes to the fact that individuals belong in groups. Jesus was moved by the individual without a *group,* the individual *isolated from his group,* and the joy and salvation of the healing of a leper or a demoniac was not merely a matter of physical restoration but that *now he belongs.* [4] He could go back to the group from which he had been alienated and tell them what the Lord had done to him (Mk. 5:19). This is the point of the three parables in Luke 15: the isolated one now belongs again; the lost sheep is no longer lost; the lost son is home again. Jesus' concepts are *collectives*—folds and flocks (Jn. 10:16). Even when he deals with individuals he has the total group in mind. The episode with the woman of Samaria is a good example of this: beyond the woman, Jesus saw the group to which she belonged. He sent her back into the village (Jn. 4:16), knowing she would talk (vv. 27-30). He saw Sychar as a field ripe unto harvest—a responsive population (v. 35)—and he was quite right, for many of the Samaritans of that city believed on him (vv. 34-43). When he preached the Gospel to the poor and deliverance to the captives, though this may have been directed to an individual at times, I believe he was speaking here of collective mankind—the communities that he desires to restore. Jesus concentrated his ministry on groups like the publicans and sinners, village groups and occupational groups (Lk. 15:2; Mk. 2:16; Jn. 1:24, etc.). He sent his disciples to households and villages (Lk. 8:1; 10:5, 8-9, etc.). Even the Great Commission is in terms of ethnic units within ecumenicity.

Therefore, from among the features of Jesus' model for mission, I have selected two only for this chapter: (1) the presupposition of the availability and the activity of the Holy Spirit as the source of power, and (2) the implication that the human group is a thing to be preserved, that the isolated individual needs to be restored to the place where he or she belongs, and that groups are winnable. Thus the two elements of the subject of this chapter are both found to have been clearly articulated in the mission of our Lord himself. As he himself determined what the apostle's model for mission was to be, this surely ought to be valid for us today. Pessimistic theology has to be rated against this model.

NEW TESTAMENT CHURCH PLANTING

Our Lord gave us to understand that the Holy Spirit would be operative within the Christian mission (Mk. 13:10-11). We also have the promise that He operates to the end, together with both the witnessing church and convert (Rev. 22:17). The whole sweep of church history lies between these points.

History of Beginning of the Church

   Pentecost itself, the historic happening when the Spirit was manifestly
given to the waiting apostles, was followed by their first missionary
proclamation (Acts 2). The proclamation was in terms of trinitarian
action. The audience was reminded of the promise of the Spirit (v. 33)
which was not, in reality, offered to a wider audience than the apostolic
band (v. 38). This is verdict theology—repentance and response. Three
thousand souls is a people movement figure (v. 41). These converts were
baptized together and immediately consolidated into a physical fellowship,
as Jesus bound together the disciples. Thereafter in their travels they left
behind little social groups as Jesus himself had left in Sychar. Thus the
churches or fellowships—with doctrine, fellowship, the breaking of bread
and prayers—began to grow organically from the very start (v. 42). They
went from house to house and praised God (vv. 46-47), and their numbers
grew day by day. Although this was a strong people movement that went
on day after day, it was not a mass movement, for the biblical recorder
speaks of *"every soul"* (v. 43).
   In the following chapter a lame individual was cured, but the incident
was used by Peter as a subject for a sermon to the total group. This
sermon to the people (men of Israel) involved an encounter with a select
group (4:1), and imprisonment. Asked by their judges to give an account
of themselves, they spoke of the Holy Spirit (v. 8). Peter spoke at length
and they were released with warning. Subsequent preaching and healing
and fellowship led to another outpouring of the Holy Spirit (4:31). The
movement had grown so much that by Acts 6 it was out of hand and
murmurings arose. The church was already bicultural. Under the leadership of the twelve, the community was called together and the multi-
individual group operated as decision maker. The ideas put forward by the
leaders were ratified by the populace (vv. 3-5), new roles were created,
and individuals were appointed—further organic growth. The three criteria
for this position were "honest report, full of the Holy Ghost and wisdom."
One of the appointees was a proselyte. They were ordained by the laying
on of hands. As a result of this organic growth under the Spirit of God, a
number of priests joined the community. This phase of the people
movement was terminated, as far as the written record shows, with the
death of Stephen, whose message was rejected in spite of the fact that he
was full of the Holy Spirit (7:55). He had pointed out plainly to his
audience that they were resisting the Holy Spirit (v. 51).
   This episode is a bridge to the story of Paul after a series of rural
incidents. Word came to Jerusalem of interest in Samaria. We might call
it a *mood of inquiry,* or a readiness to listen to the Gospel (8:14), and so
John and Peter were sent there. As yet there was no spiritual movement,
no outpouring of the Spirit (v. 16); but after prayer directed to this end
(v. 15), they of Samaria also shared the experience (v. 17). This gift of the
Spirit was so manifest that a local magician wanted to buy it, just as
animist magicians trade their secrets to this day. Thus the early church

CHAPTER 6 - THE HOLY SPIRIT AND RESPONSIVE POPULATIONS

was alerted to a danger and given a useful piece of instruction. The preaching extended through the villages (v. 25).

We are now introduced to Philip who was directed to Gaza to meet the Ethiopian and lead him to Christ, under the guidance of the Spirit (vv. 29-38). Subsequently the Spirit led him away to Azotus and the cities of Caesarea (v. 40), leaving the convert to take the Gospel to the nation where he had great authority (v. 27). Also from the Petrine narrative we have the people movements at Lydda and Sharon where whole villages ("all that dwelt at") turned collectively to the Lord. Peter was itinerating. There were already Christians at Lydda and he visited them for pastoral encouragement. These movements were sparked off by a healing miracle (9:32-25), as also happened at Joppa (vv. 36-43). In the following chapter Peter was with Cornelius at Caesarea, whither he had been called. Cornelius had "called together his kinsmen and dear friends" (10:24) and they were many (v. 27). Peter witnessed (vv. 39-41), that is, he shared his experience, and the Holy Spirit fell on those who heard (v. 44). This extended family conversion in the Gentile community surprised those "of the circumcision," but the converts were baptized because they had received the Holy Spirit (vv. 44-48).

All this demonstrates that Jesus led the apostles to expect expansion from Jerusalem, to Judea, to Samaria and to the uttermost parts of the earth when they had received the Holy Spirit (1:8). One of the reasons for this diffusion is found in chapter 11. Persecuted converts scattered to Phoenicia, Cyprus and Antioch and preached to the Jews of the dispersion. However, at Antioch some of those who had come from Cyprus and Cyrene preached to Grecians, and "a great number" believed (11:19-21). Barnabas, who was sent from Jerusalem to investigate it, rejoiced at the expansion of the Christian community, exhorted them to faithfulness, and went to Tarsus for Saul, whom he brought along in order to help him with instruction for a whole year (vv. 22-26). He knew of Saul's conversion and of his powerful testimony among the Jews at Damascus (9:22).

The Pauline missionary experiences are similar to those already summarized. The Holy Spirit was always active, some movements were quite extensive, and groups of converts were formed into congregations. From this point as the Gospel spread in the Graeco-Roman world house churches are formed (Rom. 16:11; Phile. 1). Lydia was baptized together with her household (Acts 16:15), as was the Roman centurion in the same city (v. 33). Paul preached to the household and obtained a group response (vv. 30-34). The word *all* appears three times in these verses, with respect to his preaching to all, and all believing and all being baptized. It is a good picture of the total multi-individual group. In chapter 18 there is the house of Crispus, the chief ruler of the synagogue, all of whom believed and were baptized (v. 8). The household was the social unit, the small group which made its own decisions at the level of personal religion as distinct from national loyalty.

In Acts 19 is recorded the disturbance which Demetrius the silver-smith caused. The previous episode reveals why the craftsmen were so alarmed. Verses 17-20 record a strong movement away from the magical arts to Christianity in Ephesus. It must have been a large and significant movement (because of the implications of the passage). The magical books and paraphernalia were worth 50,000 pieces of silver, and they were destroyed by burning, as animists today burn their fetishes upon conversion as an ocular demonstration of their change of faith: belief, confession, demonstration—the regular pattern (Tippett 1967a). A people movement among the magicians brought a counterdemonstration among the craftsmen whose trade was in jeopardy; it was a movement on the basis of occupation. People movements in occupational classes or castes may reach a great size, as for example, Xavier's movement among the fishermen in India.

To Paul's experiences at Antioch, Philippi and Ephesus we could add those at other places. Each place had its own uniqueness. In Asia Minor he began in the synagogues and presented a study arising out of the history of Israel as a steppingstone to Christ (Acts 13:14 ff.) Sometimes he had Jews, proselytes and Gentiles who responded (vv. 42-43), but organized opposition from the more envious Jews made these would-be converts less stable. In Iconium also, Jews and Greeks both believed (14:1). Paul now identified the troublemakers as "unbelieving Jews" (v. 2), but before departing from the district he ordained elders in the churches he had planted, so the organic church grew (vv. 22-23).

At Rome it was quite different. This Christian community emerged by migration growth. Christians who were merchants, soldiers, craftsmen and others moved into the capital along the network of Roman roads. Many of them met in Rome in private homes and secret places; they were even found in the household of Caesar. From Romans 16 it is apparent that Paul knew many of them before they had gone to Rome. Their names are often Greek or Roman—craftsmen, kinsmen, fellow prisoners. Eventually he reached the capital himself and, although a prisoner, he lived for two whole years in his own house, receiving all who came, preaching the kingdom and teaching of the Lord Jesus (Acts 28:30-31). A similar ending is used in his letter to Rome, in which the preaching of Jesus Christ was made manifest to all nations (16:25-27). Where better than at Rome! From the Scriptures he wrote to Rome, "I will confess to thee among the Gentiles, and sing unto they name . . . the God of hope fill you with all joy and peace in believing, that ye may abound in hope, through the power of the Holy Ghost" (15:9, 13).

To sum up this biblical unit, two things stand out clearly: (1) the activity of the Holy Spirit in the New Testament church planting, and (2) the operation and approval of the Spirit in the conversion of social groups. The control of the Christian mission by the Spirit may be seen in His initiation of mission (Acts 1:2; 13:2, 4) and His deployment of it

(16:6-7). As the blessing and power of the Spirit were promised the mother of our Lord when the incarnation was announced for his earthly mission (Lk. 1:35), so the same blessing and power of the Spirit were manifested in the mission of the apostles (Heb. 2:3-4). The New Testament church was planted by the apostles, through group movement patterns, by the power and under the direction of the Holy Spirit. The church grew from a recurring spiritual experience that brought conversion responses to multi-individual communities upon their receiving of the Spirit. Where they did not respond, this was said to be "resisting the Spirit."

THE SPIRIT IN THE GROWTH PROCESS

Essential to the possibility of the idea of Christian mission is the existential reality of a discrete fellowship group. We call this the church, though it has other biblical names—the flock, the body, the fellowship, the household, the temple, the priesthood (1 Jn. 1:3)—all of them corporate groups into which converts are to be incorporated (Tippett: 1970a:58-61). The Bible does not bind us to any single structural form for the church (either cultural or denominational), but it does commit us to a group of some kind. Our Lord formed the apostles into a group in his lifetime with the precise intention of leaving it behind in the world after his departure: a fellowship of those sharing the kingdom experience, says Bowman (1943), the remnant called out by the Messiah. He promised them the Holy Spirit, using another term, the Paraclete, who would dwell within them, and whom the world could not know (Jn. 14:16-18). He would remain with them after the bodily departure of our Lord (16:7). He would be their Teacher as Christ had been (14:26), and both the Paraclete and the disciples would bear witness to Christ in the world thereafter (15:26-27). This small body of material in John's gospel, where this word is used, is addressed to the disciples collectively. Jesus sees them as a group whom he sends back into the world to represent him there. The burden of this gospel is *witness to Christ* (20:31): witness for a verdict of acceptance. Yet, it recognized the possibility of rejection (1:11). Acceptance (i.e., believing) means power to become children of God (1:12) and gives one a place in the fellowship group and assurance of the presence of the Comforter, which means a peace that the world cannot give (ch. 14).

John 14 takes us far beyond the other religions, for it shows Christ as the only way to the Father (v. 6). It is thoroughly trinitarian and therefore will allow no dialogue which eliminates the uniqueness of the Son and seeks a compromise on the basis of God and Spirit. It shows the Christian's spiritual separation from the world no matter how much his or her ministry may be in it. The world cannot receive the Paraclete (v. 17) or mediate His peace (v. 27).

Jesus brought the disciples together and made them a fellowship that they might stand together and support each other. In a good deal of the New Testament teaching that calls for Christian maturity and growth in grace, the collective form, as the idea of "perfecting the saints," is used. Ephesians 4:11-12 shows both the perfecting and organic growth expected of the church. If we look forward we find the church as a body fitly joined together, with every part working effectually so that the body edifies itself in love (v. 16). If we look back we find we are instructed to keep the unity of the Spirit in the bond of peace, for there is one body and one Spirit (vv. 3-4). Here is diversity in unity. Here is the multi-individual group. This is possible only in the presence and power of the Spirit.

The moral living and virtues that are expected of converted Christians, either of individuals or groups, are also possible only in the presence and power of the Spirit. This is the Spirit who witnesses with our spirit that we are sons and daughters of God by adoption and heirs of Christ (Gal. 4:5-7; Rom. 8:8-17). Through the Spirit Christians are given spiritual gifts (1 Cor. 12:13; Rom. 5:1-5). His Christian graces are sometimes described as the fruit of the Spirit (Gal. 5:22-23; Eph. 5:9). Thus it is the Holy Spirit which enables the church to be the church ministering the life and love of Christ to the world, in New Testament times and today.

One of the features of the New Testament church which may be traced to the work of the Spirit, quite apart from the service ministry and the mutual edification within the fellowship, was the vital experience of *power, joy and faith,* which Hunter calls *the concomitants of the Spirit's presence* (1961:92-93). You will find individuals described as "full of faith and of the Holy Spirit" (Acts 6:5, NASB; 11:24, etc.), and these terms, with *joy* and *power,* cluster together in the record. These concomitants of the Spirit give a zest and thrust to the group. When the Holy Spirit falls on a group, that group becomes transformed. It is this new dynamic that gives the group outreach and makes it witness, and leads to what Roland Allen (1962) called "spontaneous expansion." In my case studies of the planting and growth of the church in the south-central Pacific, and in the archival documents on which I have worked for years, I have invariably found this to be true of the great people movements to Christianity (Tippett 1954). The narrative vibrates with power, joy and faith, in spite of the persecution and military pressure from enemy groups.

Another concomitant of the Spirit's presence which I have found in the island records is the assurance of the ultimate triumph in glory with God. This was a radiant and exciting experience and was certainly associated with the work of the Spirit. The apostle Paul spoke of the earnest of the Spirit, the Spirit being, as it were, a pledge and a promise of more to come, a foretaste of glory for Christians to enjoy here on earth (2 Cor. 1:22; 5:5; Eph. 1:13-14). This also for the island converts was a matter "to be told abroad" and shared. They communicated it with power by dialogue, dancing, chanting and proclamation. It was part of the excitement of the people movements. As Green points out, the power of the Holy Spirit was for the New Testament church a "guarantee of the coming Kingdom," and "eschatology and mission were irrevocably united in the person of the Spirit" (1970:273).

The church in the New Testament was not supported and controlled by some overseas board or other foreign sending body. True, a missionary program went out from Antioch, but the churches stood on their own feet from the beginning, and were indeed themselves missionary churches. Without organized training programs and seminaries, how did the early preachers get their messages? Without our printed resources, Bible and commentaries, how did they know what to proclaim? The message was certainly preached with power. Jesus had led them to expect that the special role of the Spirit would be to teach them all truth (Jn. 14:26) and to testify of Christ (15:26), and they were to bear witness of what they had learned from being with Him (v. 27). Paul (1 Cor. 2:13; 1 Thess. 1:5), Peter (1 Pet. 1:12; 2 Pet. 1:18-21) and John (1 Jn. 5:6) all speak of the role of the Holy Spirit in revealing the message of truth and life.

To sum up the role of the Holy Spirit in the growing process of the church, we have seen first that there must be a physical entity we call the church, a discrete group. This has been preserved and nourished by the Spirit since the departure of Jesus to the Father. From the Spirit the fellowship group has a peace the world cannot give and an experience the world cannot share. The operational pattern of the group is to have members mutually supporting each other, building each other up in virtue and service. United and diverse, they are a multi-individual group. All this is possible only in the power of the Spirit, from whom we have also the gifts of the Spirit and the fruit of the Spirit, which enable us to operate as the body of Christ in the world. Other concomitants of the Spirit are power, joy and faith, which frequently occur together and are features of the church in times of spontaneous expansion, a fact borne out also in history. These are often accompanied by a strong eschatology with assurance. Eschatology and mission unite in the person of the Spirit. The message which is preached with power is that revealed and verified by the Spirit. These are the features of a church growing at the qualitative level of what McGavran calls *perfecting* in church growth theory (1955:13-15).

RESPONSIVE POPULATIONS TODAY

Not all populations are responsive. Fields *come* ripe unto harvest. The harvest time has to be recognized, and harvesters have to be sent in at the correct season. A discussion of how fields ripen is another subject, but what happens to a crop which is not harvested when it is ripe goes without saying. In this chapter I have argued that many ripe fields exist, some of which are large and promise an abundant harvest. Responsive populations should mean many people movements and great numerical church growth. Identifiable groups are waiting to be won for Christ. When the group responds, a congregation has to be created, preferably with the same structure as the group itself. Those responsible, as the stewards of the ingathering, need common sense, humility, anthropological understanding, and a strong personal faith to be good stewards; but, above all, they need obedient submission to the Holy Spirit, without whose power and blessing there could be no mission at all.

Also related to our subject, but worthy of separate treatment of its own, is the subject of the thousands of new churches (denominations) emerging all over Africa. A large body of literature is growing, and this discloses the wide range of religious ferment in Africa (see Sundkler 1961; Turner 1967; Oosthuizen 1968; and Barrett 1968). Some of these movements seem to be quite heretical, others quite conservative as far as their Christianity goes, others are boldly experimental. All are intensely enthusiastic. Neither is this religious ferment limited to movements that are Christian or syncretistically Christian. Some relate to the other faiths and some are quite newly pagan. Neither is this confined to Africa. In Japan there are Soka Gakkai and many other movements, the statistical rise of which may be set off against an inverse fall in Christian baptismal intake figures of the traditional churches, dating from about 1957. The greatest Christian growth is among groups little known in the West, such as the Spirit of Jesus Church. What I am saying as I draw this chapter to a close is that great multitudes which no person can number are currently either modifying their religious position or changing their religious affiliation. Viewing the matter on a world scale, there probably never has been such a period in history when such a large percentage of the world's peoples have been so open for religious change. Far from being a secular age, it is intensely religious, even in our Western cities. This dynamic situation calls for reevaluation of missionary techniques, and a deployment of individuals and resources so that missionary thrust is directed where the populations are most likely to be responsive. But having said that, the thrust must carry religious conviction, it must meet both the physical and spiritual needs of mankind in society, it must have power, joy, peace and vitality, and it must not make individual converts into religious and social isolates, but bind them together into a fellowship community. All this can only be done under the direction of the Holy Spirit. As Starkey has said, "The most striking purpose of the Spirit's advent . . . is to be found in his gift of community" (1965:23).

I see no hope for the way of individualism in our modern world. The individual must feel he or she belongs. The interacting, multi-individual aspect of the community must be brought to maturity. Nearly all the basic problems of human society spring from carrying the interests of the individual too far so that they deny the rights of the neighboring individual. Individuals belong in context and the context requires balance—loving one's neighbor as oneself. All this has a superb backing from the anthropology of communal society, but this is theory. The theory has to come to

root in real life situations. The world needs not merely a world understanding, but understanding in all the cohesive subunits that make up the
various levels of human society. For us in mission this means the local
churches at grassroots level, the fellowship groups which are the body of
Christ, ministering His mind, and service, and love and mission in their
neighborhood.

In the last analysis, it is here that the church grows or does not grow.
You can take a Christian fellowship group and study it anthropologically
as an institution, and see "how it ticks," but if you carry your research to
the ultimate conclusion you will have to admit that there is still one
element which registers in your data but cannot be explained in human or
processual terms. I call this the *noncultural factor.* It is, of course, the
Holy Spirit. He is at work. Anthropologically I know how the church
ticks, but another factor has to be introduced before the ticking is
regulated as it should be. Given the current mood for religious change,
and considering the missionary program in such a responsive population, I
see no better way of handling the situation than by planting Christian
fellowship groups that fit the local social structure and encouraging the
people to pray for the gift of the Holy Spirit. If such a group is both
indigenous in character and filled with the Spirit, and the religious mood
of the location is innovative, we may expect a spontaneous expansion of
the church. This is the regular pattern of people movements, and God has
most certainly blessed it.

Notes:

1. For the place of the Holy Spirit in church growth theory and theology, see
Donald McGavran, "Authentic Spiritual Fire," *How Churches Grow* (1959:55ff.)
and my chapter, "The Non-cultural Factor," in *Church Growth and the Word of
God* (1970a:42ff.).

2. The manner in which missionary policy can be influenced by the background of
home officials came home to me some years ago when I was researching an
African situation where a rapid conversion intake was suddenly stopped. Eventually I discovered that a missionary from India, who had been in a location where
he had seen extremely small and slow growth, upon retirement was given a
portfolio with authority over this African tribal situation. He had demanded that,
as missionary staff did not permit further intake, the missionaries on the field
consolidate the existing gains, and let the accessions not begin again until the
personnel was adequate to handle the movement. It never did get started again.
Thus, a responsive movement had been sealed off, and a community which might
have been won whole was left half Christian and half pagan.

3. This theme is the subject of my *His Mission and Ours* (1960), a bound
manuscript at the School of World Mission in Pasadena.

4. For the church growth theology of belonging, see my chapters "The Convert
and His Context" and "Belonging and the Process of Incorporating," in *Church
Growth and the Word of God* (Tippett 1970a).

CHAPTER 7

A Resume of Church Growth Theology and Current Debate

The School of World Mission and Institute of Church Growth at Fuller Theological Seminary is noted for a type of missionary theory and theology known as *church growth*. The purpose of this chapter is to pinpoint some of its main theological tenets and to comment on the issues in current missionary debate in which this theology involves us. I hope that in the course of this discussion we may observe the trends of contemporary missionary theology which determine missionary policy and action.

We of the School of World Mission faculty are all field missionaries. We have come out of very different cross-cultural situations with a common conviction that the growth of the church has been less than it should have been; that, in some way the servants of the Lord have been obstructive to the immediate purposes of God. When the Old Testament writer says "They limited the Holy One of Israel" (Ps. 78:41), or when Paul warns the Thessalonians to "quench not the Spirit" (I Thess. 5:19), we think that we should speak to the matter of the harvests that God has obviously brought to ripeness but which His servants have never harvested. Our specialized training is in the social sciences. As theologians we are laymen. We come to the Bible as individuals out of the human situation for whom the Bible is a working tool—a "norm for faith and practice" if you like. Our approach is problem oriented and the answers we find have to work effectively out there in the cross-cultural world. We seek biblically based theory that works in the world. Our methodology is experimental and any theory has to interpret the facts that are observed or collected in the world. We have all learned the hard way how the theology of the home Church or mission board determines the policies, the selection of personnel, the distribution of funds and the priority of projects. Thus a field situation can be completely wrecked by an overstressed theological whim at home. The theoretical methodology of Christian mission is conditioned by its theological undergirdings. In this chapter I shall be dealing with the theology rather than the methodology. I shall first describe the scope or limits of church growth theology, and then the terminology for our discussion needs to be fixed.

DEFINITION OF THE LIMITS OF CHURCH GROWTH THEOLOGY

Church growth does not cover the whole range of Christian theology. This is not to say that we do not believe an unemphasized doctrine, or that we regard it as unimportant. Sometimes church growth has been criticized because of the omission of some doctrine that is important to the critic. Yet history shows that theological controversies tend to focus in limited areas of doctrine that have particular significance for particular situations. The battle rages at that point. The war is being fought on many fronts today and we believe that on our particular front a battle is being fought that will determine the status of Christianity in the non-Western world for a century or more to come if the world endures that long. So we do not cover the whole field of theology in this concept of church growth. For instance, we say little about the *authority of Scripture* as a doctrine that has to be argued. We are speaking and writing to evangelicals and we assume this doctrine as a vital presupposition. To a secular audience maybe we could not assume that. In the same way we believe that humans live under the purpose of God, that without God they are lost and that under God they are responsible for their stewardship. We believe in the Trinity although at any time we may be entirely expressing ourselves in terms of the action of one Person of the Trinity. These and many other points of Christian doctrine are implied, without any apology in the argument. We assume that the hearer or reader, like ourselves, accepts the particular doctrine when we mention it. Some of our critics, usually those who have read only one article, have done us injury at this point. You do not criticize a book on Africa because it does not mention the United States. Church growth theology, then, is firmly rooted in the evangelical tradition, even those doctrinal points which it seldom articulates.

When I use the phrase church growth (a term we have, I think, from McGavran) I am speaking of a *process*—a growing. And because of the adjective "church" it must be seen as a *corporate* process; that is, a process of a body growing, a body of discrete but interacting parts. We are not concerned so much with the conversion of isolated persons who ever remain as isolates. Every conversion is a conversion in a context of people. Witness, even to an individual, must lead to incorporation in the group before that individual can be an effective witness. The word *growth* implies life in the process. I am not talking of a formal or a constitutional development. It is not an organization that can be graphed or charted as some sociologists try to do with the church. It is an organism. The difference between an organization and an organism is life. They both have structure but only one has life. So I would define church growth as *the corporate growing in the Lord.* This is a process.

Although there is something about life that cannot be measured, nevertheless, there are symptoms of the healthy or unhealthy state of that life. Temperature and pulsations do say something. Church growth methodology deals with this aspect.

The theology of the process of growing in the Lord covers five dimensions. First, it calls for a clear doctrine of the *Church,* which will cover first its nature and then its role both in *space* and *time.* Second, we require a theology of *communication;* in biblical terms—*proclamation, witness* and *teaching.* This brings us in touch with the nonbiblical concept of *dialogue.* Third, we must have a theology of *conversion,* which we have often put into terms of *power encounter* because of our experiences with the conversion of animists. Fourth, we need a theology of *incorporation,* which includes also the necessity for the Christian *nurture* of believers. Finally, there is the essential theology of the *outreaching ministry* in *mission, service* and *reconciliation.*

These are the points at which church growth theology has to be articulated, but let me reiterate that this is not the full orbit of our belief. In fact, this very structure stands on a base of other theology. For instance, a disbelief in the lostness of mankind without Christ, or a dual Godhead of Father and Spirit (i.e., the humanization of Christ) would invalidate our whole theology; but then, it would invalidate the authority of Scripture also. So I submit there is a certain cohesiveness about church growth theology which is itself a reflection of the cohesion of Scripture. We draw selectively from different bodies of material in Scripture. But they are bodies of material. There is a corpus of passages on the *diffusion* of the knowledge of the Lord in the promises of God, another corpus of *growth imagery* in the parables of Jesus, the numerous *conversion* units, the idea of the *continuity* of mission "until He comes again" or until "the end of the age," the passages which depict the *inward growth* of the fellowship of believers, the *responsibility* for a *ministry outside* the world and the idea of the *group movement* to Christ. Every one of these ideas is a recurrent theme in Scripture, and when they are rearranged as a cumulative series in one place, they present an impressive picture of God's revealed purpose for His Church. I have tried to present these units for Bible study in *Church Growth and the Word of God* (1970a). The book is not written for any particular theological battle, but rather to stand beside the church growth books of theory and field case studies as part of the total picture, so that readers may see that theologically the church growth writers operate within a biblical frame of reference.

DEFINITION OF TERMS

The attack on the evangelical, and I believe biblical, concept of the Christian Mission today comes to us in a subtle form in the area of semantics. I want to put this in my own way and I do not hold my church growth colleagues to my definitions. I have come to the conclusion that wherever possible we should define our terms on a basis of the Bible, and that where there is a distinction which is philosophical or secular, we ought to chose another word rather than assign a nonbiblical meaning to a well-known biblical word. Thus, for example, I refuse to use the word *proclamation* for *any* kind of work done in the name of the Lord, such as a silent "witness" or a dialogue. A proclamation is a message, a word from a higher authority proclaimed by a herald in his name. It is a definitive announcement—not a matter for discussion or debate. Another key biblical word is *witness,* which is the person testifying to what has been seen, heard or discovered. This is normally a specific testimony. The idea of merely being in the world as a silent Christian presence is a far call from the Bible idea of witness as presented, for example in the opening verses of John's letter, or the use of the word in his gospel.

Both proclamation and witness are biblically attested means of communicating the good news—one a pronouncement under authority, to be heard but not argued with, the other a Christian's personal testimony which can be shared, even in dialogue. In between are other forms of communication. This very variety of *vocal* presentation surely prevents us from accepting the judgment of those dialogical writers who write with vigor against the monological structure of the Church and would discard proclamation entirely, throwing the proverbial baby out with the bath water. The misuse of the pulpit calls for preaching reform, not for a denial of proclamation. And as for good works: we can call them the fruit of Spirit, the Christian way, the life of holiness, Christian service, or the influence of the Gospel; but under no circumstances can they be called, as some dialogical writers do, "nonverbal proclamation." That phrase is an etymological monstrosity, a self-contradiction.

The relevance of this discussion for Christian mission today is that the definition of good works as "nonverbal proclamation" permits people who are sent in the mission of God to "kid themselves" that they are proclaiming the Gospel, when in point of fact the words of invitation to accept Christ are never articulated. Furthermore, almost anything can be defined as "good works." It could be a paternalistic charity that actually holds up indigenous development. It could be technical aid with political consequences. There is no end to this. Once you play about with your basic terminology you can classify all kinds of things as mission, and change priorities and deploy funds and personnel. Worse than all this, it is a shifting of authority in mission from God to mankind. The idea of good works as nonverbal proclamation means we have no specific word from

God for the unconverted, but the holy lives we live in service will show them the way.

I know and have visited one mission field where for the first sixteen years there were no converts. The missionaries believed they had to civilize the pagans first, improve their lot, make them industrious, and then they would be able to see themselves as sinners and intelligently seek salvation. These were evangelical missionaries. The native people rejected Christianity because to them it was a religion of hard work, fencing, cultivating, marketing and making profit.

Another word we have a good deal of trouble with today is the word *mission* itself, which like the word *dialogue,* does not come from Scripture. Nevertheless, I think the word may be traced historically, through the Latin to the *apostello* cluster in Scripture. If so, then Vicedom is right in calling the mission *the sending* (1961:45ff), and proclamation goes with it. The purpose of the sending is good news from God to mankind. John 17:18 is followed by verse 20, which suggests the disciples are sent forth to give a verbal proclamation that people might believe. Likewise, Acts 13:2 is followed by verse 5 in which Paul and Barnabus "preached the word" in their sending. So mission to me is a being sent forth to proclaim the Word of God unto salvation; that is, that individuals may respond and believe. In other words, mission is what I have called *verdict theology:* a deliberate attempt to secure a verdict for Christ. This may be achieved by proclamation, witness, teaching or preaching the Gospel, as long as the Word is articulated and a decision sought. This is implied in the Great Commission in the word *make disciples.* McGavran's phrase for the numerical growth of the Church is *discipling.* Some critics reject this because they give a different meaning to discipleship, but this term comes from Jesus and it is a single word in the Greek, and it expresses beautifully how pagan animists reject their gods and place themselves as learners under a Lord whom as yet they know only as a Lord of authority over the spirits who have hitherto plagued them. Conversion was a clear cut verdict *against* one power and *for* another. This is the church growth process. This is the discipling of the nations. Sure it is reflected in statistics, but it is a dynamic process at work, and the Holy Spirit is in it. This is the theme which runs through my *Verdict Theology in Missionary Theory* (1973a). Mission and proclamation go together, and the purpose of the sending and proclaiming or witnessing is *that individuals might believe.*

This is the traditional view of mission. The word is frequently redefined today to include every kind of work the Church does, on the assumption that the activity of the Church is a total thing. This is strongly resisted by Lindsell (1968:53), who says that "to lump everything the Church is supposed to do under the term *mission* is to do semantic violence to a good term and to divest it of a significance it always had." Now, while I grant that popular usage and new needs will bring about natural semantic change, I detect in this case a process of semantic manipulation. As a social anthropologist the study of change is my business, but I am also an applied anthropologist and I believe that beneficial change should be channeled in the right direction. In this case I am sure the change is in the wrong direction. Theoretically the motivation is good: the Church is one thing, a unity and its activities should not be fragmented; mission is everybody's business all the time and all we do for the Lord is mission. This idea grew from a realization that the *laymen* should be involved in the activities of the Church, a true and important insight. But the redefinition of mission was bad reasoning. In point of fact there is nothing in the Church which is everybody's business. Everybody's business is nobody's business. The functions of eye, ear and hand are unique and not interchangeable. The unity of the body lies in their interdependence not their standardization. To designate everything done for God as mission is to give a valuable term an imprecision which renders it useless, and to leave a void at the place from which the term is taken.

I know a church where this process is going on. Five years ago they had a strong sense of mission. Fifty-six percent of the budget was expended outside the church. With the acceptance of this new idea of mission, the overseas allocation was cut, and funds were redirected to issues on the home front. These issues were legitimate services and truly a claim on the church, but the void left further afield was the first step in a process of responsibility enclosure, and the localization of Christian concern. The void of nonaction soon became a void of nonconcern. The process enclosed still further. Today only 33 percent of the funds are spent outside the congregational property. Thousands of dollars have been turned inward instead of outward. The church has acquired more property (it already has far too much) and has launched a program whereby that property will bring more revenue. That church has become a mighty landlord because of a loss of the concept of mission. The process has become an ethical degeneration because semantic imprecision has permitted the deadening of conscience.

Then maybe you will ask me what word I would use for this idea of the total activities of the Church. The word I usually employ is *ministry*. I prefer this because it is a general word, not a specific one like mission. As there are many spiritual gifts, so there are many ministries. The outreaching ministries of the Church are at least three (with the increasing complexity of modern society we may need more): the ministry of service, the ministry of reconciliation and the ministry of mission. The total thing is the ministry of the Church, but the functional parts of the Body have different roles and require different gifts. Good, clear, functional definitions of the Church's ministries safeguard against voids and enclosure.

THE CHURCH AND ITS MINISTRIES

Perhaps we have now reached the point where I should define my doctrine of the Church. Today the Church is under fire. Many people believe it is on its way out. Hoekendijk (1964) says this. Although I go along with many of his basic ideas, I consider many of his secondary arguments dangerous and misleading. I would certainly agree that the Church is due for some drastic formal changes. But this is not necessarily the end. Anthropologically, as a social institution in a dramatically changing society, it is bound to change if it is to remain a functioning body. Just to minister the mind and love of Christ to our changing society requires change. Ten years hence the sociological structure of the Church will be quite different. This does not alarm me.

A few years ago an article of mine entitled "The Church's Cutting Edge" (1965a) appeared in an Australian paper. At the time I was much exercised by a growing movement among the younger ministers who were stressing the idea of "churchless ministries," not constructively, but very much to the injury of the existing fellowship of believers and to no particular benefit. They were advocating a form of Christian presence doctrine which dispensed with the need of the Church as a functioning body, in spite of the biblical instructions that we operate to the end of the age. I wrote of the *continuity* of the Church *within* and *throughout* change. I tried to show that the Christian witness was not merely a number of isolated individual Christian presences, voiceless in a pagan world, but a corporate power of a living body, continuing as a fellowship and witnessing as the Church. The article was reprinted outside Australia and brought more responses than anything I have written. Jesus did not leave a number of isolated individuals to be lone presences in a hostile world. He left a group. He spoke to them collectively more often than not. The Book of Acts is dotted with small fellowship groups. The process of growing in the Lord is a collective experience. The patterns were different: Lydda and Sharon, Antioch, Philippi and Rome. The *forms* of the pattern differed. The common thing was a *fellowship* in the Lord, the breaking of bread, the praising God, the singleness of heart, and the adding to the Church daily.

In my own speaking and writing about the Church I use two descriptive terms from the Bible. There are others I know but these two are adequate for my purpose. One is the *Fellowship of Believers* and the other is the *Body of Christ*. Each I use in a biblical way, though not necessarily the only possible way. I use the former when I speak of the Church as people called out from the world, meeting for prayer, praise, the preaching of the Word and the other means of grace. Christians building each other up by sharing the faith and growing in grace: this is church growth— *quantitative* with the incorporation of converts into the group, *qualitative* with the Christian nurture that builds them up so they may go forth into the world again to witness and serve. In McGavran's book (1970) the first of these is *discipling* and the second *perfecting,* as the Great Commission puts it—making disciples and teaching them all things I have commanded you. The doctrine of the Fellowship is found in 1 John 1. After two verses of personal witness, verses 3-4 show the reason for witness—to incorporate converts into the human fellowship group which is also in fellowship with the Father and with Christ. In verse 5 we have the message or word from God and in His fellowship we walk (v.6) and walking in fellowship with Him we have better fellowship with each other (v.7). When I talk of these dimensions I speak of the Fellowship of Believers.

If this was an end of the matter, as it unfortunately has become for many congregations, it would lead to congregational enclosure. Church growth theology will not stand for this, for ours is theology of outreach. When I am thinking of this dimension I usually use the phrase Body of Christ, because Christ as I read about him in Scripture was a figure in the world. His mission was *to* the world and in the world, and after he had chosen and trained his disciples he sent them forth *into* the world. The teaching about this he gave them just before his death (John 17) and reiterated it after the resurrection (John 20:21). So when the material body of Christ was removed from this world there remained, as Paul said, "the Church which is his Body" (Eph. 1:23). This is not a figure for the lone Christian. This is a body with all its multifunctional parts interacting. This is corporate. Thus is the mind of Christ, the love of Christ, the compassion of Christ and the word of Christ communicated *in* the world and *to* the world through the Church which is His Body.

This dichotomy has been a stumbling block to Christians in practice and to theologians in theory. Time and time again the Church gets imprisoned at the fellowship end and shut off from the world, or so involved at the world end that the withdrawal for fellowship is forgotten. But the concepts are both scriptural and they have to be reconciled with each other. The only solution seems to be that the fellowship cannot grow properly without the outside world in which to "work out its salvation in fear and trembling"; nor can the Body of Christ witness, serve and meet the needs of mankind without drawing on the resources of the fellowship. Church growth theology would require the process of growing in the Lord to operate at both ends of this spectrum.

I dealt with this at greater length above in Chapter 4 But let it suffice here to make one more comment on the church growth theology about the ministries of the Body of Christ in the world. I want to pause here because we are often unfairly criticized at this point. In Chapter 4 I depicted the outreaching ministries of the Church in terms of *mission, service* and *reconciliation.* I see these as the tripartite conception of the nature, and therefore the *needs* of mankind. As Figure 7 illustrates, although Christian individuals may be called to concentrate on one of the ministries, the Church is a multi-individual and a whole thing, a corporate group, the

Body of Christ in the world and multiministried. In *service* we are meeting the *bodily needs* of mankind in all its multitudinous forms, in physical struggle for life. The Church ministers to these individuals through service. A Church without a service arm is inconceivable. The ministry of *reconciliation* deals with mankind's mental turmoil, psychological disturbances and social discord. Social justice and race relations are under this head. Bringing humans to live in peace with fellow humans is certainly a ministry of the Body of Christ. But the nature of mankind is not confined to body and mind. Mankind has also a *soul* and to this is directed the ministry of *mission*. The business of the missionary, at home or abroad, clerical or lay, is to bring people face to face with Christ, and if possible secure, by witness, by prayers, by vicarious suffering, a *verdict for Christ*. A Church has to fulfil all these ministries in *equilibrium* to be a healthy, growing Church. That is the objective theological base of the church growth viewpoint.

FIGURE 7
External Ministries of the Body of Christ in the World

However, that theology has to be worked out in specific local situations by every independent congregation, which is also called a church. The local church has to realize that it is the *Church*—the Body of Christ—in that locality and must corporately fulfill all the ministries in the world. Each locality is sociologically unique. This means the needs of the people in one locality will differ from those in another. Each church will have to work out its own strategy of ministries for its own locality. It may even have to determine priorities for one ministry over another. These priorities, however, do not lie in the nature of the Church but in the nature of the situations where the Church has to minister.

In large areas of Africa and western Oceania today, millions of animists are changing their religious affiliation. Christianity is not the only option before them. Maybe it is Communism or Islam. This is not a change just being forced on them. They are seekers after a new faith, and we know this state of enquiry is not likely to last very long. These people are not asking for technical aid. Mostly these situations are basically religious. The time of the old gods has run out and the fields are ripe unto harvest. We believe that in this kind of situation there is a priority for the ministry of mission. This emphasis has led some critics to say we have no time for service projects and social justice. This we flatly deny. We recognize that there are probably some situations which offer a current priority to the service arm of the Church. We urge every young church planted to develop the total complex of ministries. What we object to most strongly is the home church or board establishing massive service projects that the national Church can never take over economically, in places where the doors are open for evangelism but may not remain open for long. We try to plant service projects that can be absorbed into the program of the local indigenous Church, but until you have an indigenous Church, how can you have an indigenous service ministry?

Before I leave this section I raise the question of church growth and denominationalism. The two have nothing to do with each other, but some have criticized us for denominational extension. We are mystified because we have always prided ourselves in our ecumenicity. Our students for the last twenty years have come from over seventy different church groups. I myself am an Australian Methodist with a strong Wesleyan background, and since I have been here I have participated in the laying on of hands at a Disciples of Christ ordination, I have had an article published in a Pentecostal journal and I have preached the sermon at an Episcopalian mass. And I am sure this is typical of the wide range of contacts of my colleagues. My course in the Anthropological Basis of Leadership, where church structures are bound to show up if they do anywhere, has been accepted by people of all denominations. I have tried to show how a denominational structure can clash with one culture pattern and be appropriate for another, how the appointment of leaders and the mechanisms for decision making should be culturally and not denominationally conditioned. Neither have I been silent in my writings on the way denominationalism hinders Christian witness. In *Solomon Islands Christianity* (1967a), one of the 13 sections in the conclusion and recommendations was given to Denominationalism, in which I advocated a plan of cooperation and intercommunion as a demonstration of Christian unity. This was at least realistic. I get a little irritated when critics who do not do their homework call church growth denominational church extension. One of the great features of the School of World Mission—Institute of Church Growth is the cross-fertilization of denominational ideas in the classes, where students from over seventy different countries look at structures of other denominations in the light of the structural needs of their indigenous churches.

What these armchair critics fail to allow for is the great difference between a church planted a century ago using a Western denominational pattern and a church planted today by a missionaries trained in church growth and anthropology, even if they go out under some denominational banner.

THE COMMUNICATION OF THE GOOD NEWS

In defining *proclamation* I mentioned the rejection of this mode of communication as unsuitable to our day and its mood, by the dialogical writers, and their substitution of the *idea of dialogue*. I agree with their motives against the monological structure of the Church where all the functional roles have tended to concentrate in one clerical person to the exclusion of the layman. This pattern has cast its shadow over the mission field, and church growth is opposed to this type of structure. However, we do not agree with the dialogical writers when they reject proclamation because it does not suit the mood of the day. People are not disposed to be told anything categorically. The mood is for dialogue and not monologue. What has been lost, though these writers do not point this out, is *the idea of the herald:* the preacher proclaiming the word from the Lord. The preacher is merely speaking his or her own mind, and speaking it categorically, and of course people will not take that today. Or, perhaps it is just a tonic talk, or something completely fuzzy without any authority. This also demands reply and so the mood is for dialogue rather than monologue. These writers argue that this mood is a cultural change to which we must accommodate ourselves.

So we communicate today by entering into *dialogue* with people who have ideas different from our own. We expose ourselves to each other, and share experiences. But, says Howe in *The Miracle of Dialogue* (1963), we must not try to convert the other person to our ideas. We enter fully into each other's experience and then we will understand each other and the truth will be discovered. Maybe the other person will adopt our position; maybe we will adopt theirs. But to consciously try to convert the other, that would create a dialogical crisis and defeat the whole object of the experiment. This is all very popular today. Dialogue is the thing. In confronting other faiths, especially Hinduism and Buddhism, this is the currently approved technique of mission. So you strive to penetrate into a Hindu mind *to find the Spirit of God there.* Maybe you hope the Hindu may meet your Christ and become Christian but you dare not ask him or her. This would be presumptuous. It would show your lack of humility, your Western arrogance. With the dialogical approach that avoids a crisis at all costs goes another theological idea, namely, that of the Presence. When you do penetrate into the other religion you find the *Presence* already there. So we have another group of writers who speak of *seeking Christ in Hinduism.*

In point of fact, all this is an accommodation to the Asian reaction to the claim of Christ, that there is *no other way* to the Father but by Him. This unique claim has always troubled the Hindu polytheist who thought of Hinduism as big enough to incorporate all others, like a great lake into which all rivers flow. I have known Hindus who have claimed to be both Christian and Hindu. The idea of having to give up the all-inclusive Hinduism because Christ claims absolute allegiance has always been one of the greatest hurdles to Hindu conversion. Now that the Asian pressure is against white civilization, the Gospel which they associated with that civilization is more dangerously advocated. The easy way out therefore is to engage in dialogue and seek the Presence of Christ or the Spirit in Hinduism. This is another reason why proclamation is out of favor today—*the mood of Asia.*

Or you may apply the same ideas to Islam. Here the idea of offence was the divinity of Christ. So you enter into dialogue and you find the Presence. In your dialogue you are careful with any mention of Christ that you do not create a dialogical crisis. Your rapport is at the cost of a *fractured doctrine of the Trinity.*

Space limits do not permit me to draw out further these aspects of communication which show how the Christian mission is being accommodated to the mood of our day and the mood of Asia. I have dealt with both dialogue and presence in *Verdict Theology in Missionary Theory* with some documentation. That book also contains a chapter on Christ's exclusive claim to be the only way to the Father, and also a typology of communicators of the Gospel in the New Testament Church. I concluded that the method of dialogue, as I define it, could be used by an evangelist, a teacher or a witness. However, an acceptance of Howe's proscription of the dialogical crisis makes it impossible for a disciple to witness for a verdict, and this would invalidate it for communication as defined in Scripture.

The accommodation of missionary theology to the mood of the day and the mood of Asia is undoubtedly due in part to the fact that the outspoken theologians of today come from one of three areas: those who bear the marks and influences of the Germany of Hitler; those who would regard themselves as the secular theologians; or those missiological writers who have come from the resistant mission fields. With the exception of Vicedom, we do not have a good biblical missionary theologian who has come from missionary experience where he has seen people coming to the Lord with New Testament pentecostal fervor.

For the want of a better place, I might mention here another point of attack on our missionary approach to the other faiths. This comes from the *universalists*. We can never have a discussion with these people because we can never find a basis for discussion—the Bible is not the same thing to us. They describe us as *pre-critical* and say we can never win modern men and women because we deal in myths. They reject the Bible and any idea of a supernatural Figure. Their rationale is *evolutionary*, classifying Christianity as *pre-critical, critical* and *post-critical*. They reject the evangelical approach as *mythical* and the liberal approach as *humanistic*, and see the hope of the world in post-critical Christianity measured in terms of *social service, education* and *philosophy* and moving in harmony with *modern science*. They think the mood of modern missions is now bypassing the pre-critical and critical approaches, though both of these hold up progress. Nevertheless, a universal soil is being prepared for a *universal religion for mankind*. This is surely as far out as a Christian missionary could get. It is a philosophical view that has some tragic ramifications on the mission field, but the idea of a universal religion has real anthropological problems, unless it is conceptualized in some way after the picture in Rev. 7:9-17, which is far from their idea.

These problems of the mode of communicating the Gospel, under close analysis, are all found to be basically problems of the *content* of the Gospel. The same may be said about the juggling with semantics, the accommodation to the mood of the day and the mood of Asia. Church growth stands squarely on the traditional view that *mission means being sent out under authority to proclaim, teach and witness to what God has done for mankind in Christ*, bringing people to Christ and pressing for a *positive act of acceptance*. In other words, to win converts.

THE THEOLOGY OF CONVERSION

There is only one way the Church can really grow. That is by *conversion. Externally* individuals have to be won from paganism or from materialism; *internally* each generation has to be brought face to face with Christ for itself. In each case there has to be a *positive act* of acceptance, submission and an experience of faith. Without conversion the warmth of the Fellowship falls and the church statistics begin to reflect it. The basis of all church growth is conversion.

There are two scriptural ways of looking at conversion: as *an act of God* (the work of the Holy Spirit) and as an *act of mankind*. If we have said more of the latter in church growth writing it is because the former is part of our basic presuppositional structure. We fully recognize that there could be no real conversion without the activity of the Holy Spirit. The human side of the experience is covered in the Bible by such terms as *turning* to the Lord, *repenting, confessing* and *believing*—four strong action verbs in a context of acceptance or rejection with eternal consequences. Repeated refusal to respond is sinning against the Holy Spirit. Already there are signs of tampering with the semantics of this biblical terminology. "Turning to the Lord" for instance is open for a wide range of interpretation if removed from its context. Christian mission needs a book which attempts something like Snaith's *Distinctive Ideas of the Old Testament* (1944) did in tracing the key theological terms through the Bible, into the New Testament.

When we are confronted with conversion experiences at the grass roots level; when people are turning to the Lord in groups as they did at Lydda and Sharon in New Testament times; then we are facing an experiential phenomenon rather than a theological construct. Yet the two most certainly relate. When people take their fetishes within whom the fearful powers of the spirits have been contained, and now at a precise point of time voluntarily cast them on the fire or into the sea (a thing they had not thought possible before), and have done this in a newly found power of One who has power over all power (the *exousia* over the *dunamis,* as Luke puts it in his record of the words of Jesus), so that suddenly they are free; they are new creatures and are prepared to put themselves under Christian instruction. This is what I mean by an experiential situation. The evangelist has to handle it. When that evangelist is trained in a Western seminary, Bultmann and Hoekendijk have not given him or her much equipment to deal with it for the Lord. In church growth theology we call this the aspect of *power encounter.* Biblical examples can be found in 1 Kings 18, Luke 10:19 and other places. We find it leads us to a biblical theology—but not by any means to the same passages of Scripture as we are normally led to by Reformed theology. One is brought to realize the tremendous range of Scripture for dealing with multitudinous cross-cultural situations that Westerners never dream of. We have a biblical thrust in a cultural structure which is not covered in any Master of Divinity curriculum that I know. Anthropology has helped me more in this than anything I had in seminary. If one can move within the philosophy of animism one can deal with its structures and discover that Christ can be understood there. This is not, as the Christian Presence people sometimes say—to seek the Spirit in Animism. If you bring Christ into animism you bring Him into encounter with the spirits that are there and this is verdict theology *par excellence.* There is no dialogue here. It is a clear-cut issue of Christ or Satan (see Tippett 1973a:88-91; cf. also chs. 8 and 25, below).

If we think of conversion in the anthropological terms of *decision-making* it can be researched *as a process.* In the study of *innovation* as the basis of cultural change (Barnett, 1953) conversion falls under the study of *acceptance and rejection of new ideas.* Presenting the Gospel falls under the head of *advocacy.* This is a large area of study with some well-developed anthropological tools and methods of analysis. In church growth methodology we are much indebted to Barnett, the leading authority in this field since 1953. In *Verdict Theology* and other writings I have made use of a model of the conversion process. This research, as seen in Figure 8, shows the process psychologically as a period of *awareness,* a point of *realization,* a period of *decision-making,* a precise point of *encounter* and finally a period of *incorporation.* The value of a model like this is that it permits missionaries who use it to realize the points at which they must have strength, and the points where they can fail. Thus by seeing what they are doing missionaries become better communicators. This anthropology has a biblical base, because the communicator is a co-worker (*sunergoi*) of God—the steward appointed to a task and held responsible for his stewardship, for God has manifested His method of *winning people through people.* Hence our emphasis on *responsibility.*

FIGURE 8

Model Showing the Dynamics of the Process of Conversion and Incorporation

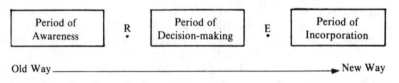

In church growth we have little doubt about the devotional sincerity of the average missionary. I wish we could say the same thing about our diligence in trying to discover exactly what is the nature of missionary stewardship and what it means to be a good steward in a given situation. Obedience to God and leaving results all to Him is not enough, because He calls individuals to be shepherds, stewards, soldiers, builders, fisher-men, co-workers—all of whom have a craft or task in which they are expected to be proficient and will be held responsible.

THE THEOLOGY OF INCORPORATION

Conversion is not the end of the trail. It is the beginning. The experience has to be consumated. Converts now cut off from the old way, have to be made to feel at home in the Fellowship of Believers. They have to discover the resources of the promises of God and the new values in sharing the Christian life. They have to discover their own particular gifts and find an active roles as *participants* in the Fellowship of Believers. It is just at this point that many missions fail. It is here more than at any other point that the Westernism of a missionary can impose itself on the church being planted. If we assume that the situation calls for an indigenous church that will carry on and function healthily after the departure of the missionary, we need to remember that those new Christians will belong to a cultural milieu quite non-Western in its values. The language, music, liturgical forms, patterns of decision-making, type of building, hours of worship, and many other things, should be determined by the converts themselves. It is here that a Western or denominational structure will slow up the *process of incorporation* of converts. A foreign congregational structure and leadership pattern will also hinder the congregation from becoming a fellowship of believers. People have to *share cultural values* in order to establish a fellowship. Jesus told the disciples that there were other sheep who were not of their fold, although they were His sheep and belonged to His flock.

Within the fellowship, as I have already indicated, the converts need to grow in grace, build each other up in the faith, absorb the truth of the written Word and share the corporate Christian experience. Of course, it must not end there. Thus strengthened they go forth to the ministry in the outside world; to the world *where they were once known as pagans,* to demonstrate and to testify what great things the Lord has done unto them. In one sense they go out as individuals but there is another way in which they bear *a corporate witness.* As in New Testament times, they are spoken of in the plural. These Christians are indeed the people who turn the world upside down.

In communal society the news that Visawaqa has become a Christian —if that is the end of the matter—will raise a number of problem questions, but in that it has isolated him from his lineage it will not impress anyone and may lead to serious persecution. But news that Visawaqa *and his household* have become Christian will influence every other household in the lineage. And the news that Visawaqa's lineage has turned to Christ and that each individual has burnt their fetishes is really "headline news." All the other lineages now move from the period of *mere awareness,* past the point of realization into the period of potential *decision-making.* From now on, in every household of the neighboring lineages, the evening conversation is about Christianity. There may not even be a missionary in the vicinity. But one by one over the months and years there are households who come through that period of decision-making to the point of *actual encounter*. They decide together, because after many months they have reached a *consensus,* that next Lord's Day they will publically burn their fetishes and become Christian. Then they will journey many miles to some missionary, who may not even know their language, and demand to be *incorporated.* That missionary had better have a pretty good idea of the road they have travelled and what incorporation into the fellowship means to them, because they will put themselves completely in the missionary's hands. It is at that point the missionary plants either an *indigenous* or a *foreign* church. I wonder how many theological seminaries are preparing their graduates for such a time as that.

In communal society where the people have an intense awareness of the social group, where the group means social cohesion, security and perpetuity in an uncertain world, one of the greatest cultural feelings of satisfaction is the idea of belonging, *or having a place of your own in the group, and being able to play your own specific role in the group life. This is why it is so tremendously important for converts, who come out of the pagan group, to feel that they are not without some group to which to belong. They come out of something into something.* They must know who they are and how they participate. Even in our own society so often converts come in the front door and after a few months go out the back door, for this precise reason—that they have not been incorporated. This, I think, is what 1 John 1 is saying in the opening verses.

So the converts are incorporated into the Fellowship; the Fellowship brings them to perfection (maturity) and sends them forth into the world into the ministries of *service, reconciliation* and *mission.* This is true for every Christian individual but it is also true that these ministries are corporate. It is because they are corporate and because individuals are endowed with differing gifts that the total ministry goes on in equilibrium and continuity. The cycle goes on and on because it is corporate, and because the Church endures through time until He comes again.

As the Church moves outwards in mission from land to land, so too it reaches out from one generation to another. It has dimensions in both *space and time.* As the Vatican II "Decree on the Mission of the Church" put it, that which began with the first coming of our Lord goes on until his second coming.

CHAPTER 8

Trends in the Theology of Mission

Note

PRESUPPOSITIONS

In this chapter I want to focus on seven practical areas of Christian mission. I think that perhaps they are more than just "trends." They are movements which mark the emerging contours of missiology in this Post-colonial Era of Christian mission.

Before I discuss these, however, I must first specify three presuppositions which I am going to assume without discussion, and which I hope we can take as read.

The use of the word "trends" suggests something dynamic and not static. It suggests a process of change going on. In this chapter I shall presuppose three things about the nature of that changing situation in Christian mission.

First of all, I presume: that all of us now recognize as a fact that we have indeed already passed from the Colonial to the Post-colonial Age in Christian mission; that the situational givens have changed; that the colonial structures have either gone or been modified; and that paternalism has had its day, and a new set of relationships have come into being for cross-cultural workers. I hope we all recognize this as a fact, and thus may discuss the character of and new requirements of the changes rather than the fact of the change itself.

Secondly, I assume also that we have grown out of the depressing notion, which was argued in the 1960's, that the day of Christian missions is dead and the missionary should just go home. I trust that we have taken another look at the Great Commission and recognized that the mandate is for a continuing program, as Vatican II put it, from His first until His second coming. What has changed is not "the termination of cross-cultural mission" but the passage from colony to nation, from mission to church, from paternalism to partnership.

On the theoretical level I presume, last of all, that we all recognize that *missiology* has emerged as a science of mission, an interdisciplinary field drawing on the social sciences, especially anthropology. I presume we recognize that every mission field is unique and that every situation is open for research. In such research we expose reasons for growth and nongrowth, theological problems like "syncretism," problems of identity like "indigeneity" and the incorporation of converts into Christian congregations. And we are discovering that theological issues have cultural aspects.

Thus the three presuppositions on which I proceed with my discussion are that we recognize that (1) we have passed from an old period of mission to a new one, (2) that Christian mission is continuous whatever the social changes, and (3) that we have in missiology an accepted research technique to explore our socio-theological problems. We may now go ahead and look at seven trends in the theology of mission with which we face this new Post-colonial Age.

TREND 1: TAKING A NEW LOOK AT THE THEOLOGY OF GOD THE CREATOR

The battle over evolution has forced evangelical Christians into a truncated theology of God as Creator, and it has caused some serious problems on the mission field. We have thrust the Creator into the distant past as if His work were completely finished after the formations recorded in the Genesis account. We have overlooked the fact that God is the Creator still, that His work is ongoing and has also a future or eschatological dimension still to come.

The book of Psalms in particular is built round the notion that God the Creator *is*—not *was*. The Psalmist talks with God and praises His ongoing work (Ps. 145, 146, etc.). He sees the Creator continuing His creative operations through the ongoing cycle of the seasons and of day and night. The Creator is a living God involved in human life today. He made the ear and hears. He formed the eye and sees. He teaches knowledge and knows (cf. Ps. 19, 33, and 148). His creating work is more than physical. He forgives the penitent by creating a new heart within. There is a network of theological concepts tied up with the Creator God in the Psalms—all in terms of current or continuing action.

This current action of the Creator and Provider God is not confined to the Psalms. His actions are shown in the prayer of Jeremiah (32:17-19), in the Levite proclamation in Nehemiah 9:6, in the Lord's own oratorical questions out of the whirlwind to Job (chs. 38 and 39), the continuity of winds and rains (24-26), the productivity of the earth (27), and the keeping of the stars in their course (31). In Isaiah 40:28-31 God the Creator both renews our strength today and shows that He is an everlasting God. As Jesus Himself put it, "My Father worketh until now, and I work" (Jn. 5:17).

The creativity of God is also manifest in His spiritual work, the work of *re-creation* by which an individual becomes in Christ "a new creature." The road from the Old Testament to the New follows the promises of this spiritual rebirth: "The Lord hath created a new thing" (Jer. 31:22). Isaiah foretold the creation of a new heaven and a new earth (65:17). Thus the notion of God as Re-creator is tied up with the eschatological hope of the people of God.

One doctrine for which the mission field cries aloud is that of the Creator God, whose work is perpetual, both a present reality and a future hope. We need to articulate that the Creator God whose work is continuous is also Provider, Redeemer, Renewer, and Father (see Ps. 103); that He is one God and available to people now, to meet their contemporary felt needs.

Now there are two aspects of missionary activity in which this doctrine becomes vital today.

First, the doctrine of God as Creator is vital in every place where people worship idols or fetishes or celestial bodies, where they elevate created objects and worship them instead of the Creator. There are some powerful passages in Scripture for the guidance of the missionary at this point. Read for yourself Ps. 115:2-9; 135:13-18; Isa. 44:9-24; 45:20-22; Rom. 1:25. This theme of the tragedy of worshiping the creature or creation, instead of the Creator, runs beyond the Scriptures into early Christian literature (for example, the Epistle to Diognetus). The biblical attitude to idol worship is rooted in the doctrine of the Creator.

John Williams used this passage in Isaiah 44 for preaching on board ship in the presence of a number of Polynesians, when suddenly a chief sprang up and stamped his foot on the deck. "What fools we have been!" he shouted; "we have confused the *moah* for the *noah* (the sacred for the profane). To the day of my death I shall never again worship an idol with eyes that cannot see and hands that handle not" (Tippett 1973a:4). What we have here is a good example of how modern tribal, subsistence communities often come to the Gospel via the Old Testament. The Hebrews, surrounded by idol worshipping nations, were often tempted or involved with the precise problems of many of our mission fields today.

Secondly, many tribal communities have a doctrine of a creator god who made the heavens and earth. It is an easy road from this concept to the God of the Bible—but it is filled with danger, because this pagan deity is a god who created, and having finished his work, retired, as it were. He is remembered in the tribal myths as the one who created the earth; but he is not a living god now, no one worships him, he is cut off and remote from the life of the ordinary people. The gods of daily life who receive the religious attention of the people are the gods of the garden and of the house, the fishing spirits, the gods of war and the healing gods. The only way of distinguishing this retired creator from the God of the Bible is to insist that our Creator God is alive, still creating and providing, and indeed is the same One as our Heavenly Father.

One of the greatest tragedies I have met in my missionary travels was to find a syncretistic breakaway movement of over twenty whole villages who rejected their Christian church after fifty years of Christian instruction. Over that fifty years they had never eradicated their pre-Christian notions of a retired and departed creator, and that failure in Christian education opened the way for the charismatic leader of the movement to assert, "God, the Creator, did His work and retired; Jesus Christ went to the cross and died having finished His work; and now we are in the age of the Spirit, and I am His spokesman in your presence." And twenty villages broke away and put themselves under his heretical instruction. Quite apart from the fact that the mission's teaching on the resurrection and the work of the Spirit must also have been defective, it all started from a truncated doctrine of the Creator and His creative activity. All my informants started from this point.

We need to be careful when we use the many different names for God to stress His diverse activities, that we do not allow converts from polytheism to compartmentalize these as different gods. We need to stress that God *was* and *is* and ever *shall be;* and that He is *one* God. The Creator is also the Heavenly Father, here and now, and much of His creative activity springs from His fatherliness. Because He is Father, we can call on Him. Because He is still Creator, He can meet our felt needs.

The Colonial Age of missions ended with a plethora of Cargo Cults, which demonstrated that converts ascribed meanings to the Gospel which the missionaries never intended. Christian doctrine has to be examined through the eyes of the polytheist, that appropriate instruction may be given. Truncated creationism is a good (or bad) example of this wider principle.

TREND 2: DEVELOPING A THEOLOGY OF POWER ENCOUNTER

Many evangelical believers confine themselves to the New Testament and forget that God has given us a whole Bible. I feel no doubt at all about the value of the Old Testament to the missionary, especially in a tribal situation where the people, like the Hebrews, live close to the soil. We have been talking about the problem of getting a people from their pagan gods to the Christian faith. Arnold van Gennep (1960), the French anthropologist, demonstrated from the study of rites of passage how the first stage of the process was always an act or *rite of separation* from the old ties and loyalties. It is the same with conversion from paganism. There can be no effective incorporation of the convert into the fellowship of believers unless there has first been a specific *cutting off* from paganism.

This step is often a very spectacular ritual—fetishes are burned, sacred totemic taboo fish are eaten, idols are stripped of their decorations and thrown into a fire, skulls are buried in a grave or cast overboard into the salt water, groves are cut down, or sacred paraphernalia is thrown into the river. The forms of ceremonial cutting off from the past are many, and vary according to the locality. These are symbolic acts, with their focus on the *locus of power* of the rejected religion. They are *power encounters* in which converts show their change of faith and demonstrate that they no longer fear the old gods. For them they have died. It is an intensely meaningful focal point in the story of their conversion, and the missionary must go to the Old Testament to understand it. It is in the New Testament too, but the roots and exegesis of it are found in the Old. Paul Minear says the encounter shifts in the New Testament from idols to Satan: "the radii of theological ideas diverge, but the centre of experience remains the same" (1948:68-69).

To the animists it is not purely their own encounter but an encounter between their old and their new God. They have rejected the supernatural resources on which they once relied, and are challenging the old power to harm them. This cutoff point may be a highly emotional and stressful experience, but until the battle is won here, their old gods will never leave them alone, and they will not be able to share the experiences of the Christian fellowship. The conversion of animists is not a passage from nonfaith to faith. It is a passage from wrong faith to right faith, from the false god to the true God.

Paul met this problem at Corinth where the symbolic focal point was the "cup." He said, "Ye cannot drink the cup of the Lord and the cup of devils" (I Cor. 10:21). Whose *koinonoi* are you—Christ's or Satan's? The Corinthians were trying to be Christian and also to hold on to their paganism at the same time. Polytheists do this. But Christianity demands an individed loyalty—there is to be no coexistence and no syncretism. In this, Scripture has had a single voice throughout every period of Hebrew and Christian history.

The rule is laid down that the people of God are to be God's alone. There is to be no rival god (Deut. 6:14). Any turning to other gods is sin and will be punished. Several reasons are given. God will have no competition—the loyalty argument (Deut. 6:4-14). He wants a people who are like Him—holy (Deut. 7:6). The destruction of heathen altars is authorized (Deut. 7:5, 25; Ex. 23:24; 34:13; II Kgs. 23:4-20). When Israel is condemned in a prophetic woe, breaking the covenant relationship is specified as the nature of her sin (Isa. 1:1-4; 2:6-8, 17-18). Israel is warned against making idols (Deut. 4:16-18), worshiping the celestial bodies (v. 19), and forgetting the covenant (v. 23). When she is faithless, she is described as a harlot (Hos. 1:2).

When there is a return to the Lord, there is a ritual demonstration of some kind—the heathen altars are torn down and those of the Lord rebuilt (Judg. 6:25-26), a stone of witness is set up (Josh. 24:26), or a competitive encounter of gods is enacted, as at Carmel (1 Kgs. 18:18-39). Thus does

Elijah defeat the prophets of Baal, but not by himself, for the power is of his God. Elijah's merit is that he was prepared to act for his God and trust in Him for victory. This is the theology of pagans who burn their fetishes and expose themselves to the vengeance of its spirit force because they are confident that the power of their new Lord is greater.

When Kapiolani, the Hawaiian, climbed the sacred fire-mountain and defied the fire goddess, Pele, to harm her as she broke the taboos, walked over the edge, and cast secular objects into the sacred volcano, it was for her indeed a power encounter. No one had dared to do it before. By her victory she cut off the past (Selwyn 1897).

The pagan converts have to be free to follow their own path to Christ, especially at that point where they themselves feel they are cutting themselves off from old gods. The missionary has no right to order the destruction of sacred paraphernalia or to stop it. It has to be a voluntary act on the part of the convert. Only the pagans themselves can cut themselves off from their old resources, and it has to be an act of faith. They put their faith to the test, though they do it in a very different way from a Western Christian.

Power encounter operates also on the mission field in the confrontation with sorcery, spiritism, or other similar phenomena. These have to be taken seriously. The missionary who ridicules these things as unscientific immediately terminates the credibility of the missionary witness. Only by greater power can these powers be overcome, and that through an act of faith. Neither is it effective for the missionary to say "as long as this fellow believes he is under the power of sorcery, I must work with him *as if* he were indeed so victimized, though I do not believe it myself." This is very quickly detected as unbelief, and the victim of sorcery left to an unbelieving missionary will most certainly die. The only cure for such a victim is the assurance of a power greater than that which binds him, and this surely lies with Him who said, "All power is given unto me" (Mt. 28:18), and who promised His disciples to give them "power (*eksousia*) . . . over all the power (*dunamis*) of the enemy" (Lk. 10:19).

Ratu Apakuki was a Fijian chief, young and competent. Near him dwelt a higher chief who was older and less competent. Apakuki was appointed to a government post on his merits. The older man wanted the post and employed sorcery against the young chief, who now grew weaker and weaker and was indeed at death's door. Everyone had given him up. He was a good man and had helped with the preaching at the church, but he knew he was dying. The Fijian pastor, much lower in social status, visited him in true prophetic style and rebuked him for his unbelief. "You know why you are dying, and you will indeed die, because you are a hypocrite. You have preached in the church and yet you have no faith in the power of Christ, who said He had *all* power and that you could draw on this. You believe the power of sorcery is stronger than the power of Christ." Apakuki was not used to being so addressed by the pastor, who he thought might rather have prayed for him. But as he reflected on the matter, he recognized the prophetic nature of his word. He called for a little light food. In repentance his faith revived. In two days he was on his feet again, and something new came into his preaching.

Missionaries who are sent to work among this kind of people had better escape the Western philosophical worldview as soon as possible. Their ministry will be within a worldview quite different from their own, and their message has to be both *credible* and *relevant* within that more dynamic frame of reference. If they cling to their foreignness and refuse to let themselves go, they will be the more manifestly foreign. If, on the other hand, they become part of this worldview and take their Bible with them, so much so that they learn to take it at its face value and act on it, they may discover the Bible a completely new book to them. We are all so terribly Western in the way we use and dissect the Bible. It can be better understood when we view it from a worldview more approaching that in which it was originally written. And power encounter is only one of the new dimensions that will open to us. The world of Hebrew seasonal festivals, for example, is another, and also the realm of sacrifice.

(This entire area of power encounter is crucial to missions today—so much so that I have devoted Chapter 25 to it in the "Cluster of Missiological Problems" section of this *Introduction to Missiology*.)

TREND 3: DISCOVERING NEW ASPECTS OF THE THEOLOGY OF INDIGENEITY

The concept of the indigenous church goes far back into the 1840s, when Henry Venn, the secretary of the Church Missionary Society, was seeking ways of dealing with certain mission fields, in particular New Zealand and Sierra Leone. The key word of his missionary theory was "euthanasia"—the notion that the mission had to die that the church might be born. He wrote many memoranda on this subject over the years, for he had a long term in office. Forgetting the historical origins, let me say merely that the way the theory of the indigenous church has come down to us in our day has been termed "the three self theory." The aim of this theory was to bring a mission to such a state that it could become an indigenous church, standing on its feet with respect to "self-support," "self-determination," and "self-propagation." Even though this theory was widely accepted by mission boards and field missions, it was very seldom tried. Missionary paternalism and their lack of faith in the ability of their converts to take control prevented their letting go. This can be documented in scores of mission fields and may be taken as a general weakness of missions in the Colonial Age. Even after a century or more of Christian instruction very few indigenous churches came into being. The few more effective cases of indigenous church emergence have been the result of specifically planned programs. In some cases the home board came to a sudden decision and cut off support without planned preparation. These cases failed sadly.

The demise of the colonial system forced many mission fields to become churches on their own resources, but what is more significant is the theological reinterpretation of the whole concept of an indigenous church. The three-self idea fell short of the ideal in any case. Financial independence, organizational autonomy, and missionary outreach were not in any way a total complex of the marks of a church. It was obviously an artificial structure, and the minimum structure at that, to permit the freeing of the local group from missionary overlordship. This was, at best, a strategical rather than a theological motive. It was defective also because all three criteria had foreign Western and often denominational models and did not relate to the local lifestyle and economy. Moreover, there was nothing biblical about it. Neither did it relate in any way to a theology of indigeneity—yet the Bible told me years ago there should be such a thing.

The apostle Paul, who is the biblical model for church planting, planted churches, not missions. He was sent forth on a mission, but he stayed in a place only long enough to identify the natural leaders and form them into churches. Sometimes he visited them again on a later journey. He wrote letters to them. He sent his representatives to look into their problem situations from time to time. But he did not plant mission stations which dominated the Christian group, gave it a foreign denominational structure and theology, and created the problem of getting, after many years, from mision to church. I saw this and reasoned this way on the mission field long before I read Sidney J.W. Clark and Roland Allen. However, it was Clark (1928) who gave us the concepts of *construction* and *reconstruction* to distinguish missionary church planting from the passage from mission to church, and pointed out that the latter was a matter of necessity in our present missionary predicament, but that all future work should be construction of churches from the start. Then he laid down rules for reconstruction where it was needed. This was as early as 1928; he was a post-colonial strategist long before his time.

Now I must state what I believe to be the theology of the indigenous church. A church is indigenous: when it is culturally a part of its own world; when its witness is relevant in meeting the needs of its congregation and the world about it; when its message is meaningful in the context where it belongs; when its physical form and operating structures are suitable for the culture; when it acts on its own initiative in the service ministries arising from local needs and crises and in missionary outreach; and above all, when it is aware of its own theological identity—in other words, it sees itself as the Body of Christ ministering the love of Christ, the mind of Christ, the Word of Christ, and His ministry of reconciliation and comfort in the location where it is set in the world. And let me point out that this does not depend on any Western models for budget, organizational structure, or nineteenth century missionary patterns. Its indigeneity lies within its own sense of selfhood as the Body of Christ communicating relevantly in that community. The concept of indigeneity has nothing whatever to do with the three selfs. Its true selfhood requires anthropological relevance and theological awareness and effective pastoral ministry—nothing more and nothing less. It may even draw from outside resources and personnel as long as they do not infringe on these requirements.

This theological and anthropological redefinition of indigeneity has really changed the pattern of pioneering mission on some fields I know. I know a missionary among the Navaho Indians who is helping the people plant church structures and worship forms far nearer to those of another denomination than his own because he knows they are more indigenously relevant. He is involved in a church planting cooperative program rather than a large station complex, which his own denomination is still saddled with in other mission fields. I have both done research and worshiped with these people and know they have a fine sense of selfhood, which is missing in many of the other groups on this same reservation.

The notion of indigeneity has changed from a halfbaked strategy to a full-orbed theology, and this is one of the greatest changes emerging in the era of post-colonial missions and a sign of greatest hope for the future.

TREND 4: REINTERPRETING THE THEOLOGY OF SOCIAL CHANGE

Christian mission is deeply involved in the processes of social and religious change. Evangelization is itself a change process. The old approach to mission was based on a wrong assumption that change was a one-way process. The stronger controlled the weak, the superior the inferior, the adult the child—and likewise the "advanced" people supervised the growth of the "child" races. Colonialism was based on these fallacies, and colonial missions consciously or unconsciously went along with them. This was the root cause of our ingrained superiority and our paternalism. We spoke of *culture clash,* envisaging the civilized countries imposing their will on the uncivilized and raising them to a civilized state. We regarded ourselves as agents of change as if the changes we brought about were literally the changes we intended.

In recent years this view has been radically changed. Anthropologists no longer speak of culture clash, but rather of *culture contact* to allow for the fact that it was not a one-way imposition but a two-way interaction. The indigenes accepted the white man's institutions and artifacts on their own terms, used them in their own way, and gave them their own meanings. To put this in terms of Barnett's anthropological theory: the missionaries were the *advocates* of change, the indigenous *acceptors* or *rejectors* were the real *innovators* because in accepting the innovation they adapted it to their own need, in their own way, and frequently gave it quite a new meaning which the missionaries never intended. There are scores of examples of this in Oceania—in liturgy, in religious language, and in indigenous theology. But it also bears on economics and social values. Anthropologists (Belshaw 1954) and historians (Shineberg 1967) have alike demonstrated the part played by the indigenes themselves in the change process.

I think the most interesting spin-off of this new orientation of the data of the history of missions is the light it throws on the *problem of meaning* for the advocate (who is, in our case, the evangelist). When a missionary explains the atoning sacrifice of Christ, say, to a pagan hearer who comes from a sacrifice-oriented tribal society and does so in words derived from the pagan religious vocabulary (and there is no other alternative), is the explanation the missionary articulates the same as the explanation that is heard by the potential convert? When the missionary explains that God is our Father, to people of a matrilineal society in which the father is only a social addition to the family by marriage and what we think of as the father role is played by the mother's brother, what does the potential convert hear the evangelist saying about God the Father? What kind of a theology does the potential convert come out with? In any case, it will be the acceptor and not the evangelist who gives the doctrine its ultimate meaning.

Or, to give another example, say the evangelist is teaching the relation of the Father, Son, and Spirit as a Trinity to a people with no such idea in their worldview, and the Trinity is translated literally as "God in three persons" (which is itself an idiom from the classical theater anyway), however careful the evangelist's teaching, once the term concocted reaches out beyond the immediate audience the people probably will hear it as "three gods," especially if they are converting from polytheism.

A previous generation of anthropologists criticized the missions for stimulating religious change in non-Christian societies, for "destroying culture," as they put it. These salvage anthropologists were also under the delusion of the static nature of tribal society which had to be preserved for posterity. But the development of the anthropological study of acculturation and culture change itself virtually has done away with this criticism. Change is not a bad thing. Indeed, it is necessary for survival. All societies have their inbuilt mechanisms for change and adaptation. What the missionary has to learn is to operate through those cultural mechanisms rather than against them. Our Lord has commissioned us to bring about change and to do it cross-culturally. We are called to be advocates seeking response to the Gospel and the renewal of human societies. There is no question about this. What is to be critically questioned is how we go about our advocacy. Here we are involved with the *problems of identification and empathy*. This requires that the missionary understand the social institutions and decision making mechanisms and the indigenous manner of presenting a case for change with respect, and to do so on a person-to-people basis, not an adult-to-children one. In any case the final decision is with the hearers, not the advocate.

No discussion of the theology of social change would be adequate without an attempt to enumerate some of the *change processes* which are features of our contemporary world. These are inevitable processes because of the nature and circumstances of our times. If our theology is to be relevant, it must speak precisely to the point of what these changes mean to the program of evangelization in the modern world. They call for new techniques and forms of communication and new types of ministry. I shall have time to mention only three such processes.

First, there is the *process of modernization.* Modernization is manifest in the changing lifestyle of most communities as the world shrinks in size and modern structures and inventions are diffused to the earth's remotest corners. You see it in the transition from subsistence farming to wage earning systems, from self-sufficiency to specialization, changing hours of work, and capacity for spending. You see it in the diffusion of electronics, so that a tape recorder, which a few years ago was feared, like a camera, as a box for catching a person's soul (his voice or likeness), is now a common thing in remote villages, and all children want to hear their own voice or see their own portrait. You feel it everywhere; the films of Hollywood have spread and projected a distorted view of changing Western values. These aspects of modernization have created a whole new set of ethical and theological problems for the communicator of the Gospel—for example, the loss of traditional marriage and family safeguards and the increase of divorce. Traditional values, which evolved to give equilibrium to a former lifestyle, are found to be inadequate in the transitions of modernization.

Second, we have the *process of urbanization,* which is not merely a statistical matter but a radical change of living conditions and lifestyle, with new values and legal restrictions. Tremendous experiments in the sociology of living close together in restricted units are going on all the time, and each new experiment raises a new set of problems for the evangelist.

For example, a few years ago I was in Mexico City and interested in the growth process of the squatters in the vacant allotments and how the government dealt with these by clearing the locations and building huge high-rise establishments. When completed, these buildings contained everything needed for the life of their inhabitants. They had their supermarkets, their swimming pools, their recreation sections and theaters. Everyone in a given establishment was in a common level of wage scale. Everyone was a Mexican. No foreigner could live there. What is the requirement for evangelism in such an establishment? The government's agnostic attitude and laws forbade the building of a church or the residence of a foreign missionary there. Two things were apparent: (1) the evangelist had to be a resident, therefore a national Mexican, and one living within a given wage scale; and (2) whatever *koinonia* was planted there had to be of the house church or the coffeehouse type. But one cannot assume that because these factors apply for Mexico City, they will suit all high-rise experiments in other places. Every experiment has to stand as unique in itself. When it is fully developed, the theology of the evangelization of high-rise apartments will be extremely varied. In Hong Kong, for example, rooftop evangelism is often employed.

I may very briefly mention a third, the *process of mobility*. I am not thinking so much here of the nomadic tribes of the world, although they do present their own set of problems for evangelization, but the general mobility of the human race in our day. A few years ago a national magazine calculated that 38 million Americans changed their place of residence every year. Today the figure is undoubtedly higher. Can you imagine over 800,000 families moving in one month? The moving van has replaced the covered wagon. This raises problems for both evangelization and for pastoral care. In the latter case I recall doing a survey for the Episcopalians at one of their Navaho Indian areas and finding a huge discrepancy between their baptismal records and their resident local constituency. Unrecorded mobility had robbed them of 37.5 percent of their adherents and reflected a lack of pastoral responsibility over the years. More positively, human mobility means the emergence of cross-cultural homogeneous units in every big city, awaiting evangelism. Aware of this opportunity, one Church in America with 2,000 congregations worshiping in Spanish, 250 in other European languages, 50 in Asian languages, and 400 in American Indian languages has been formed of mobile groups looking for a place to settle. Thus I would argue that in our day mobility means a problem of pastoral care but also an opportunity for cross-cultural evangelism even at home.

TREND 5: REDISCOVERING A THEOLOGY OF THE CORPORATE GROUP

One of the major causes of paternalism in colonial missions was Western individualism and competitiveness. The missionaries often failed to recognize that this was their own peculiar worldview but that, in point of fact, they were actually conducting their program of evangelization within an altogether different worldview, a thought-world of group structures, where the equilibrium of the corporate unit was the primary value. There are two points where Western missionaries sometimes had theological trouble because of this. They did not always allow for the homogeneity of the corporate unit in decision making—which, for the missionary, meant conversion. Likewise they did not always appreciate

the multi-individual homogeneity in the worship structures of the congregations they planted. In each case this led to a foreign character of
conversion and worship patterns. The Western missionaries did not
always see that they were looking at things from their own Western
worldview and that the Gospel could be seen without distortion from
worldviews other than their own.

Not all missionaries knew how to handle a group conversion movement of some hundreds of persons coming together to the Christian faith. I
know of one case of missionaries saying this could not be of the Spirit of
God and so held the inquirers off at gun point, because they thought the
only mode of conversion was the form they had known at home. They did
not recognize that this rejection of paganism had come after months of
multi-individual discussion in their proper decision making institutions for
matters of religious change. This was their way of doing it meaningfully,
and as yet they knew no other. They were open to be put under instruction
but their coming was rejected, and rejected in a most offensive way.

I have worshiped in two Melanesian congregations, both were of the
same denomination and supported by the same home churches but very
different in their worship patterns. In the first the people were called by
the beating of a native drum. Before the service they chanted the catechism
in the pre-Christian indigenous liturgical manner. They sat as they would
normally sit in a culturally oriented gathering. The sermon, hymn singing,
and Bible reading were in the vernacular language. The officials, according
to their different functional roles, welcomed the members, received the
offering, and made the announcements. They were all indigenes, and their
appointment reflected the social structure of the worshiping community.
The women's group and the choir were participant and indigenous. The
equilibrium of this congregation was indigenous and homogeneous.

In the second case the missionary, who kept the key, unlocked the
church, rang a church bell, led the service, read the lesson, gave the
announcements, called for the offering, and blessed it. The choir was led
by a foreigner, and they sang a Western anthem. The hymns, the reading,
and the sermon were in English. What equilibrium there was in this
service was monostructured round the foreign missionary. From the
Melanesian worshipers there was no participation save their half-hearted
hymn singing. Culturally, the first church was an operating homogeneous
unit; the second was utterly foreign and monostructured.

The theological problem arises when, through the human process of
migration or mobility, people from one kind of homogeneity find themselves in a Western (English-, German-, or French-speaking) urban
locality and find they either have to become assimilated into Western
monolingual congregations or separate themselves as homogeneous unit
churches. This raises the question of the unity and diversity of the Church
and is an issue of current theological debate.

In June 1977 a follow-up consultation of the Lausanne Congress met in Pasadena to discuss the homogeneous unit and its significance for evangelization. It agreed that a homogeneous unit church could be quite authentic and does not have to upset the unity of the Church as a whole. It differentiated between *unity* and *uniformity,* but it went on to say that that same homogeneous unit congregation needed to see that it also belonged to the Church universal and to demonstrate in some way that belonging. Let me quote from the official statement:

> We are unanimous in celebrating the colorful mosaic of the human race that God has created. This rich variety should be preserved, not destroyed by the Gospel. The attempt to impose another culture on a people, who have their own, is cultural imperialism. The attempt to level all the colorless uniformity is a denial of the Creator and an affront to his creation. The preservation of cultural diversity honors God, respects man, enriches life and promotes evangelization. Each church, if it is to be truly indigenous, should be rooted in the soil of its local culture (L.C.W.E. 1978a:3).

Then after an hour or so discussing specific attempts to retain the diversity within the unity the following was added:

> All of us are agreed that in many situations a homogeneous unit church can be a legitimate and authentic church. Yet we are also agreed that it can never be complete in itself. . . . In isolation it cannot reflect the universality and diversity of the Body of Christ, nor grow into maturity. Therefore every homogeneous unit church must take active steps to broaden its fellowship to demonstrate visibly the unity and variety of Christ's Church (4).

This was perhaps the most significant item in the Pasadena statement which, coming from a selected post-Lausanne work group, shows how far evangelical missionary theory and theology has progressed since the Berlin Congress of 1966—which belonged utterly to the Colonial Age of missions.

TREND 6: ALLOWING A THEOLOGY OF CONTEXTUALIZATION TO EMERGE

Over the last decade an area of interaction between theology and anthropology, often spoken of as ethnotheology, has claimed increasing attention. It has come from anthropology and in particular from the linguists—mainly Bible translators. How do the language and the culture of the communities to whom we try to communicate impose themselves on the forms and structures with which we communicate? How do we get a dynamic equivalent for the New Testament message or a New Testament church in a culture different both from the biblical one and from our own? Anything relevant to the Bible translator at this point is relevant in the same way to the preacher, teacher, witness, or evangelist. It raises again the problem of meaning. Does the convert hear what we say, or think we say? Another body of evangelical missiologists was attacking the same problem from a slightly different angle. They used the term *contextualization*. What does it mean to put the Gospel into a context different from that in which it originated? These two streams met at the Lausanne Congress, where one of the work groups was wholly devoted to the subject.

As a result of this a post-Lausanne consultation was called at Bermuda to discuss the contextualization of the Gospel in different cultures. Bible scholars, theologians and anthropologists from all continents were brought together for discussion on an advanced level for several days. My own impression as a participant was that the theology of the contextualization of the Gospel was speaking to us at four distinct levels at least.

The first of these levels was with respect to the *communication* of the Gospel itself — that means Bible translation on the one hand, and preaching/teaching/witness on the other. This further means that we are responsible for the words we choose and the forms with which we communicate. How do we obtain, not a literal sequence of words from the Bible, but the spiritual content of the passage as it would be required for meeting the felt needs in a particular cultural context? How may grammar and semantics be used to communicate a relevant theology?

The second level is at the point of *church formation.* We are not there to plant a Western denominational structure which came perhaps out of the European Reformation or some other historical event of no concern whatever to people in the context where we are communicating. What is to be the form of the *koinonia*? What kind of a leadership structure does it need to be meaningful to that kind of people and within which they can work happily? What kind of building, if any, should they provide for their worship? How can the people be led to feel that the worship is their own and to participate in what is going on before God? Are the liturgies indigenous? Does the organization of the church program meet the felt needs of the community so that the church serves as the Body of Christ in that locality? These are all theological questions because they deal with the relations of Christians with God and mankind. The physical character of the church has to be culturally congenial to the people. The means of grace must be spiritually adequate within that cultural context.

Third, we look at the *local leaders,* not just the system by which they are appointed, but the leaders as persons and their acceptability to the congregation, the precise nature of their functional roles, and the methods by which they are trained for leadership. In all these matters culture is very much involved, and a system of training may have to be specially created to meet the circumstances. Can you imagine a situation, a gerontocracy, say, where rule is by the old men? The highest value in this society is mature experience. The old men have faced the variety of human crises—floods, famines, fires, wars, pestilence—if anyone knows how to deal with a crisis it would be an old man. Then their missionary wants a leader for the church being planted among them. The missionary selects a young man in the prime of his strength who has studied the Bible and knows it well and is a good preacher. The experiment fails. It fails, because in the opinion of the group, a leader must have lived long enough to face all the spiritual crises that the group can meet. In our society the youth may be ideal—but not in this one. The whole complex of leadership has to be contextualized, and it is a theological matter because the leader and people have to relate to each other personally before God.

Then there is a fourth area where the Gospel has to be contextualized, namely, the application of *Christian ethics*. This may be *direct* or *indirect*. When pagans become Christian, manifestly many things have to go. The old Fijians, for example, knew that cannibalism, widow strangling, patricide, infanticide, and other pre-Christian institutions had to be discarded. The theology of humans relating to other humans before God demanded the ethical change. Other issues were indirect. They did not emerge until the converts began to live the Christian life, and suddenly they found themselves confronted with ethical decisions. Some of these came out of the cultural context. They related to social relations, marriage, and perhaps trade, and they called for quality of Christian life and maturity. Some of them brought two different moral values into conflict and the convert had to make a choice—like telling the truth against loyalty to one's family, which was a difficult choice in a society based on family solidarity.

One thing needs to be said: both the spiritual opportunities and the moral temptations that a Christian convert may meet will vary according to the cultural context from which he or she comes. Appropriately the Bermuda Report ends:

> Our consultation has left us in no doubt of the pervasive importance of culture. The writing and reading of the Bible, the presentation of the Gospel, conversion, church and conduct—all these are influenced by culture. It is essential therefore that all churches contextualize the Gospel in order to share it effectively in their own cultures. For this task of evangelization we know our urgent need of the ministry of the Holy Spirit. . . . (L.C.W.E. 1978b:33).

TREND 7: DEMANDING A NEW THEOLOGY OF MISSIONARY TRAINING

If we presume that before candidates for missionary service are even considered for appointment they have had some basic biblical and theological training in a theological institution or Bible school and have themselves made a personal commitment to Christ and have had at least a course on pastoral or missionary formation, we may ask what remains to make them suitable for missionary service.

When I first went out as a missionary, that was all that was available, except a little comparative religion that I hoped would help me and about which the least said the better. I was so enthusiastic about my calling that I would have left my job in Melbourne there and then and gone out without any training at all; but my good father convinced me that I needed the standard ministerial and biblical training and a little pastoral experience. He was absolutely right, and I often thanked him in my heart afterwards. But even so, I was a typical colonial missionary. Frequently I have reflected on those disillusioning first years of culture shock and thought that, had I been able to do a course in anthropology before going to the field, I could have reached in two years the point of effectiveness that took seven or eight.

After fifteen years on the field I felt so urgently the need for anthropological study (I was trying to learn anthropology from the authorities who lived at the turn of the century) that I left the field and went back to school in America. Then, armed with at least a partially updated knowledge of the discipline, I returned for the most fruitful period of my missionary ministry. Then the door opened for me as a teacher and researcher in missiology, and I knew that I could never be truly a missiologist without an advanced degree in anthropology. So, when I urge the importance of this discipline for the training of missionaries, I am speaking from experience. I know personally the difference it made to me as a communicator of the Gospel and as a cross-cultural pastor, and beyond this I know how it opened to me new vistas of biblical insight that I never got from any preacher, teacher, or commentary.

The missionary candidate today has two things that we never had in my day: (1) anthropology as a discipline has developed into a tremendously enriched data base of information, a more refined and accurate body of theory, and a whole new area of applied science. It is a tremendous resource; (2) not only is it better than in my day, but it is more easily accessible. In the light of its availability, missionaries who avoid it today must be held responsible if they commit a cultural blunder when they evangelize on the field.

I have now addressed several new trends in missionary theology for the Post-colonial Era. Every point that I have had grows out of the colonial missionary's inadequate anthropological preparation. This too becomes a theological issue, because it is a matter of Christian responsibility if we fail to recognize the essentiality of cross-cultural preparation, cultural awareness and linguistic proficiency when we send out our missionaries.

I was involved in a meeting of the Committee on the Curriculum for Missionary Training. It included evangelicals, liberals, and Catholics, but in spite of their theological differences they were all convinced of the rightness of Christian mission and were of one mind on the essentiality of anthropological training for it. Here is the first item of their declaration:

The training of cross-cultural missionaries for the changing times and
conditions of the mission fields of the world in our day, requires more and
more understanding and empathy. For many years the discipline of
anthropology (especially such aspects as social and applied anthropology,
acculturation, cultural dynamics, the phenomenology of religion and
ethnolinguistics) has been inadequately utilized in the majority of educational institutions where missionaries are trained. With the availability of
this kind of education in our day, the sending forth of missionaries untrained
in anthropology is no longer justifiable (C.C.M.T. 1974:1).

This statement throws the responsibility also on the sending church or
mission board responsible for the training program, and when we talk of
responsibility, we are in the area of moral theology.

The Committee also devised a recommended model for a curriculum
of study for institutions involved in the training of missionaries. The
model is highlighted in Figure 9. Such a model presupposes that each
missionary candidate would have already received a thorough general
education as well as the proper theological and biblical training. Furthermore, "the fields set out in the model are related to preparation for service
in Christian *cross-cultural* mission, not the home ministry, which may or
may not overlap with this, according to the circumstances" (1974:2).
Today there is a growing number of seminaries, like Fuller's School of
World Mission, which are preparing missionary candidates and missionary
veterans in just such a thorough way.

In conclusion I return to the title of this chapter, "Trends in the
Theology of Mission." The word *trends* suggests change. I reiterate that
the biblical theology of God's saving purpose for mankind, mankind's
lostness without Christ, and our mandate for mission are abiding and
basic. There is nothing that has changed about the missionary imperative
and purpose. The changes all come from the need for a better and more
empathetic method of communicating that unchanging truth in an amazing
diversity of cultural contexts. Thus the real change of mission in this Post-
colonial Age is the theological effect of the injection of anthropology into
the missionary operation.

FIGURE 9

A Suggested Curriculum Model for the Training of Missionary Candidates

1. Simplified	2. More Developed	3. Most Deversified
1. History of Missions	History of Missions to the Reformation History of Missions Since the Reformation	Expansion of the Early Church Missions—Middle Ages to Reformation History of Modern Missions & Ecumenics
2. Theology of Mission	Theology of Mission—Gospels Theology of Mission—New Testament Church	People of God in the Old Testament Theology of Mission—Gospels Theology of Mission—New Testament Church
3. Principles and Practice	Principles and Practice Indigenous Church	Principles and Practice Indigenous Church Theological Education by Extension
4. Cultural Anthropology	Cultural Anthropology Social Structure and Authority Patterns	Cultural Anthropology Social Structure and Authority Patterns Contemporary Trends in Missiology
5. Comparative Religion	Hinduism and Buddhism Islam	Hinduism and Buddhism Islam Other Eastern Religions
6. Applied Anthropology	Applied Anthropology Theory of Anthropology	Applied Anthropology Theory of Anthropology Data Collecting (Research Method)
7. Traditional Religions	Phenomenology of Traditional Religion Traditional Religious Practices and Practitioners	Phenomenology of Traditional Religion Traditional Religious Practices and Practitioners Nativistic and Revitalization Movements
8. Church Growth Case Studies	Case Studies from Africa Case Studies from Asia and Latin America	Case Studies from Africa Case Studies from Asia and Latin America
9. Language Learning	Language Learning Language and Culture	Language Learning Language and Culture Translation
10. Missionary Internship	Missionary Internship Mission Project	Missionary Internship Mission Project Reading Courses
11. Global Awareness and World Affairs	Global Awareness and World Affairs Cultural Dynamics	Global Awareness and World Affairs Cultural Dynamics

12. Spiritual Formation and Growth of the Missionary

PART II

The Anthropological Dimension

PART II

The Anthropological Dimension

The real significance of understanding the basic ideas of social anthropology and a working knowledge of its methods and techniques for the Christian missionary has to be *discovered*. This is essential in every cross-cultural situation for the evangelist, doctor, health worker, teacher, agriculturist or Peace Corps worker. All people are naturally *ethnocentric* and this ethnocentricity is not reduced until one becomes *aware* of the cross-cultural situation and the validity of diverse *values* for different people. Above all, the advocate of a new religion must both demonstrate empathy and establish rapport if there is to be effective cross-cultural communication. One dare not ignore a culture. There needs to be a clear understanding of the institutional structures and personal relationships within them, and familiarity with the language of the society, if the missionary is to work within those structures and relationships. Few individuals are born with this kind of understanding. Normally it has to come with training. People are so conditioned by their own *enculturation* that they do not appreciate the process of enculturation in other ethnic systems. This appreciation has to be acquired by deliberate and conscious effort.

The first essay in this section, "Anthropology: Luxury or Necessity for Missions?", was an attempt to deal with the question of training missionaries. Under the pressures of the field experience I had been critical of my own training. But later, when I became immersed in the work of training missionaries and I took a hard look at the curriculum and the relevance of training programs, the discipline of missiology began to formulate itself, and with it the dimension of anthropology.

76705

"Changes in Anthropological Orientation and its Bearing on Missiology" discusses the theoretical, methodological and interpretive changes which have modified the pre-war attitudes of anthropology. "Anthropology for its own sake" has given way to applied anthropology—science which has to justify its existence by application in the world programs of human betterment. Thus anthropology is generally more in step with missiology and its positive or helpful values are more readily available to the missionary.

The mission field has changed dramatically. The day when missionaries could present a foreign theology in a foreign language and plant a foreign church has gone. The study of anthropology tells us why. We have lived through a period when anthropologists have been extremely critical of missionary methods and ethnocentricity (not without some justification), although they themselves have been much indebted to missionaries for their cultural descriptions and linguistics. A great deal of the earliest anthropological writing was done by missionaries who had learned their anthropology the hard way: on the field without any preliminary training. Their memory now stands among the real pioneers of the discipline: Williams, Codrington, Gill, Fison and Fox, to name only a few in my area. The strongest wave of criticism came with the salvage anthropologists who stressed the anthropological offences of the missionaries. They were more concerned with exposing error and destructive criticism than with offering any positive and constructive assistance. However, over against the negative (critical and corrective) voice of anthropology there ought to be a balancing positive (directive) word. If the former shows what the missionary should not do, the latter should point out ways of more effective missioning on a sound anthropological base. These concepts of error and approval I have tried to set out in "The Negative and Positive Value of Anthropology to the Missionary." I hope its criticism is constructive. My purpose is to warn the missionaries of the dangers of *action against social structure,* and suggest their more considered *action through social structure.*

Christian mission is involved in the flood of culture change. Its thrust is especially at the configuration of religion but the effects are felt in all directions. In "Anthropological Processual Models in Missiology" I attempt to study the effects of culture change on the rites of passage from one world to another—from the animist world to that of the Christian. The anthropological dimension of culture change, culture and identity, and salvation in this modern era of Christian mission is the theme of "Salvation and Cultural Identity." The role of religion as *integrator* of society is discussed in "Patterns of Religious Change in Communal Society." Here also I discuss four types of religious change experienced by collective mankind in the animist environment: demoralization, submersion, conversion and revitalization. Perhaps this is a step in the direction of a typology, but it is comparative rather than exclusive. The importance of finding adequate functional substitutes for cultures undergoing change is addressed in "The Functional Substitute in Church Planting."

My *Introduction to Missiology* has been cast mainly in rural or insular communal societies, because that is where I have given my missionary service; but the manifest patterns of human mobility suggest that the major missionary operations of the last years of the twentieth century will fall into the industrial and urban situations. The process is rapid in this direction. I have addresssed this tremendous migration of rural peoples to the confines of the city in "Urban and Industrial Situations: A Solomon Islands Case Study." Although it addresses a particular Solomon Islands situation, the principle insights of this study are readily applicable to many of the burgeoning urban situations today. It is a good example of the beginnings of the process of urbanization. It shows the social structure of a city beginning to form. It shows that the flow or influence in the rural-urban situation is as much centripetal as centrifugal. It shows the consequences of new forms of culture clash for the Christian mission. Here is an area of anthropological research we have not yet adequately incorporated into missiology, but it is high time we did so. Chapters on "The Dynamics of the Bicultural Church" and "Membership Shrinkage" in Part IV also speak to the urban situation.

The missiological use of anthropology is selective. We are more concerned with the study of collective mankind as "interacting beings in social groups" than with humans as animals. Only occasionally do we use physical anthropology in a church growth study; for example, when a researcher wants to distinguish between two ethnic groups. But there are other branches of anthropology which speak to missiology: culture and personality, linguistics, ethnolinguistics, and so forth. Culture and personality frequently impinges itself on a case study where personality factors seem to bear on religious conversion. I firmly believe that as yet we have hardly scratched the surface of the resources of anthropology that are at our disposal.

CHAPTER 9

Anthropology: Luxury or Necessity for Missions?

The beginning of courses in anthropology at the School of World Mission at Fuller Theological Seminary brought a quantity of correspondence from Bible school and seminary professors of mission asking for information, course outlines, and reading lists. The correspondence reflected the feeling on the part of some professors of mission that anthropology ought to be included in their program and an uncertainty of how to go about it.

The following observations are offered in the hope that they will help clarify the situation and thereby give some direction to the planning of courses in missionary anthropology. Such courses cannot be planned by collecting outlines and bibliographies for different levels and purposes. The first requirement in planning a training course is to be aware of the need and to set the goal that meets it. This problem ultimately resolves itself into six basic questions which must be answered.

The original version of this chapter was published in *Evangelical Missions Quarterly*, January 1968, Vol. V, No. 1, pp. 7-19. Gratitude is hereby expressed to the publisher for permission to include it here.

BASIC QUESTIONS

1. *Is the Anthropological Training Given to Missionary Candidates Adequate and Relevant?*

Every institution involved in the training of missionaries has to face up to this. I should have kept a census of the many missionaries who have told me how they wished they had been trained in anthropology. I myself have often felt I could have reached that point of effectiveness in two years which took me ten as it was. In the end I had to take an extended furlough without pay to make up the deficiency. Courses in comparative religion are frequently of little value when one gets to the field. Much of the subject matter has come from the theory of the early armchair anthropologists, or it is related to the philosophical superstructure of the great religions rather than the real encounter at grassroots level where people are open for conversion.

A number of missionaries, it is true, must be trained for this academic encounter, but proportionately these are few in the total complex of world mission. Missionaries need to be trained in the way the animist thinks. They need to be able to reason in the logic and imagery of the medicine man. They need to be brought to an awareness of the difference between *encounter* and *dialogue* in cultural as well as theological dimensions. They need to be able to diagnose the character of acculturation processes at work in their specific situations and recognize readiness for innovation when they see it.

To some extent the adequacy or relevance of the course will depend on the theological outlook of the seminary concerned; but even a sound biblical theology has to be communicated effectively across cultural barriers. barriers. We are involved with the problems of cross-cultural advocacy and are confronted with the possibilities of *acceptance* or *rejection*—or perhaps *modification,* which brings us into the area of syncretism. Even if syncretism is dealt with on a sound theological level, it may still be academic and theoretical and totally unrelated to the specific forms of, say Africa and Latin America. A relevant course will introduce missionary candidates to these things.

And there is the problem of meaning. When pagans accept the Gospel, what do they take it to mean? Does it mean the same thing to the foreign advocate as the indigenous acceptor? There are problems of expressing theological concepts in pre-Christian terminology—or do you invent new vocabulary? If so, is it a foreign imposition?

What is the function of the social structure? What are the patterns of relationship in the family? Who marries who and why? How do you explain the fatherhood of God in a matrilineal society? Do you demand of a pagan polygamist that he divorce his wives before you baptize him? Are the rites which honor the ancestor matters of reverence or worship? These and thousands of other questions are the stuff of anthropology and, whether we like it or not, they are also the burden of the missionary. Anthropology is certainly no substitute for ethics, but it examines all these things and asks why. What is the function? How do they meet the felt needs of the society? What are we doing when we change them? If we know and understand what is involved, we will be wiser by far in our thinking, our acting, and our praying.

If missionaries go out into their fields of service without having been made aware of the type of problems they are to meet, their training can hardly be described as adequate or relevant. Anthropology is a must. More and more this is being realized by seminaries and missionaries alike. The missionary situation itself demands it.

Moreover, the course should be undergirded with sound theology. If such an institution has no care whether there be any real acceptance, how can it teach the techniques of advocacy?

2. What are Missionary Candidates Entitled to Expect of the Training?

Missionary candidates are entitled to expect four things of the training:

a. A training in the content and message of the Scriptures and a knowledge of how to explore and use their resources, which are presumably gotten in prior divinity courses.

b. The skill of his or her particular missionary craft—as preacher, teacher, doctor, nurse, or agriculturalist, etc.

c. An appreciation of the significance of the Great Commission, combined with the missionary's specialist skills, in this particular missionary situation in this present hour. This is on a personal level and no specific course is available. The candidates may be seeking this personally. Yet they are entitled to expect that somewhere advisors will show them how *their* skill, *their* call can be meaningful in *their* time and place of service. They are entitled to be confronted with the personal relevance of God's demands on them.

d. But this is not enough. Missionary candidates need to learn how to be effective across cultural barriers, where the Bible is viewed differently; where there is dialogue with orator, herald, teacher, medicine man, and craftsman; where the logic of reasoning follows a strange pattern and where he or she will use an inadequate technical vocabulary.

The young candidates subject themselves to training in the belief that the course will prepare them for their new roles. They are entitled to this. It is not a mere degree they seek. They seek to be prepared for the life role to which God calls them. At this point they rely on the seminary.

3. *What is the Problem Faced by the Professor of Missions?*

This problem has two different forms. In the first situation we have a seminary with a strong department of missions carried by several professors, with one of them perhaps assigned to anthropology. It ought to be so, but, in point of fact, I cannot say that it actually is. In any case, this is an ideal toward which seminaries should aim. The problem is a personal one. In a seminary for training missionaries the anthropologist selected should be a dedicated person with Christian convictions. The anthropologist's faith should be in tune with the missionary cause. Preferably the anthropologist has served a term as a missionary, or at least has been closely identified with missionary activity on the field.

It may be argued that an objective anthropologist with no personal commitment to the Christian mission can inject many a critical stimulus into classes with good effect. This is undoubtedly true, but we should never lose sight of the fact that the anthropologist teaches in an interdisciplinary area and must be able to appreciate both the disciplines which are trying to be bridged. No purely objective scientist can really appreciate the ideals and problems of the missionary without some subjective involvement in mission. Furthermore, anthropologists and journalists have long hammered away at missionary inadequacies through lack of anthropological knowledge. To some extent the criticisms have been valid, but the point is made, and we are aware of it, and the matter has been critically evaluated from within our own ranks. The time has now come where positive guidance must take the place of negative criticism. The negative aspects can be handled in a few classes, but we need whole courses to show what anthropology can do positively for the missionary. This requires a teacher who has been involved in mission and knows what it is about, or at least has travelled widely in missionary situations and shared the burdens of missionaries.

The second form of the problem is met in those seminaries where all dimensions of missionary thought and activity are left to a single professor of missions. Many such appointments are based on three areas of knowledge—missionary service, wide reading in the history of missions, familiarity with the philosophy of the great religions, their sacred literature, and political movements. Usually individuals selected for this role have not gone far in anthropology, because courses in anthropology were not taught to missionary trainees in their day, and to familiarize oneself with this discipline requires a mighty lot of reading. One is confronted with a time-consuming ground work that just has to be done, and this quite apart from keeping up to date in the new material coming out all the time. The all-inclusive role of professor of missions is an unenviable task.

As these individuals struggle with anthropology, they discover the discipline has many sub-areas which are of little direct value. They find also a great deal of opinion critical of missions and manifestly agnostic.

Here and there they find promising items which fit their missionary experience, and they build up something of their own without a proper frame of reference or scientific methodology. They long for a suitable text written by a believer. The best text in applied anthropology is written by a Roman Catholic (Luzbetak 1963) and colored by the missionary orientation of that church; but in any case because it is published by a Roman Catholic press it might well be passed by.

One possible solution is to have the candidates attend a secular university for anthropology courses. This has the advantages of (1) having the courses taught by a specialist in that field, (2) making missionary candidates take an objective and critical look at the missionary image before they become part of it themselves, and (3) providing them with a basic anthropological frame of reference on which to build their own experience.

It has the disadvantages of (1) possible distortion due to the philosophical bias of the secular teacher, (2) being unrelated positively to mission, (3) involving the candidates in digesting areas of anthropology of no direct value to their life work. However, in spite of this, where seminaries are close to universities it is preferable to draw on the secular resources at hand than burden the solitary professor of missions with this unwelcome task, which should never be regarded as just an extra course that has to be fitted in somehow. My own relationships with secular university departments of anthropology have been most cordial, yet the fact remains that there is now a new discipline of *missionary anthropology* not normally supplied by a secular university.

4. What is the Indigenous Church Entitled to Expect of Missionaries Sent to Them by the Home Church for Cross-cultural Mission?

Missionaries sent to the young churches should be only those who can supply those elements and roles that the churches cannot supply for themselves. The young churches are entitled to expect the seminaries at home will bear this in mind as they train their missionaries and fraternal workers.These elements may be analyzed briefly under four headings: *knowledge, attitudes, emphases,* and *methods.*

They are expected to have *knowledge* that people need and which they are ready to share. This includes knowledge of the Gospel itself and the Scriptures which record it. It also includes knowledge of their area of specialization—medicine, education, preaching, and so forth. They work for that day when their own contribution is no longer necessary, because the young church provides its own specialists. However, as new areas of specialized knowledge emerge, the young church may have occasional roles for fraternal workers with the right kind of knowledge.

The missionaries sent out by the seminary need a right *attitude.* They are foreigners entering another culture. It is not their role to impose supposedly superior Western patterns on the people they serve, but to enter their own realms of thought and make their contribution *within*, not *against* that culture. The young church that welcomes these men and women is entitled to expect a certain empathy. I remember the welcome speech of an old Fijian minister to a young Australian appointed to a leadership role. His predecessor had frequently tempered his advice from the chair with the words, "We are here to advise you," after which he pressed his will upon them. Now the time had come for a change. The old pastor said to the young man, "We're glad to be led by a young man full of strength and vigor, but we want to say one thing as you take over. Your task is not to tell us what you want, but to show us how to get what we want." A new day in Fiji began from that moment. The young church expects this attitude of its fraternal workers.

But the missionaries or fraternal workers still have an important *emphasis* to make. They make this against the background of acculturation and modern Western theology. They are aware of such things as universalism and syncretism and know these forces from their theological depths. The young church may not fully understand these, but it feels the drag at the grassroots level. It expects the evangelical fraternal workers to expose the *peculiar local manifestations* of universalism and syncretism and show *where* and *why* they are a danger. They also keep the young church aware of the importance of outreach. There is still a major theological contribution here that the foreigner can make to the emerging church. This is an emphasis, not an imposition.

We have learned a great deal in the matter of new *methods* which can and should be passed on to the young churches—methods of study, communication and counseling. The young churches have to take their place in the modern world. Materialism, commerce, other religions and ideologies are all advocates for their souls. They are entitled to expect of our Christian seminaries that those we send out as their fellow workers have the best methodological know-how.

These four things do not come purely as natural gifts. There is a degree of training involved in each. If each has its theological dimension, each also has its anthropological dimension. A right knowledge, a right attitude, a right emphasis, and right methods—what a tremendous responsibility this throws on the seminary! This is what a young church is entitled to expect of those the home church sends out as equipped missionaries for service. The young church accepts these candidates on the assumption that they have been adequately prepared to enter into the life and thought of the world so different from their own.

5. Has Anthropology Any Contribution to Make to Missionary Theology?

As we have already seen in Part I: "The Theological Dimension" (above) anthropology certainly raises questions for theology. Some of these call for a widening of the scope of theological thinking as we know it.

Let me take a simple text that creates no problem whatever to us. "As a man disciplines his son, the Lord your God disciplines you" (Deut. 8:5). This comes from a nomadic patriarchal community. It also fits our way of life, though it threatens to become less meaningful for each generation. I know a community where a father *never* disciplines his son. The mother's brother would be offended if his role were so usurped, and it might well lead to divorce. Note what theology is involved—the concepts of *fatherhood* and *sonship, their relationships,* the *authority* and *providence* of the Father, and so on. When our Christian theology stems from imagery derived from culture forms and patterns and the missionary has to communicate these in symbols of quite different culture, is there a textbook in theology anywhere that will help that missionary?

If we believe the Bible is a sufficient rule for life and practice, then what does Deuteronomy 8:5 mean in a matriarchal society, where many missionaries have to communicate today? Anthropology does not provide the answer, but it does clarify the issue so the problem may be clearly stated. The anthropologist will ask, for instance, "Does this say that a woman-dominated society is sinful because its ways are not patriarchal like those of the Jews, and therefore the mission is justified in changing their patterns of descent and inheritance?" "Or does it rather mean," the anthropologist goes on, "that particular truth about God is put this way for the benefit of patriarchal people? Would it not be better restated for a matriarchal group?"

The anthropologist might even suggest a way of putting it: "As a mother's brother disciplines his nephew, so the Lord your God disciplines you." Has the truth been lost by the change? The meaning is certainly transmitted correctly, but the literal text is lost. Is the missionary entitled to this freedom, say in Scripture translation? The *anthropologist* exposes the problem. The *theologian* has to give the answer. But in the final analysis it is the *field missionaries* who face the problem in the real life communication situation. It is no theoretical or philosophical matter for them; they know the spiritual destiny of people is involved.

That is only one example of many. So much of our theology is based on the imagery of personal relationships within the Greco-Roman or Hebrew complexes: concepts like *reconciliation, redemption, adoption, atonement, sacrifice, fellowship* and so on *ad infinitum.* Even our worship patterns and our ethics are culturally conditioned.

Suppose missionaries find themselves in a community where a sacrificial configuration ramifies throughout the whole way of life. They want to transmit the idea of the sacrifice of Christ. This is not merely a matter of translation. Pagan theology arises at every point. For a start, finding the right word is itself a problem. They are confronted with a highly refined vocabulary of sacrificial forms from which to select, with a whole set of differentiations that do not coincide with the English or Greek meanings. Here is a completely different frame of reference. They have to learn to *think sacrificially*. They are like a musician trained only in the chords of the octave, who is trying to record something sung in a pentatonic scale. Anthropology helps them recognize that there are two completely different kinds of harmony, or two different sacrificial frames of reference. Theology has to determine whether or not the transposing has been legitimate. But once again it is the field missionaries who have to face the desperate question: How can this person be brought to a decision for Christ? If I give this person a score in the octave of the West, will it be meaningful? Can I transpose it into his or her own scale? And if I do, is the harmony of the cross valid in the pentatonic scale?

The role of the missionary anthropologist is to bring together the seminary theologian and the field missionary. Where the missionary has clung to these patterns of the West, quite frequently the young church has ultimately split off and become an independent church, perhaps with some quite heretical tendencies. This, in itself, shows the missionary religion did not satisfy the felt needs of the group concerned. This is the day for interdisciplinary understanding between theology and anthropology. In any case, seminary students preparing for the mission field should at least be made aware of the approaching confrontation with this kind of problem. If we neglect to prepare them for this, they may well try to impose a purely Western theological way of thinking, which is not meaningful but learned by rote and creates an entirely wrong idea of the Christian faith. Many an enclosed, nongrowing, foreign-patterned mission church has come from this.

6. What Is the Missionary Role in "Directed Cultural Change"?

Not so long ago anthropologists (usually spoken of as "salvage" anthropologists) were highly critical of missions for destroying the cultures of their converts. There was perhaps some justification for the criticism, although the critics themselves never understood either the facts or the dynamics involved. Today there is more emphasis on the fact of change itself. Every culture is subject to change.

It is largely because of this that missionaries can communicate their ideas to other cultural situations. While the anthropologist is interested in *how, why* and *when* people innovate, the missionary and social worker, the health officer and agriculturalist, the administrator and educator, are all concerned with the same complex of social and psychological forces. However, while the anthropologist is an objective observer interested in cultural dynamics, *per se,* these others are all subjectively involved in *directing the change* to the greatest benefit of the society. They all have their successes and their failures, and often an anthropological analysis can expose the reasons. It follows that sound anthropological training is, therefore, a valid addition to the course for the preparation of missionaries who are to be engaged in cross-cultural communication of the Gospel. And not only evangelism is involved; even service projects can be injurious if they are not anthropologically administered. If the excessive giving of aid leads to a state of dependence, it only builds trouble for the future. Many a community of "rice Christians" has been established this way. They came into being with some relief or aid program and after a century are still the same numerical strength as when they began. Aid itself may be good and right, but it requires administration with anthropological insight, lest it be directed to paternalism rather than to indigenous activity, outreach, and initiative.

The process of change needs to be smooth rather than disruptive. Excessive shock has to be avoided. There are three types of component in each situation of culture change: (1) features that ought to be preserved, (2) features that must be discarded, and (3) features that may be preserved with a little modification. I once served this philosophy to a committee of Fijian chiefs and pastors, and found they accepted it with common consent as a basis for discussion of a constructive program of reform. Smooth change is possible, but one has to be sensitive to the signs of the group's readiness for that change. It has to be relevant, it has to meet the felt needs, and it has to be timely. If missionaries are to be aware of these qualities in a situation, they are more likely to be able to interpret them if they have been trained in anthropology. Being a missionary requires common sense, grace and guidance, but also a good understanding of why people behave as they do in a cross-cultural situation. This understanding viewed negatively is a good safeguard against serious error, and viewed positively is a great aid in knowing how to take command of an opportunity and direct change toward the growth of the church and the glory of God.

Some evangelicals may ask, "Does this not take the emphasis off the divine role in mission and put it on mankind?" I do not think so. To me, God is always in the pattern, ever constant and ever faithful. Mankind is the variable. Yet God has accepted humans as His fellow workers (1 Cor. 3:9). We are responsible for our pounds (Lk. 19:11-28) or talents (Mt. 25:14-30). The vinedresser (Lk. 13:6-9), harvesters (Jn. 4:35), servants (Mt. 22:8-10), and shepherds (1 Pet. 5:2) were all human agents responsible to the Lord, knowing their respective crafts and open for judgment if their service was irresponsible (Mt. 25:26-27).

SUMMARY

Clearly then, anthropological training for missions is a necessity which can no longer be neglected. All seminaries involved in the training of missionary candidates need to seriously consider including anthropology courses into their curriculum. One lone professor of missions is not enough.

Missionary candidates, likewise, need to avail themselves of those seminaries which offer anthropology courses along with the standard theological regimen. In lieu of this, candidates need to incorporate anthropological courses taken from area universities into their program of study. Another alternative is to take such courses at the undergraduate level. Either way, anthropological study can no longer be seen by missionary candidates as a luxury to be taken advantage of when and if time permits. Too many missionaries have wasted far too much time on the mission field with just such an attitude.

CHAPTER 10

Changes in Anthropological Orientation and their Bearing on Missiology

Theoretical, methodological and interpretive changes in anthropology over the century have transformed this discipline and thereby affected the relationship of anthropologists and missionaries. True, the missionary has corrected many wrong attitudes to other cultures and their values, perhaps because of criticism from anthropology, but changes in anthropological orientation are even more significant. Missionary changes have come in methods of communication and awareness of other values. Anthropology has modified some of its basic theory and goals. As a result, the disciplines and their practitioners are now better able to help each other.

Until now the anthropologist's criticisms of missionary work have been mostly negative, even if some have been well taken. However the anthropologist is now recognizing that (1) much can be learned from a good missionary who knows the language well and identifies effectively with the people, (2) anthropology itself has not by any means all the answers, and (3) much of anthropology's own basic theory has had to be modified in the light of field experience. With these changes on both sides there should be a new atmosphere for coexistence and cooperation in problem-solving between anthropology and missiology.

Anthropologists vary in theory as much as missionaries do in doctrine, nevertheless the re-orientation in the last fifty years justifies a re-examination of the missionary-anthropologist relationship. This becomes urgent because of (1) the emergence of missiology as a discrete discipline and a field for degree granting, and (2) the creation of the role of missionary anthropologist in the area of applied anthropology. The purpose of this chapter, then, is to survey briefly the changes that have taken place and show what they signify for missiology.

CHANGES IN ANTHROPOLOGY

With no claim for presenting a total picture I classify the changes under four headings, each with several aspects. I present these observations in two columns, indicating the *earlier* and *modified* viewpoints in the left and right columns respectively.

1. Changes in the Anthropological View of Humanity and Society

1.	Mankind was once studied as an individual, "inner-directed," without adequate regard for the complexities of life in community.	Mankind is now studied in text, in both simple and complex groups. The individual is never an isolate.
2.	Living "primitives" were studied as survivals of evolutionary childhood, and treated as children.	All societies are seen as adult, with equally long history. Many of their differences may be explained by environmental factors — problems, needs and raw materials.
3.	The nature of society was described in clear-cut categories —economics, religion, war, politics, etc. The view was atomistic, analytic.	Societies compries sets of people and institutions in relationship or interplay, and beyond this in the interplay of sets within sets. The view is symbiotic.
4.	Culture was regarded as mainly transmitted from individual to individual, father to son, priest to priest, craftsman to craftsman, etc.	Individual transmission operates within group mechanisms and institutions, communal rites, prescriptions, etc. It aims at staisfying communal needs and maintaining social entity.
5.	Small groups were studied as independent ethnic units, each isolated from the next, as microcosms of human society. Social stability was reinforced by colonial authority.	Small groups, though still studied as ethnically discrete, are nevertheless seen in a holistic manner as neighbors in large regions, who must relate to survive. Independent and autonomous.

2. Changes in the Approach to and Study of Material Culture

6.	The collection of isolated artifacts began with the antiquarians, who classified them on the basis of form. Methods were experimental.	Archeologists now reconstruct communal units, artifacts in relationship, reflecting living patterns of the real people who used them.
7.	Material was arranged in supposed evolutionary series on a basis of physical form. The artifact "showed" the advanced or retarded state of its creator.	Material culture is now interperted in the light of its function in its specific context and time. It links the creator, user and group in a specific complex of rites, institutions, customs, etc.
8.	Interpretation was speculative.	Interpretation employs historical documents, new technology, radio-carbon, etc., and can be verified.

3. Changes in the View of Acculturation

9.	In the face of disappearing races, high value was set on collecting information, myths, artifacts, etc., that were in danger of being lost.	The fact of the inevitability of change is recognized. People survive by adjustment. Cultures have their own mechanisms for this.
10.	Emphasis on salvage is tended to preserve cultures for their own sakes. Culture change was resisted. A static view of culture.	Applied Anthropology and group dynamics explore how to bring about change in an acceptable manner. Emphasis is on what to preserve, what to change, and what to introduce. A dynamic view of culture.
11.	Emphasis fell on the concept of culture clash: foreign versus traditional culture, with the fittest surviving, or with a melting pot fusion.	It is now recognized that culture contact need not lead to chaos or destruction. A better concept is that of a new autonomous entity, based on an interplay on constituent elements and persons — diversity in unity.

4. Changes in Anthropological Theory and Research Method

12.	Much anthropological data was interpreted on a basis of academic investigation (using classical and biological models) by armchair theorists.	Speculative interpretation has to be modified in the light of cultural performance. New theory must be based on specific field work.
13.	The objectives of Anthropology were description, data collecting, and "science for science sake." Objectivity was demanded. Early Applied Anthropology was strongly resisted.	The objectives of Anthropology are problem-solving for human progress. Applied Anthropology has established itself. The science of mankind has to justify its existence by serving mankind.
14.	Anthropology in the colonial frame of reference treated underdeveloped peoples like laboratory animals for research by Western experts (and not-so-expert Ph.D. candidates).	Young nations are disposed to help anthropologists only when they align themselves with national goals and cooperate as colleagues.
15.	For many years, Cultural Relatativism was an end in itself. Emphasis fell on cultural diversity, and the preservation of societies in isolation. This was a static view of society.	Cultural Relativism is no longer the goal, but a resting place on the way, which provides understanding and empathy for directing change without creating chaos. Peoples survive by interrelating, not by insolation. This is the dynamic view of society.

5. Changes Within the Anthropological Value System Itself

16.	A survey of the *American Anthropologist,* 1888–1938 (50 years) showed only four references to morals and ethics.	*Anthropological ethics is a new field of study,* especially in methods of data collecting and use of information. Ethics on the frontiers of human life must go with new knowledge as mankind faces the future.

17.	As long as anthropology was objective, detached, amoral, it had no sense of responsibility.	Anthropology must control its data, because it must be responsible for the use of its knowledge.
18.	Anthropological knowledge could be mere information — not used — or if used it could be done either for right or wrong. Anthropology observes human life but stands off from it at a distance.	The recognition of ethics and responsibility transforms anthropology into creativity which seeks to make the transformations in human life which are found to be essential. Anthropology becomes a tool of social reformation.

WHAT THESE CHANGES SIGNIFY FOR MISSIOLOGY

These are the changes I see as I read the history of anthropological theory. I do not hold other readers of the subject to the same set of ideas, but for my part I see the anthropologist and missionary more and more falling into step with each another. This has a number of major consequences for missiology.

1. It is now legitimate to view a human being, not as an inner-directed *specimen,* but as a *person within a context.* Each individual influences others and is influenced by them. The social group is a vital entity, seeking solidarity and perpetuity, and claiming loyalty from its members. We meet this view of life in the Bible, with its hundreds of references to families, households, tribes and its house churches. This means the social anthropologist may consider the church planting process as a legitimate procedure of human endeavor. By the same measure the growing and strengthening of Christian fellowship groups by the incorporation and education of converts may be researched as a process of group formation and the fixing of group norms. It can be measured in a scientific manner. Thus *missiological research is open for exposure to the methods and techniques of social anthropological investigation.*

2. The object of the social anthropologist's research is to achieve an understanding of the behavior of mankind in context, why they have their own peculiar set of values, why they think and act as they do, why these features are common to the group, and why some things are approved and others disapproved. It is not what an isolated individual would think or do, but what individuals in groups think or do that becomes important. We see people binding themselves together to meet common needs and reach

common goals. Social anthropology studies the *way of life*. This fits the missionary idea of concerning itself with the *higher way of life*. The presentation of the Gospel becomes, not destructive to a people's way of life, but the advocacy of a better way, a functional substitution. The criticisms of the salvage anthropologist lessen in our day because, for the social anthropologist, *the preservation of groups of people has become more important than the preservation of their ancient artifacts*. Society has passed from a museum piece to a human situation. And on the world level nations have to learn to live together and interact as do individuals in the corporate group. Thus while we recognize cultural diversity we balance it off against the common values shared by mankind as a whole.

3. *Applied Anthropology is now free to speak to missionary method.* Rather than striving to preserve antiquated structures, it now recognizes the inevitability of change and the impossibility of a community surviving in this modern world without continual self-modifications. This shift of attitude is of major significance for the Christian mission, because it legitimatizes what we sometimes call *directed change*. The anthropologist, F.E. Williams, laid down a set of criteria in *The Blending of Cultures,* and paid considerable attention to the missionary role in this study. He insisted that many things ought to be preserved, that others should be discarded and still others could be preserved if modified. He considered that a so-called primitive society needed some infusion from without to permit its survival in the modern world. This is important to missions, evangelists and church planters. He also pointed out that directed change like this implied grave responsibilities.

4. Moreover, I believe that *there is harmony between the tempers of applied anthropology and applied missiology.* If applied anthropology attacks social problems and sets up problem solving programs, and applies group dynamics to achieve the acceptance of beneficial innovations, and these are valid for health, medical, educational, agricultural, economic and welfare improvement, does it not follow that they should likewise be valid for moral and religious betterment? If it is legitimate for governments or their departments to employ an applied anthropologist for directing change along lines of progressive humanitarianism, then the Christian mission also stands in a new position in our day—provided, of course, that the churches we plant really do meet the social and spiritual needs of the indigenous people and are not foreign impositions; and provided also that the advocates of change recognize their responsibility for the changes they bring about. It may well be pointed out that in recent years anthropologists have given more recognition to the validity of the religious dimension in social analysis. One even meets an agnostic anthropologist admitting that, for the time being, peoples in transition cannot do without religion.

Thus a program of Christian mission, like any program of social reform, derives its social status from a moral and an anthropological base and is a case of sharing special knowledge and experience where felt needs are yet to be met and satisfied. Social anthropology (especially those aspects of it which deal with culture change and value systems) forms an integral part of the science of missiology. The advocacy, acceptance and rejection of the Christian message can be conceptualized in terms of the anthropology of innovation as expounded, for example, by Barnett (1953). Renewal of second generation congregations and problem solving by role creation (organic church growth) can often be analyzed in the frame of reference of Wallace's revitalization theory (1956). A whole world of conceptual tools is now at our disposal.

In step with anthropological theory we may argue that there is such a thing as a propitious time for major social change, like the conversion of a people from animism to Christianity. If some areas of the world are currently resistant to such change, others are manifestly ripe for it. In these ripe fields Christianity is not the only option being advocated for acceptance. The question asked by some opponents of Christian mission is "Are you justified in changing the animism of these people? Why not leave them as they are?" However large parts of the animist world are currently at their "moment of truth" and are considering a multiplicity of options. In a few years they will be no longer animists—but Muslim, Bahai, Communist, or maybe Christian. If Christianity has something better to offer than animism, Christians have the moral obligation to advocate it. Some applied anthropologists would say that all the options should be presented—Christianity most certainly among them.

5. I believe I detect in current anthropological writing *a new value for anthropology itself as a responsible science.* Even a secular anthropologist would advocate technical aid to the underdeveloped: a Christian anthropologist would go further. Increasingly anthropologists are seeing that what they do in their profession entails a responsibility to society. This is a far cry from the "ivory towers" of pursuing anthropology for its own sake, or for survival. Anthropology is being called to relevance in a needy world. The same may be said of missiology. In each we have valuable accumulations of knowledge, techniques and experience. With this priceless possession lies a twofold responsibility—it must be shared and used for the benefit of mankind, and it must be so used that it be not abused. Hence, in anthropology today we find a strong move for establishing ethical codes for its application.

6. For years anthropology has been analytical. It has broken down societies into segments, and regions into tribes. It has learned much by studying mankind in microcosms and in many ways these small, discrete, ethnic units must still be recognized. The minority problem of entity is far from solved. However they have to find their place of belonging in the

whole. Analysis has to give way to synthesis. The anthropological vision expands again, with a holistic view of interrelating groups. Anthropology is in step with biblical ecumenicity, aware that (at least in material terms) the only hope is in a *community of communities,* recognizing the rights and integrity of each ethnic unit within the larger whole: interacting, interresponsible and in equilibrium. To this point anthropology and missiology would seem to be companions on the road leading to tomorrow. There is much we can draw from each other.

But the very last step of the road requires a Christian anthropology— an anthropology which sees the science of mankind leading us to the Perfect Human, the Perfect Son of the Perfect Father. Ultimately, is there any other way to the unity of mankind but via the road of becoming "new men and women in Christ?" Anthropology carried to the ultimate degree leaves us with a theological question.

7. Anthropology is taking a new look at missionaries, at their past activities, and particularly at the documentary sources they left. These are no longer being dismissed as just biased. Missionaries have another chance to speak for themselves, they are welcomed at anthropological conferences and given a hearing as long as they are willing to field questions like any other scholar. The study of Christian mission itself is now a valid one for anthropological discussion.

8. But, the most significant new development has been the tendency of anthropology to come together with other disciplines to explore the points of their encounter. Interdisciplinary research is a feature of the last 20 or 30 years, and out of this a new terminology has been born: ethnopsychology, ethnolinguistics, ethnomusicology, ethnohistory, and now ethnotheology. In several of these fields, new journals have appeared. Every one of them has consequences for missiology:

ethnopsychology bears on the personal and group dynamics of
 cross-cultural advocacy of the Gospel,

ethnomusicology bears on the selection of functional
 substitutes for Christian worship,

ethnolinguistics on the selection of terminology for
 Scripture translation, preaching and worship,

ethnohistory provides the only reliable methodology for the
 reconstruction of church growth case studies, and

 ethnotheology bears on relevancy in the interpretation of
 the Christian faith in non-Western thought and idiom—
 i.e., the problem of meaning.

There is a dynamic process of maturation going on at every one of these points of encounter. Something new is being born—a missiological mutation is unfolding before our eyes, and God is demonstrating the new processes of mission for us to use in these last years of this 20th century. God in His goodness is giving us another chance in mission, a new set of resources for improving our stewardship in His vineyard, so that our methods may be contemporaneously relevant for the communication of the Gospel which is abiding until he comes again. Now, with all the resources of anthropology at our disposal, to improve our methods of understanding and communicating cross-culturally, we must say with Paul, "Woe unto me if I preach not the Gospel!" (1 Cor. 9:16).

CHAPTER 11

The Negative and Positive Value of Anthropology to the Missionary

Many quite conscientious Western Christians fail to distinguish between two different types of behavior patterns met by missionaries among the people they seek to bring to Christ. These are both stressed by Paul in the situations with which he deals in the Pastoral Epistles.

1. There is a wealth of instruction about the need for would-be Christians to discard the moral evils of his or her old way of life— murder, lying, fornication, blaspheming, greed, false accusation, lust and so on. These are the bad habits of unregenerate mankind, and may be either individual or collective. With conversion to Christ they are discarded.

2. But there are many references in Paul to other behavior patterns which Christians are not expected to discard, although they are expected to transform them. These are the accepted behavior patterns of organized society—what the anthropologist calls the social structure. It is important to distinguish between the bad customs which converts must discard and the social structure within which they have to operate.

Missionaries who set their faces against a social structure are taking upon themselves a grave responsibility and they have no biblical precedent or injunction for it. Of course social structures are changing all the time and Christianity will certainly influence those changes; but Paul's attitude was rather "What is God's will for me in this situation? How can I win these people for Christ within their structures?"

Thus, in the Pastorals Paul urges Christians to pray for "kings and rulers and those in authority" for the worthy motive that people may live in peace, which he considers "good and acceptable in the sight of God" (1 Tim. 2:2-3). He also tells Titus that civil powers should be obeyed (Tit. 3:1). On another social level we find the structured family, which Paul also recognized when he gave rules for governing the home (1 Tim. 3:4-5, 12) and rules for husband/wife relationships (Tit. 2:5). He recognizes the responsibilities of master and servant as a two-way process and a religious duty (1 Tim. 6:1; Tit. 2:9-19).

In maintaining the community peace Paul recognized the useful function of law as a controlling force: "The law is good, if a man use it lawfully" (1 Tim. 1:8). He also recognized that society was stratified and that people from each stratum had their respective responsibilities to maintain the balance of society, but especially those in the favored groups were to help the less fortunate. The very fact that an individual was rich rendered that person responsible for community service (1 Tim. 6:17-18). Paul's reasoning on the classification of widows due for hospitality in the church shows a genuine awareness of social stratification and responsibility (1 Tim. Ch. 5).

In 2 Timothy, Paul uses a series of allegories based on the social groupings of his day. He recognizes the rules for the life and training of the soldier (2 Tim. 2:4), and the athlete (v. 5) and the patterns of cultivating and harvesting used by the farmer (v. 6). His religion is not isolated from life but operating within the world of mankind.

Thus, as one reads the Pastorals one gets a picture like this:

1. Within the church—one is to preach the word and when necessary to reprove and rebuke (2 Tim. 4:2).

2. Outside the church—one is to "do the work of an evangelist and make a full proof of his ministry" (2 Tim. 4:5), as Paul said of himself "that the Gentiles might hear" (4:17).

To equip oneself for this role one is to form fixed habits of prayer (2 Tim. 2:1) and Scripture study (2 Tim. 3:14-15). While the Christians are not to embroil themselves in worldliness they still have to live the Christian life "in this present world" (Tit. 2:12).

What then is the will of God for missionaries *within the structure of the society* He sends them to evangelize? As Christ was sent "into the world," so He sends His servant "into the world" (John 17:16). *To what extent* should the missionaries identify themselves and *how* should they identify themselves? Should they change the culture patterns or win those structures for Christ? Are they there to establish their Western denominational Church or to help an indigenous Church to emerge within their own way of life?

If these are valid questions, and I believe they are, then every missionary needs training in anthropology, especially those aspects of anthropology which involve family and other social structures and inter-personal relationships.

The Roman Catholic missionary anthropologists have out-stripped us in this dimension of missionary training. Not only have they explored new fields but they have drawn on the resources opened by Protestant research, especially that of the American Bible Society and the publication, *Missiology* (formerly *Practical Anthropology*).

Dr. Luzbetak speaks of *cultural relevancy* as "an important apostolic principle." A full understanding of the *cultural context* is necessary because wittingly or unwittingly the missionary is an agent in culture change. Anthropological understanding is necessary for the spiritual guidance and social action of the missionary. Luzbetak attacks the view that anthropology is merely a side branch of missionary training but insists it is "an essential aspect of missionary formation." Any missionary, he says, without a good knowledge of the cultural context is a dangerous "expert" (1963:18-19, f.n.). Roman Catholic research work is being undertaken today in many centers and secular universities. For years the only Protestant institutions of this kind were the School of World Mission and Institute of Church Growth at Fuller and a smaller body in Scandinavia, though the World Council of Churches had employed a number of inde-pendent research anthropologists and sociologists for individual projects. Evangelical Protestantism had just not alerted itself to this basic need. Fortunately, this has changed rapidly in the last few years with the advent of Schools of World Mission and Evangelism at Trinity Evangelical Divinity School and Asbury Theological Seminary, and the like. Yet, the need to "catch up" is still great.

THE NEGATIVE OR CORRECTIVE VALUE OF ANTHROPOLOGY

I have made the point that missioning is set always within some specific cultural context, different for each missionary according to his or her field of service. I now come to the basic question: *what has anthropology to say to missionaries at work in cross-cultural situations?*

Firstly it is *corrective to bad policy.* Let me deal first with the negative aspect. We must admit that missionaries, despite their spiritual enthusiasm and worthy purposes, have made some tragic mistakes and sometimes by winning one convert they have turned the remainder of the whole village against them. Eugene Nida's book *Customs and Cultures* (1954) is concerned with this problem.

I call to mind five ways in which missionary technique can hinder the work of the Holy Spirit, or *quench the Spirit* as Paul puts it. I can do no more than summarize these, but each is worth a whole chapter in itself. They would make a discouraging volume.

1. Mistakes of Misunderstanding

These mistakes of misunderstanding are caused through ignorance of custom, through treating people of another culture as if you are dealing with Westerners at home. Our value patterns, courtesies and discourtesies, orientation to life, attitudes to work and personal relationships, felt needs and the meanings of our idioms are so different, that until we really know each other we are liable to make these mistakes of misunderstanding.

There is a well-known story of an administrator whose attitude towards a golden stool led to a series of wars, purely because of his ignorance. This was applied to Christian mission by Edwin Smith. When one goes to mission among folk of another culture, he is bound to try to understand that culture.

2. Mistakes of Offence

These mistakes of offence spring from different values placed on things and approaches by the missionaries and the people whom they seek to win. The most common form of this is a clash between missionary individualism and tribal or family collectivism. If an evangelical missionary wins one convert out of his tribe and thereby builds a barrier of the whole tribe against him, so that no church can be planted and the lone convert remains as an isolate, the most likely thing is that when the tribe is eventually won it will turn to Roman Catholicism or some other denomination because this evangelical missionary gave offence. Thus a denominational issue is introduced as a permanent schismatic effect. Another cause of offence is a blatant disregard for pagan taboos when people are still pagan.

3. Mistakes of Causing Opposition

There are mistakes by which the missionaries themselves create active opposition. The pagans are thus not just indifferent to the Gospel but actively hostile. A missionary can cause this by failing to observe the cultural paths of communication, ignoring the community officials—chief, priest and elders—or by any approach which threatens the solidarity of the group, or disregards the indigenous rules of protocol.

4. Mistakes of Imposition

One of the most common missionary methodological mistakes has been the imposition of foreign forms and practices, especially denominational patterns. I refer to organizational machinery, leadership patterns, worship patterns, foreign ethical values, modes of dress, financial patterns and missionary supervision and controls. All these things hinder the emergence of an indigenous church, and once they have been established it is well nigh impossible to change over from a dependent mission to a self-reliant church.

Frequently the missionary, especially after three or four generations of Christian influence, is blind to these impositions; but many enclosed foreign churches with congregations of 50 to 100 Christians after 100 years of missionary work show the same old story: "killed by foreign imposition."

5. Mistakes of Void Creation

Finally, there is the creation of voids (vacuums as Nida calls them). When social practices, cultural mechanisms and economic procedures of pre-Christian times have been discarded and no functional substitutes have been provided, the social needs originally met by these pre-Christian devices are liable to lead to discontent in the second generation. Many nativistic movements resulting in great loss to the Church can be traced to this cause.

I have merely mentioned five specific types of obstruction to church planting and church growth which can be caused by bad missionary method. The list is by no means exhaustive. Good anthropological training would help the missionary to avoid all these mistakes. So much for the negative or corrective value of anthropology to the missionary!

THE POSITIVE OR DIRECTIVE VALUE OF ANTHROPOLOGY

Secondly, on the positive side, a knowledge of anthropology has value to the missionary who will make use of it in many more aspects than I can deal with here. I shall mention only some, letting each point lead on to the next as I make it.

Procedure

With respect to procedure, anthropological training helps a person to understand the significance of pattern in a community, how the pattern is composed, what classes of people form the society and how people (individuals and groups) interact and interrelate. This helps one to know how things ought to be done or said to gain sympathetic hearing. It is a good thing to know the correct and courteous procedure. How do I give? How do I receive? How do I ask, act, respond, resist, complain, praise or interact without offence? To do and say things with the correct procedure is half the battle in gaining rapport.

If individuals enter into a missionary situation as foreigners, as a representatives of a Church from the West, and do things in the Western fashion, they are seen as agents of the West itself, of the white race with all its unhappy attributes, and all its questionable history. If, on the other hand, missionaries adopt to *their* regular procedure and operate through *their* culture patterns, at least the form and procedure of the church they plant should be more indigenous than Western. In other words, to approach the people we seek to win for Christ within procedural patterns that are *theirs* and *not ours* is one of the positive things anthropology has to show us: that the first step in identification is to accept as many indigenous forms and procedures as can legitimately be retained as Christian.

Communication
Arising from this is the whole area of communication. What are the indigenous methods and mechanisms for the communication of ideas? What is the approved decision-making body? How is an issue for major decision presented to the tribe, group, family or whatever unit applies as the decision-making body? What characters have been institutionalized within the society for this role of communication? Are there traditional heralds, mediators, orators, or spokespersons through whom a case is presented, or may individuals speak for themselves? How is a new message traditionally presented? Does one go first to the chief of the tribe or the head of the household? Or does one call together the whole group for a public meeting? What kind of a council exists for decision-making? Who has the right to admit one to the community so that he can communicate at all?

All these are particularly important with new missionary ventures in tribal or hamlet societies, thousands of which are open for evangelization today. If you communicate through the normal channels the people know what is being done and are ready to concentrate on the message or matter presented for decision. If you do not do this you are an obstruction as a person, you are regarded with suspicion and public feeling is weighted against the acceptance of your requests. Surely there are enough obstacles without creating more.

Proficiency in the Language
Anthropology would also indicate the need for missionary proficiency in the language of the people for effective communication. This is necessary: (1) for the communication of the Gospel to the individual in conversion; (2) for the translation of Scripture; (3) for the effective conduct of Christian worship; and (4) for the regular instruction of the new convert in the faith, for composition of hymns, catechisms or other aids. In all these cases theological concepts have to be expressed, and the

faith of future generations can be adversely influenced by the selection of unfortunate terms. Missionaries have to become thoroughly proficient in the relation of custom and language to be sure they are not building up some heresy for their successors. The selection of the word for God or the term for the Three Persons of the Trinity can lead one into polytheism, or the terminology used for Holy Communion may have pagan overtones. It is not good enough to allow some other person to do one's translation. If a person is to be a missionary he or she is obliged to see that the communication is effective. The matter of *meaning* is extremely complex when we start to investigate it.

Anthropology has explored both the areas of linguistics and the relation between language and culture (ethnolinguistics) and these resources are available for the missionary.

Innovation

In the study of innovation as the dynamics of culture change, anthropology has taught us much which has bearing on conversion as a process. Why do people change their traditional religion? Do they accept the new religion with the same meanings as those intended by the advocates? What are the motivations for such decisions? What factors suggest people are ready for large scale innovation change—or in other words are "ripe for conversion"? This branch of theory and research has much to give the missionary and is a new area opened up in 1953 by Barnett's researches on innovation, which made use of some conversion data.

Methodology

Quite apart from these basic concepts which are relevant to missionaries and help them understand the processes being used by the Holy Spirit, there is a tremendous wealth of methodology which anthropology has made available in our day. These include: techniques for observing and recording data, resources for study (including many fine surveys), documented material on the meaning of change and behavior, classified knowledge of whole culture patterns, devices to aid the learning and exploration of foreign languages, and mechanical aids for communication, both individual and group.

The anthropologist and missionary are not the same. The former observes and records culture change; the latter tries to channel it in a specific direction. Anthropology is no adequate substitute for the Christian mission, because it only asks *why*; it does not *do*, though it might suggest what to do. Therefore to any persons truly dedicated to Christ, anthropology offers tremendous resources, methods and information that will aid the consecrated missionaries in their church planting and building up of converts in the new faith.

Anthropology also has a great reflex value for missionaries. It widens their outlook and knowledge of their pastorate, it opens new horizons of biblical understanding, and reveals Christ for who He is—our Universal Contemporary, bigger than the Graeco-Roman world or Reformation theology, bigger than geography, time or language. Granted, individuals may discover this without anthropology, but anthropology will develop their capacity for it, and help them to recognize the warnings and opportunities of the cross-cultural situation where their missioning is performed.

CHAPTER 12

Anthropological Processual Models in Missiology

One night a few years ago I picked up a book to read before going off to sleep. It chanced to be an essay of de Quincey's, entitled "On the Knocking at the Gate in Macbeth." It is not only a beautiful piece of English prose, but it is a subtle and critical perception of what Shakespeare was doing in the play.

From his boyhood de Quincey had been challenged by the repeated knocking at the door at the end of Act 2, where Duncan has been murdered. Even as a boy de Quincey had felt there was something beyond the factual information in the meaning of the words of the play. Something was suggested in that scene, or implied, which was beyond his understanding. What was the sound of knocking meant to say to the audience? Why the repeated knocking at the gate? Some years later when an historic murder case was in the news he suddenly perceived the dramatic function of Shakespeare's technique in using this sound effect from off stage. When we study a murder story, we tend to sympathize with the victim, or at least to focus on him. But the focus here is on the murderer. We have to sympathize with the perpetrator of the crime; today we would say emphathize with him. Shakespeare wanted the audience to think Macbeth, not Duncan, at this point.

The knocking marks the transition from the world of passion back to the world of reality. Here are some of the lines of de Quincey, who sees the knocking on the door, four times in a dozen or so lines, marking that after "the retiring of the human heart and the entrance of the fiendish heart" when "another world had stepped in" and the ghastly deed was done, "the world of darkness passes away like a pageantry in the clouds: the knocking on the gate is heard; and it makes known audibly: that human life has made its reflux upon the fiendish; the impulses of life are beginning to beat again." Both murderer and the audience are "profoundly sensible of the awful parenthesis that has suspended them."

This is my theme in this chapter: the study of the passage from one world to another, from the old life to the new, from the animist world to that of the Christian. As an anthropologist I am interested in rites of passage, the study of the grey period between the old and the new. This is a pan-human experience. Although it is strongly culturally conditioned, the psychological and spiritual basics are universal. *Liminality* is a real experience in the process, and there is no entry into the structured *koinonia*—except by this journey. In the missionary process a vital experience and a period of transition lie between the witness and incorporation into the fellowship.

The process is the witness, the transition, the incorporation. This is my theme.

This notion lies at the back of five or six research articles I have written, and the book, *People Movements in Southern Polynesia* (1971). In *Solomon Islands Christianity* (1967a) there is an important chapter on "The Process from Animist to Christian Forms." In that process lies a whole complex of significant missiological problems. Thus, for example, my experience as a field missionary observing the transition from the old way to the new led me to research and emphasize the significance of functional substitutes, without which the church planting will be foreign in character. The cutoff from the old has to be real. The incorporation into the new has to be real. But if the new is to be indigenous and not foreign, a cultural entity and belongingness has to be achieved.

My purpose in this chapter is to discuss the problem of "getting from there to here," from "the old way to the new," the transition, the liminality, and to do so in anthropological frames of reference. I mean, I shall use anthropological models which I believe provide us with the equipment for studying the process of conversion as a social experience. Finally, I shall identify these models with their biblical counterparts and thereby try to establish a relationship between anthropology and missiology.

The basic anthropological question is: "How do we get from there to here?" Or, asked another way, "What is the process from the old steady state, through the crisis situation, to the new steady state?" Or, "What are the cultural dynamics of an act of advocacy and an act of acceptance?" Or, "What are the rites of transition?" Or, "What do we know of the period of liminality?" Or, "What does it mean to cut oneself off from 'there' and to be incorporated 'here'?" A whole library of anthropological inquiry is devoted to this type of processual problem, and we should be able to use some of their models in missiology.

If I restate the issue in the form of a missiological question, I must ask: "How do I witness in the world so that I not only bring the person (or family) to the Lord but get him or her incorporated into a fellowship group where that person's experience may mature?" Or, "How do I bring a community of animist fetish-worshipers from their pagan forms to Christian worship without destroying their communal entity?" Or, "What functional substitutes are required to make the new belongingness of incorporation permanent?" These are problems of conversion and church planting, but I should point out that they are also valid for prophetic movements, secret societies, and Cargo Cults. If we are to deal cross-culturally with animists, we had better acquaint ourselves well with the dynamics of liminality. Shakespeare was not the only creative individual to make use of the symbol of the gate. John Frumm, who established a nativistic movement in the New Hebrides, used a gate as a key symbol (Attenborough 1960:154). One would come upon a clearing in the forest and there he would find a gate. The gate would open and shut, but there were no paths leading to it or from it. The first impression is one of futility—provision for going nowhere. It is, however, a symbol of the liminal. It is a spiritual concept of getting from the present distress to a millenarian paradise, from the burden of the white man to the true Melanesian inheritance.

ORGANIZING IMAGES TO INTERPRET EXPERIENCE

The question of using scientific models in the study of religion is discussed at length by Ian Barbour. He defines a model as:

. . . a symbolic representation of selected aspects of the behaviour of a complex system for particulalr purposes. It is an imaginative tool for ordering experience, rather than a description of the world (1974:6).

Again, they are "organizing images," he says, "used to order and interpret experience." In this presentation I, too, am using the models, or images, not so much for descriptive purposes, but "to order and interpret experience." We are in the area of ethnopsychology, in particular as it bears on religious experience. Barbour's case for the use of scientific models to this end opens a wide area of research technique and exploration to missiologists.

We can only glance at some of the possibilities in passing, but the reader is directed to his book, *Myths, Models and Paradigms* (1974), which has for its subtitle "A Comparative Study in Science and Religion."

First, if I may coin a phrase and say, Barbour's "model for a model" is not static but processual. It is intelligible only when used *as a whole unit*. I myself have always argued that static models are dangerous, that they lead to compartmentalization and the destruction of wholeness. In this chapter we are discussing processual models that get "from there to here." We observe process in experience. We focus on the "there" and the "here" and the transition between; but we do not isolate them or compartmentalize them (a point at which church growth theory is perhaps most vulnerable). A model is "a summary of complex relationships" (33).

Second, the models are meant to aid in the interpretation of *social experience,* such as, for instance, that which evokes the *numinous* and/or the *mystical.* The process takes place in a social context and it cannot be interpreted without consideration of the context. Barbour's phrase is the "social context of experience," and again he speaks of the social "continuity and cumulative identity" in which the experience is evoked (121). Here is a model we need for a study of individuals and their corporate role in the fellowship for church planting and for church growth. Barbour goes on to distinguish between the "conceptual structures, which are culturally conditioned" and the experience itself (122-123), to which I shall return in a moment.

Third, the models are based on the assumption of the existence of what (for the want of a better word) we might call "tradition," the experience of which is ongoing—*dynamic* and *developing*—"not an unchanging legacy from the past" (149). Like a living organism, it is historically continuous and yet always growing. Barbour continues to show the value of this for a community, which can see its exemplars and its history in new ways "and can adapt to new circumstances and new problems" (149). The crises faced by the early church in Acts 6 and later at the Jerusalem Conference (Acts 15), both of which led to organic church growth in new structures and policies, can be discussed in terms of this model.

Fourth, both on the individual and the collective levels we are dealing with what Barbour calls "the experience of *reorientation* and *reconciliation,*" or what Tillich, in *The Shaking of the Foundations* (1948), called "the transition from estrangement to reconciliation." We are dealing here with pan-human experience: the models are as valid for mission at home as abroad.

Fifth, the models are open to a biblical view of history, of God acting in and expressing Himself in history and bringing human communities into being because of what He has done in history—communities which feel their corporate entity and are aware of their growing. As Barbour says:

> Response to historical events brings concrete religious communities into being; the celebration of these events is a continuing source of corporate identity and personal renewal and an occasion for worship (151).

This opens the door for relating the actions of God recorded in Scripture to the activities of God in the history of Christian expansion and the contemporary Christian mission. It is a model for the corporate community which is emerging and growing. It is, in terms of Barbour's definition, an imaginative tool for organizing and interpreting experience, rather than description, and it permits our interpretation to be made in terms of a scriptural view of history.

PARADIGM CHOICE AND PARADIGM SHIFT

Essential to the use of scientific models for religious purposes is the recognition of the existence of paradigms in all scientific and religious research. According to Barbour, a paradigm is "a cluster of . . . conceptual and methodological presuppositions," and it exists in every scientific community, where it becomes the formulation of norms and key concepts (103). The paradigm dominates for a scientist committed to a research program (101-102). It is this truth which validates missiology as a field for research. Our research is determined and conditioned, for example, by the Great Commission. It is our paradigm on the level of missionary action. On the widest level of all, the Scriptures themselves are our paradigm. They are our testing tools. They condition our research. As long as we are committed to the paradigm and measure everything by it, we hold a perfectly scientific position. But if we fiddle with the semantics of mission, and interfere with its value as a testing tool, we can hardly claim to be scientific. Of course, the onus is on us continually to test the tool itself in the light of experience.

Thus, to return to Barbour, he maintains the importance of commitment to the paradigm and the tenacity in sticking to it throughout a research program. The importance of the conjunction of commitment and inquiry, if applied to theology, for example, demands that research be both *confessional* and *self-critical,* because we are in a paradigm community (180-181).

However, the Christian (missionary) community is not the only paradigm community. This may be said also of the animist community to which the missionary goes, which has its own faith commitment and value system. What we confront here is an advocacy for the rejection of one paradigm commitment for another.

At this point Barbour argues for "the rationality of paradigm choice," or "paradigm shift," borrowing considerably from Kuhn's *The Structure of Scientific Revolutions* (1962). He points out that every significant revolution is a paradigm shift—from Aristotelian to Newtonian physics, or from the latter to relativity, or that away from Ptolemaic astronomy. But it requires an act of conversion. "A new paradigm prevails only when the older generation has been 'converted' to it, or has died off and been replaced by a new generation" (104-105). Paradigms determine the way the scientists see the world and therefore their observations are *paradigm-dependent,* as also indeed are their criteria. Thus the "adoption of a new paradigm is a 'conversion' " (105). A revolution is thus a community's "rejection of one time-honoured scientific theory in favour of another incompatible with it" because of new data available or new insights.

Kuhn's view of scientific revolutions as paradigm shifts is based on the idea of the paradigm shared by the whole scientific community. Although the shift may be preceded by a competitive period between the two rival theories (each with its individual adherents), nevertheless a revolution or paradigm shift requires corporate acceptance. "Like the gestalt switch it must occur all at once or not at all" (Kuhn cited in Barbour 1974:104-105). Although Kuhn's model has been subject to criticism from some quarters at the point of paradigm-dependent criteria, nevertheless the paradigm shift may be effectively advocated if it can be shown that the needs which the old paradigm left unsatisfied, and the problems it left unsolved (and which therefore probably caused a state of crisis) can be solved by the new paradigm. This has manifest significance for the advocate of the Gospel in Christian mission.

The model of the paradigm shift permits a useful analysis of a people movement into Christianity, which focuses on the group action, the cutoff point and the adoption point, i.e., the rejection of the old way and the acceptance of the new, which is what a paradigm choice amounts to. There is indeed good reason for using a model that explains a scientific revolution for interpreting a tribal acceptance of Christianity.

RITES OF PASSAGE

Perhaps of all anthropological processual models none has been more widely tested than Arnold van Gennep's concept of the *Rites of Passage*, articulated about eighty years ago but only translated into English in 1960. The subject of van Gennep's concern was the ceremonial patterns of the passage of persons from one social or cosmic level to another: marriage, initiation into adulthood, funerary rites, and so forth. Van Gennep found that they fall into three categories, which he called *rites of separation, rites of transition,* and *rites of incorporation.* Although he found the rites unevenly developed by different peoples, he invariably found some evidence of each of the three aspects of the process in almost every case. In my own anthropological field research I have been astonished at the quantity of evidence I have collected that is quite clearly either (1) evidence of a cutoff from the former state, (2) evidence of the process of transition, or (3) evidence of the incorporation into the new. There is probably no more useful model in anthropology for pinpointing for the missionary and national pastor the importance of such things as the break with paganism and the adequate incorporation of converts into the new fellowship group. In that van Gennep concentrates on the ceremonial and ritual of the process, the model should be useful also in interpreting conversion movements in terms of ritual—for example, baptism as a rite of passage.

When I was doing my doctoral examinations, I struggled through van Gennep's French, and I believe it must have influenced me more than I realized at the time. I saw conversion and incorporation into the Christian fellowship as a process, and developed my own model along the lines of van Gennep's. By that I mean I accepted his idea of separation from the old way, the transition, and the incorporation, though my transition was the "Period of Decision Making," and I had more focus on the significant points of experience. I did not consciously borrow anything from van Gennep, but now as I look back I think he probably influenced me.

I used my conversion model in three "Research in Progress Papers" (1967c, 1969b, 1971a), and also in *Verdict Theology in Missionary Theory* (1973a:122-130). The model came out of my data. This, I believe, is the only valid way of developing new models. (Of course, you can test someone else's model from your data, but you should never create a model on a purely theoretical base.) It was not until my summer in New Guinea, when I was confronted with what is known as the "cargo mentality" and the failure of the missionaries adequately to consummate the people movements described by Vicedom (1961) and Frericks (1957), that I realized that church growth towards Christian maturity needed still another stage (Tippett 1974a). As I see it now, this is a vulnerable point in church growth theory, which badly needs deeper research. However, there is no way of organizing the data of conversion and consummation but with the aid of a processual model, and I have yet to find one better than this.

LIMINALITY AND INTERSTRUCTURAL PERSONS

n Gennep devoted the second chapter of his book to "The Territorial Passage," and discussed the quality of sanctity or taboo associated with the transition from "there" to "here"—boyhood to manhood, etc. He concentrated for some time on the "ritual of the threshold." The threshold is only part of the door, a place of departure or entrance or waiting. The contemporary anthropologist who deals with this is Victor Turner, who calls it "the period of margin or 'liminality' [van Gennep used both terms] as an interstructural situation" (1967:93). He studied initiation rites at depth and sought indigenous concepts about the "nature of 'interstructural' human beings." By the way, were this transferred from Ndembu initiation to Christian baptism, say, in Latin America, we could study persons spoken of as "sympathizers" who attend church but do not accept baptism and are indeed "interstructural human beings." These are margin (*limen*) persons. Turner, in *The Forest of Symbols* (1967), found that the *"liminal persona"* had a name, an established behavior pattern, and was identified as a transitional person, but did not yet belong—was not yet truly classified. Furthermore, the liminal person as yet really had nothing: no status, no insignia, no role. Turner sees them as structurally invisible, ambigious, and neutral (99). Their positive aspect is the possibility of growth, the possibility of transformation into a new pattern, and the availability of instruction—but having withdrawn from the old way and not yet having been classified in the new, they do not draw fully from the values and norms of either structural position. Turner was very much involved in the elaborate symbolism of an animistic rite of passage, much of which hardly concerns us when dealing with sympathizers, yet he does make the above points and one is struck with their relevance to the missionary confronting the sympathizer problem. He ends with a chapter called "Betwixt and Between: Liminal Period" in *The Forest of Symbols* by inviting investigators "to focus their attention on the phenomena and processes of mid-transition" (110).

THE RECOMBINATION THESIS

Also associated with the conversion process but focusing on the precise innovative act is the recombination thesis of Homer Barnett. Barnett devotes a book of over 450 pages to the exposition of this theory and its ramifications in *Innovation: The Basis of Cultural Change* (1953). After more than three decades it still remains the classical work on the subject. The basic processes are explained in Chapter VII, in which the mental configuration of the innovative process is analyzed and schematized. A configuration is a mental activity pattern which depicts the linkages and fusion of elements and how they are reorganized in an act of innovation. Thus new things may be conceptualized by the recombination of known parts. By abstraction one has to get from "Y" to "B," from "there" to "here." The model is enlightening either for demonstrating what actually happened when an innovation took place or what has to happen for it to take place.

A missionary understanding the model will think more clearly about how to advocate the Gospel, and will see what has to happen for the advocacy to be accepted. The theory also demonstrates the existence of the common factor, through which "Y" and "B" can be identified or equated for purposes of the recombination (195), and this should help sharpen one's advocacy. I think that perhaps there was no other single concept I learned from anthropology that so transformed my thinking on the advocacy of the Gospel and the dynamics of its acceptance and rejection, unless perhaps it was his application of Muzafer Sherif's experiments on the fixing of group norms (116-118), which he tied into his discussion on subliminal striving for meaning. I used this in my "Research in Progress Paper" on group conversion (1967c), and in *People Movements in Southern Polynesia* (1971:210-214), which was written when I was with Barnett.

I tangled with Walter Houston Clark in the first John G. Finch Symposium on Psychology and Religion (Tippett 1973b) on the manner in which he presented conversion as a change of attitude from a "nonfaith" to a faith orientation, from unbelief and disintegration to integration, and especially in his use of Saul of Tarsus as his illustration. This led to my discussion (1973b: Appendix) of the nature of conversion in terms of Barnett's recombination thesis. Saul's (X) Hebrew orientation produced his defending (R2) Judaism (Y) in terms of the persecution pattern of his behavior in the relationship (XR2Y) and conversion meant a change to a new behavior pattern similar to that of the Christian converts (A) preaching (R1) the Christian Gospel (B) the new relationship for Paul being (XR1B). This is what Barnett calls *projection,* because Saul the Jew is now projected into the familiar configuration of Christians, like Peter and John, preaching the Christian Gospel (1953:346).

In terms of this present chapter getting Paul away from Y (there) to B (here) in the new Christian relationship in the schema of the recombination thesis is a useful corrective to the false notion of nonfaith, or faith voids. The presupposition of a faith void will misguide us into forgetting that an individual has to be converted from something quite precise. One of the addages which Dr. Barnett used to repeat with almost monotonous regularity was "Every act of acceptance is also an act of rejection." In the process of conversion it is extremely important, both in the jungle community and the Western city, that the old fetishes be destroyed.

REVITALIZATION AND ORGANIC CHURCH GROWTH

In *Church Growth and the Word of God* (1970a:67-70) I discussed organic church growth in terms of *revitalization,* a concept we have from Anthony F.C. Wallace's article "Revitalization Movements" (1956), in which he described the main features of a major culture system innovation pattern by means of which a society confronting stress returns to normal. The basic structure of his model is illustrated in Figure 10.

FIGURE 10
Wallace's Revitalization Model

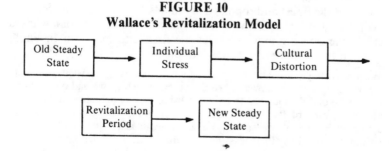

This is again the process of getting "from there to here." The period of revitalization is one of mazeway reformulation, from which the new social institution, which relieves the stress, emerges.

Many of the independent churches of Africa are, in point of fact, revitalization movements, and also Cargo Cults if they bring about a new steady state and relieve the stress. In our church growth studies I have used the concept for modification made within the indigenous church, and especially for constitutional and operational reorganization.

Some writers have used the term for a conversion movement. However, this could be so only if the movement came from within the group itself — i.e., they have lost confidence in their old gods, and have fallen into a state of stress, from which they have ultimately extricated themselves by becoming Christian and accepting the new way of life. This has happened and is a revitalization movement. But there cannot be a revitalization movement on a basis of foreign missionary advocacy — not as Wallace used the term. It is better to stick to the term people movement for that. According to Wallace, a revitalization movement is a "deliberate, organized, conscious effort by the members of the society to construct a more satisfying structure" (1956:265, repeated 279). It is because of this aspect that I retain it for discussion on the indigenous church.

The period of increasing individual stress before the general state of cultural distortion and community stress reminds us, as do all models of this type, of the multi-individual character of these societies. Likewise the period of revitalization, the drama of the reformulation of new structures, which ultimately provide the new steady state, are seen to be multi-individual: a concept widely used in church growth theory (Tippett 1971:85, 199-206, 262).

A BIBLICAL MODEL AND THE BIBLICAL PARADIGM

The question now arises: how do these anthropological models in missiology line up with Scripture? For purposes of comparative analysis let me take a biblical model and a biblical paradigm.

One of the finest anthropological models I know, not only for church growth, but also for my own personal motivations in Christian witness is found in the opening four verses of the first letter of John. In Phillips' translation (or paraphrase) it runs like this:

> We are writing to you about something which has always existed yet which we ourselves actually saw and heard: something which we had opportunity to observe closely and even to hold in our hands, and yet, as we know now, was something of the very Word of life himself! For it was life which appeared before us: we saw it, we are eyewitnesses of it, and are now writing to you about it. It was the very life of all ages, the life which has

always existed with the Father, which actually became visible in person to us mortal men. We repeat, we really saw and heard what we are now writing to you about. We want you to be with us in this—in this fellowship with the Father, and Jesus Christ his Son. We must write and tell you about it, because the more that fellowship extends the greater joy it brings to us who are already in it.

That is a model for Christian witness. It indicates the importance of corroborative evidence, and demonstrates that a witness must know and believe that to which he or she testifies. It specifies precisely what God did for mankind in Christ: this is the burden of his witness. It demands that the person(s) responding to the advocacy must be led on and incorporated into a collective group, a fellowship, a koinonia. For this to be widely possible these fellowship groups must be diffused abroad: it implies church planting. It is a two-dimensional fellowship, not only with other converts (we want you to be with us), but with the Father and Jesus, His Son (Tippett 1974b). Furthermore, once incorporated into the group the convert(s) must grow in the joy of the Lord. It is a beautiful model for getting "from there to here." This is not the only biblical model of this type, or even the only processual model. It preserves the concept of flow or momentum, through witness (advocacy), to acceptance of the Gospel, to incorporation into the fellowship group.

A paradigm, as we have seen, is a cluster of methodological pre-suppositions which formulates the norms and key concepts on which the group operates. How and why do we behave according to that pattern of witness and incorporation, that getting the converts "from there to here?" The paradigm is based on an historical event and utterance, when Jesus came to His disciples and commissioned them. He said:

All power is given unto me . . .
Go ye therefore and teach all nations,
Baptizing them in the name of the Father, Son and Holy Ghost
Teaching them to observe all things I have commanded you,
    And lo, I am with you always, even to the end of the age
(Mt. 28:18-20).

The assurance of His power, the commission to go (i.e., the apostolic mission), baptizing (i.e., the rite of incorporation into fellowships), teaching them to observe (Christian instruction and living), the promise of His presence, and finally the reference to "the end of the age" (i.e., the continuity of the commission until He comes again)—this was the model for the early Christians. In like manner, we too are a paradigm-community. Our research and our mission are dominated by those instructions, communicated as an event in history.

TO THE END OF THE AGE

The biblical paradigm for the missionary function of the church specifies an ongoing operation to the end of the age. How then are there some Christians who argue that the apostolic mission was terminated with the closing of the biblical canon? The anthropological models I have borrowed have come from contemporary data bases in most cases, although some have ethnohistorical dimensions. My own research throughout the Pacific, which can be documented from records that were certainly not made with posterity in mind, have a strongly biblical ring about them. They support the biblical view of history, and they manifest remarkable parallels with the apostolic church (1971: see Index p. 280 for about 30 entries).

But one does not need to be confined to the Third World. The same things are demonstrated, for example, in the life and experience of John Wesley, which will perhaps serve to terminate this chapter. I raise the case of John Wesley because he is so often cited as a great example of instantaneous conversion. The entry in his journal for 24 May, 1738 has been cited thousands of times, supposedly to prove what we really cannot claim. As far as his theological knowledge was concerned he went through no change. He had preached this theological knowledge before that date and through it the condemned prisoner had found peace and faith.

Wesley's experience was a process. It comprised a series of pre-conversion experiences and a sequence of post-conversion ones in sanctification. The experience of "the warmed heart" was a point in a *contextual stream of events,* not an isolated event without a context. This is not just an opinion. Read his *Journal* over February, March, and April, his confrontations with Peter Bohler (Feb. 7 to Mar. 4), which reflect the experiential continuum, which at so many points he shared with his brother. Even the Aldersgate experience which began with his morning devotions—"thou art not far from the kingdom"—had a sequence. Wesley was well informed in scriptural theology long before that date; his account of sanctification, written as early as 1725, was very much the same as he believed at the time of his death. What happened at Aldersgate Street was that he took the step of faith. He was prepared to rely on and act on that faith, and in doing so he experienced what Wesleyans to this day call the experience of *assurance.* It was the vital point in an experiential continuum. And his brother shared the same experience about the same time.

Following this, after a brief trip to Germany, Wesley entered the period of his life when the frustrations of rejection that preceded the Aldersgate Street experience gave way largely to one when small communities of searching sinners and believers began to multiply. By September he had a society sharing the new experience with condemned prisoners in Newgate Prison, and another society in Bear Yard. On November 3 he started prayers at Bocardo Prison; two days later he began prayers and preaching in the workhouse at Gloucester Green, and two days after that in the workhouse at St. Thomas. The following year he began field preaching. There was such a difference after May 24, 1738 that it is easy to see why folk think of it as an instantaneous conversion. But you cannot read the *Journal* without sensing the continuum of the work of the Spirit in the soul of this man who already knew the text and theology of the Bible as very few saved men did.

I stand myself in the Wesley tradition, and I share an experience with a similar sequence of events. I could have illustrated this chapter from the data in his *Works*. Whether I look at Scripture or at the experience of Wesley or at my own missionary experiences as reflected in my writings and notebooks, I end up where Barbour stands, arguing the importance of "the recurring theme of the *experiential basis* of religion, as essential for religious vitality in practice as for defensible epistemology in theory" (1974b:278).

CHAPTER 13

Salvation and Cultural Identity

Margaret Mead, in *Culture and Commitment,* insists that the new
question of our day is, "Can I commit my life to anything? Is there
anything in human cultures as they exist today worth saving, worth
committing my life to?" (1968:xii). She includes belief in God, in science,
in society, in anything at all. It is the question humans face when
confronted with "the responsibility of not destroying the human race." I
latch on to the word "commit" rather than to the pessimism of the
question. My own commitment is to Christian mission in a world that is
ready for it. I am also committed to a belief in both oral and scientific
values, and stand with Horowitz (1968), who says, "the presence of
moral components does not prevent a scientific view of society, but, to the
contrary, is its *necessary condition*" (my emphasis). Such a commitment
is required in missionary anthropology in this new era of rapid cultural
change.

ANTHROPOLOGY AND CHRISTIAN MISSION

An increasing literature on certain subsections of applied anthropology
—educational, medical and missionary anthropology[1] indicate a significant
attitudinal shift among anthropologists. Once applied anthropology of any
kind had to fight for existence. The study of mankind was supposedly a

---

The original version of this chapter was published in the *International Review of
Mission,* Vol. LXI, pp. 236-251, under the title, "Conceptual Dyads in the
Ethnotheology of 'Salvation Today'." Gratitude is hereby expressed to the
publisher for permission to include it here.

strictly objective and scientific description. Today anthropology has to justify its existence by application to the felt needs of mankind. It is called out of its "ivory towers" of "science for science's sake" to be responsible for society. This notion was developed by Gjessing in an article "The Social Responsibility of the Social Scientist" (1968:397-403).

Furthermore the region between mission studies and anthropology, long a kind of no-man's-land, can no longer be so regarded. A new type of missionary case study has appeared, with either an anthropological section or anthropological themes running through it. These studies speak to wider circles than the particular countries they research.[2] They show, what Luzbetak has articulated, that "the most basic human problem in missionary work" is "the socio-cultural context" and thus anthropology is "an essential aspect of missionary formation—not a 'side-branch' " (1963:18-19). This chapter explores some anthropological dimensions of culture change, culture and identity, and salvation in this new era of Christian mission. In the study of mankind's "consciousness" (identity) anthropologists, because of their cross-cultural explorations, have been called "intensified" humans (King 1969). Anthropological theory requires a data base of tested and measured information from precisely defined localities, groups of people or themes. Techniques vary, but good theory must be built on case studies.

The same is good for missiology. Publications like the Lausanne Committee for World Evangelization Occasional Papers and the Church Growth Series coming from Fuller Seminary's School of World Mission, are serious attempts at developing missiological theory on a basis of field research. Without this theory/research "marriage" accomplishments and failures of the churches could not be fully shared. Although each situation is unique, nevertheless there are consistencies and continuities which need to be understood if we are to be efficient in our stewardship under God.

We ought to be, Janus-like, looking both backwards and forwards. Mission, like culture, has a past, present and future. The operational dynamics and opportunities of today must take cognizance of the collective experiences of yesterday and keep an eye on the goals of tomorrow. We reject the lessons of the past to our peril. We look forward into an unknown future, the contours of which are beginning to form. Some braver souls, like David Barrett, (1969:362-366) dare to project what may be expected. Barrett sees a strong black Christianity with African values by the year 2000. Against this we set sociological predictions without number, foretelling the demise of Christianity by that date. For most people the only certainty is "today." Here we stand at a point of time, trying to be aware of its dangers and alert to its opportunities. We would eliminate the errors of the past but preserve its abiding values. On the other hand we must articulate programs for tomorrow that are credible and realistic. Something has to be terminated; but something has to be transmitted forward. Today is a *synapse*. Impulses of energy generated yesterday have to pass on into the systems of tomorrow. At this point of space and time, and from this mental set, we consider salvation, and culture and identify.

The danger of conflict in debates in the theory of both anthropology and mission is semantic. Nothing holds up progress (i.e. the application of adequate theory to real life needs and situations) like disputations over semantics. We strive for a statement to which all may subscribe, knowing full well that when we come to act on it we will interpret it differently. I hope what follows will point up the confluence of issues of possible misunderstanding and encounter. There are fundamental distinctions that need to be recognized before Christian mission can set forth its goals clearly, or discover adequate methodologies for presenting salvation today and understanding cultural identity.

CHANGE AND CONTINUITY

No aspect of anthropology has claimed more attention since the war than culture change. More and more the agents of change (including medical, educational and agricultural workers, missionaries and traders) are receiving advice from applied anthropologists.[3] Before the war "primitive" societies were studied frantically lest their cultures should disappear. Anthropologists protected them and told missionaries to go home. Cultural relativism was common talk. True there is something about cultural relativism which every anthropologist and missionary has to learn—namely, that every society has its own patterns, values, world-view, and right to make its own decisions and to do things in its own way. But it is just as bad to "cage" a community and treat a people as guinea pigs for experiment or museum display as to inflict paternalistic, Western, ecclesiastical systems upon them. The survival anthropologists were, in their own way, just as ethnocentric and paternalistic as any missionary. Cross-cultural agents of change must tread the road to cultural relativism (if only to understand), but they must not bog down there (Goldschmidt 1966:138). This would leave them with a static view of society that just is not true. Important research today is considering the cultural significance of mankind as human. This does not ignore the relativity of cultural groups in this pluralistic world (indeed early relativists like Herskovits [1951] and Linton [1936] also searched for universals in human societies), but recognizes that these diverse homogeneous groups have to live in close proximity and to interact. To cut off tribes by isolation for survival sake is to condemn them to stagnation and extinction. But the more they interact the more they change.

Anthropology speaks to Christian mission about the nature of change. First, change is going on all the time. The notion that tribal societies are static is a myth. There always has been change, however slight. The speed varies, but this is nothing new. Change is not necessarily bad. It indicates when a society is ready for it. Every society has inbuilt mechanisms for effecting change. The cross-cultural agent of change needs to be aware of them and operate through these indigenous institutions, procedures and persons.

Second, any changes advocated by the agent of change, have to be seen, not as foreign impositions, but as options advocated, which will be accepted or rejected by the target group. The community will have its own pattern for decision making. Except where Christianization has come with military conquest, Christian missions were advocated and accepted, not imposed. If the Protestant missionaries were to blame for the Western form of their advocacy of the Gospel, their fault was the same as that of every salesman and TV commercial—namely, they presented only one option. Their convictions were ethnocentrically Western. Often they failed to see that Christian worship, and indeed the Gospel itself, could have "indigenous garments." (I generalize. Some early missionaries were good anthropologists.) They intended to oversimplify the option as a "package deal": the old way or the new, the darkness or the light. However, for whatever motivation, the people made the choice.

In the new era of mission two things should be kept in mind. First, the option of an indigenous theology and form of worship must always be presented. The target people must never be confronted with a foreign ecclesiology and theology as the only option to their old way. Second, and quite apart from this, Christianity is not the only foreign option today. Millions in African, New Guinea and Indonesia, for instance, have discovered that their old religious system is no longer adequate for the new day, and have reached the psychological and cultural moment for change, as described by Kroeber (1948) and Barnett (1953, 1956). Innovate they certainly will, but Christianity is competing with Islam, Secularism, Communism and maybe Neo-pagan Syncretism. The basic difference between the old and new eras of mission is the current multi-option. In the light of this, conversions may have a better motivation in the new era. Some anthropologists have stressed that agents of change should deliberately confront peoples considering change with all the options, and discuss the compatibility of possible options with their own way of life (Foster 1962:269). By the same token, this demands the presence of a Christian advocate in every dynamic situation, as I think the scriptural commission obligates the Church anyway. I see only two valid reasons for withdrawing missionaries: (1) if they are foreigners and a strong local witness has already been established, and (2) because of repeated rejection (Lk. 10:10 ff.).

Third, culture change does not have to be chaotic or violent. Violence and revolution may remove certain obstructions, but they always leave scars on the society. Some priceless values are inevitably lost. Many effective cultural and social changes have been won by less destructive methods: literature, music, drama, recreation, revival, to mention a few. The battle against slavery in England was fought in pulpit and parliament, as were also the labor reforms after the industrial revolution.

Over against culture change stand the essential cultural continuities. When societies change slowly these continuities stand out as stabilizers which permit change without serious dislocation. They relate in particular to the moral fiber. A society which loses these is in a bad way. For example, a fundamental unit of social stability is the family. When the family falls apart, a whole complex of personal relationships, enculturative education, interdependence, security and responsibility is dismembered with it. This is so whether the family is monogamous or polygamous, nuclear or extended. It is reinforced by rites of passage, the value system and religion. The family, then, is one of these continuities. The value system itself is another, and so is religion. When any of these breaks down, the society passes into a state of severe stress. A functional substitute may be found for the broken institution: but a society without a value system or religion (communism is a religion, or faith system, at the negative pole) or a family pattern is heading for anarchy and extinction.

The Christian missionary enterprise has operated under many changing forms, but its essential continuity, its value base, down through history has been the Bible, where the commission to bring salvation to the nations is set forth. As long as this is regarded as the revelation of God it survives as a continuity through changing techniques of mission and changing situations in which mission operates. But if the notion of the Bible as the revealed word of God to "individuals in mission" be allowed to disintegrate, we have merely a cultural artifact from ancient times, a museum piece, with no relevances beyond that of "any one's opinion."

"Development," "humanization" and "liberation" are politico-ethical terms. If we desire to use them theologically, then we presuppose that the notion of the Bible as the revelation of God in mission is one of the continuities, which must be preserved through change in the new era of mission, and the terms acquire an evangelical meaning. Thus the attitude to the Bible is crucial. Unless we agree that it provides the criteria for mission, and place it in the continuity rather than the change category, there is little hope for agreement about the nature of salvation today.

DESTRUCTION AND CONSTRUCTION

Margaret Mead's question arises from the current process of cultural change. It raises ethical and theological problems because it affects the human situation and mankind's survival. Fifty years ago Alexis Carrel (1935) pointed out that mankind was heading for trouble because the various branches of intellectual endeavor were not progressing at the same rate. She doubted the spiritual capacity of humans to control responsibly the new knowledge being acquired. The daily news, the war reports, the existence of terrifying bombs remind us that we live in a dramatically dynamic world with "terrible powers of destruction" set over against "limitless powers of construction"—all in the hands of humans. Margaret Meat told this to the American Association for the Advancement of Science years ago. She saw in this "capacity of man to destroy or construct" a sore need for vision, a realization that the world was unsafe, a need to understand the magnitude of this power and to use it responsibly.

About the same time Charles Coulson (1956) addressed the World Methodist Conference on "Nuclear Power and Christian Responsibility." He concluded with a dramatic illustration of this dichotomy—a single person with one hand on a single lever to push or to pull, to launch an atomic weapon on the Atlantic coast or to light an inland city with atomic power. He asked if scientific mankind who now had in their hands the powers of God, had yet learned enough of the mind of God to use them responsibly. After the sixties and seventies we agree with Mead that humans need vision of meaning and responsibility.

In the face of mankind's inhumanity to mankind, of fear in all its forms, the threat of destruction, the possibility of another world war from which no victor could emerge, certainly there is need for salvation in social terms—quite apart from the traditional meaning. This is ethical in that it deals with human relationships. "The unity of man" wrote Wolf (1964:95) "is a process of the involvement of man with man, through the medium of human culture." Theoretically this kind of salvation should merely require humans living with their kind in peace and achieving Mead's "vision of meaning and responsibility." Secular anthropology can go no further than that—and that is only theoretically possible, however worthy a goal. The problem, of course, is human nature, mankind's proneness to sin and their stubborn refusal to love their neighbor as themselves.

The point McGavran (1955) keeps raising is that you must get humans right with God before you can get them right with their fellow humans. You can go so far with dialogue and constitutional procedures, but as Colin Morris once reacted to an appealing address on the relief of poverty, in the final analysis the iniquities behind poverty spring from human sin. Ultimately it is a theological issue. Then, as believers who have come to terms with God and draw from His resources, redeemed mankind look again on the human condition. "Vision of meaning and responsibility" now has new significance, not as a hope or wish, but as stewardship under God. Then we must certainly play our part in the "saving" of society, first by resisting its injustices and then by appropriating its constructive opportunities. This is *Christian,* not secular anthropology. The articulation hangs together because the culmination of a science of mankind is the "new person in Christ."

RESTATEMENT AND REFORMULATION

I have discussed the creative tension between change and continuity. The inherent capacity of society for change is itself a continuity. What has been said of cultural values applies also to both anthropological and missiological theory. New theoretical dimensions are continually being explored, but they spring from existing theory. The great anthropological theorists—Tylor, Codrington, Frazer, Boas, Malinowski—have all had later anthropologists modify their theory. Yet their basic discoveries have been restated from time to time.

Tylor's possession theory (1891:Vol. 2) was a valid frame of reference for researching the phenomenon, but he tied it to unilinear evolution and the phase of savagery, a notion subsequently discarded. The theory had to be restated without erroneous presuppositions. The part which stood the test of time is still used for possession studies.

Likewise, Malinowski's (1938) concept of a new autonomous entity was put forward within the colonial situation, which he believed to be the "given" within which it was to work. Colonialism broke down but there is still vital truth in the concept, which calls for restatement for post-colonial situations. Malinowski resisted the dualism of culture clash, the weaker perishing before the dominant. He saw the new autonomous entity (identity) with administrator, missionary, trader, farmer and chief interacting and interrelating. A restatement of this principle currently operates in some young nations were British planters, for example, have taken out local citizenship.

Restatement is significant also in missiological theory. Many church growth studies show how remarkable growth has been achieved by the restatement of some biblical principle for new conditions. Acts 13 has been adapted as a model for many church planting missions, and Acts 6 for organic church growth by role creation. The Great Commission has been repeatedly restated for new situations through history; Brancati, Carey, John Williams all did so, with significant effect.

Over against these restatements of theory, and distinguished from them, have been radical reformulations of missionary procedures and techniques, which the new situations demand. Thus Carey's *Enquiry* (1792) brings out clearly how he was concerned with the world changes of his times: the discoveries of the great navigators, new navigational techniques, newly discovered tribes and languages; and how he himself became involved in a mission beyond the technology of the apostles. He saw what was wrong with the Church of his day, with abundant resources and no outreach, and corrected this by methodological reformulations. The restatement of the Great Commission for the new era was one thing. Reformulation of methods and policies to act upon it was another. They are found side by side in his *Enquiry*. It is axiomatic that any reformation of missionary technique should begin with a restatement of the Great Commission.

UNITY AND UNIFORMITY

One must admit that our progress in understanding the identity of minority groups, ethnic or social, has been either slow or unrealistic. The Western world has a questionable notion of the rightness of majority rule. The wrongness of minority rule that is despotic and oppressive is apparent, but at the opposite pole is something which can become just as destructive. Anthropological case studies have frequently shown that social and ethnic groups, caught in the networks of a large nation, frequently have to forfeit their cultural identity or face possible extinction.

When I visit an Indian reservation I find that people want to retain their cultural identity, to follow their traditional way of life, to preserve their values and skills, and speak their own language. But there is no real hope for survival as such, no economic future unless they accept the values and languages of the "main culture." They hear the country saying, "Retain your cultural identity and die, or adapt and compete with us, for you belong to the nation, and the main culture is the national culture." Either minority or majority rule can become inconsiderate and despotic.

The same situation exists in bicultural or multicultural communities or congregations. A Hispanic pastor in Los Angeles has English and Spanish speaking members in the congregation and possibly other groups. If any group is neglected, it will probably be a minority one. But without the opportunity for participation in the ongoing program they lose identity. There is no belongingness.

Integration and assimilation have been presented as "salvation." Sermons by the hundred have been preached on "being one in Christ" and on there being "neither Jew nor Gentile." We all understand that somehow we must learn to live together; but we advocate it in two very different ways. I believe the notion of Unity or Uniformity exposes the problem.

Before people can live happily together they have to see themselves biologically as the same: human beings. Anthropology has long been saying that our ideas about race are a tragic myth. A good, short statement on this is Kluckhohn's chapter on it in his book, *Mirror for Man* (1969).

On the other hand we make a bad mistake when we confuse race and culture. Every individual, anthropologically speaking, has two identities—one as a member of the human race (which means theologically, that he or she is one for whom Christ died) and the other as a member of some specific culture, from which he or she derives habits, language and outlook on life. A pastor or missionary may be well aware of human identity, but tragically oblivious to cultural identity. The former concerns the right of every person to hear the Gospel and to have the option of accepting or rejecting it. The latter determines the languages and manner in which it should be communicated, and also the patterns in which one's new life in Christ is nurtured and exercised. If we decline to offer the "Gospel in mission" we deny people their true identity. If we offer it in culturally unacceptable forms we reject the cultural identity.

In theological debates this often surfaces as the Unity-Uniformity issue. Uniformity presupposes a "melting pot" and claims integration on a basis of human identity. Unity operates on a biological model, like the scriptural Body of Christ, with differing parts functioning in interrelationship, doing his saving work in the world; or alternatively as many folds whose sheep belong to one flock under one Shepherd. I cannot find the concept of uniformity in the Scriptures. Moreover the validity of the "melting pot idea" in the megalopolis has been heavily attacked by critics. The reader might read the book *Beyond the Melting Pot* (Glazer and Moynihan 1963). Scripture and anthropology seem to be in step in recognizing the importance of diversity in unity; which suggests that the true meaning of integration is discovering how blacks and whites, Europeans and Africans, can live and work together without giving up their cultural identities.

If we state salvation in terms of sociology (instead of eschatologically), it would seem to me that such social salvation should stimulate some experience wherein people of various cultures would come to respect each other's ways of life, share dialogue in love, bear mutual burdens and manifest different gifts without the sacrifice of identity. However, this cannot be accomplished on any common base from the social sciences. I can only see it as a possibility when the parties concerned become new people in Christ: but that is a Christian and not a secular anthropology. Then, as parts of the Body of Christ, they would need to retain their distinctiveness, their cultural gifts and identify.

Missionaries who have succeeded in escaping from the house on the hilltop, have itinerated frequently, learned to eat the food, speak the language, sleep in the leaf house, and cultivated deep friendships across cultures, have invariably found a deepening of their own Christian theology because of the rapport. I believe we will never appreciate the wholeness of Christian theology until "the nations" have added their contributions to it.[4] My Fijian brethren taught me to love the Old Testament. Diversity in loving unity brings this, not living in uniformity.

This is a postconversion experience. I am not speaking of dialogue with those of other faiths, but with Christians of other cultures. We still have much of the "working out of our salvation" to discover, and having discovered it, I am sure we will witness better to those of other faiths. I recall how the poetry of the Indian Christians, Tilak, came through to me with the startling discovery that there was far more in theology of sacrifice than I had dreamed. Tilak retained his cultural identity in his poetry, and my life would have been poorer and less dedicated had this not come my way. When we recognize cultural diversity we begin to draw from it.

LIBERATION AND RECONCILIATION

A large part of the world is in a violent mode today, and this is reflected in revolution and the theology of liberation. This is an interesting anthropological phenomenon. The theology itself has a biblical undergirding and the cry for liberation is a just cause. I believe the doctrine can be stated evangelically; but, on the other hand, it is often politically manipulated with political goals. A Marxist interpretation is prominent among its many uses. Nevertheless, it is a salvation motif, and in Christian terms has something worth saying. The idea of liberation for individual and community is a valid goal.

On the other hand, a purely sociological liberation, in spite of physical improvement attained by the effort, is no guarantee for a liberated spirit. Without this liberation of spirit the "alienated," "truncated" person, who by liberation is supposedly "integrated and made whole" is, in point of fact, neither integrated nor whole.

A graduate defending his thesis a few years back narrated his experiences with Latin American informants, who reacted against the word "reconciliation." Reconciliation mechanisms are not peculiarly Christian. They are widespread across the world in non-Western societies. The informants' rejection of the term was due to their feeling that reconciliation was a passive procedure, an act of resignation, or at best a compromise. They could not conceptualize salvation in this term and talked of liberation, which suited better their feelings of aggression.

Now, reconciliation is by no means passive. It is an active thrust against the existence of social discord and often takes much courage to initiate. From a remote island in the Solomons to the hunting forest-dwellers of Southern Ethiopia I have seen non-Christian reconciliation mechanisms in operation—religious acts in the name of some deity, positive and premediated. They differ from liberation by being corrective procedures within a social structure. Liberation is a destructive procedure of cultural change, setting people free from some form of oppression.

Anthropologically, reconciliation and liberation are opposites—one restoring society, the other resisting it. Yet both are forms of social salvation.

Interestingly enough, both can be used as analogies for the work of Christ—as Reconciler and Liberator. In each case the earthly prototype is tentative, only effective within limitations, and confined to the here and now. In Christian terms reconciliation and liberation are results or outcomes of humans meeting the Reconciler or Liberator face to face. Two questions arise for consideration: (1) Is a purely sociological liberation or reconciliation adequate? (2) To what extent is mankind so recreated in Christ that they become themselves liberators and reconcilers in the community where God has placed them? Once again, secular anthropology takes us only so far. Are we to stop there, with the ultimate limited by mankind's own capacity? Christian anthropology is a better *finale*. In Christ, the perfect Human, humans transcend the limitations of their natural capacities, and as new people in Christ they find a new dimension for their selfhood.

CONCLUSIONS

I have been pressing throughout that in an age of rapid cultural change, like the present, dramatic discontinuities are inevitable. Frequently they are absolutely essential. They do not necessarily have to lead to chaos. They are often opportunities for new beginnings after failure. Nevertheless, these discontinuities (sometimes conceptual, more often perhaps methodological, technical or practical) must be held in a state of reasonable equilibrium by certain continuities (more often conceptual). Some things survive. Certain principles and laws (as also in business, economics or science) have to be restated repeatedly. Machines, operations, techniques and patterns may change, but principles go on, at least until better substitutes are found. If mission is to remain Christian, certain ideas must be recognized as basic. People must go on believing them. When context and environment change, new communicative approaches must be found for the very reason that fundamentals still have to be transmitted.

Discontinuities, revolutions, new beginnings and new eras are never quite absolute, however drastic. Much literature supporting such discontinuities fails to recognize the essential continuities—and I do not exclude writing on salvation today. If an understanding of salvation is limited to terms of contemporary experience, the danger is that, being enthused over necessary innovations and programs, such an understanding may fail to relate to our Lord's idea of mission itself.

A sad commentary on our unwillingness to be realistic is that four decades after a plea for "a typology of minority groups"[5] to identify problems of minority-dominant group relations, and hundreds of anthropological monographs on our pluralistic societies, our preaching should still be bogged down, trying to enforce main-culture uniformity. A systematic survey by a research team is still required. Where cultural pluralism exists it must be recognized. Unrecognized, ignored or suppressed and the whole community (world on the largest panorama) is under stress; but recognized and allowed for, it may become a positive value. Roger Keesing called it "a crucial human resource," and went on:

> The cancelling out of cultural differences and the emergence of a standard-ized world culture might—while solving some problems of political integration—deprive men of sources of wisdom and vision, and a reservoir of diversity and alternatives, he cannot afford to lose (1968:365).

Any study of salvation today must recognize: (1) the character of the human situation, within which we are to engage in mission, so that the thrust of the operation may be culturally, relevantly and appropriately equipped for effective engagement with the real issues; and (2) the character of the human condition and the abiding theological principles which speak to it, without which the effort can be no more than a benevolent humanitarianism, not necessarily Christian at all; and which would lead to an age of "mission" even more exposed to paternalism and ethnocentricity than that from which we are emerging.

As a missionary anthropologist I see the basic components of a currently valid missiological theory as anthropological and theological, (1969a), the former speaking to the human situation and the latter to the human condition. Our Lord clearly indicated to his disciples an approach-ing ministry _in the world_ and _to the world_ (Jn. 17:18); yet individuals were to be brought to him as the only way to the Father (14:6). After his departure the subsequent record indicates that they both restated and acted upon this directive. In those days of shock following the crucifixion, the risen Lord reinforced their confidence by pointing out two basic continuities: the written and living Word (Lk. 24:25-27, 30-32).

Notes:

1. Missionary anthropology is covered by such works as: Smalley (1967), Nida (1954, 1960), Smith (1945), Law (1968), Luzbetak (1963), and also by the journals _Missiology_ (formerly _Practical Anthropology_) and _Anthropological Quarterly_.

2. D'Epinay (1969), Taylor and Lehmann (1961), and Tippett (1967) are examples of this kind of missiology.

3. For example, Arsberg and Niehoff (1964), Spicer (1952), Barnett (1956), Mead (1955), Foster (1962, 1969), Linton (1945), and Bunker and Adair (1959), to mention only a few.

4. All the Americas, for example, have yet to learn from the Black person who "does not come empty-handed seeking equality; he possesses values that need to be added to American culture(s)" (Mitchell 1969:10-15).

5. Wirth (1944) proposed the criteria for such measurement: (1) identification of number, size and location; (2) degree of friction and amount of exclusion or participation; (3) nature of social arrangements governing relationships, and (4) possible goals for both groups.

How Does Religion Replace Animism?

CHAPTER 14

Patterns of Religious Change in Communal Society

The title of this chapter relates religion and society. People live in organized communities and within those structures they have a religious faith and practice. Before we can discuss the significance of any manifestations of religious change in a given society, we must understand how the religion and the society relate.

This will take us into the anthropological theory of primitive religion, although we use the term "primitive" with caution and with qualification. All religion has tremendous time depth and it is not for one to call another "primitive." Even those forms which seem so simple to us, are more complex than we imagine. They have their own logical system, symbolism, theology and ritual, frequently set against a complex worldview which certainly did not emerge overnight. Often we stand under the shadow of Darwin and his contemporaries, and the comparative religionists who constructed an evolutionary theory of religion which imagined belief to have evolved towards the great religions and with Christianity as the ultimate goal of the process. This theory required that the seemingly simple forms be represented as survivals of the early stage in the evolutionary process. These ideas came from the armchair scholars. As anthropology developed its methods and techniques, and stress was placed on field research, it became increasingly apparent that primitive religion was intensely complex and diverse. The possibility of these being survivals in a line of unilineal evolution was rejected. Although we still hear the names of E.B. Tylor and Sir James Fraser, who early alerted us to new dimensions for the study of primitive religion, we have gone far beyond them. Some of the problems they raised have never been solved, but they were mostly speculative matters, like the origin of religion and

157

the idea of where the soul came from. Emphasis today is on description of the religious structures, how the systems operate, and the processes of change they are undergoing. Tylor gave us the word *Animism,* which we still use. Fraser tried to differentiate between magic, religion and science, and though we do not accept his distinctions we recognize that these things are different. Certain names stand out in the history of anthropology and still speak to our study of animism: Marett, van Gennep, Lowie, Radin, Malinowski, Rivers and Wallace. There are others, but from these missiology has borrowed.

THEORY OF PRIMITIVE RELIGION IN MISSIOLOGY

Among the students of "primitive" religion the notion has been held that religion is the *integrator* of society. Radin has said that:

> Religion among primitive people is concerned with the maintenance of life-values and, since no other means of stressing and maintaining them exist there, it permeates every phase of existence (1937:15).

More recently Wallace, discussing the process of a new religion establishing itself and having reached its "plateau," says that thereafter

> religion functions for a kind of *governor for society,* stabilizing its members and correcting the tendency of institutions to wobble or drift (1966:4— emphasis mine).

Lowie, in an article on "Religion in Human Life," published posthumously in 1963, tells how he came from a position of rank atheism to belief in the fundamental importance of religion in human society. This is an anthropological study, not a Christian one. Here *religion* is integrator. In his *Primitive Religion* (1952:xiv-xvi) he indicates his acceptance of religion as a universal feature of human culture (xvi); he rejects Tylor's definition in *Primitive Culture* (1871) as minimal because it is purely intellectual (desire for explanation) and leaves out the emotional element (xiv-xv); and then differentiates between the rational and supernatural (xv). "In every society," he says, "there is a spontaneous division of the sphere of experience into the ordinary and the extraordinary." Theoretically he is indebted to Marett, who saw the primitive's workaday world of reason and experience as one of cause and effect, but with the sense of the Supernatural set over against mere practical rationalism (1914), and also to Soderblom for his idea of the Sacred (with qualifications). Goldenweiser (1946:416ff.) also had spoken of "supernaturalism." These were interpretive scholars, but they were not without a good body of data for examination. It seemed to them that though the supernatural stood over against the practical conceptually, yet, to the primitive, both bore on cause and effect in life as he knew it.

With Malinowski, the students of primitive religion broke away from the evolutionary theory of Frazer, and the respective roles of magic, religion and science became more clear-cut. Frazer saw human progress from magic (mankind's manipulation of supposed hidden powers), to religion (appeal to supposed powers outside themselves) to science (rational explanation of the universe). Malinowski saw them as three different responses. Science is human achievement. Magic is the attempt to coerce the unpredictable. Religion is an appeal to the higher powers for its own sake. In his article in the symposium *Science and Religion* (1931:81) he sums it up thus:

> Religion gives man the mastery of his fate, even as science gives him the control of natural forces, and magic the grip of chance, luck and accident.

Rivers, who came into anthropology from medicine, struggled with the same differentiations in magic, religion and medicine, and found in religion mankind's belief in, and drawing from, powers outside and greater than themselves; whereas magic depended on mankind's manipulative skill with rites (he was especially concerned with sorcery), and medicine comprised knowledge and control of practices which regulate natural phenomena that lower human vitality and cause death (1927:4). From these differentiations Rivers derived his classification of sickness among primitives as due to the human agency, nonhuman agencies and natural causes (7). As prognosis depends on diagnosis, sorcery has to be met by counter-sorcery, but spirit-sickness by, say, sacrifice. At least some kinds of sickness can only be handled by religious means—where neither sorcerer nor medicineman can cure.

The difference between Malinowski and Rivers is probably due to their different quests. They gathered data in the same part of the world and agree in differentiating religion from magic, and magic from sicence, and in recognizing the role of the Supernatural in human life. From my reading of Rivers, I believe he would have agreed with Malinowski's contention that religion standardizes social impulses and assures the victory of custom and tradition over the mere response of thwarted instinct. Rivers' acceptance of the need for cure by sacrifice would suggest his acceptance also of Malinowski's view of the public and festive character of religion and its importance in dealing with a crisis, and reestablishing morale. Malinowski has put this:

> ... religion counteracts the centrifugal forces of fear, dismay, demoraliza-
> tion, and provides the most powerful means of reintegration of the group's
> shaken solidarity and of the re-establishment of its morale (1948:53).

About the same time as Malinowski was working out these theories within the field situation in Oceania, Radin, working from different field data and in a different frame of reference, had reached some parallel conclusions. He was concerned with the dichotomy and tension of ideals in society, and expressed his conviction that "the religious-ethical ideal" challenges and criticizes the "purely mundane ideal" because it is more likely to achieve the desired "happiness and prosperity" by emphasizing "the cardinal fact of life, the sense of proportion which alone saves man from destruction and misery" (1927:90). To the function of religion in integrating the group by standardizing its values and reestablishing its morale, we have now added the element of its moral influence. This is in line with Malinowski also, to whom I now return.

Malinowski set out his views on the social and individual significance of primitive religion in the following terms:

1. Social cooperation is needed to unveil sacred things and approach supernatural beings. Wholehearted community ritual creates the atmosphere of homogeneous belief for those who need it.

2. Public performance of religious dogma is indispensable for maintaining morals in primitive communities. Every article of faith wields a moral influence. For morals to be active they must be universal.

3. The transition and conservation of sacred tradition entails publicity, or at least collective performance. Dogma is inviolable. The believer must be convinced that what it accepted as truth is safely preserved. Every religion requires tangible, reliable safeguards to guarantee its authenticity (1948:66-69, much abbreviated, but Malinowski's terminology retained).

It has been argued that religions differ from one another because of what are called *identity values*, those features which are essential for integration and survival in whatever environment and economy the society might prefer or require by necessity. As Wallace points out (1966:26), this tends to give religion a class, ethnic or racial identity, and of course it depends on the integration of the society. The relation between the society and its religion is certainly very close. The class or ethnic identity values—language or dialect. creative arts and forms, authority patterns, occupational traditions, and so forth—make for an extremely cohesive religion. When such an animist faith is confronted with the possibility of change to Christianity, the agent of change needs to understand the nature of that cohesion. It explains both people movements to Christianity and group resistance to the conversion of individuals.

Even Durkheim, whose thesis that religion venerates not the god but the society is by no means proved, believed that the function of religion was to establish such attitudes and notions as were deemed necessary for the perpetuity of society (1912). Indeed so many scholars, with such divergent views of religion, and who have come to grips at so many points, nevertheless seem to accept the idea of the function of religion being to assure the security and survival of society. I think it needs no further comment. In passing, however, I may suggest that even in our modern society, if religion today seems to have become dispensable, it is probably because the Church has come dangerously near to forgetting its responsibility to society and has concerned itself too much with its own survival. It is just at this corresponding point of time, when the witchdoctors turn from being social "benefactors" to being social "parasites" that the populace of animist societies turns to Christianity. I have seen this process in operation on more than one mission field (Tippett 1970b:178-198).

If the religion of a society is oriented towards the survival of the society, and its own traditional authenticity has to be safeguarded, how can the religion ever be changed? Who can initiate such change?

In discussing the normative, functional thesis (that religious institutions represent central values and integrate the society because they are internalized by the members) Wallace has pointed out that this conviction offers religion "a degree of primacy in culture change" (1966:25). This notion suggests two things to me: (1) that a great many of the social changes, the approved innovations, that take place in a society pass through the sieve of religion, either initiated by it or with its approval, and (2) that any normal change to the religious structure (conceptional or manifest) will come from within. If religion is the integrator of society, only the integrator itself can really change the character of its role without demoralizing the society. Even when it initiates change in its own character, that change has to be accepted by the society. This is not to say that there are no unnatural ways of changing religion: military conquest, for example, or internal rebellion or natural catastrophe. These are disruptive crisis situations where the function of religion is to restore not the old order, but equilibrium. The change may be drastic and a compromise, but it will have to be accepted first by the religious system and then by the populace. Here again it is Wallace who has reminded us that the function of religion "is not merely to support and inculcate values, but also to devise some means for resolving the conflicts" of society (1966:27-28). He is speaking mainly of tensions generated within the society, but who else can deal with tensions imposed by external pressures? The whole question of the *stress situation,* especially that situation great enough to affect the whole social group, is charged with significance for the agent of directed change.

Such an agent of change is the Christian missionary or pastor, regardless of whether or not that one is operating cross-culturally. It bears on his or her operations at two points: (1) at the point of the possible conversion of a group, and (2), when a stress situation has created a state of dysequilibrium within the existing group and some modifications (structural or theological) are called for. The quantitative impact of the first is a group conversion of some kind, and the organic renewal of the second I have usually described in my church growth writing by borrowing

Wallace's term (1956) *revitalization movement* (Tippett, 1967a:348, 350, 352; 1970a:67-70). In both cases significant religious changes have taken place, but after the process has been completed society is once more in what Wallace calls "a steady state," and the renewed religion carries on as the integrator or governor of society. Despite the precise differences in the structure and operation of the new society or religion, the basics of the second steady state are the same as those of the first, as I think I can demonstrate by the use of a simple model, as demonstrated in Figure 11. With cases of religious change by Western one-by-one conversion, demoralization under acculturation, and submersion due to oppression, the model will be different. But group conversion and revitalization bring the society out of crisis to a similar steady state.

FIGURE 11
The Place of Religion in Society

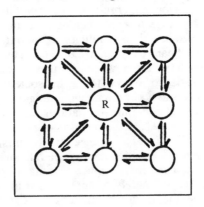

R = Religion

Many of the anthropologists I have met face to face are agnostics. For the time being, they recognize the necessity of religion in a tribal society, as a social mechanism for integration and preservation of the way of life; but they regard it as dispensable. They live under the shadow of Frazer. Some day these societies will have evolved beyond the stage of religion to the stage of science and then there will be no further need for religion. But there are others who have thought the matter out more carefully. Answering the question, will religion "outlast the apparently triumphant spread of scientific enlightenment?" Lowie says that it assuredly will because history shows "the transfer of the religious sentiment to new manifestations of the Extraordinary or Holy, never the extinction of the sentiment itself" (152:345).

I shall now turn from this theoretical preamble to examine four basic types of religious change related to the passage from animism to Christianity, and endeavor to pinpoint how the new state may be either satisfactory or unsatisfactory, and the consequences of this for the stability of the young Church so planted.

DEMORALIZATION

A historical study of the record of colonialism—both imperialistic and commercial types—over the last two hundred years shows how whole tribes have been demoralized by acculturation, how population has declined and a sinister malaise has overcome the people. Scores of once powerful and productive communities have disappeared altogether, whole tribes have died out completely. Others survive only as tiny groups, with too few people to provide the numbers and balance required for the functioning of their traditional institutions, for example, the religious institutions of the Bororo (Heustis 1963). Scores of the now still empty islands of the Pacific were depopulated by culture contact and in particular by the blackbirding trade of the last century (Tippett 1956a; 1967a:20ff). Even where the victims were not exterminated, there was terrific population displacement and those who remained had lost their population distribution and balance so that social institutions fell to pieces. The British anthropologist, Rivers, edited a book of essays on the *Depopulation of Melanesia* (1922), in which his own essay was concerned with the psychological factor: a loss of interest in life. He shows the interrelationship of the various aspects of society and how the loss of one affected the other. Mission and government were responsible in that they removed heathen and immoral customs without ascertaining first what their functions were, and providing substitutes. The result was that they left cultural voids which deprived the people of essential cultural activity and zest for life. This is an important and much quoted essay. (For its application to the Church, see Tippett 1967a:25-26, 147-159).

In some places population declined steadily for seventy or eighty years, and alarmed administrators and missionaries conducted surveys to discover causes. Eventually the people adjusted themselves to acculturation and their numbers began to increase again. It was only because of their virility and great numbers that they were able to endure long enough to make the adjustments. It was so with Fiji, where the missionary vigilance forced the government to act and appoint a commission to examine the depopulation. The Fijian population had dropped to less than a hundred thousand—a third of its number when culture contact began. It is almost a quarter of a million today. Hawaii's experience has been less satisfactory. Only ten thousand pure Hawaiians survive today. There are

about a hundred thousand part-Hawaiians. There are less than ten
thousand part-Fijians. This reversion of figures tells another tale of
culture contact. The historian, Derrick, attributes the Hawaiian population
decline largely to liquor (1936). Sandalwooding, whaling, trade in arms
and ammunition, blackbirding and venereal disease were all responsible.
Against these evils the missionaries were virtually the only corrective.
They fought a noble battle against one evil after another for a century, and
for it they were abused by sea captains and sailor novelists. The recent
availability of so many primary sources on the Pacific of the last century
tends to support the missionary claims about what was really going on.

I hold no brief for some of the policy and techniques of the early
mission to Hawaii, but I insist that it be evaluated in the historic sense, on
a basis of the character of American Puritanism of that day; but having
said this, I must add that both the missionaries and the American Board
have had a raw deal from the beginning to this present day. If there is
justice and judgment with God, then I am convinced that some day James
Michener and the Mirisch Corporation will have to answer for what they
have done. But for our present purpose, the relevance of the Hawaiian
mission lies in what it says to the notion of demoralization. The process of
demoralization under acculturative influences, for which the missionaries
are often wrongly blamed, began long before the islands ever saw a
missionary. During the three decades between the arrival of Captain Cook
and the first missionaries, the disruptive factors I have listed above did
their awful work, and Hawaii was thus in a bad state of demoralization
when the *Thaddeus* arrived in 1820.

The best and most reliable picture of the early mission to Hawaii,
which covers only the first seven years, is Albertine Loomis' *Grapes of
Canaan: Hawaii 1820* (1951). It is entirely compiled from primary
sources, and I know the record is true, as I too have worked over the
documents. Miss Loomis, in the "Prelude" speaks of the demoralization
of the pre-missionary period in this way:

> . . . many sorts of white men came to Hawaii. They came for provisioning
> and for escape. They fought for the king, connived at rebellion and sought
> concessions for far-off business houses; built fortunes, became royal
> favorites, espoused chiefesses and reared half-caste families; drank,
> gambled, brawled, rioted, deserted their ships, dallied with brown girls and
> sired unnumbered "orphans".

And again she tells of references in the ships' logs to the acquisition of
provisions—hogs, vegetables and fowls—at first for a song, but then with
prices rising:

> And when iron hoops and chisels no longer sufficed, the traders broke out
> rum and wine from their stores or broadcloth and linen or beaver hats and
> writing desks. The island chiefs grew shrewd as the game of commerce went
> forward. They learned to take more from the farmers and fishermen, to ask

more from the eagerly competing foreigners. In time they refused to bargain for anything but the biggest, showiest—and often the deadliest—items the white man could bring: muskets and ammunition, brass field pieces or battery guns from ships' decks—and sometimes the ships themselves. In exchange for these, the chiefs had found in their sandalwood forests a product for which the white traders would mortgage their souls, and the gaunt commoner was hounded into the hills to cut, strip and haul the fragrant timber.

Eventually the trade became a monopoly, the chiefs supplying only to Kamehameha, and the white men being able to buy only through him:

> He adorned his palaces, crammed his storehouses, glutted his treasury with bright Spanish dollars and filled his harbors with foreign-built vessels.

This is only the economic part of the process. It does not touch such matters as the prostitution, which the missionaries ran into every time a ship came into port, and was a well-established pattern when they arrived. A glance back over those descriptions will suffice to note that many of the basic features of the social structure were breaking down—farmers and fishermen were being exploited by the chiefs beyond their normal authority; rum and wine was leading to brawling and rioting and destroying social relations and work programs, gambling was introducing an undesirable value, Western clothing was acquired as a status symbol, arms and ammunition in the hands of one chief gave him a paramountcy that he would not have otherwise achieved, and this led to a trade monopoly. The islands were slowly denuded of their great sandalwood forests, commoners were enslaved to carry on the trade, island generosity gave way to bargaining for profit and extortion; and beachcombing whites, for whom there was no "slot" in the social system, became permanent figures in the scene.

All these evidences of demoralization can be well documented. I can do this myself from primary sources. This is what the missionaries found when they arrived—as Michener must have known quite well. Any one of these points can be treated at length. The popular myth has it, for example, that the missionary forced the people to wear clothes. I think I could find twenty or more references to show this predated their arrival. The chief Kalanimoku met the missionary party on its arrival in a "white dimity jacket, black silk vest, nankeen pantaloons, white cotton stockings, shoes, a plaid cravat and a top hat"; he was the "prime minister" and this was his status symbol. No missionary could have persuaded the proud chief to wear these things. It was his own idea. This demoralization was an increasing condition over the years between Cook's visit and the arrival of the missionaries.

More and more it must have become apparent to both the king and his chief priest that their religious system just did not have the resources to hold the society together. Many of the real Hawaiian social values had been thrown to the wind. The country was torn by wars, administered by white men. The new class of white trader had no place in the system. White visitors did not distinguish between a prostitute and a taboo woman. Nor do we wonder that both the king and his chief priest were ready to give up the religious system. It had long become an anachronism. The first intelligence the missionary party received, before ever setting foot on Hawaii was (and I quote from a Hawaiian letter of 1820):

> Tamahamaha is dead. The taboos are broken. The idols are burnt. The Moreeahs are destroyed and the priesthood abolished.

And this is witnessed by five signatures: Bingham, Chamberlain, Whitney, Ruggles and Loomis. Nor is this the only account of this historic event. In the missionary journal we find the taboo reference explained in these terms: "the men are all Inoahs, that is, they eat with the women" and that this is so "in all the islands"—showing the scope of the movement and its general diffusion. The journal expresses fear on account of the general instability and the new king's lack of sobriety. It speaks of his indifference to religion as being longstanding, about his relationships with the whites, and his readiness to improve his learning. I have also seen the text of another contemporary letter on this subject, written by a sailor. The event took place in 1819. The taboos were broken by the king himself. The torch was set to the sacred paraphernalia and the shrines were despoiled by the highest priest, Hewahewa. The place immediately broke out into civil war, the religious iconoclasm being used as an excuse for political aspiration, but traditionalist-rebels went down before the iconoclast-king's forces. It was all over before the missionaries arrived. Nothing had yet replaced the old taboos. It was a country without law and order—except the arm of a drunken king and an economic exploiter (H.M.C.S. 1967:2). The person who looks the silliest over all this is James Michener, who supposedly did five years work on his novel, and who has the demoralization as the result of missionary activity.

The reenactment of the arrival of the first missionaries was presented as a feature of the Sesquicentenary Celebrations in Honolulu. I was happy to witness the event and to hear an Hawaiian, who knows his Hawaiian history, speak on the theme "Why I Am Glad They Came." He began by reminding the audience that the Hawaiians had rejected their religious system and their gods before the missionaries came and they were in a perilous social situation. He said:

> When a people loses the foundations by which they determine what is right and wrong, just and unjust, they are on their death bed and ready to die. Unless there comes a new way, they cannot live. The missionaries brought that new foundation.

That is word for word as Abraham Akaka put it. Anthropologically it was worth the trip to Hawaii to hear an Hawaiian say that. It shows first, the function of religion in society, and second, the vulnerability of a society whose religion does not fulfill its true function of holding together the society itself and its moral system, and third, he knew that the Hawaiians were demoralized and ready to die in 1820.

Michner's novel *Hawaii* (1959), which claims to be "true to the spirit and history of Hawaii" and the film based on it, distort both the spirit and history of Hawaii by picturing the demoralization as due to the missionary effort, and this effort being a failure as far as conversion is concerned. This is not good enough for an "historical" novel. In point of fact, the conversion movement was both extensive and effective; and far from demoralization, much of Hawaiian life was revitalized because of the missionary presence. What has been saved, not what has been lost of Hawaiian society, is largely due to the missionaries. With all its Christian shortcomings, the religion of the Puritan missionaries (a 19th century movement, not 17th or 18th) to some real extent replaced religion in the center of Hawaiian life; and if it did not link up with all the cultural configurations with fully adequate relationships, it did with many of them. It also created some new configurations like education and publishing, which were adequate for the new day and helped to bring some of the disturbing features of culture contact under control. Thus a new steady state was produced which enabled the society to survive. The number of missionaries who were released to go into government service—education, medicine, legislature and so forth—demonstrates the close relationships between religion and the social structure and the existence of a new steady state.

The basic model for a state of demoralization can be seen in Figure 12.

FIGURE 12
Demoralization

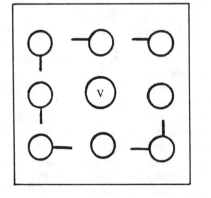

V = Void

The model for the new steady state in Hawaii after the missionary evangelization was complete would probably work out as follows in Figure 13, allowing for the fact that all cultural connections were not established:

FIGURE 13
The Place of Religion in Hawaii After the Missionaries

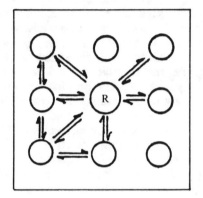

R = Religion

SUBMERSION

In passing to *submersion,* the second type of religious change, once again we are confronted by a change that is brought about by external pressures. Both demoralization and submersion are more or less unwilling responses to imposed conditions. They are acceptances, not by approval or acquiescence. but by despair in the face of the inevitable. The common causes of submersion are *military conquest, economic sanctions* and *legislation.*

Although I am mainly concerned with changes in animism, I should point out that any religion can be submerged in this way, even one of the great religions. In many places in Europe Protestantism was so submerged under the oppression of the inquisition.

We like to think that when people change from animism to Christianity it has been a voluntary and an acceptable decision, but we know that it has not always been so. My history book tells me that Olaf Tryggveson and his fleet put in at the island of Rolandsa and found that the pagan earl had only one fighting ship. Olaf told him of the benefits of becoming Christian. Before the might of the visitor's fleet and the option of baptism or execution, the pagan earl could hardly be called a voluntary convert, especially as the earl's son was taken away as a hostage against the stability of the baptism of the island of Rolandsa (Robinson 1917). The question of immediate concern to us here is: what kind of a Christianity emerges after this kind of religious change?

The religion with possibly the worst record of this kind is Islam, which overran northern Africa and wiped out what remained of early Christianity there. The symbol of the sword was written into their war cry. Many of their methods were most infuriating to the Christians, especially when they kidnapped Christian children and raised them as fanatical Moslem warriors to be turned against their own Christian flesh and blood.

But military action is not the only form of pressure that has been applied for purposes of securing religious change. Social pressures inside the country and economic sanctions have been used both to prevent secession from the one religion to another and to achieve conversion. This has been so within Christianity in the history of the sects. The geographer, P.W. English, has written a fine volume, which would qualify as history or anthropology as well as geography, *City and Village in Iran* (1966). In one place he demonstrates how social pressures and economic sanctions were deliberately used by the Moslems to achieve the conversion of the seventh century Zoroastrians (1966:23-24).

Another oppressive procedure for securing conversion is legislation. There was a period of English history, for example, when the fortunes of the country were fluctuating between Roman Catholicism and Protestantism, when the changing monarchs and their administrations had a strong disposition to one or the other form of Christianity; when the general public was virtually pushed one way or the other by the legislation. The result was that there never was a period of English history more riddled with intrigue. Always the submerged religion refused to die and plotted against the ruling faith. The internal and the international politics of the country were mere reflections of the religious forces at work, one trying to rule by legislation and the other trying to resist the legislation by intrigue. For England in the periods of the Tudors, the Commonwealth and the Stuarts we see the central place of religion in the society; but as there were two religions, one in control and the other submerged, there was no peace.

Now what, we may ask, has this to do with conversion from animism to Christianity, which is really the subject of this chapter? The story of Christian mission over the last century and this, whether we like it or not, has gone "hand in glove" with the march of colonialism, both the imperial and commercial forms. Frequently we must admit it was deliberately planned this way, the representatives of Government, Commerce and Church, operating together; for example, the Niger Experiment (Walker 1930:18). Once a colony was established, the impact of each of those three forces was increased many fold. Each of them in its own way bore down on the animistic faith of the inhabitants. The actual acceptance of the new faith—Christianity—was a voluntary matter, and economic pressures were little used in recent times to effect conversions. But a change from animism is a negative as well as a positive thing, an act of rejection or deprivation as well as the acceptance of a new way, and these do not necessarily have to take place at the same point of time. as we have seen in the case of the demoralization of Hawaii. Such things as cannibalism, widow strangling, infanticide, patricide, feuding, raiding and sorcery (to name only a few of the customs in mind) have all religious significance. To administrator, trader and missionary alike, these were undesirable and disruptive to his program. Each of these foreigners depended on the maintenance of what he called "law and order." What he meant was a kind of law and order which he called civilized. Actually all these customs operated under law and order, but few of the foreigners saw this. A state of law and order was achieved by legislation, and legislation was more concrete, it was written down, and we can now look back at it and study it historically.

Even in the most enlightened colonial administrations, where the claim of freedom of religion has been made, legislation has been disruptive to the aboriginal animism. Thus when cannibalism had to go, the acquisitions of religious power for facing danger, producing fertility and curing sickness were seriously interfered with; when widow strangling had to go, the beliefs and provisions for life beyond the grave were all disturbed; when patricide had to go, the continued physical presence of the senile elder interfered with the social rights and controls of the active elder in public life; when feuding had to go, a mechanism of leadership selection was lost to the tribe; when headhunting had to go, much of the philosophy of *mana* had to go with it; and when sorcery had to go, society was left with scores of moral and religious problems for which the people had no means of solving. When the system of taboo was legislated against, hygiene declined and body waste was left lying about the villages. All these religious disturbances can be documented without going outside Melanesia.

I know nothing so disruptive to animist religion and the social life, of which it is the integrator, equal to colonial legislation. The missionaries at least put something in place of the religion they took away, even if it was so often, alas, a foreign substitute. But legislation was an end in itself. It was a negative approach to life. It needed a gospel to give a positive dimension.

Quite apart from the negative aspect of colonial legislation against animist institutions, it is appalling for the abysmal ignorance it displays of what it legislates against. Nothing shows this up better than the laws of the African colonies against witchcraft. One would surely assume that such a legislator would at least need to know the difference between a witch, a witch doctor and a witch finder, seeing the legislation will need to deal with them all; and their measure of social guilt or misfortune is certainly not equal. These countries have now their independence and I do not know whether the national legislators have modified these laws or not, but writing in 1958, Parrinder in his book on *Witchcraft* discussed the Laws and Ordinances of Nigeria, Tanganyika, Uganda and Kenya in an illuminating passage (1958:126-127). A law stating that "any person who represents himself to be a witch . . . ." is a foreign and not an African notion. Normally the witch does not profess to be such except under accusation and pressure from the witch finders. No one is a witch by choice. The social penalties are too great. A law which punishes the individual who seeks to preserve society from witchcraft, mistaking him for a sorcerer, is surely to punish the innocent with the guilty. A law covering everything by means of a blanket phrase "occult power and knowledge" is inadequate for definition and dangerous in its scope, open for abuse. The same may be said of a Kenya Ordinance (1928) which covered any person claiming "to exercise supernatural power." A pentecostal type of priest or prophet in any harmless movement or a Christian church could be charged under such a law.

Witchcraft is only one of the many religious problems which have been brought under colonial legislation without a clear understanding of their nature and function; but it is a good example of *foreign imposition*. It also shows how legislation about witchcraft, without any clear understanding of what the institution is and how it operates, can undermine the religious configuration which is the integrator of the society, in spite of the Colony's boast of freedom of religion.

If the place became a Colony by military conquest, and this was followed immediately by foreign land settlement, the establishment of schools and medical services, the establishment of plantations and the codification of laws (quite apart from the presence or otherwise of a Christian mission), the chances of the survival of the original animism would be remote. Several things could happen. There might be a general demoralization and the people might even die out altogether. The people might modify their animism and settle down to an unhealthy coexistence with the foreigners. Or the people might elect to accept Christianity in a nominal fashion and try to fall into step with the foreigners—and this might be for any of a number of motives. They might consider it politic or prestigious to accept the religion of the foreigner because he is the conqueror, or because he is wealthy or because he has so many amazing things. These are nominal Christians at best. I am not speaking here of genuine conversion movements, with which I will deal under the next heading, and which are classed by themselves because they have an inner dynamic, a self-image and a healthy creativity in spite of the colonial situation.

The nominal Christians and also the modified animist coexisters whose religious change is due in some way to imposed foreign controls, commerce, instruction and legislation, because their *manifest* religion is formal and "a thing of convenience," will frequently have also a *latent* religion. It will be this latent religion that speaks to their deepest feelings. In this, one will discover significant elements of the old animism, or at least what the believer thinks his or her old animism was (because this can recur in a later generation which is not clear about the old religious beliefs and rites). It may be an individual retires surreptitiously to the forest and explores the past. It may be a whole village breaks away openly under some native prophet who claims to have a revelation from the past and to have recovered what the people have lost by accepting the foreign religion.

The old religion used to hold their life together. Now there is a void and the foreigner rules the land. If the current religion is nominal, formal, not dynamic, you can be quite sure that some animism is latent. The term I use for this is *submersion*. It does not require much to fan this coal into fire. Normally submerged animism is not organized. It is scattered about in hidden places; but if there are enough of these coals smoldering away, it only takes a single prophet to arise and the organization can emerge with startling rapidity. This kind of outburst has been a feature of the post-war situation in many parts of the world. It would be appropriate at this point, if I had the space, to discuss a nativistic movement out of a second or third generation Christian community, but I refer the reader to *Solomon Islands Christianity* (1967a), where this is dealt with at length. It must suffice here to modify my model to illustrate submersion, as seen in Figure 14.

FIGURE 14
Relationship Between Religious Void and Submerged Animism

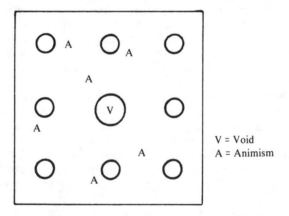

V = Void
A = Animism

There are degrees of submersion of animism in nominal Christianity. It may be deep, or it may be very shallow—just beneath the Christian veneer. Evangelicals are disposed to speak of this as *syncretism* or as *Christopaganism*. Syncretism may be quite manifest, of course, but on investigation one is shocked at the amount of submerged animism which is found.

It is submerged because it is driven underground by military conquest, land alienation, economic pressures and legislation; all of which frequently suggest to the indigene that the foreigners lack sympathy. It is possible for years to become centuries, and for that submerged animism to go on building itself stronger and stronger into the substructure of the nominal Christianity.

For years I used to wonder if an evangelical mission could be regarded as justifiable in a community where the people were already Christian—as in a Spanish colonial location which was strongly Catholic. It was not until I eventually did some research in Mexico and found so much manifest animism that I could hardly recognize the Church as Christian at all. I saw devotees (whose devotion I do not doubt) crossing a cement plaza on their knees to a shrine more Aztec than Christian, while others put paper or cloth under their bloodstained knees to get it charged with power for magical or healing purposes;, vendors selling magical herbs whose efficacy came from the blessing of the saints rather than any medicinal property, and this on the steps of the church; worshippers carrying shrines of straw and corn in some way after the manner of an old fertility cult; and a stream of persons one by one kissing away the toe of a stone statue to obtain thereby blessing on their lives and household; and all this was done in the name of Christianity.

This I saw in Mexico, and I knew that any evangelical mission to these persons was without doubt a mission to animists. I saw much the same thing in a rural city in Guatemala. I was speaking about these things to a gathering of Mayan pastors in Guatemala and described a Mexican situation without naming the place. My Mayan friends said they recognized the place from my description, but I had never been to the place they thought it was, so I am led to think it typical.

Such is the nominality of the Christianity that has come in the train of the Spanish military conquest: a Christianity which merely drove the animism underground. I saw a group of Mayan converts in a Guatemalan village. They registered their public confession by surrendering their wooden crosses to the evangelist. In conversation afterwards I discovered that they were Mayan, not Christian crosses. From the way they viewed and used those symbols I knew they were fetishes—nothing else, however much they appeared to be Catholic and Christian. Other fetishes included a root which seemed to have a face and an ancient pre-Catholic Mayan figurine. Supposedly this was Catholic Christian; in reality it was submerged animism.

Take, for example, that amazing autobiographical story of *Juan the Chamula* (1962) which the translator anthropologist, himself a Mexican, insists is the story of a typical person. Here then is a typical Mexican Indian Catholic, emotional and crude in many ways, yet deeply religious, always attending to his "Christian" duties. I read through this book and marked the religious features. The veneer of Christianity of the Catholic type featured the Virgin and the continual patronage of the saints, the use of the symbol of the cross (as much Mayan as Christian), adoration of and making vows at the cross, and the trinitarian formula. These are the features of Catholicism open for animisation. In reality the saints are Mayan deities with Christian names. Many features are quite syncretistic— the ritual and beliefs of the Cult of Saint John, the role of the Savior, the festival performances and processions, a large corpus of mythology, ideas about disease and healing—and although Christian strands of thought can be detected here and there, they are dominantly animistic. On the other hand, many features of the religious life of this man are completely animist: the attitude to the spirits of the dead, the worship of the sun, the communion with the ancestors, the burial ritual and its religious pre- suppositions, the association of spirit animals with the sickness and health of human beings,the magic of curing the spilling of libations of liquor, the function of charms, sacred objects and taboos and the means of diagnosis or divination.

> A man is sick because his spirit animal in the forest is sick. A curer is brought, and candles, resin, liquor, a rooster and flowers for the curing rite. The curer pours an oblation on the ground and drinks the rest of the liquor. The flowers are put on the altar. After the oblation the curer prays to the Christian God and the Son, the Earth and the Heaven, offers the gifts brought by the sick man, with incense, and prays to the spirit of the Moon and the Earth Mother, and while praying wrings the neck of the rooster. At the moment of this sacrifice the sick man suddenly feels free (cf. 88-91).

The old animism has gone, along with its organized priesthood and its pre- Christian structure. Once the Spanish swept over the land it could never be the same again. The Spanish brought their Christian organization with them and the people nominally accepted the new religion. But at heart they were still animist, and, inasmuch as I have myself observed and read, they still are: a case of submersion.

CONVERSION

When I speak of the third type of religious change as *conversion* I should remind the reader that we are discussing change from an original animistic state in communal society. We are dealing with change that affects social groups, so that a large body of people as an entity fits the description. I am not speaking of one-by-one conversion such as we are familiar with in Western individualistic society. I am speaking of what we call a *people movement* in church growth theory. I have discussed the nature of this process in a long essay in *People Movements of Southern Polynesia* (1971) and McGavran has a chapter in *Understanding Church Growth* (1970). The phrase was suggested to avoid the stigma of the term, *mass movement,* which was so misleading.

In communal society people make their decisions and act on them in group patterns. Psychologically this is good. It maintains the solidarity of the group and if the group is not unanimous the step of change is not taken. This has obvious advantages over the Western "civilized" system where the public action is determined by the majority vote, and the minority is so often left without any rights at all. Most of the schisms in the Western Church and cleavages in the country are due to this inequity. Because of this characteristic of communal life—action on unanimity—when people change from the old religion the new substitute should be able to take over as the integrator of the society as was the role of its predecessor. This is why a church that grows from a people movement can be largely indigenous from the start, whereas a mission church planted by one-by-one conversions may still be a dependent mission congregation with maybe no more than a hundred adherents after a hundred years.

Another reason for the rejection of the term "mass movement" was the impression that individuals are completely submerged in the primitive mass and have no scope for individualism and initiative or for making a personal commitment to Christ. No one who has ever lived in the milieu of communal activity could accept such an erroneous idea. We are dealing with groups of people, every individual having a precise role and knowing his or her relationship to every other person, with their approved ways of sharing, discussing, and deciding what ought to be done in a given situation or even in an unstructured stimulus field. Although the group as a whole has its group values, there is nevertheless considerable individual variability within the group as long as individual values and initiative do not ignore the group values. Although I am indebted to Homer Barnett for being made aware of the multi-individual character of the communal group, I know it had been written into anthropological theory before this. For instance, Lowie (1952), in dealing with primitive religion spoke of individual variability within the social group:

> The individual is not merged completely into his social milieu—he reacts to it as an individual, that is, differently from every other group member. The cultural tradition of his people dominates him, but it is reflected in a distinctive fashion by each psyche (221).

He goes on to argue that we cannot study individual responses apart from the cultural milieu, and that it is not until there has been individual exposure to common cultural norms that the individual responses have any meaning (224). Thus the member of the communal group has much to teach the Western individualist about decision making; namely, that decisions are not made by individuals for their own sake alone, or in spite of their neighbor, but rather for their own and their neighbor's sake. They ask themselves: what does my decision mean for my neighbor? This question seldom occurs to a Western individualist.

Radin, also in his *Primitive Man as a Philosopher*, (1927) rejects the idea of the social group in terms of an impersonal mass. He sees the group as a "medley of contacts" and the "impingement of personality on personality" (38). He resists the assumption that the group activities of "primitive" mankind can be seen as an "automaton incapable of self-realization" and he is critical of the idea of "the tyranny of the group" (41) as held by some Westerners. He shows that the tendency for group action is not tyranny but deliberate individual choice, in which the individual realizes his dependence on the group and vice versa: "each man's tacit assessment of himself." Consciously and unconsciously each individual strives for "the psychic unity of the group" and resists anything that would destroy this. And if anything does destroy it there is the feeling that their "personal worth and personal dignity has been outraged" (51). Radin devotes a whole chapter in this book to "primitive" mankind's "Freedom of Thought," and this is not just theoretical. His data is drawn from the field of mythology, which he analyses from the point of view of interpretation.

In church growth writing, Pickett, McGavran and myself began in the field situations we knew, struggling with the phenomena of these group movements out of animism and into Christianity, and without any theoretical framework on which to build. We each used the commonly accepted term—mass movement. Yet for each of us our early and more recent work can be recognized by our rejection of that term in favor of *people movement* or *group movement*.

In a fairly long monograph on the conversion movements of Fiji (Tippett, 1954) based entirely on primary sources, many of them from records in Fijian, I have set out the series of group discussions which led up to the conversion of Ratu Cakobau and his family. Here we see that these discussions occupied a number of distinct groups; religious, social, kin, and national and went on for several days. Points were referred to the missionary for clarification. Objections were raised, discussed and dismissed. Possible consequences of group decision were examined. Here we have Radin's "medley of contacts" and his "impingement of personality on personality." Thus the force of the data drove us away from the idea of *mass* movement. We were dealing with *groups* of *people*.

Obviously, if a large social group is to change from its old religion to a new one, the question of precisely when a change is possible is important. The study of culture change in social anthropology reveals that societies do reach points of time propitious for major change. Major changes are difficult unless a society is ripe for it. Kroeber (1948) has shown how the discoveries of Mendel were not acceptable because society was not ready for them. Some decades later three scientists almost simultaneously came to the same conclusions, but now society was ready to make use of them. Likewise the Gospel, which is always true, nevertheless can be rejected because the time is not ripe. Our Lord was known to say "My hour has not yet come." The Scriptures allow for the place of the psychological moment, even for God's action in history: "when the fullness of time was come God sent forth his son . . . ." The development of the theory of the people movement in conversion from animism to Christianity has permitted us to pinpoint an extremely important fact: that societies move towards "their hour" or towards their "fullness of time." This is due to a combination of factors—historical, social, psychological and spiritual. It would seem that God brings social groups to these points of crisis when they are ripe for decision. As He brings the fruit of the orchard to ripeness by a multitude of forces which He himself has initiated, He says to the orchardist: Your harvest is ready, gather it in. And the orchardist knows that if it is not gathered at that precise point of time, the fruit will fall or rot on the trees and another cycle of the seasons will have to pass by before the crop ripens unto harvest again. Anthropology shows that societies are like that too. The right time comes for major change. But it is always possible for the opportunity for innovation to be lost. This truth has been stated and restated in church growth writing, but mission boards and missionaries never fully learn the lesson of the importance of sending harvesters into the *harvest*.

As a result, the harvest is often gathered in by others. The Christian "harvesters" are in the unripe fields and the harvests are left either to rot or to be gathered by non-Christian groups: Hinduism, Islam, Buddhism, Communism—they are all missionary organizations.

They have handed me tracts in the streets of Honolulu and of Hollywood: Hindus and Buddhists. In Japan, Soka Gokhai has grown by means of Christian evangelistic techniques. Over thirty years ago now, we had to be told by a secular anthropologist that:

> Buddhism, may function as the psychological equivalent of Christianity, or any other of the faiths of Western Civilization (Lowie 1952:xv).

And again, Socialism could be studied as "a phenomenon of social psychology" (343), which makes it a potential rival to Christianity as something that can be advocated for acceptance at any time when the mood of a people is ripe for innovation, as Barnett would put it. The basic harvest theology of church growth writing has to be seen against this anthropological and psychological "backdrop."

There is also a phenomenological or experiential way of looking at a people movement from animism to Christianity. In this chapter I am contrasting types of religious change, thus to set conversion over against demoralization and submersion I shall need to pinpoint how it differs from them as a religious experience. The model for such a society, as seen in Figure 15, is identical with that with which we began, because this is a new steady state with Christianity in the place of the old religion as integrator of the whole. This is an ideal, of course, but it is far more than a mere theoretical abstraction.

FIGURE 15
The Place of Christianity in Society

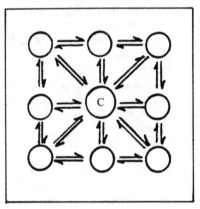

C = Christianity

REVITALIZATION

The term *revitalization* in movements of religious change has been borrowed from Wallace (1956). Although I certainly do not accept all of Wallace's ideas on religion, I consider him one of the most important theorists in the area of religious change today. In his more recent work (1966), in which he works out a number of significant religious typologies, he develops a number of forms of revitalization movement. Many of his basic ideas have been taken over in church growth writing, in the areas we know as *qualitative* and *organic growth*. This means that the concept has been used, not for movements of change from animism (conversion), but for subsequent movements in the second, third or later generations of Christian history. Thus revitalization movements are group responses of renewal when the Church has "run down" somewhat.

Several aspects of Wallace's revitalization theory have related to church growth theory in those areas which McGavran has opened up but not developed in his writing (1955:13-16)—the second of his "'Stages in Christianization" which he calls "Perfecting the People." McGavran himself has mainly used the term *perfecting* for the follow-up of *discipling*; that is, for such things as post-baptismal care after conversion, and applying it to that same generation (1970: 325-329). Even so, his initial statement declared that holy living, social, racial and political justice were all part of the perfection growth and that both the discipling and perfecting processes should go on generation after generation (1955:15). Most of what he has written of the subsequent generations has come under the rubric of "biological growth" of the Church, and this is mostly found in his case studies. He regards it as important but has said little about it. The theoretical dimensions of *qualitative and organic* church growth, in addition to the *quantitative,* and the need for these to be in a state of *equilibrium* and to be *continuous* through the generations, has been developed by his colleagues (Tippett 1966; 1967a:29-32, 347; 1970a; 1973a:126-128; Winter 1969:339) and his students. In 1966 the idea of the continuity of harvests was introduced into church growth theology and several sections in *Church Growth and the Word of God* (1970a) are devoted to different aspects of continuity.

In church growth theory the Church goes on until He comes again and thus it becomes imperative to examine the growing of the Church in each successive generation. As every graph of growth indicates, churches run into periods of decline, variously known as *fatigue, entropy* or *anomie.* There is need for reformation, revival, renewal or revitalization, that a church which has become static and is about to die may begin to grow again. At this point Wallace's revitalization theory has been useful in helping us to describe and understand the processes involved.

In a nutshell, Wallace has explained things like this. We begin with a steady state, a period of moving equilibrium. In the course of time this is disturbed by increased individual stress that eventually becomes a period of real cultural distortion, a general stress situation for the whole communal group—the entropy or anomie. I have seen many second and third generation churches in this condition. When a whole society is like this, it is ready to die. Most revitalization movements have produced a prophetic type of person who has been able to meet the need and gain popular support. Wallace has worked out the stages of this process— *formulation of a code, communication, organization, adaptation, cultural transformation* and *routinization* (1956; 1966:159-163). This is the process required to save the church (or society) from disintegrating, splitting up, or being absorbed by some other group. It restores the church (or group) to a new steady state of moving equilibrium. The routinization was the phase which shifted the movement's function from *innovation* to *maintenance.*

This has provided us with a number of theoretical reference points. First, we are dealing with a *communal stress situation,* which must be resolved lest the group split or die. Second, the revitalization movement is consciously *organized from within the group itself.* This permits us to distinguish between a revival and a revitalization movement.

> It may well be that a Church or congregation is dying and needs renewal. That need may be spiritual or organic. The cure for the former is *revival*; the cure for the latter is *revitalization.* Revival is something that comes from without; it is the work of the Holy Spirit and may come unexpectedly. . . . But revitalization is a renewal of the structure. It comes out of the crisis situation when the members of the society endeavor to deal with the crisis. It comes from within. It is a human program which can be observed, tested and measured. . . . Revival links up with divine resources, and revitalization restores organic structures by better techniques and methods of operation (Tippett, 1970a:67-68).

The structures need not necessarily be physical. They may be doctrinal, moral or social, as for example the crises facing the seven churches of Asia in the Revelation. God did not promise to *revive* their churches. He called on them to *overcome,* to revitalize by communal congregational effort. The word "overcome" recurs seven times in two chapters.

One of the best examples of revitalization in the New Testament is mentioned in Acts 6. The service life of the Church was growing more complex. Its physical structure was inadequate. A stress situation developed around the priorities of proclamation and service and the debate had a racial aspect. The whole group met together and faced the crisis realistically by creating a new functional role and allowing for the racial dimension. If Acts 2 is a revival experience, Acts 6 is revitalization.

In Acts 6 the people in a state of crisis are restored to normality and as a result the Christian community multiplies. This is one of the many types of salvation experience in Scripture—the group relief from tension.

Wallace has said that "the essential theme of the religious event is the dialect of disorganization and organization. ... This dialectic, "the struggle" ... between entropy and organization is what religion is all about. ... Religion ... offers a solution that assures the believer that life and organization will win, that death and disorganization will lose ..." (1966:38).

One of the key words of church growth theology is responsibility (see Tippett 1970a:index). It does not accept the presupposition that Christians in mission have merely to be Christians where they are, to do their "thing" obediently and leave everything to God, who will determine the results as He wills. Although it certainly presupposes that Christians work under the sovereignty of God, God has made them His agents, servants, stewards, and these are responsible offices. As each Christian is responsible, the same may be said of the collective group. The fellowship of believers is responsible. This responsibility is not confined to the ministry of mission. It is responsible under God to so order its communal life that disorganization gives way to organization, discord to peace, death to life. The research project which I did in the Solomon Islands kept saying to me over and over again that the weak spot was at the level of the village congregation. The battle was clearly being won or lost there. The demand was revitalization (Tippett 1967a:348, 350, 352), and revitalization on the level of belief as much as structure. I felt the people had forgotten that the Christian experience itself needs to be *continuous*; that each new generation needs to come in crisis to Christ afresh collectively (1973a:10).

In the Scriptures the idea of renewal by revitalization is not confined to the New Testament. It is a biblical concept. God was continually renewing His people. I have devoted a chapter to this idea in the Old Testament in *Verdict Theology in Missionary Theory,* where I call it "the inward dimension of mission." The story of Israel turning back to God as a result of the contest between the prophets of Baal and Elijah in I Kings 18 was "a revitalization based on a right decision in an existential situation at a precise point of time." The prophet at the right point of time is a regular feature of revitalization movements. Part of the mission of God through history has been to revitalize His people through the agency of the Wycliffes, the Wesleys, the Whitfields, and many others in the midst of their real life situation, "that no generation be satisfied to live on the experience of its fathers. The method of the mission of God has continually called men to decision within the group itself" (1973a:14-15).

In this study I have been dealing with group movements in societies with an animist background, and I have chosen to describe the group responses to a prophet or evangelist, whereby a young Church is renewed and the loss of vitality is restored as a "revitalization movement," following Wallace. Of course, not all revitalization movements are Christian. Some even move away from Christianity. The distinguishing features are (1) they come from within the group, (2) they alleviate the stress situation (perhaps by restructuring) and (3) they restore society to a steady state of moving equilibrium. The new steady state has something new in it—maybe a reform, or the modification of older and outworn forms, or a new element of worship, or a new program, or that the felt needs of the group are met in a more satisfactory manner. The revitalization movement could be a renewal of Christianity, or a cession to Islam, or Communism, or a return to some kind of Neopaganism, if this acceptance relieved the tension of the crisis and was initiated from within the group and was not imposed from without. The fact that a revitalization movement could be either towards or away from Christianity reminds us of the grim truth that Christianity is not the only advocate for innovative acceptance today. We are also reminded that unless the religion which is accepted (and Communism may be classed as a religion at the negative pole for our purpose here) becomes the *integrator of the society* (after the model) it is not likely to be steady for any length of time. Religion has to *relate to culture* and not leave a *cultural void* by being separated from the integrating parts.

We are not to suppose that this breakdown of group movements under the heads of *demoralization, submersion, conversion* (people movements) and *revitalization* is all that there is to say on this matter. This is a theoretical essay and these four classifications have been presented mainly as a grid for the data that permits a discussion of the idea of religion as the integrator of society, and the consequences of interference with the relationships of religion and the other configurations in the culture pattern. This, as we have seen, gives rise to a cultural void over a period of time. Some writers have called this a cultural vacuum. It has also been described as "a loss of interest in life," and as *anomie*. It is the psychological factor which leads to population decline and extinction under acculturation and it is due to a large extent to the displacement of religion as the social integrator. I mean religion—not the old religion. The old religion may be displaced, but it has to be replaced by a functional substitute that a steady state of moving social equilibrium be preserved.

CHAPTER 15

The Functional Substitute in Church Planting

THEORETICAL PREAMBLE

The "Functional Theory of Culture," as put forward by Malinowski in *The Dynamics of Cultural Change* (1945), argues (among other things) that a society organizes "the whole body of implements, the charters of its social groups, human ideas, beliefs and customs" in such a way as to permit an individual "to cope with the concrete, specific problems which face him in his adaptation to his environment in the course of the satisfaction of his needs" (42). Within the complex configuration of the total society will be found a number of subordinate configurations. Malinowski calls them the *integral institutions* of a tribe and discusses their complicated character. He points out that "an institution like the family or chieftainship, ancestor worship or agriculture, has its roots in all aspects of culture" (52). To change any of these institutions, therefore, has serious ramifications on every aspect of social life. Nevertheless, under certain circumstances a society may engage in major structural social change without chaos, or even losing its cohesion or entity, if these functional networks are not overlooked. "One kind of institution," he says with caution, "can be replaced by another, *which fills a similar function*" (52, emphasis mine). This is a complex process. Changing the chieftaincy, for example, would also involve changes in law, authority patterns, family life and religion, and these changes would need to be synchronized. They would have to be substitutions which met the needs of the total group and gave group satisfactions.

A comprehensive institution endures because it is organically connected and satisfies an essential need of society. It can be suppressed, but it is then driven underground. It can be mutilated, deprived of this or that aspect or

183

prerogative, but it disappears only with the destruction of the whole cultural identity of a people. Either this, or else it can be replaced by a more adequate institution, fulfilling the same function, satisfying the same needs. . . (53).

And again:

While change is possible, in order for it to be satisfactory, permanent and real, it must be complete, in the sense that an equilibrium is again restored among all the institutions which together constitute the culture (54).

To pass from Malinowski's functional adaptations to the theory of *innovation*—the dynamics of social change (Barnett 1953), we are reminded that these functional substitutes have to be *accepted*. They may be perfectly adequate alternatives to the advocate, but they are not effective until accepted by the social group (in this chapter—converts to Christianity), and even if accepted a completely different meaning may be attributed to them by the acceptors. There is always a possibility of rejection. Missionaries speak of resistant and responsive fields. Acceptor groups are those who feel the innovation is an adequate, functional substitute which meets the existing wants or felt needs better than the institution it is proposed to discard (Barnett 1940, 1953).

Herskovits (1951) speaks of the acceptance of *functional eguivalents,* by means of which *older functions* are retained with *new forms.* To this I should add that a functional substitute may be an *old form* with a *new value;* it frequently is with the conversion to Christianity. Herskovits also refers to "the corollary that when no functional equivalence can be achieved" the imposition of new ways by the donor society "leads to demoralization of the recipient group." To this I should add that if the supposed target group is strong, it may simply react by rejecting the substitute altogether.

Malinowski (1945) pointed out:

. . . the piecemeal attack on pregnancy taboos, on occasional sexual excesses, and on certain marriage customs in some tribes by missionaries, who have been unable to relate these rites to the fundamental institutions of family and marriage, has been, in my opinion, the main cause of the failure of Christian endeavor in raising permanently the moral standards of the African in those communities (41-42).

Malinowski is not criticising the missionaries for making changes. He realizes that change is inevitable and expects the missionary "to be true to his vocation"; but he is critical of attacks on cultural institutions which give no consideration to basic functions of the institutions.

Luzbetak (1963) has pointed out that, in his experience, substitutions may be *complete* or *partial,* and attributes the partial displacement to "the fact that innovations, as a rule, are unable to fill all the functions of the corresponding traditional pattern."

Nida (1962) suggested that functional substitutes attempted by missionaries have been "almost wholly unsuccessful" because of the "highly integrated character" of the non-Christian rites to be modified, because the changes have been imposed from outside, and because they have not aimed at solving the basic psychological needs. Certainly, any of these reasons may defeat the purposes of the advocate of change, but it is quite wrong to say the missionary functional substitutes have been almost wholly unsuccessful. On the contrary, in this chapter, my data will be drawn from successful cases from my own experience.

With respect to my own additions to this body of theory, I wish to stress a few points. First, missionaries, even though in one sense they are truly agents of change, are not really the innovators. We should not bypass the truth that the convert is the acceptor, and that unless he or she is, then the innovator or substitute will not be permanent. Second, most functional substitutes which I know to have failed, have only been tried years after the eradication of the original institution, when a quasi-Christianized generation has arisen with another set of values—partly Western and only slightly indigenous. Sure, a functional substitute is difficult to apply when a later generation of missionaries repents at the loss of cultural heritage. On the other hand, when good functional substitutes have been proposed and accepted at the time of the primary religious change (conversion), "in my book" these have stood the test of time and have proved effective (Tippett 1963). Third, if conversion (like any other major social change) is to be accepted by a communal group, some adequate substitute or substitutes are essential, otherwise a cultural *void* of some kind will most certainly emerge due to the felt but unmet needs. These voids produce tensions which inevitably burst forth in some form of nativism (Tippett 1963, 1967a). Fourth, when conversions are individual (one by one Western type) functional substitutes are difficult to innovate because they are *social* mechanisms and they cannot be applied to the whole group when only a few individuals are Christian. When social groups become Christian as groups, by means of their own communal decision making patterns within the social structure, functional substitutes are frequent and effective. Fifth, in the process of incorporating converts into their new fellowship group or congregation, indigenous forms, rites, festivals and so forth, which can be given a new Christian value content, have greater likelihood of finding permanent acceptance than foreign forms and rituals (Tippett 1967b). Sixth, it may be pointed out in passing that people movements to Christianity (as also people movements out of Christianity, cf. Tippett 1967a) occur when social and religious conditions call for change; i.e., a *need for change* is felt. A time propitious for the change of religious belief is also a time propitious for making functional substitutes. The greater the time that lapses after the original conversion movement before the establishment of functional substitutes, the less likelihood they have of being permanent, and the more difficulty will be found in planting an indigenous church. The battle for an indigenous church (i.e., belonging to the people and to the culture) can be lost or won at this point. Finally, the concept of the functional substitute permits amazing diversity in application. A functional substitute may be a form, a ritual, a symbol, a role, an idea, a craft, an occupation, an artifact, an economic pattern, or it may even be the Christian religion itself under certain ideal circumstances.

The notion of functional substitutes is highly significant for all the so-called agents of change: missionaries, administrators, agriculturists, teachers, veterinarians, Peace Corps, health and medical workers and so forth. A great deal more research needs to be done on the subject, both in theory and in practice. This is true because the one who dares to change the culture patterns of other people is surely to be held responsible for what is done. Malinowski (1945) points out that the anthropologist must be concerned for changing because no primitive culture nowadays is in isolation but is always "in contact and in the process of change." He also insists that anthropologists have a moral obligation to interpret the Native. And the missionaries in their turn should learn from the anthropologists so that in the changes they feel bound to advocate they investigate first the functional integrity of the society and strive to retain the equilibrium that guarantees its perpetuity.

CLASSIFICATION AND DESCRIPTION OF FUNCTIONAL SUBSTITUTES

Culture change may be analyzed by arranging innovations according to a classificatory system structured on the basic configurations which, when brought together in interaction, comprise a given culture pattern. These may be described in the following manner:

1. The **Normative System,** including the social structure itself, its controls, authority, roles, legal apparatus and other features which preserve the organizational cohesion.

2. The **Enculturative System,** including the machinery for education, initiation, rites of passage and so forth.

3. The **Economic System,** including wealth, food supply, agriculture, trade exchange and so on; in other words, mechanisms for production, distribution and consumption.

4. The **Theological System,** comprises mythology, beliefs and religious practices: ritual, prayers, sacrifices, taboos and religious duty.

5. The **Technological System,** with its technical skills, arts and

crafts, industry, aesthetic expressions, music—both the prodution and use, technical paraphernalia and machinery and also the artifacts produced by a society for all purposes.

These *functional systems* are something like Malinowski's *instrumental imperatives* but I have avoided that term because his descriptors are not clearly enough delineated for my purposes. The reader must not suppose that a society or its culture pattern can really be fragmented into five parts in this way. This is merely an abstraction for the purposes of analysis and the classification of data.[1] It should not be assumed that these are water-tight compartments. For example, if I take a fine Maori greenstone club, or a *tiki,* normally I should classify this under the technological system as it is most naturally described as an artifact in terms of craftsmanship or art style. However, it is also a sacred object, created by a sacred person (*tohunga*), a member of a class who alone know the techniques, ritual and taboos associated with the craft. Thus it could be described in terms of the theological system as a religious exercise, or as normative as it relates to the role of a class of persons and the exercise of their unique responsibility and authority in the tribe.

The scheme of functional systems is therefore only a convenient device for the purposes of classification and description of (in this chapter) functional substitutes whereby Christianity has been made more or less indigenous by converts from animism. I believe that, by this means, I can demonstrate the value of the functional substitute for incorporating converts into the organized fellowship, which we may call the indigenous church. The functional substitute will preserve something of the pre-Christian tradition—probably the formal aspect, although it may be a value or an occasion—but it must be recognized as essentially Christian; otherwise we have syncretism and not a true functional substitute.

Let me cite a couple of examples. Wiant (1946) described a pre-Communist collection of Chinese hymns set to Chinese tunes. His article in the I.R.M. suggests a new perspective that was coming all too late in China.[2] These hymns concerned themes from the Chinese life pattern and several significant elements of Chinese life were given a Christian inter-pretation. These hymns were based on the idea that the indigenous music satisfied an emotional need felt by the people and would bring the Christian truth in a meaningful and appreciated form. Or the felt need may spring from an occasion. Thus a Bechuanaland missionary was approached by the chief of a newly converted group. They were about to plant their principal food crop—the first time they had done so since their conversion. They had never previously engaged in planting without some pagan ritual for the productivity and protection of the crop and the cultivating group. What did the new faith require at this point? The missionary had the insight to realize the consequences of his reply: did Christianity mean the secularization of agriculture or was it to be done in the name of the Christian God? He wisely judged that the visit of the tribal chief with this problem indicated a real felt need and so he prepared a Christian ritual to be memorized. Determining to give it a scriptural base, he found himself driven mostly to the Old Testament, which deals more with a people living close to the soil. The new Christian rite was addressed to God the Creator and Provider, the Lord of the harvests (Welch 1953). Pagan religious rites and festivals pinpoint occasions when felt needs are met and converts from this kind of society need to be built up in the new faith by making full use of the festival potential of the Christian year. Both forms of traditional music with Christian content and Christian planting rituals and prayers do preserve indigenous values. This is not syncretism because we cannot say they are "neither truly pagan nor truly Christian": they are Christian, whatever the form. This is indigenous Christianity achieved by means of functional substitutes.

When we study the functional substitute we are in the areas of both material and immaterial culture. Architecture, design, ornamentation and the physical arrangements of a Melanesian church building are quite material, but the structure rhythm and values of the oral chant heard inside the building are much less tangible. Yet both may be functional substitutes, by means of which the Christian religion becomes relevant in this Melanesian world. The question the missionary has to face and answer is: does Christianity have to be in Western forms to be accepted in a non-Western culture? This chapter says: No! If it is to be relevant in Melanesia, it must be Melanesian. Nothing demonstrates this better than a study of functional substitutes that have been, not just advocated, but accepted by the people. This does not mean that there is no place for white missionaries in an indigenous church system. As long as they have a precise role, accepted by the group and controlled by the group, and as long as they contribute to the group's functional cohesion, it is possible for foreigners to belong. In one of my books I show that a white trader or planter can be accepted by the people of Malaita as an essential part of the indigenous economic system without disrupting it; i.e., the system continues to operate an to meet the felt needs in spite of the changes in it (1967a:174).

I now purpose examining a body of data within the categories set out above in my functional systems. This material comes from mission fields and young churches I know personally and from my own researches and note books. This is mostly from Oceania, Fiji and the Solomons in particularly, but also Tonga, Samoa and a few cases from Ethiopia and the Navaho Indians.

The Normative System

At several points in *Solomon Islands Christianity* (1967a) and other writings I have discussed the high degree of natural capacity for pastoral leadership found among converted priests and magic-men. I believe that this is not merely due to the natural status and respect they have in the tribal community. A great many competent Fijian ministers, long after the disappearance of the native priesthood, have in point of fact come from *na bete* (the priestly segment of society). The Fijian Church, having emerged because of a fairly complete people movement, has accepted the Christian ministry, *per se,* as a straight functional substitute for the pre-Christian priestly leadership. Both conceptually and geographically the church as the religious configuration is set centrally in the life of the village. Religion is still, as Lowie put it (1963), the integrator of society. (For the geographical centrality see Tippett 1958:114; 1968a:163; Sahlins 1962:70 and my comment on the same 1968a:17).

The concept of *mediation* in Fijian life involves the traditional social roles of heralds, representatives, priests and prophets. These functions continue to the present day, although both Government and Church have created new positions, similarly structured, and have given them new titles. These are functional substitutes, by means of which the current business of administration and religion is carried on in the same old and meaningful patterns (Tippett 1958:107-117). Both the lay and clerical officers of the Fijian Church (*na mata turaga and nai talatala,* lay representatives and stewards at different levels and the ordained miisters) are the counterparts of the old *mata-ni-vanua* and *na bete,* heralds and priests. This network of officials is open for much extension of the counterparts as both the pre-Christian and the Christian patterns had many ramifications. The nearer these administrative and church counterparts are, formally and functionally, to the endemic officials the more effective they are in operation. All over the colonial world both Governments and Missions have run into the problem of selecting their agents (representatives, mediators and so forth) on a basis of education and acculturation, as against such tribal values as social status, seniority and maybe even birth. Many a new office has been created, with great potential because it could meet some felt need, only to be rejected by the people involved because it ignores the social values of the group.

In Samoa the head of the household (*matai*) was originally the domestic priest and leader of the family rituals. When the Christian Church emerged in that country the same character was found to be responsible for the Christian family devotions, and the whole pattern of the communal councils (*fono*) on various levels had become Christian. The Church just took over the system and likewise the authority values and controls. The writer has analyzed Samoan organized Christianity against the social structure in an essay, "Cultural Determinants and the Acceptance of Christianity" (Tippett 1971:137-170). Keesing, in *Modern Samoa* (1934:400) put it this way:

... the chiefs and orators merely rejected one set of interpretations and functions and took over the other without any vital blow being struck at the fundamentals of the existing order. The *tala aitu* [priestly class] was replaced by the white missionary and the *faife'au* [native Christian ministry], the old theology, by the new. The matai, from being the family mediator with the gods, became a deacon in the church and conducted the regular evening service, which has become an essential part of Samoan household life; his authority was bulwarked by Biblical injunctions—indeed from the first there could not have been much basic difference between the patriarchal system of the Old Testament and the *matai* organization.

The white missionaries to Samoa, having been what they were, would never have agreed to the appointment of church leaders who failed to demonstrate spiritual capacities. Those scholars who insist that the religious leaders of communal or tribal societies come from "the lunatic fringe" will find no supporting data from Oceania, where Christianity spread by people movements, and took over whole social structures. Converts established their churches on the normative models they knew. Many journalists and a few historians have criticized what they call "missionary laws," but my researches over many years with primary sources have shown these laws coming from indigenous Christian leaders. Normally they took the initiative, put forward the laws, discussed and ratified them. If they showed missionary influence it was not due to missionary imposition but was probably due to the new standards that came with the acceptance of the missionary's message. I know that in the case of Tahiti (probably the most criticized of the "missionary laws") the initiative was taken by the chief and the details of the council discussion are still preserved and I have read them.

The Enculturative System

Enculturation is the process within the social group or community, whereby the members pass through the life stages and become, say, adults, or married persons, or elders. It is the internal educational process. It includes what van Gennep called the "rites of passage" (1960). A society cannot survive without these institutions. When a Christian group, a fellowship, a congregation is planted, it must have some organic form and provide in its internal system for its members to pass through the recognized stages of growth to religious maturity.

Thus, for instance, the rite of baptism is frequently conceptualized by converts from animism in terms of a Christian rite of passage. It has the same features: it provides an educative program of preparation for the rite, it achieves a change of status in the group, it is a symbolic and ritual demonstration, it receives individuals into membership and gives them a sense of belonging, and so forth. Such similarities would seem to suggest that the nearer the forms of the Christian rite are to indigenous institutions, the more effectively the new Christian content (meaning) should be communicable. The same applies to the Sacrament of the Lord's Supper, say for the Western Dani of the Baleim Valley, for whom sweet potato has been substituted for bread. Such substitutions are easier when the rite concerned is an educative one.

Fijian Christians have a series of small domestic festivals along the life span of the growing boy and on into manhood. These bear on such things as birth, birthdays, circumcision, courtship, marriage, fatherhood and so forth. Some of these have no Christian origin and come down from ancient times and may be simply "so many days (four, ten or one hundred) after some event" the meaning of which is lost in antiquity. Yet they are observed as times when "it is good to come together and value the ties of the family." The Christian pastor or catechist will be there and they will have suitable prayers to God. The solidarity and perpetuity of the group is felt, and if they are following the life of a person they will pray for him or her. Thus the individual never stands alone. He or she is always "an individual within a group" which is why Christian baptism has frequently deeper meaning for Fijian than Western Christians. Here are indigenous values at a point of Western weakness. They do not deny the significance of the individual, but recognize that the individual needs a context of relationships to give his life meaning—maybe a family or fellowship, by whom acceptance is given.

Animist societies who have highly developed initiation rites are bound to expect much from Christian rites when they face conversion. As initiation ceremonies are intensely educative any failure to find adequate functional substitutes will probably leave an educational void in the Christian society. This is exactly what has happened on many mission fields. If the initiation rites of the animist society are phallic, the missionary has quite a problem on his hands, with a practical and a theological level. Invariably we discover that if no substitute is found, a community of Christians emerges without any sex education. The parents, the pastors and the Christian school all avoid it and leave it to the others (see Chapter 28, below). The theological problem lies in the fact that to the phallic animist this phallicism is his basic mechanism of social security, of survival, and of the perpetuity of the group. This is the symbolic ceremony for the increase of life; and they are completely honest about it. Can we lead them from the "increase of life" to the "increase of Life," from something that is "life-centered" to that which is "Life-centered," from the "source of life" to the "Source of Life?" I believe that a society with phallic initiation rites, when it becomes Christian, will still need sex education and I think the Church could deal with it with a theological undergirding (cf. Tippett 1963).

Funerary rites, the last of the rites of passage, have also an educative value for the living, who frequently feel bound to their dead ancestors in some way. Shearer (1967) has narrated how the missionaries to Korea demanded of their converts a clear-cut break with ancestor worship; and now after many years he finds memorial services being held with the approval of some Korean pastors and their surreptitious participation. Undoubtedly this indicates a felt but unmet need. I pointed out in my subeditorial comments on Shearer's article that the missionaries had considered only two options syncretism and prohibition—and now after many years the Korean pastors are seeking a functional substitute for the non-Christian ceremonies; the option which was not considered in the first place.

Many animist communities have naming ceremonies. Where these exist the Christian community needs to be sure it has adequate functional substitutes, as near as possible to the same points of time in the life cycle of the individual. In doing some research recently in Ethiopia among the Highland Tishena I discovered that a marriage ceremony is always preceded by a purification rite, whereby the parties are cleansed of all youthful indiscretions and the marriage begins "with a clean slate." Some of these people seemed to me to be about to become Christian. It seems essential to me that any Christian marriages among these people should begin with a rite of purification (1970b:135).

I have in my possession two photographs of mission field marriages. One from the South Pacific shows the bride and groom dressed in stenciled bark cloth after the traditional manner, their hair sprinkled with tumeric and carrying a whale's tooth for their ceremonial presentation to the officiating minister. The other comes from Africa and depicts the bride and groom sitting on chairs and dressed in foreign clothes—the man in tails and a top hat, the woman in a full wedding gown and veil. One recognizes the indigenous values, the other values the foreign. The bark cloth, the whale's tooth and the tumeric come from the pre-Christian religion, but they symbolize a culture, its craft occupations, its way of life, the cohesion of society, a marriage pattern in which two extended families are bound together to reinforce the marriage, a village in which to live and work communally, and finally, security in one's old age. All these things were pre-Christian values, but they did not come into focus in a marriage ceremony and its symbolism. This is a Christian not a pagan marriage as the ritual, the hymns, the Christian pastor and congregational worship of Christ indicate. For a pagan chief there may have been a polygamous element, for the commoner there may have been no marriage. The divination, the magical rites, the cannibal associations, the animist priest, and the ultimate possibility of patricide for the man and widow strangling for the woman. Thus are the pagan values eliminated, but those values capable of sanctification are preserved in functional substitutes—a Christian marriage ceremony which is nevertheless thoroughly indigenous. It is a Christian rite, yet it sanctifies needs that were felt before Christian times.

The Economic System

In *Solomon Islands Christianity* I narrate two cases of economic distress among Christian converts due to a failure to provide a functional substitute, and I show how, in each case, the situation was corrected by the creation of a Christian rite to meet the felt need. In the Polynesian community of Rennel Island (a Polynesian outlier in Melanesia) the S.S.E.M. converts had abandoned their economic pursuit of shark fishing because of its pagan ritual associations. The people, discomforted by the economic loss, asked their native pastor to prepare a Christian prayer and ritual for shark fishing and were thereby able to return to the productive enterprise. The Anglicans had a similar experience in Malaita. They were porpoise fishers, porpoise teeth being used for necklaces, a form of wealth, and the project was normally community wide. The pursuit was abandoned for the same reason—its heathen associations. Eventually a national pastor introduced a Christian service and prayers. Because the time lapse of nonparticipation was greater in this case, he met a great deal of opposition. The pagan claims to the fishing had been established and the first attempts of the Christians to regain an interest were something like a contest. Not until the Christian claim was proved by a remarkable catch could the impoverished Christians regain their rights and see their economic security restored. In each case the idea of Christian prayers serving as a functional substitute for the heathen rites was put forward by island Christians—not by the missionaries (Tippett 1967a:270-272). In the same book in a section on economic patterns (173-171) we find functional substitutes mentioned with respect to "bride price," peace ceremonials, trade exchange, wealth concepts, transport of goods and the minting of money. The exchange system goes on in spite of change. These changes are due to cultural borrowing and frequently the presence of a Christian mission (especially if it has a store) will speed up the process. A mission airstrip or a plantation is a major instrument of change. Many things which are bought by the island people are used for quite different purposes from those for which they were intended: they become functional substitutes to meet other needs. Many low-priced, gaudy, Western trade goods have been bought purely to serve as ornaments or status symbols. As a mark of the last world war, discarded brass shell cases are used in churches as flower vases all over the islands. I remember among the nomadic Gulebs of Ethiopia in the wilderness country how poorer people obtained cardboard cartons from the mission station to use as covering on their houses as the wealthier herdsmen used skins.

These functional substitutes are found in every walk of life, a great many of them in the life of the church. Sometimes they represent a novel use of some foreign object to serve an old purpose, sometimes in reverse, a new and Christian use for an old artifact. Often there is an economic reason behind the acceptance of the innovation.

The early church offerings in Fiji were mostly made in terms of native artifacts (which the missionaries evaluated for export), or foodstuffs (which the missionaries purchased for their own consumption or shared with their native preachers) or oil (which was sold overseas). Artifacts, foodstuffs and oil may be said to have been functional substitutes for "money" with which to run the church program. It shows a sense of stewardship from the beginning, but only that actually sent to England was converted into money. Like the society, the Church lived on a subsistence economy. The church collections were not gathered by an official who passed a plate or bag to the accompaniment of an organ. They were presented in the old traditional ceremonial manner, the contributors coming forward, single file to a central "table" according to social group, family or household, with any musical accompaniment being provided by the group contributing at any point of time, and this was always in the true Fijian form of song or chant. Out in the leeward islands, where a greater number of Polynesians dwell, the forms tended to be more Tongan and you met the *polotu* type of musical chant. This is still true today after more than a century (Tippett 1958:118-125).

As time went on and Fiji began cultivating cotton and sugar and produced copra commercially, a money economy gradually took over and this was reflected in the church finances, not because the missionaries demanded it, but because the people now had money to give. From the archival records of the Methodist Church in Fiji you can reconstruct a picture of this process. This was a Church which always paid its own way, trained its own ministers and paid them, built its own churches and financed them. I have never found another place where the Church and society have so marched in step, slowly but steadily, along the way of acculturation. There are functional substitutes at every corner. The district annual meetings of the Church are patterned on the regional gatherings (*solevu*) which have come down from pre-Christian Fiji as periodic meeting places where every interrelationship of the socio-rligious network was in operation. On the highest level the representatives go to the Council of Chiefs (*na vanua*—the land) and the Conference (*na Lotu*—the Church).

The Theological System

The early Fijian Church explored with delight the potential for Christian liturgy and worship. The Morning and Evening Worship, the Lord's Prayer, the Ten Commandments, the Beatitudes, the Confession, the Te Deum, introits and vespers were among the first things translated. They were accepted as substitutes for the old pre-Christian priestly rituals and the dynamic personal experiences that came with the early people movements at Ono, Viwa, Bau, Kadavu and other places guaranteed a participating congregation. The Te Deum was used spontaneously when converts registered their public decision by "bending the knee" to the

Lord. The Fijian matrons appropriated the role of leading the chanting—this itself a functional substitute for their pagan role in the pre-Christian festivities after victory in war. Now they chanted the catechism, one as leader asking the questions and the group responding in pre-Christian rhythms and intonations (Tippett 1958:68-72).

Moral and didactic passages from the Scriptures and especially the epic descriptions—the creation, the flood, the building of the temple and the New Jerusalem—were chanted by the congregation in the pre-Christian rhythm, the women with the theme and the men with the accompaniment (85-89, 136, 142). The seasons and the harvests, a significant feature of the pre-Christian religion, are covered annually by *na lotu ni sevu* (which literally means "Christian first fruits," 96-106). Oral tradition is still used, though the Fijians are all literate today (140), and the people are called to worship by the Fijian drum, not a bell. Once it called the gathering for war, but now for worship, using the same beat. The joyful hymns which are composed on the theme of "gospel bells," inasmuch as they have been translated, are rendered "beating drums" (157).

The Fijian version of *Pilgrim's Progress* became the greatest and most used functional substitute for the old mythology (141) and still remains as part and parcel of the older Fijian thinking to this day. Certain Scripture passages of little interest in the West are treated with respect in Fiji—the chronologies for instance. They also use the passages of Hebrew migration and accounts of the promised land, like their old sagas, for communal recital.

The Western critics of missionary work from the early whalers to the modern novelists have never seen the moral restrictions and sabbatarianism of the Polynesian churches as anything but narrow Puritanism. But they fail to allow for the fact an innovation advocated has to be *accepted* before it becomes a feature of the culture. Both Polynesia and Melanesia had strong systems of taboo and a new religion without some taboo would have been no religion at all. So the idea of the sabbath was itself a functional substitute and the islanders accepted it because they valued the taboo system and felt it met a social need. There is documentary evidence to indicate that they saw it this way at the time.

In the Church of England missionary area of the Solomon Islands we find many useful functional substitutes, and it is just at this point where that denomination gets the best participation from the people. They see the sacrificial aspect of the Lord's Supper as having taken the place of the old sacrifices (Tippett 1967a:298).

On the level of the individual Melanesian Christian farmer in Malaita I found them religiously bringing the first basket of sweet potatoes from a new crop and placing it before the altar in the church, even though the priest did not know who made the offering. Frequently, I saw such a basket when I went to Evensong. The religious rituals associated with the whole area of food supply are well developed—both for fishing and agriculture. The liturgy of Rogationtide leads the convert from the old belief to the idea that "This is my Father's world": The Rogationtide ritual and an appreciation of it are found in *Solomon Islands Christianity* (269-270). The Anglican prayers for the locality where the worshippers dwell, for travellers along the coast and into the mountains, for seasonable weather and for the sick, being set and printed prayers which are regularly used, serve as functional substitutes for the old religion, which was certainly concerned with the affairs of daily life (272). Far away from the Pacific, but in the same area of thought, I was once privileged to participate with some Episcopalians in a small domestic ritual performed on a Navaho Indian outfit in the Upper Fruitlands area of New Mexico. It was a house blessing ceremony which called on the Lord to protect the house and the household from troublesome spirit forces—a point at which many Navaho have real felt needs.

Another dimension of the theological system lies in the area of dramatic art used for the presentation of religious knowledge. If one visualizes a trip around the world, thinking of the younger churches, I am sure he or she would have a huge list of forms taken from the animist way of life and used for the presentation of Christian truth. In Fiji one finds every kind of drama, from concert items to three act Bible plays in the vernacular, group recitation in unison, and even dirges. And there is dancing of every conceivable type, some with the message in the dance and some with it in the accompanying words. Educational and narrative material from the Bible is dramatized or presented as a pageant, inside and outside, especially on the occasions of the great festivals of the Christian year, most widespread of all at Christmas. I have met with this in Mexico where evangelicals, having often come from a Roman Catholic Christopagan background, have a penchant for festivals. When I have run into Christian Asians far away from their homes they might well be presenting the evangel by means of shadow shows or a puppet display. This might be in a church service or in the marketplace. Many of these forms are neither New Testament nor Western. Many of them come out of the non-Christian religions. There is no apparent end of these indigenous expressions for presenting the thoughts and feelings of the heart in drama and music. In that they are used for communicating the Christian Gospel they may be taken as functional substitutes. Individuals feel the desire to dance and they communicate the love of Christ in their hearts by means of their non-Christian art, and thus they make it Christian.

The Technological System

A great many of the functional substitutes which fall under the head of the technological system are creative, aesthetic expressions in arts and crafts, indigenous and secular forms which have been given new meaning and Christian content. We might have included under this head the many rhythmic, responsive and musical forms in the theological system, but I shall confine myself to craftwork of one kind or another.

The importance of these functional substitutes in the creative crafts is that (1) they preserve the indigenous value of the *symbolic* as the craftsman's method of self-expression, and (2) they preserve the technical skills that have hitherto been associated with pagan systems and are in danger of being lost because of the change of religion.

Let me give an example of each of these factors. (1) In another place I have narrated a contest between a small Christian party and the heathen gods, represented symbolically in an ancient banyan tree, extremely sacred and much feared. The daring Christians cut it down with their axes, leaving their pagan friends horrified and afraid. This in itself was a symbolic act and was interpreted by all in terms of a "trial by contest" after the style of Boniface and the oak of Geissmar. Having completed their work of destruction and having cut up the wood in a utilitarian manner, the Christian party did not leave the scene until they had set up a Christian cross where the tree had originally stood. This was surely symbolic of the power in which they had undertaken the contest. More still, it was a functional substitute—the cross in place of the tree, a symbol of sacrifice and victory in place of a symbol of fear (1967a:100-101). (2) The fame of the great black pre-Christian war canoes of the Solomon Islands was not purely on account of their horrible headhunting missions, but also because of their superb inlaying of mother-of-pearl design. With the coming of the mission and government, headhunting and skull cults which demanded more and more heads declined. Furthermore, it was only the size of the raiding that made such large craft necessary. With changes under acculturation smaller canoes were built. The magnificent canoes have disappeared and the inferior counterparts of today are more than adequate for the demands of the religion and the economy. This is how arts and crafts disappear. Fortunately, the Anglican Christians have preserved the art of mother-of-pearl inlaying in their beautiful baptismal fonts which seem to declare to the Melanesian world that the finest workmanship should still be dedicated to God. Here is the preservation of a craft which was always dedicated to religion.

I had the opportunity of speaking to a small group of Navaho Christians at a sawmill. They met for a worship service in a house and I spoke to them from a Navaho rug rather than a pulpit. Originally, the designs of these rugs depicted the activities of the holy people or the corn spirits. This one, I noticed, was a Christian design. A cross was woven into the wool. Here was a symbolic expression of the new faith substituted for the corn spirits. At the same time at least for the woman who had woven it, it was preserving her craft skills. Behind this mat lay the whole pastoral life of the Navaho, the woman's flock and her children's daily task, the spinning of the thread, the collection of the dyes and dyeing of the wool, the manufacture of the loom, the weaving of the rug and the creativity in working out the new Christian design. All this was preserved by the dedication of this rug to God.

If the craft work preserved in a Christian functional substitute was performed with the aid of a religious rite in the old pagan pattern, there most certainly should be a Christian rite, or at least a prayer, associated with the Christian craft. Or if work songs were used (cf. the Banana Boat Song, the Song of the Volga Boatman, etc.) then Christian work songs should be composed. In the first Fijian Christian schools the craft work was taught to the accompaniment of such songs (Tippett 1958:134). When crafts are communally organized, the Church should preserve the group's character and not train odd individuals to set up in rivalry to the group or destroy its equilibrium and the weightage of its authority pattern. Thus a government or mission industrial school which trains many isolated individuals as carpenters on a basis of individual merit, can throw the clan of traditional carpenters into unemployment and poverty. But if those industrial school facilities are offered to the carpenters' clan, then this is a functional substitute which maintains the equilibrium of the society.

This came home to me with some force when I was resident on the island of Bau. The people had argued for years about the restoration of their church building, which had been damaged in an earthquake and much of the timber work had been riddled by borers. They had the money for the work, but a number of the young men who were not traditionally carpenters (I think from memory they belonged to the fishermen) had learned the carpentry trade and commuted daily to the capital working for wages. They did little to aid the communal stability, but were good carpenters. The authorities could not agree on which of them should be employed and how they should be paid or whether to give the contract to an outside builder. At last in desperation the church steward came to me for an opinion, which I certainly did not want to give. I chanced to ask what would have been done in olden times and learned that the chiefs would have asked the people of Daku with the usually traditional ceremony. The whole elaborate pattern was described with its inter-responsibilities and interrelationships, and then I did express my opinion. Within a week or so the Daku carpenters moved in. As the building was a church, the chief of carpenters had selected a team of workmen of the highest moral character. The materials and men were assembled and dedicated to God in an act of worship and the work began. When the work was done it was a fine piece of craftsmanship and everybody was entirely satisfied.

This program was a complete network of interresponsibilities, the two communities cooperating within the chiefly system, with rituals, music and feasting and a grand ceremonial reopening—a huge complex of functional substitutes, which stimulated a great deal of spiritual enthusiasm in the countryside for miles around.

This church itself is a fine functional substitute for a pre-Christian temple. It has been described in detail in *Fijian Material Culture* (1968a:167-172) and elsewhere (1958:80-81). Many of the features of this building are functional substitutes in their own right. For instance, the old cannibal killing stone on which prisoners had their heads bashed before offering their bodies to the war gods, was taken at the time of the conversion of the people and a baptismal font was carved from it. This is now set in the church and is still a religious symbol, but now of the new way of life and faith. The old chief himself wanted it preserved as a reminder to his people of the greatness of their salvation. I heard the Bauan herald rebuke a tourist for calling it a gruesome thing: it wasn't put there for the tourists, he said, but as a reminder to people who remembered the cannibal ovens.

The Bau church has walls three feet thick. They are made of the stone foundations of seventeen heathen temples. Here again is the symbol of the passing of the old way, but the claim that worship of some kind must continue. The same psychology was associated with the conversion of the people of Viwa, the island opposite Bau. The sacred groves were cut down and the timber derived thereby was used to build the first church on the site of the grove. These were what Luzbetak (1963) calls *complete* functional substitutes—the new religion for the old.

The central position of the church building in the village structure I have sketched with a typical Fijian model (1968a:163). Sahlins observed the ruins of a pre-Christian village at Navucinamasi, Moala, and noted that the platform of the temple was in the same relative position as the modern churches (1962:70). This is often so, but not always.

The Anglican churches in the Eastern Solomons are wonderful examples of the use of real indigenous design and ornamentation with native materials—both outside and inside. The rafters, screens, lecterns, altars and the designs on the back of the sanctuaries; the painting, the carving, the sinnet work, the inlaying—it is all quite Anglican, but it is aesthetically indigenous. The people like it and seem to get a great deal out of their worship.

The design behind the altar in St. Michael's Episcopalian Church in Upper Fruitlands in Navaholand is thoroughly Navaho in art style. In the same church, which preserves some of the architectural style of a hogan, at least internally, by developing the central part of the otherwise cruciform structure, here I have seen Old Testament stories presented pictorially in functional substitutes of sand painting designs.

When the Togan chief Taufa'ahau became Christian he manumitted all his slaves, rejected his war philosophy, and built a fine church in the Togan architectural style. He then had his prized military heirlooms worked by his carpenters into the design of the communion rail and the pulpit steps. The symbolism of this was that his hitherto highest pagan value was now brought low before the true God, and its physical accoutrements were to be transformed into the physical elements of the means of grace, where the people would rather hear the preaching of the Word and receive the sacrament instead of his message of war. This he declared was his way of testifying to his contemporaries (Tippett 1971:96-97).

THE CULTURAL VOID

The importance of countering the apparent cultural deprivation due to, say, the moral demands of the new religion, by means of adequate functional substitutes is quite manifest when we consider the phenomenon spoken of as a *cultural void*

> We Westerners often fail to see what a void we leave in the lives of people who are deprived of a rite because we see no particular value for it. The rejection of initiation rites is one of these void-creators, though the danger of the void may not work itself out for a generation or two (Tippett 1963:68).

I have already mentioned a few cases in which cultural voids have been left after conversion. Some of these, like the economic poverty due to the loss of shark fishing and a supply of porpoise teeth wealth, were subsequently corrected by the provision of acts of worship which changed the pagan pursuits into Christian. Others, like the failure to provide sex education, may be brought out into the open by discussion and ways and means of dealing with it provided (Tippett 1965b). The feeling of lack of respect for one's deceased father felt in Korea because of the abandonment of ancestor worship, we have seen, has led this current generation to introduce memorial services and to do so "behind the back of" the missionary.

The most aggressive form of reaction to a cultural void is the *nativistic movement,* sometimes called a *Cargo Cult.* A large social segment breaks off from the young church (it invariably has a clear-cut social structure, maybe an extended family or a village, or a group of related villages) and forms a cohesive and autonomous religious group: a sect if you like. The movement frequently is led by a prophet and may be messianic. Its motivation is to regain something believed to have been lost—taken away by the white man. This recovery is usually expressed in a millinarian doctrine. Maybe some Christian elements are retained but the traditional will be uppermost. The result will be syncretistic; the very thing the missionaries tried to avoid. The Bible may be retained, but if so, it will be interpreted in terms of traditional values. If the movement is brought under control, say by the government, it will recur from time to time whenever a suitable situation develops. We sometimes speak of this as "the continuity of the cults" (Tippett 1967a:216). The basic felt needs must be dealt with before there is rest. (For a detailed analysis of this kind of phenomena cf. Tippett 1967a:201-266.) The literature on this is abundant. The failure to provide adequate functional substitutes in the newly planted church leaves a void. Voids create longings. Longings lead to unrest and unrest in time to violent reaction.

In the same volume I have also discussed the loss of leadership training institutions with the termination of pre-Christian war and feuding in Choiseul and the void left and felt to this day (200). Of course, war and feuding had to go but in that they did have a social function (viz. to train leaders) a functional substitute to train leaders in the community social life (not just church leaders) should have been instituted. Even more so, we may pinpoint the headhunting complex operating from Roviana. I have discussed this in chapter ten of the same volume. The same question was first raised by the British anthropologist, Rivers, in a book of essays on the depopulation of Melanesia, in which his own article discussed "The Psychological Factor." He made the point that the most important factor in the capacity of a people for survival is "an interest in life." He attributes depopulation to the loss of this interest. It is interesting to note that, although the term "functional substitute" was not used in that day, the suggestions he had to offer for the solving of the problem could be described as a series of functional substitutes. With the loss of headhunting the business of canoe building fell off seriously. So he seeks a new motive for making canoes, exploring the economic and recreational possibilities (1922:109).

The cultural void, like the intellectual and spiritual voids, is a danger spot because it always has room for the "wrong thing" if the "right thing" is denied. As the nativistic movement brings syncretism to the place where Christian truth would normally be expected, so the possibilities of distortion of the new faith are related to the number of voids in the lives of the converts. We have a parable of Jesus which speaks to this situation. The house was swept and garnished but left empty. The expelled spirit returned with seven others and the last state was worse than the first (Lk. 11:24-26).

For the purpose of this chapter and its bearing on missiological theory I suggest that, in the newly planted church of animist converts, a direct relationship exists between the effectiveness of the functional substitutes and the possibilities of reaction against cultural voids. Cultural voids might be reduced by paying greater attention to any cultural institution rejected upon the acceptance of Christianity: what are its functions in society and what kind of Christian substitutes might be advocated? Headhunting, cannibalism, slaving and the like had to go, but the social needs they once met still continue. The Christian evangelist cannot just pass them by, saying they are unethical. They have to be met squarely. It is at this point that the functional substitute is indispensable. The correct time to make these innovations is when the people are becoming Christian. In a recent survey I did for a mission working among the tribal peoples of

Southwest Ethiopia, where the people seem to be moving towards the Church, I found myself pointing out cultural features time after time: features which would require functional substitutes. I would hope that if I went that way a decade hence I would recognize a Guleb Church, a Masongo Church and a Tishena Church, rather than a foreign Church. I would expect to find this in the leadership patterns, the enculturative systems, the stewardship patterns, the presentation of the message, the meeting places, the structure of the worship and so forth. Because the three peoples I have mentioned are, one of them nomadic, one settled agriculturalist and the other forest dwelling, we may expect the innovations and functional substitutes to be responsible for three entirely different patterns. If I find a Western denominational pattern over them all, I shall feel very discouraged, as I have made this point clearly in *Peoples of Southwest Ethiopia* (1970b).

Notes:

1. A society is an integrated thing, a network of relationships, a totality. Even though a society may be described journalistically as segregated (not integrated) because of group differences within, anthropologically it is integrated because those groups face each other in precise relationships—be it sometimes a hostile one. Those relationships are part of the totality at any given point of time and thus the totality is never merely the sum of the parts.

2. Missionary policy in China was generally against the use of Chinese music as being associated with Buddhism as distinct from Western music which was regarded as Christian. The missionaries sought to avoid syncretism by rejecting the indigenous and thus the Chinese Church was foreign. The change of perspective came too late.

CHAPTER 16

Urban and Industrial Situations: A Solomon Islands Case Study

The New Testament congregation at imperial Rome emerged as a result of migration growth, without any evangelistic mission or missionary visit. Many folk mentioned in Paul's letter were known personally to him and had worshipped in congregations farther east. There they had learned the interdependence within the fellowship, and having migrated to the capital they sought each other out and the Church emerged spontaneously. Before long it was reaching out even into "Caesar's household." Statistically, migration or transfer growth is not growth at all, but in the formation of a new congregation there is always organic growth, and such a new cell should achieve numerical growth by its outreach within the new environment. When we consider the Roman Church as against those of Greece, we realize the biblical precedents offer us more than one pattern of church planting.

The New Testament situation in Rome has something to say to Honiara, the only place in the Solomon Islands which can really be called a town. Clearly Honiara, more than any other place in the Solomons, is open for new ideas and experiments. In one sense it is the center of diffusion and therefore the key to the Solomons, but this statement needs considerable qualification. The popular idea that roads and other communications, laws based on official enactments, officials implementing

The original version of this chapter was published in *Solomon Islands Christianity*, (London: Lutterworth Press, 1967), pp. 330-345, under the title, "Urban and Industrial Situations." Reprinted in 1975 by William Carey Labrary, 1705 N. Sierra Bonita Avenue, Pasadena, CA 91104. Gratitude is hereby expressed to the publisher for permission to include it here.

them, and many other forces radiate over the rural areas from the capital, is a matter for debate. Strong evidence exists for centripetal rather centrifugal forces being dominant. It is certain that the movement of people is more *to* the town than *from* it. For missionary policy and technique, the important question is whether the town is key to the country or the country is key to the town. The Roman Christian community had its roots in the outposts of the empire and their deaconess was sent from Greece (Rom. 16:1). However, that young Church was operating on principles of self-determination and self-propagation, reaching out into places where civil authority ruled.

Missionary theory in this area was developed some sixty years ago by Clark, who based his research mainly on Asia, North China in particular. Unfortunately the war and subsequent events of a political character have changed the face of China, but his research is still relevant. He also told of an Anglican bishop pointing out to him that whereas 80 percent of the people of India were living the country, 80 percent of the missionaries were resident in the cities. He was investigating the comparative merits of city and country as strategic points for church growth, and was impressed by the fact that city converts did not plant churches in the country but that many city churches were built of communicants who had been converted in the rural areas. In my own experience of over twenty years in Melanesia, I must admit that this is undeniable. Clark traced the dissemination of Christianity to rural focal points, especially the hundreds of rural market centers, the regular meeting places of rural folk. He devoted years of study to village situations where doors were open for evangelism (1928:12ff.). Those areas where missionaries acted on his proposals soon had very encouraging results to report.

Dr. Peill, a medical missionary, took up the same theme and reached very much the same conclusions, developing the significance of migrations *to* rather than *from* the cities. Those who sought employment became permanent city dwellers, returning to the country only for the Chinese New Year. Those who obtained their education *away from* the villages, lost their sympathy for them and cared even less for village betterment than the foreigners. Peill believed that far more flowed from the villages into the cities than vice versa, and thereafter concerned himself with developing techniques of village church planting (1930).

Rowlands applied Clark's methods in Siaochang with good results. He concentrated on the rural markets rather than the towns, and planted simple self-supporting churches which certainly produced some spontaneous growth (1930). Peill and Rowlands worked in an area where nine million people lived in 11,400 villages. Each of the rural markets served as the meeting place for folk of some twenty to thirty villages. Clark's theory is founded on a solid body of objective data, and the truth these men established is too valuable to be allowed to perish because Communism has changed the situation. If anything, the fact that it involved the last pre-Communist research makes it all the more important as valid for other areas not yet under Communist domination.

While it is true that some ideas do become diffused from an administrative center in all directions, we must not overlook the importance of movements in the opposite direction. If we are to understand the Honiara situation we must first master those elements, characteristics, beliefs and practices from the scores of rural areas which are being thrown together as the constituents of the Honiara situation.

THE HONIARA SITUATION

Migration Growth and Innovation

The churches grow in Honiara, but I cannot answer for their degree of conversion growth from the world or from paganism. It is largely migration growth at the expense of the villages. The Anglican cause in Honiara is composed mainly of folk from the Eastern and Central Solomons and Polynesian outliers. The Methodists come from New Georgia and Choiseul. By agreement with the London Missionary Society, they are trying to incorporate the Gilbertese. The Fijians also are Methodists in the main, and some of the local initiative, as for example in the choir work, comes from this direction. The Roman Catholic, Seventh Day and South Sea Evangelical causes in Honiara are all found to have strongly regional bases for their respective congregations. In this way the denominations of Honiara reflect the country from which their adherents have migrated.

The New Testament congregation in Rome produced a spontaneous expansion in the imperial capital, so much so that before long Nero had to do something about it. There was, of course, no foreign mission organization in Rome to take them under its paternal (or maternal) wing, no organization which could supply a chaplain. If they were to emerge at all, they had to do it of their own accord, and of course they did. The missions are very busy in Honiara. They have numerous projects in the settlements that are springing up like mushrooms about the town. The missionaries are trying to bring these groups to self-support and one can honestly say that much good work is being done. The official Methodist policy conceives their work as that of a chaplaincy caring for "our people who have migrated to the capital." This grows from a long policy of comity. The post-war capital has been established in an Anglican comity area. This confinement is admittedly honorable but it in no way lines up with the New Testament concept of a church, having no outreach. It will never win "saints in Caesar's household." It will become enclosed—sealed off from the world in which it is called to witness. There is a real dilemma here. It is an issue in all the emerging towns of Oceania. I see no justification for establishing chaplaincies to circumvent comity agreements, because we are called to plant churches and churches are called to

outreach. Comity agreements were made in the Pacific to avoid denominationalism and maintain Christian unity within regions. If in our post-war
world these comity regions are no longer discrete, then the comity pattern
has become obsolete.[1] If obsolete it becomes an obstruction. Whether the
time has come for interdenominational cooperation in joint projects or for
organic union, I am not sure, but of one thing I am quite certain—
chaplaincies to care for "our people who have migrated" are spiritually
wrong if they are to be denied outreach. Enclosed congregations are not
only static but they exert a negative witness in the community, because
they advertise Christianity as enclosure. I trust that what I have said will
not be taken as a criticism of the missionaries personally—I am criticizing
the policy under which they have to labor. Neither are the Methodists the
only folk who have chaplaincies in other comity areas.

This policy may seem the easy way out, but it is thoroughly paternal
and inhibitory to spontaneous indigenous growth. Honiara, and to a lesser
extent Gizo and Auki, are new situations which call for vital church
planting free from enclosure and colonialism. Paternalism and colonialism
go together. The whole orientation and terminology of the Europeans of
Honiara is colonial—and it has not many years left for peaceful change.[2]

Although the growth of the town brings new forms of materialism and
social problems, these need not necessarily be bad for the Church—if for
instance they provide stimuli for an emerging Church to struggle towards
its own entity as a relevant organism within the changing scene. It is true
that folk who have drifted from their villages have great adjustments to
make. They receive many shocks. Their lives are suddenly opened for
re-evaluation. Thousands of innovations are thrust before them for
acceptance or rejection. The town also has opened their eyes to denominationalism. Many of them have come from areas where there was little
competition. They have insular perspectives, controlled by linguistic and
cultural differences and possibly reinforced by denominationalism. It
operates against the unification of the Solomons as a country and against
the united witness of the Christian Church in the face of the materialism of
the capital. Yet a real indigenous Church can emerge in this very type of
situation, if it can free itself from paternal controls and be allowed to
struggle for its selfhood.

The town is a loosely held agglomeration. It has not the social
solidarity and structural cohesion of a village. Religion is no longer the
integrator of society. If there is any integrator at all, it is the economic
concept of "work for wages." Materialism and money usurp the place of
religion. I have pointed out that the church communities comprise migrants
from rural areas, but many migrants are lost altogether to the Church.
Folk from dependent communities are not always able to stand alone
when they reach the temptations of the town. So there is disequilibrium
and change everywhere. The new class structure of Honiara is beginning
to take shape on a thoroughly colonial pattern, but it could be subjected to

a major social upheaval of a formative character before the pattern becomes stable. Times of migration and the emergence of towns are propitious for innovation. This means that religion itself comes up for re-evaluation: for reacceptance, for adjustment, or for rejection. The churches of Honiara are therefore faced with specific problems of advocacy. What do they offer or advocate in their programs? Do they offer the same paternalistic patterns of the last generation missions, or is the program modified? If modified, how is it modified? Is it "modernized" to bring it into line with changes in the Western patterns of the home church of the missionaries, or is the modification rooted in the soil of the Solomons? Is it still colonial with the white man running the affairs of the Church and making the decisions, or is it so geared that the missionaries could hand over entirely to an indigenous Church without injury? Who actually runs the age group activities, the women's groups, the work projects? Who makes the announcements in church—the indigenous laymen and women, or the white missionary?

Times of migration from village to town, I have said, are propitious for innovation. The day which offers regular wages, materialism and escape from churchgoing to the young islander who migrates to town, also offers to the Church an opportunity to modify her advocacy and swing from paternalism to indigeneity. The urgency of the situation lies in the fact that almost every boat entering the port of Honiara from the other islands brings persons who will personally re-evaluate religion as they have known it—either for escape from it or loyalty to it.

Rural Roots in Urban Society

The situation at Honiara is very different from the emerging town or industrial area in Western society. Despite its modern aspects, materialism, money, gambling, liquor, hours of labor, facility for spending and being entertained, and so on, the situation remains a *Solomon Island situation* and must not be appraised by Western industrial criteria. It is just here that administrators, educationalists, social workers and missionaries can go wrong. It does not follow that an organization effective in New Zealand will be effective in the Solomons, or that a Western health policy will be acceptable to the islanders. Neither does it follow that a young islander sent overseas to study youth work, social work, or some other branch of learning and practice, will be able to handle the island situation upon his return. The town and industrial situations in the islands are built up, as we have seen, by hundreds of individuals who have been plucked out of rural configurations. Some of them are second generation Christians and some are pagans.[3] For many of them the socio-religious background is a Christian-pagan coexistence. The issue of magic versus sorcery, the prestige of an accumulation of shell money, the traditional method of obtaining a wife, together with the numerous ties and responsibilities within the kinship organization, are the big factors which still determine their principal decisions. This is another way in which the village is the key to the town rather than vice versa.

No one will deny that the town situation has features of its own not common to the rural area, and these have to be faced. However, it is often better to allow the indigenous leaders in the complex itself to evolve their own solutions, with just a little inconspicuous guidance, than to equate these situations with overseas "counterparts," which on the surface seem to be similar because they are urban and industrial. These new features of the town are still innovations being advocated—not yet fully accepted. The really abiding features of the new town way of life may well turn out to be matters of rural orientation which the migrants have brought with them.

It is sometimes thought that an islander with an overseas education is a natural choice for handling a town or industrial situation. This does not necessarily follow. He or she may be the right person, but the overseas education may be the very thing that disqualifies him or her for the role. Every group has its natural leader. It may be more profitable to take the natural leaders, with or without education, and give them opportunities to lead, the missionary keeping in the background.[4] Natural leadership and acceptance by the group is something overseas training cannot provide. It is easy to hold up growth by overlooking natural leaders because they do not measure up to required academic standards. This means that leadership is being determined by foreign rather than indigenous criteria. If new indigenous labor groups are emerging in urban situations, we may be quite certain that those groups will stabilize only as the natural leaders emerge. Writing of the rural region Clark said:

> Leaders exist in every community. To find, help and get out of the way of these is one of the best pieces of work to which missionaries can address themselves. Abundant proofs can be found of the capacity of these leaders to do the work required. . . . The most difficult task before the missionary is perhaps to get out of the way. . . .

and again

> To be able to distinguish natural leaders, to give them the fullest opportunity to lead, to encourage and support them in their leadership, is one of the chief services a missionary can render (1928:28-29).

The concentrations of laborers in the town are groups of villagers, not Westerners, and they retain the orientation of the rural world from which they have migrated for at least one generation. Their children, born in the town, will present a different situation, but when they mature it is hoped that that generation will produce leaders from its own numbers. Any growing church should supply its own leadership, commensurate with its social and academic levels at any given point of time.[5] If a congregation fails to produce leaders, then the fault must lie with its own methods of organization for growth. I do not know any group of islanders in sport, labor or social life, in country or town, that has not sought out some natural leader round whom the group stabilizes itself. No church needs to be built round a missionary. The role of the missionary is to recognize the natural leaders, open facilities to them and support them.

A good example of the power of a natural leader to consolidate a new situation may be seen in the village of Roroni in Guadalcanal. This village has social units from very different regions and people of three different denominations. Their social stability has been established round a natural leader, a strong personality who sees that each social segment, while maintaining its own domestic unit, does so in an orderly and tidy manner. The village is a credit to its purely indigenous leadership.[6] While it is true that every group does not produce a leader of this caliber, every group does produce a leader. This is a profound fact which assures any emerging group or church of indigenous capacity. With respect to the town situation, we need to realize that it is a composite pattern of emerging groups, each group with its natural leaders. The Church must seek out those leaders, win them if they are not Christian, and give them scope for leadership in spiritual matters, so that the groups that are forming may have Christian orientation. The criteria for selection of leaders will be indigenous, and missionaries must not try to force this in other directions. If the members of the group come from one culture or linguistic region the rural criteria of that locality will most certainly apply in the choice of leaders. If it is a work group from different cultural and linguistic areas, the group may work out new criteria, but we can be certain they will have Melanesian rather than Western dimensions. Here again the key to the town situation is in the rural areas.

But the folk in the town are more open for innovation than their relations back in the village, and in this respect the town is to some extent the key to innovation and experiment. Innovations that are acceptable in the town may be expected soon to be diffused throughout the country. I said, *"acceptable."* It is not right to assume that things *advocated* in the town will spread to the country; but if they are *accepted* by the rural migrants to the town we may anticipate diffusion. Here again there is a relation between town and country.[7] The fact that radical behavior in the town (like marriage outside a kin pattern) brings a violent reaction when the news reaches the village, shows that migration to the town does not mean separation from ethnic responsibilities and perceptions. Furthermore, migration involves the town dwellers in continuous hospitality obligations for any casual visitors from the village. In many ways a community of Solomon Islanders in the town is still essentially an island community. It may in time achieve a greater degree of education and sophistication but it will take more than one generation to change its basic orientation.

Honiara "Collective Man"

Much of what has been written of rural work in this study is valid also for the town congregations. However, the town environment is certainly different. Congregations are not ethnic units, they are interracial, and their worship may be in English. Social outworkings of the faith in service will certainly differ. In either case the Church must demonstrate that it is a community mediating Christ's program to all within its reach in its own specific situation. In both cases Christ depends on the Church to win those who are not religiously committed to him. However, the two entirely different environments—one rural, subsistent and ethnic, the other urban, commercial and interracial—cause us to ask whether they require entirely different approaches and methods of evangelism. We may ask, for instance, if town dwellers are now individualists who can be dealt with outside the group. This assumption is common among missionaries working in many cities. It has made some very lonely Christians. My experience is that the islanders find isolation difficult. Even though they never return to their village, the ties hold fast. In the city they seek out some other group, even though it be some loosely held sodality that meets for gambling in a Chinese cafe, some group to serve as a substitute for that which they know. They have lost by migrating to the town. For good or bad, they transfer their loyalties to this adopted group. Basically, a human being is a gregarious creature and the Melanesian is no exception.

In bringing people to Christ, we are not asked to isolate them as individuals, but to see them incorporated into a group, a *fellowship,* as the apostle John called it (1 Jn. 1:3). There is something to be said for winning groups whole, and this means winning also industrial groups for Christ, *as groups*—even in modern Western society there is something to be said for this. The evangelist, Bryan Green, has raised this very point, asking whether the missionary experience of the winning of whole communities for Christ (which he admits removes many of the problems faced by the isolated convert) has not after all something to offer in respect of methods of evangelizing "the more sophisticated collective of the industrial man. Should the evangelistic approach here too," he asks, "be to win the group over into baptism, and then individuals to personal conversion?" (1951:148). He leaves the question unanswered. I react in two ways to this suggestion. He does not allow for the fact that these great movements require a period of (to use his own term) *pre-evangelism,* which brings the individuals who comprise the group to unanimity and thus permits the manifest collective action. However, he certainly had a point in finding some similarity between the two *collective man* situations. Both groups will have a cohesion derived from structure, loyalties and leadership, from which both security and satisfactions are derived. In one case they are based on personal qualities alone, and in the other cultural and kin factors may also be involved. Nevertheless they are similarly structured. In the case of the groups in Honiara, the labor having been gathered from communal societies, the solidarity of the group is more or less assumed. The laborer expects that there will be a cohesive group, and even if it be a purely work group he or she transfers normal loyalties to the new group. The ties are less strong in that they know they can break with them at will, but as long as they remain with the group they submit to its cohesive discipline.

For residence they will attach themselves to a household that has previously migrated to the town from their own island and there they remain within the kin cohesion. Thus they compartmentalize their life and divide their time between a work sodality and a kin unit. They find no difficulty in being loyal to both, because they live one life at a time. They think of both collectively and act with the group after having had their say in the discussions that ultimately determine the group action.

It is therefore hoped that the role of the group will not be overlooked by the Church as it deals with the migrants to the town. The fact that islanders have demonstrated a readiness to transfer loyalty to a town group which offers leadership, cohesion and satisfaction, surely offers opportunity to bring the pagan migrants into a Christian experience in the town. Can they be brought to see in the Christian fellowship such a group as meets their needs? There are certainly opportunities for church growth in the town.

On the other hand, this dualism of loyalty to work group and kin group may well cut across the Christian connections. What happens when a young Christian takes up residence with pagan relations, or works with a group that is purely materialistic?

In Honiara the growth or nongrowth of the Church lies with the congregations themselves. If the indigenous Christians set out to win others and to incorporate them into the group, there are certainly opportunities for growth. If, on the other hand, the Christian groups are enclosed, and if the Christians in the social and industrial groups do not stir themselves into action, the town has overwhelming dangers and the ever-increasing migration to the town will usually mean secularization. So once again, as we found in the village studies, the emphasis falls on the role of the local congregation. Can the Church in the town become a self-propagating community? The door is certainly open if Christian migrants retain their allegiance and town Christians have the *will* to evangelize. A foreign mission has little hope; an indigenous Church has great opportunity.

Diffusion of Religion and Morals

In the earlier units of this report we saw that much of the magico-religion and sorcery of Roviana and Simbo had been imported from Ysabel, Vella Lavella and Choiseul. Hogbin reported that the Kaoka people of Guadalcanal, with whom he lived, had also imported much from outside, from Florida, Maurau and San Cristoval. In our study of the nativistic movements we saw how Pokokoqoro obtained his samuka from

Malaita, and how Marching Rule borrowed some of its ideals and methods from the Chair and Rule Movement. In connection with the latter we saw something of its inter-island communication. Within historic times, no matter how strongly these islands have fought to retain their independent entities, there has nevertheless been a widespread diffusion of indigenous concepts, both religious and political. The medium of such diffusion was once the headhunting and slavery configuration. In more recent days the instrument of diffusion of political ideas has usually been the labor system, either for commerce or for war.

Since the disappearance of the headhunting and slavery complex, the diffusion of magico-religion and sorcery has been transferred to the labor system of recruitment and employment. As long as labor recruitment is pursued among the pagan communities, the purely *nominal* Christians (and a large percentage of nominals are interested in the proposition of labor for wages), who live and work with them in the labor concentrations in towns, will be tempted to explore again the lost mysteries of their ancestors.

If the majority of laborers recruited were *nuclear* Christians, the diffusion of religion would no doubt be a more healthy one in the opposite direction. We seem to have here a kind of spiritual "osmosis"—a nuclear Christian tends to draw the pagan to conversion; but in the case of a mere nominal the attraction is reversed, as the root draws water into itself, or has its water withdrawn if the salts outside are too strong.

Christian witness in the labor concentrations is further weakened by its denominational division. It lacks a united front and is therefore inclined to be argumentative and is confusing to the pagan who might be attracted to it otherwise. It is difficult to suggest a solution for this problem. To encourage the enlistment of nuclear Christians would hardly meet the need, for denominationalism would continue and the village congregations would be considerably weakened. The only real solution is a drive to reduce the number of marginal and nominal Christians in the villages, so that whoever signs on for labor, his or her witness will be true. Time after time we are brought back to this fundamental issue: the need for deepening the spiritual life of the local congregations.

The important fact that we have established is that Honiara and the smaller towns are the "clearinghouses" for trade in all kinds of magico-religious formulae and rites, for sorcery and for sexual experiments. The origin is back in the still pagan villages. The market exists because of the marginality and nominality of many of the Christians who sign up as labor. If the town patterns are new, the patterns of the magico-religious trade are survivals from the past. The only safe cure I can see is a revival of true religion in the second generation Christian villages which supply labor for these concentrations.

Hogbin, the anthropologist, found the plantations in the Solomon Islands (what we have said about Honiara applies to the plantations as well) a focal point for the increase of homosexual practices. He correctly pointed out that there was no standard sex pattern for the young man of the Solomon Islands, that each locality had its own peculiar moral orientation. Take three adjacent islands as examples. There was chastity in Malaita (which accounts for their hostile reactions to a sex offense), considerable freedom in San Cristoval, and instituted prostitution in Guadalcanal. When laborers from such different orientations meet and live together for a prolonged period, there is naturally some resultant cross-fertilization of ideas. One of these effects has been a lessening of sex controls when a group of young Malaita-men return home from service (1939:163-165). This is deeply resented at home and often leads to bloodshed. The problem of welding the Solomon Islands into a political and social entity is an extremely complex one.

Analysis of Marginality
    For some time there has been an awareness in Sociology of Religion of the problem of marginality. Among the numerous research projects in this matter, one Roman Catholic study known as the *Southern Parish* seems to offer something for setting over against the Honiara situation (Fichter 1957). The community investigated was analyzed in four categories, which the sociologist, Fichter, has called *nuclear* (active participants and faithful believers), *modal* (normal practising Roman Catholics), *marginal* (conforming to a bare arbitrary minimum of expected patterns) and *dormant* (those who had given up Catholicism but had not joined any other denomination). The study was scientifically computed on a basis of specific questions and answers in three southern urban localities for persons over the age of seven years, who numbered 14,838 baptized people. Of these, 5,786 were recorded as *dormant* and were eliminated from the study. Of the 9,052 remaining, 11 percent were recorded as nuclear, 68 percent modal and 21 percent marginal. To include the dormant as I have done in my piety curves for Rarumana and Fouia ("E"), rough computation would give us the following percentages:

nuclear	7
modal	42
marginal	12
dormant	39
	100%[8]

In spite of the important facts that these figures are Roman Catholic and not Protestant, Western and not Oceania, urban and not rural, yet they present some similar features. From my personal observations (but without any statistical analysis), I imagine this would approximate fairly closely to the overall strength and weakness of collective Christianity in Honiara. When we study constituencies whole, i.e. including my nominals or Fichter's dormants, it would seem that bimodal curves are a feature of our age. Fichter is right in focusing on the marginals, for these are the most unstable category. They are still in the Church but have negative attitudes to religious obligation and are the most vulnerable.

This sociologist put forward four generalizations as reasons for the instability of this segment of marginals. He admitted these factors work on all Catholics, but that the effect was least on the nuclear and increased as it moved to the dormant end of the scale.

The first he calls *contrasting assumptions,* the problem of reconciling patterns of conduct with religious values that are contradictory. The second is a *relative morality,* acceptance of the idea that the Church's position is right, but that it does not allow for "my" particular case. God, of course, would understand "my" special circumstances. The third is *antiauthoritarianism,* because of the ideal of personal independence. The fourth is the *dysfunctional parish,* the fact that the social structure and values of urban society have interfered with the parish as a *community of persons* (429-432). These are important insights and are not confined to Roman Catholics or to Western society. In these respects the urban life of Honiara has similarities with urban life of the West. I do not think they exhaust the kinds of pressure felt by Christians in urban society, nor do I think that ours is the first generation to have felt them, but they are useful concepts for self-examination and offer a suitable frame of reference for studying the problem of marginality. They could be used by missionaries who minister within the Honiara environment, as a tool for analysing their situation.

It must be pointed out that these are general principles. The mode of their outworkings will differ in each type of urban society. For the Melanesians in Honiara we must remember that they are migrants from communal units—different types of communal units, with different patterns of authority, status, prestige and responsibility. They come from subsistence economy into a Western money economy, from technological specialization for exchange trade into labor for a foreigner for weekly wages. They come from a society in which they had the choice between paganism and one form of Christianity to a confrontation with a host of Christian denominations, on one hand, and agnosticism and materialism on the other. These are all new experiences. Fichter's generalizations may be applied to any urban society, but where an urban community is emerging because of migration from communal villages, each one of those generalizations is immensely complicated by the factor of *acculturation.*

However, it is one thing to discover the reasons for marginality and the drift of marginals into nominality, and it is quite another thing to discover how to deal with it. We know the process goes on. We know that any form of migration permits people to slip from the marginal state to the nominal or dormant almost unnoticed—what missionary Miller of Korea (1939) used to call the problem of *shrinkage* in church membership. Perhaps methods and approaches can be modified to keep in step with the changes on the cultural scene, but in the final analysis it comes back to a matter of personal decision and the acceptance of a relevant faith for life. Each generation in the Church has to come to this for itself. Is the Church to modify itself to fit the changing environment, or is it to press its own claims as a factor causing change in the environment? Is the Church to adjust itself to new secular values, or is it to strive to ensure that the new values have spiritual dimensions? Can the encounter with the world ever be avoided? Why must Christian relevance be found *within* the secular world, unless for the very purpose of winning that world?

To classify marginals into categories should tell us much about why they are marginals; but nothing other than direct confrontation with Christ will bring the transformation which the Church must continually strive to achieve.

The Church's problem in Honiara has been accentuated by the fact that the laborers have not constituted a representative cross section of village Christian community, but have largely comprised marginals and nominals. The character and standards of such groups do not line up with those of the villages. A great many indeed just stop going to church at all. The only effective counter to this lies with the better type of migrants who do link up with the Church in town—they should be impressed with the urgency of being missionaries to their own marginals and nominals.

Notes:

1. In the course of this research the writer accumulated a great deal of material on the comity agreements and denominational relationships. Owing to the length of this manuscript, this had to be eliminated. It is indeed the subject for a whole monograph.

2. Many day to day adjustments are called for, speaking of adult labor force as "the boys," of adult cooks and domestic workers as "house boys," of talking in a superior manner about "the natives" in their presence, all of which betray a paternalistic and superior attitude. One of the first impressions I had when I arrived in Honiara was that of returning in time to a day I had hoped was dead.

3. A recruiter who was operating in the Tai Lagoon while I was there was obtaining more pagan than Christian labor from that locality.

4. This presupposes that the person has a Christian experience. If not, then he or she should be the object of personal evangelism. The Christian group will find it hard to prosper if their accepted leaders are not Christian.

5. The theology of this position has biblical roots. Moses' farewell blessing to Asher was "as thy days so shall thy strength be" (Deut. 33:25). The Christian Church has had no reason to doubt this aspect of the goodness and providence of God. Yet Christian missions are so frequently straining at raising standards for tomorrow's leadership that they fail to make use of the indigenous leadership available for today on its own levels. This is just another aspect of our paternalism.

6. The story of this interesting leader has been published (Macquarrie 1945), although the building of this village belongs to his later years. I visited this village without warning and believe I found things as they normally are. Most of the people were out engaged on a communal project but they had left the streets well swept, and many of the domestic units were hedged with crotons and Vouza's own house had a quantity of modern equipment—sleeping nets, sewing machine, and so on. An armchair from some wartime aircraft was set up for comfort by the window. There were two church buildings and each denominational group had its residential segment. The original group was Anglican. The South Sea Evangelicals had come from Ngalibia River country in Qasibatu. The Roman Catholics comprised three families. One of my committee men drove me out to this village on my last day in Honiara, when I asked to see another village which differed from the types I had come to know.

7. Even in cases of the youth who have signed up to escape village authority or their low social status, for they would unconsciously retain their traditional solidarity with folk at home.

8. I have used five categories because my data fell naturally into such a breakdown of classes. The fact that Fichter shows that 42 percent (and 68 percent of the dormant class be excluded) classify as modal rather suggests a subdivision would have been possible. Working with nuclear, modal and marginal Christians, one gets a curve like my hypothetical average. This is to ignore the fact that 39 percent have drifted away from church. They have not joined another church, and if pressed would say they were Catholics. This gives a bimodal curve and explains why I avoid the term "modal."

PART III

The Historical Dimension

The Historical Dimension

One of the numerous interesting functions of history is to record two apparently opposite forces which maintain a state of tension through time; namely, *continuity* and *change*, or *stability* and *instability*. Precisely the same two forces are a major concern of anthropology. The *equilibrium* or *dysequilibrium* of human society should be measurable, to some extent, by the degree of balance or imbalance in social institutions. For example, to what extent has the magical system of this or that animist people been undermined and how far are they from a major communal religious change? Both traditional resistance to culture change on the one hand and rapid social change on the other may be examined, described, measured and discussed within a frame of reference of anthropological analysis in a diachronic arrangement through time. When anthropologists research in what is called "culture contact" or "social change" or "acculturation" (an area of social anthropology) they are concerned with historical methods of data collecting and are as much involved with restructuring patterns through time as with observing what surrounds them today. One might argue that anthropologists are historians, yet they are more than historians. They are experts in social patterning in a way that only few historians are really proficient.

The history of social (including religious) change and/or stability is also the study of *acceptance* and/or *rejection* of *innovation*. This again is the business of the missionary, who in terms of Barnett's innovation theory is the *advocate* for change when seeking to bring about conversion, for example. Once again we may well ask if this is historical or anthropological research in which we are involved. To us in missiology the great theme is the Christian mission, but the research adventures lead us forth with both anthropological and historical methodology and equipment. Yet if either discipline claimed us this would injure our completeness.

In this section of *Introduction to Missiology* we explore briefly the historical dimension in missiology. In the first chapter we examine some of the issues which have persisted in the "Church's Confrontation with the World." We find that certain *configurations* and reactions to the growth of the Church are peculiar to no single age of history but are recurrent. They emerged at the very beginning in the first Christian century and they must be recognized as continuous conditions of the battle. In the second chapter we turn from the happenings to the "Themes of the Christian Church," which also abide through history. We go on to consider the matter of authority and mode of communication and again we find constants with their historical roots in the New Testament Church. If the history of the expansion of the Church says anything to the Church of today, it must surely be that her cultural forms may vary from time to time and place to place but there are certain basic themes which come from the New Testament Church and continue through history in spite of formal change. In our own day we also find these themes in live and growing churches. The historical dimension ties us right into the fibers of continuing Christian experience, the origins of which are in the Bible itself. Missiology (and especially the church growth case study) reinforces its biblical base through the study of history. This is explored further in " 'Contours of Reality' in the History of Mission."

The middle ages speak to us in mission today because of the great advances of that time into the heart of European animism. This has many similarities with Africa today. Despite the wide separation of these two areas in time and culture and the differences of their outside worlds (for example, the state of civilization), nevertheless the nature of their pagan animism and the psychological factors of group conversion had many common features. Thus the waves of history, which have broken at their crests in the times of Constantine, Boniface and John Williams are breaking again today in Africa, Indonesia and the New Guinea highlands.

One of the major research problems which confronts us here is the very practical one that few historians have anthropological training and few anthropologists will wade through hundreds of pages of "irrelevant" material for a single reference. The time and labor problem is serious (Pargellis 1957; Washburn 1961; Sturtevant 1966). Clearly, here is a symbiotic situation. However, the need to take the time to wade through the historical documents must be recognized by missionaries. Without such painstaking efforts we will be left to the mercy of the scholarship of others who are oftentimes predisposed against past missionary activities and, thus, interpret the historical facts in prejudiced ways. This issue is pointedly demonstrated in "A Statement on the Use of Documents: The Complexity of the Conversion of the Tahitians." From all this a relatively new discipline—ethnohistory—has emerged, a discipline which very much concerns us in missiology. Ethnohistory seeks to integrate history and anthropology. Such integration makes for tremendous insights into the past efforts of missionaries; especially useful is the case study approach. This section ends with two examples of ethnohistorical case studies, each illustrating the insights which only the historical dimension can give us.

CHAPTER 17

The Church's Confrontation
with the World

The historical dimension of missiology permits us to study forces over a period of time. Only by increasing the time depth of a study like that of the spreading and growing Church can we really distinguish between *happenings* or *events* on the one hand and *trends* or continuing *forces* on the other. So frequently when we look at the condition of institutions we are told that "this particular state or condition" of the institution was due to "that particular event or happening." In my reading of history I have acquired a general tendency to resist this approach, without very critical examination. I believe that far more often the condition of an institution at some given time of examination is the result of an *evolutionary* rather than a *revolutionary* process. I agree that a happening or event may bring a process to a point of definite decision or action, but a revolution cannot be effective unless it is *accepted by the people*. Great social, political and religious changes are more the result of developing situations than single events. Revolutionary individuals can do what they do only because the conditions of the country and the feelings of the people they win to their cause are as they are.

Religious change from paganism to Christian faith is a complex process. Frequently we hear that "so-and-so became a Christian because of such-and-such a happening" as if it was a single thing in a moment of time. Undoubtedly there was a moment of truth but who knows the full complex of experiences that permitted that moment of truth to be valid for that person? With individuals, groups and societies happenings are results rather than causes. The anthropologist, Kroeber, showed how certain clearly demonstrated theories were not acceptable to the scientific world at the time, and their potential was not tapped for forty years. The

222

ultimate acceptance of these scientific laws was determined, not by the event of their discovery, but by the development of a scientific mood which made them acceptable.

Thus it may be argued with a good deal of truth that people become Christian, not because of the event or preacher, but because the event or message provides an adequate answer to the felt needs of the convert(s). That is the way an anthropologist would put it. The theologian also recognizes these preliminary factors which make the conversion possible. Wesley said in his sermon on "The Means of Grace" that "Providence and the Spirit of God go before and open up the way." This is the doctrine of *prevenient grace*. In church growth theory I have put it myself in *Church Growth and the Word of God*:

> Church growth method therefore recognizes the operation of noncultural (or divine) factors in bringing situations to a ripeness for decision (1970a:46).

So too, although we stress the coming of Christ as an event when God acted in history, even so the Bible sets it "in the fullness of time," suggesting that God's activity was continuous and that somehow the world was ready for Christ's revelation when he came.

Having satisfied myself that there is no anthropological or theological difficulty with this idea I turn to the historical aspect, which is the subject of this chapter. I believe that it can be established that history is dynamic and charged with forces or phenomena which are more significant than *events* in bringing about social or religious change. It is difficult to define or delimit these forces, but one is made aware of their existence by investigating social tensions, moods, attitudes and felt needs. For present-day cultural and religious change the anthropologist could perhaps measure these forces by his normal techniques for collecting quantified data (interviews, schedules, questionnaires and participant observation) but you cannot go back far in history by these methods. Therefore one is confined to written documents and records, a limiting factor for the researcher. Even so, my reading of the history of the expansion of the Christian Church from the New Testament beginnings until it had spread over Europe, for example, convinces me of the existence of these forces with a mood-attitude-need composition.

Thus a large people movement from paganism to Christianity is always immediately preceded by some form of social or religious dis-equilibrium. Again, when the Church so established begins to grow, a mood-attitude of pagan alarm develops, which creates a state of tension between the Church and the world, and manifests itself in a new pagan policy—misrepresentation, private or official persecution or social ostra-cism. Or, within the Church, especially in the second generation, if a price still has to be paid for being a Christian, there is a severe temptation within the Church to surrender to rationalization or syncretism. These three quite different mood-attitude forces—the first the large social unit

being led to a communal decision, the second the pagan concern for
solidarity and security, and the third the Christian fear that tends to
accommodation—are recurring features down through the history of the
Church. They are more causal in the history of church planting and
growth than any specific person or event.

THREE CENTURIES OF CHURCH GROWTH

The Christian Church at Jerusalem comprised a community under
the republican control, but when the refugees scattered throughout Judea
and Samaria the Gospel began to spread by people movements among the
non-republican communities. Lydda and Sharon were whole community
movements. The Gospel also spread along the sea coast. Ptolmais, Tyre
and Sidon, the seaports were republican and the converts there came from
the Jewish population a cultural movement.

Something entirely new happened when the message reached Syrian
Antioch: non-Jews were converted. The Church had leaped over a cultural
barrier. The non-Jews of Antioch, once their relations had been established
with Jerusalem, put Christianity on a new footing. They became a sending
Church. Normally, the mission procedure was to send itinerant preachers
who went first to Jews and then to Gentiles. The churches which gathered
varied in size and in racial mixture—some were house churches, some
comprised ethnic groups and some had a class structure. The Church in
Rome grew by migration growth. Both Asia Minor and Greece soon had
strong networks of churches which maintained contact with each other.

In the Sub-apostolic Age the Church spread through the Hellenistic
world along the roads and trade routes and beyond the bounds of
Hellenism. This was a period of cultural instability. People were interested
in the Christian approach to life. Based on Scripture, which was soon
accepted as authoritative, Christianity offered a good frame of reference
as a rule for faith and practice. Individuals could act on it. It suggested a
patterned way for life and service. It satisfied human needs.

Christian communities were relatively small until about 180 A.D.,
and were mostly family based. They spread along family lines of what the
anthropologist calls the "extended family." Usually they were regarded as
one of the many cults, the multiplicity of which demonstrated a "hungry"
world, restless and searching for satisfaction for its unmet needs. The
depth of Christian penetration was uneven, which suggests that the
feelings of unsatisfied needs were uneven.

The Church spread more rapidly from the urban centers. These were
the cultural and commercial centers of diffusion, the points of contact
between one area and another, and some of them were major cross-
cultural meeting places. The seven churches of Asia, already significant in
New Testament times and the recipients of several of Paul's letters, were
not only meeting places but places of diffusion—two way communication.

This was very much the situation until the internal disorder and foreign wars after 180 A.D.

No individual arose to take the place of Paul. Christianity was communicated by tradesmen, merchants, artisans and others, who gathered for commercial purposes in the trade centers. In the course of their travels they had access to numerous Scripture versions: Egyptian, Syriac, Latin and Greek. From a missionary college at Alexandria, trained missionaries went forth to Asia, Europe and Africa. In the middle of the second century Justin Martyr wrote:

> There is no people, Greek or barbarian, or of any other race, by whatever appellation or manners they may be distinguished, however ignorant of art and agriculture, whether they dwell in tents or wander about in covered wagons, among whom prayers and thanksgivings are not offered, in the name of the crucified Jesus, to the Father and Creator of all things.

This interesting reference, which shows the writer's view of culture and the limits of "the world," indicates both the focal points of his Christian faith and also the degree of its penetration into the world. It suggests to me also that Christians comprised household groups.

A mission from Smyrna planted the Church in Gaul, where Syrian merchants were scattered even to the Rhine Valley. Ephesian Christianity reached the Rhone, and other Greek communities had come from Ionia. The martyrdoms of Lyons and Vienne (177 A.D.) drew attention to the strength of Greek Christians in Gaul. Greek, and not Latin, was the language of the educated people, but many Christians there were Celtic, and Irenaeus preached to them in their own language. The earlier Christians in Britain seem to have been connected with the survivors of the massacres in Lyons and Vienne (cf. Hole n.d.), thus showing a flow of Christianity from Greece through Gaul to Britain.

The paganism of the north was quite decadent. It had become unstable under the impact of Roman civilization. The Anglo-Saxon leaders were unlettered and had no literacy supports for their traditional system. In the first place, it had been displaced from the mainland forest country and had migrated to an island of civilized towns; all of which adds up to one thing—England was eventually converted in a day of acculturation.

Figures computed by various authorities before 325 A.D. are so varied that they must be regarded as unreliable although they seem to be estimated on the basis of concrete descriptions. Because it seems most reasonable, we might perhaps accept Robinson's figure (1917), based I believe on the research of Harnack (1962 [1908]). This gives us four million Christians in 325 A.D. distributed in the following intensity throughout Europe:

> Thrace and Cyprus—the areas of greatest numerical strength, where Christians numbered fifty percent or more.

Rome, Italy, Macedonia and Southern Gaul—where Christianity held its own with other religions because of influential persons and leading classes among its ranks.

Northern Italy and parts of Greece—where Christianity was thinly scattered.

Western and Upper Italy, Upper Gaul and Germany—mostly pagan with a few Christian clusters.

(Note: This is the European distribution only. There must have been large numbers in Asia and Africa.)

Hodgkins' figure (1903) for all the Empire was ten million. This was about ten percent of his population figure. A hundred years earlier, by Gibbon's (1923) computations, Christians were figured at one twentieth of the total population, but there had been considerable growth in that century. At the same time as that last statistic, the Christians in Rome numbered 50,000 out of a total population of one million. Smith (1897) claims this estimate is confirmed by the monuments.

I think these figures should warn us that although the documents do report great movements from paganism to Christianity, these only represent a small percentage of the total population at this stage of history. Origen spoke of "tens of thousands who have left their national laws and customary gods for the law of Moses and the word of Jesus Christ" and again "preaching of that word has found its way into every part of the world." Yet that same writer described the Christians as "very few indeed" in comparison with the total population.

Even in Syrian Antioch, which we might perhaps expect to have been Christian by, say, 400 A.D., was described by Chrysostom as having a Christian population which was "a bare majority." If we can project backwards some of the things we have learned from church growth case studies, the statistical pattern seems to suggest that the spread of the Church in the first three Christian centuries, was a regular people movement pattern in which family groups, social segments, classes, villages and small clans were won, and these were able to survive as cultural entities. Admittedly I am speculating, but I see no other way of explaining all the facts in the records. Lydda and Sharon suggest this, and so does the case of the chief town of Pontus from 240 to 265 A.D.

THE MOOD-ATTITUDE TOWARDS
THE ACCEPTANCE OF CHRISTIANITY

The view was put forward by a church historian about a century ago that the Greeks and Romans had failed to accept the role for which they had been divinely called, so God transferred it to other peoples from the north. The Goths, Franks, Burgundians and Saxons were to sit on the thrones now taken from the Greeks and Romans and to succeed to their spiritual privileges. From these northern barbarians, Merivale suggested much of modern Christianity has been derived, colored and molded. He found many Germanic ideas which could have served as steppingstones for the Gospel—the struggle between good and evil, the great sacrifice, the moral virtues, the final judgment and triumph and so on. His point is that the people were ready, indeed waiting for the new religion. Greece and Rome had despised them and their glory was taken from them as the Gospel spread among the barbarians of its own accord. He cites Jerome:

Lo the Armenian lays down his quiver; the Huns are learning the Psalter; the frosts of Scythia glow with the warmth of faith; the ruddy armies of the Goths bear about them the tabernacles of the Church, and therefore, perhaps, do they fight with equal fortune against us, because equally they trust in the religion of Christ (1866:96).

Merivale's point is philosophical and perhaps ethnocentric, but the source he cites is more than interesting. Jerome shows the barbarians as *acceptors* of the new faith but he mentions no *advocates* who presented it to them. Anthropologically they must certainly have been ripe for conversion. Christianity, however primitive its form, must have satisfied their felt needs.

The African coast is a fine field for the study of religious innovation during the third century. The Church was strong and soon rivaled Asia Minor. Here was a region of racial mixture. Phoenecians and Italians had settled beside the older stocks, known as Berbers, who were rural people. The Phoenecians were urban workers and middle class; the Italians were landowners and upper class, who had come as colonizers after the Punic Wars. The cities multiplied and depended on the rural agriculture, so interaction was inevitable. The process of Romanization was rapid, older institutions declined, Latin replaced Greek, and the whole place was receptive to new ideas. The population increased rapidly. All these features led to a mood for innovation. We are not in the least surprised then that the Church bounded ahead in people movements in the third century, that Latin Christian literature emerged and that the Church was strongest in the cities and in the Latin-speaking communities where the preaching was in Latin. Some limited progress was achieved among the non-Latin groups but it was slight. These groups became Christian only as they were Latinized.

In the same century, a major people movement from paganism to Christianity was experienced under Gregory Thaumaturgos in Pontus. It is said that it began with seventeen Christians and ended with only seventeen left as pagans. It had some interesting anthropological features. Christian festivals were established to serve as functional substitutes so that the transition from paganism to Christianity would be meaningfully Christian, yet Christian standards were demanded, nominality resisted and compromise was disciplined.

I have argued that the Church has grown in periods of cultural instability or acculturation, in places where the people have been "ripe for change," with a "mood-attitude" really receptive to new ideas. The nineteenth century was such a period of history, largely because of culture contact. This current post-war period in which we live is another, but there is one major difference. In the last century there was only one option to paganism—Christianity. Today, in some places, the pagan has a choice of Christianity or Islam, in another, Christianity or Buddhism, and in still another Christianity or Communism. It was something like this in the period of which I am writing. It was a religious age, and it was an age ripe for innovation. The period from 200 A.D. to 800 A.D. saw the face of the world completely changed. While Christianity was spreading through Europe and a few Christian missionaries were reaching out into India and China, Buddhism was challenging the Christian cause in the Mediterranean and spreading in China, Mithraism was another rival to Christianity in the same areas, using the same forms and methods in the hope of countering its attractions. In the sixth and seventh centuries, while Christianity was evangelizing the British Isles and Germany, Islam was taking possession of North Africa and the Middle East and was indeed a threat to Europe until the days of Luther. True, Islam had a military aspect, but Buddhism spread, according to Latourette (1938b), by her "religious vitality" *when existing institutions were weakened.* The acceptance of Buddhism was preceded by a weakening of social structures and traditions and Chinese cultural instability created an innovative attitude.

THE MOOD-ATTITUDE AGAINST CHRISTIANITY

The hostile reception of Christianity by the self-satisfied world differed greatly from the responsiveness of those with felt needs. Where the traditional structure and economic system are stable and provides such satisfactions as power and profit, the mood-attitude is one of resistance to change. This psychology is partly responsible for the existence of resistant and nonresistant fields in Christian missions. Perhaps this was foreshadowed even in the days of Our Lord in the episode of the exorcism of the demons from the unhappy maniac and the demonstration of his healing their possession of the swine, which were immediately drowned in the sea. The point is that the demons were drowned. However, no matter how good this release was for the victim and his friends, the owners of the pigs had a different point of view. For them it was an economic matter and they wanted no prophet in their coasts whose operations threatened their economic stability.

Christianity also began its existence in a state of tension with the world. No description illustrates this better than Acts 19. Here Christianity clashes with the guild or collegia of the silversmiths. These guilds were not trade unions, Blaiklock points out, for their functions ramified throughout the whole social life, meeting needs much wider than wages and labor conditions. As structures broader than the family but narrower than the State, they provided for pleasure, social interaction and its self-expression for the populace. Besides the silversmiths were guilds of bankers, gardeners, farmers, cooks, transport workers and so forth. Such social clubs, when adroitly controlled, could well be political weapons if by any chance something threatened the economic interests of the leaders. Acts 19:24-29a demonstrates this.

If we go back to verses 18 to 20 in that same chapter and look at the reason for the disturbance, we will see that a great many people had confessed Christ in that city. These converts would seem to have been largely another guild, for by profession they were magicians and sorcerers. They demonstrated their loss of faith in the magical arts and new allegiance to Christ by publicly burning their paraphernalia, the quantity of which may be judged by its value—fifty thousand pieces of silver. We seem to have a people movement here, the sociological structure of which was the guild of magicians. No other guild in the city could so threaten the economic stability of the silversmiths. We could want no better example of a responsive block with a mood-attitude for acceptance producing a hostile response from an unresponsive block which felt its interests were threatened. This has been repeated over and over again in history and accounts for much of the persecution which Christianity has suffered. The simple fact that people saw fit to turn from traditional ways and gods and thereby threaten everything dependent on them, as Origen said "incurred the hatred of idolaters" and endangered Christians because of "the risk of death."

The pagan fear for their family ties, their laws, their customs and their gods produced a mood-attitude of hostility. They saw the Christians as athiests. They regarded the followers of Christ as disloyal to the Empire because they proclaimed Christ, and not the Emperor, as Lord and Savior. The educated critics accused Christianity of destroying the social structure of the Roman way of life. The ordinary people saw Christianity as a *disease*—the idiom of Tacitus. Tertullus also called Paul a disease. Pliny's term was the "contagion of this superstitution." It appears also in the rescript of Claudius. The general Roman attitude to the Christians, then, was that they were social misfits. They withdrew from idolatrous amusements, gladiatorial combats and religious festivals and dropped from any trades which had religious undergirding. They replaced the religious symbols of their houses with Christian ones and generally marked themselves off from society either by their temperaments or their convictions.

Yet, the Christians lived and worked with their neighbors, lived a peaceful life, were disposed to helping others and were noted for general reliability. The only charges that could be brought against the Christians were their rejection of the gods and those social institutions which were associated with the pagan religion. So difficult was it for the enemies of Christianity to pin down Christians to actual offences against the law that these enemies had to resort to *misrepresentation*. The "disloyalty" of Christians became a serious charge. They were accused of incendiarism. Their sacraments were said to be inhuman secret rites, even of cannibalism. Thus in time it became an adequate accusation to call a person Christian.

One can hardly discuss the persecution of Christians without mentioning the Bithynia letters of Pliny in the second century. These letters describe how Christianity was spreading in cities, villages and rural districts and this spread could not be checked. The temple worship and pagan festivals were suffering from the want of support and the demands for sacrificial meat had fallen off in the markets. Pliny was unable to nominate any moral charge against the Christians but regarded their neglect of Roman religion as economically serious and due for correction. They were judged, not under the law, but under his imperium for punishing sacrilegious people. The admission of the name of Jesus was all that was required for conviction. Pliny himself had been under great pressure from the temple priests and the guild of butchers who supplied the sacrificial meat to do something about it. The mood-attitude towards persecution of the Christians had built up because Christianity had threatened vested interests.

Persecution varied in type—sporadic or organized, petty and surreptitious or official—or it might have been aimed at preventing conversions and restoring the stability of the old faith, or extermination on the score that Rome's military problems were due to the neglect of the gods. These are common patterns of anti-Christian persecution down through history. Natural calamities like floods, earthquakes and famines have frequently been blamed on Christians and have led to persecution. Such misrepresentations may be due to events, but they are possible only because of deep-seated mood-attitudes behind which lie some threat to security: authority, religion or vested interests. This is a recurring phenomenon when the Church begins to spread. Consciously or unconsciously Christian converts in pioneering days of mission have striven to come into the Church in groups as a protective device against persecution. In that the group has also provided converts with facilities for spiritual growth and action, and is itself a biblical concept, it has served the Church well.

The tendency to misrepresent the Christians and thereby to bring them under the judgment of society is not confined to mission in pagan lands. It is a regular feature of the Church's encounter with the "secular" world. It has also been responsible for denigrating the missionary image in our own day. One does not have to excuse missionaries for their mistakes to say this. I mean, for example, that in my own area of Oceania, the great critics of the missionary have been those whose unChristian interests have been threatened by missionary endeavor—sexually permissive mariners with some literary skill, blackbirders who made profit by slavery, sea captains who supplied arms and ammunition and participated in native wars, investors who tried to corner holdings in native lands, administrators who used punitive expeditions to settle disputes with the islanders, and so forth. Or maybe the threat sprang from international rivalry or from religion itself. These critics attacked the missionaries (and therefore the Church they represented) by misrepresentation in order to destroy their image in the world at large. The mood-attitude against the Church manifests itself with every expansion of the Church. And did not the Lord warn his disciples that it would be so? Part of the Church's encounter with the world is a readiness to take up the cross, to endure misrepresentation, persecution and social ostracism.

CHRISTIAN MOOD-ATTITUDES TOWARD SYNCRETISM

The Book of Revelation reflects the intense persecution of a first century period. One does not wonder that the early Christians would seek some way to avoid this burden. Already in the New Testament times the Church faced the temptation to compromise. A number of passages in Paul's letters deal with it. In the Revelation we have references to Balaam, Jezebel and the Nicolaitans, three cases of the temptation to compromise. The covetous Balaam longed for wealth and this jeopardized his fellowship with God. He had influence and ability, but abused them and seduced the religion of Jehovah by sacrificing his moral standards. Jezebel of Thyatira claimed that behind the pagan worship system there stands the general idea of God, who can be acknowledged in either one form or another. So you perform the sacrifice but in doing so you think of Christ instead of the pagan deity. You attend the feasts but you indulge in moderation. The letter of Our Lord condemns her, as it does any of our own day who adopt this same approach to the non-Christian religions or commit fornication with an "honest" heart (Rev. 2:20).

This was a deep-seated problem within the Church itself. It had many forms but basic to them all was a mood-attitude that feared to accept the cross in Christianity: I mean the cross Christians themselves have to bear. Yet history shows that the Church stood firm on this. Paul told the Corinthians that they could not accept the cup of the Lord and also the

cup of devils. In the fifth century there arose a group of so-called
Christians who were spoken of as the Tanit Cult. They worshipped the
Queen of Heaven on Sunday mornings before church. The apologist,
Salvian, fought this issue on the exegesis of the passage just cited from
Paul. Here is a continual temptation: compromise, rationalization,
accommodation, syncretism. Although the Church has been continually
plagued with this attitude on the part of nominal Christians, it has usually
maintained the New Testament position. In our own day, in a book on
syncretism, *No Other Name,* Visser't Hooft put it briefly and clearly:

> When God reveals himself man cannot say: "I accept up to a certain point
> and on condition that I remain free to look around in other directions also."
> He can only say "Yes" or "No" (1963:89).

All kinds of pagan ideas have crept back into the Church from time to
time, but sure enough before long some prophet will arise and expose the
accommodation. One of the wonderful things about the Church is that
despite its many human failings it has always, sooner or later, demonstrated its capacity for reform. It has been subject to repeated bursts of
repentance and evival. Thus, for instance, in the fifth century, when
Christians had introduced astrology into the practice of the Church
(borrowing from the heathen cult *Sol invictus* and interpreting their fate
from the stars, and even bowing to the sun before entering church) Leo,
bishop of Rome made this heathen departure a matter of preaching as he
urged his flock against the temptation to compromise. If the failings of the
people indicate the mood-attitude to compromise, it is the responsibility of
the voice from the pulpit to restate the basic New Testament criteria for
their decision making. A study of sermons down through history not only
throws light on the moods and attitudes of the congregation, but also
indicates how the spokesmen of the Church saw their own role. It tells us
quite a lot about temptation and the capacity for reform.

The theme of this chapter was "The Church's Confrontation with the
World." I have tried to deal with this subject on a basis of group feelings
and forces rather than events, because I regard events as effects rather
than causes. Using mostly examples from the early history of the Church
I have tried to isolate three of these complexes of group feelings: the
feeling of social disequilibrium which makes a people movement to Christ
possible, the feeling of alarm which creates the kind of tension that gives
rise to persecution, and the feeling of fear that often arises among nominal
Christians when confronted with the cost of full commitment and manifests
itself in a temptation to accommodate to non-Christian forces. These
group feelings or forces have been common to every age of the Christian
mission. Among themselves they have the common point that they all
relate in some way to the Church's encounter with the world: first, the
world ready to be won; second, the world being won; and third, the world
trying to win back those only nominally won.

CHAPTER 18

The Themes of the Church

The idea of a human society having a limited number of discrete *themes* whereby it could be recognized and distinguished from any other society was put forward by the anthropologist, Opler (1946), in response to Benedict's contention in *Patterns of Culture* (1934), that each society was recognizable by a single dominant *configuration* and its ethnic personality quality. Forty years ago, when I was first struggling with systematic theology, I was taught to conceptualize the character of the Church by its *marks*. This theology was somewhat conditioned by the organizational structure of the Christian religion as it emerged in the West and was obviously just a convenient frame of reference for systematic theological instruction. It occurs to me now that Opler's more natural concept of cultural themes might well be applied to the Christian Church through history.

The question is: "When we study the history of the Church from its beginning down to the present day, when we consider the Church as a society of human beings with its distinctive pattern that marks it off from other societies, what does history show to be its continuous themes?" This is not to construct an artificial *schema* for theological discussion. I am not even depicting the Church as it ought to be according to the Scriptures. I am looking at history and I am asking what are the abiding or recurring themes that are manifest as I contemplate the Church as a society, community or a fellowship. What features stand out as *the great continuities* of her history? Such a consideration has value to us today, because through the two thousand years of her history the Church has existed in many different environments, faced many different crises, and penetrated many different cultures. Any abiding themes may be investigated as possibly *supracultural,* bigger than culture as Christ is bigger than culture. In a day of rapid social change when the Church's physical and aesthetic forms are open for dramatic modification, what may we expect to survive? If the Church is still to be the Church in spite of change, by what basic themes may she be recognized?

The Church's strong characteristics, witness patterns and service programs, have been conditioned by environmental and cultural factors, historical pressures and opportunities. These were variables. Each had a validity in its own time, place and culture, but is a manifestation of the Christian life, not an abiding theme. Rather they spring from those themes.

Both synchronic studies of the Church across the world and diachronic studies through history indicate four basic and abiding themes, which may be called *faith, entity, mission* and *application*. These are the universals of Christianity. I do not suggest that the Church has always been perfect in these dimensions, or that she has been without her serious lapses. But there has never been a time when these four themes have been completely missing, wherever there has been a Church. When they have declined the Church has been weak (no matter how powerful or active it has been in other ways) and when the Church has been revived these four features have shone through. Now let us look at each of these themes in turn.

THE ABIDING THEMES

Faith

Faith has continually demonstrated itself through history in two clear dimensions—frequently more than two, but two I believe have always been present. First, there has been a belief in a *Supreme* and *Living God.* He has been personal—that is, able to communicate His will and love to mankind and mankind has been able to share fellowship with Him. As a Living God He has been marked off clearly from idols of wood and stone. He is also the Supreme Being, there are no other gods beside Him and neither is mankind to imagine themselves a god. This faith has marked the Christian off as distinct from other religions and reaches its highest point in the concept of the Fatherhood of God, without which there can be no true brotherhood among humans. So the faith in the Supreme and Living God has marked the experience of people coming out of paganism into Christianity at any point of time in history.

A second aspect of this theme of faith is that it has been more than a thing believed: it has been a personal experience, a *salvation experience.* From New Testament times down to the present day this has been a continuous demand by the Church of its converts and communicants. There is a place where believers have surrendered their wills to Christ and accepted the rule of Christ over their lives. That many professing Christian individuals have not experienced a personal encounter with Christ and found him as Saviour I do not deny, but this has always been a *problem* for the Church and the very fact that it is regarded as a problem reinforces the idea that one should *surrender* one's will to Christ. It is the recognition that humans cannot save themselves. I know no period of history, whatever the culture, where no Christian records (if there be records) suggest the theme of Christian faith in terms of the sovereignty of God and the salvation experience of mankind in Christ.

Entity

The fellowship group, the worshipping and witnessing congregation, the Christian tribe or village, or the Christian community scattered throughout the land (whatever the Church's physical structure) will have some idea of *Selfhood.* Here is the *Body of Christ* in the world and the *Fellowship of Believers.* Here are the believers who have renounced the world and accepted a new scale of values. They are bound together by their experience. When they meet they organize for worship and prayer. If they are persecuted they meet in secret; it happened all through history. When, under persecution, the scattered families were able to get together for one solitary occasion, they would discover their numbers were far greater than they had imagined. Always they were encouraged by their new awareness of their entity as the Christian Church scattered throughout the pagan world. In my reading of the documents of the planting of the Church in the islands of the Pacific, I repeatedly came across this awareness of the entity of the flock. It was the same in the early periods of persecution. It was the same in the days of the Reformation. The anthropologist speaks of the "awareness of selfhood." The theologian speaks of the "fellowship of believers" or the "Body of Christ." The idea of the corporate Christian group in action with its inner and outreaching life, the Church's own image of itself in the world, is an abiding theme.

How have these Christian individuals conceptualized themselves as a Church? The group concept comes from the biblical figure: the body, the flock, the temple, the vine and branches and the fellowship. They saw themselves as a *saved group* separated from the world, as an *interacting group,* building themselves up in the faith, helping, encouraging, praying and mutually supporting each other; as a *witnessing group,* reaching out to bring others into the fellowship; as a *serving group* applying Christian principles in the world; and as an *organized group,* with an authority pattern, a worshipping pattern, a proclamation pattern, an instruction pattern, a service pattern—all under approved leaders with all persons participating.

When the Christian converts withdrew from the world's value system and adopted a new one of their own, when they cut themselves off from pagan worship, a fellowship group became essential. This was so in New Testament times. It is so in the New Guinea highlands today. As their entity developed and extended it had to become more structured. We see the process as early as Acts 6. Leadership became established. Support was organized. Worship and instruction were provided. Simple liturgies, hymns and statements of belief came into being. Discipline patterns were initiated and membership in the group was formulated. This process began in the New Testament and it went through much the same growth process wherever the Church has been planted.

The anthropologist tells us the group seeks its entity for a number of practical reasons: for security, for unity, to secure perpetuity, for protection and for functional operation. A study of the growth of the Church through, say, the first three centuries along these lines would be a legitimate research project for a social anthropologist. In any case, the idea of the Church as a corporate and functional organism with its own entity and role in the world is an abiding theme of its history.

Mission

The Church started from the Great Commission. Frequently in history it has lost sight of this vision, but whenever it has returned, a period of missionary endeavor has followed. Only when the Church has had missionary vision has it grown. Missionary vision has meant a number of things for the Church through history: (1) a return to biblical criteria for Christian action in general, (2) a demand for clear-cut separation from paganism and the world value system, (3) a more intensive concentration on Scripture (and in many cases its translation), (4) the training of interpreters of the Word (laymen, catechists, nationals, etc.), and (5) greater participation in the fellowship group (including indigenous participation on a foreign field).

Although Christians are not of the world, their commission is *to* the world and *in* the world. Mission is (in the historical use of the term) a witness for a verdict: specific persuasion, seeking decision for Christ.

Each burst of missionary activity through history has represented a confluence of two streams of activity. Certain factors (variables), political, social, technological or historical, have opened up a door for mission. To change the metaphor, a field has ripened and is ready for harvest. Then secondly, the Church has returned to the biblical authority of the Great Commission as being still valid for the day in question. William Carey argued with vigor that the explorers having opened up a new world in his day, and nautical facilities being so much better, the Great Commission had a new significance for the time.

Despite the static periods in the history of the Church, one cannot help but notice that the periods of her relevance have certainly been those with a strong accent on the theme of mission.

Application

Christianity must be applied. I find in history that the Christian faith works itself out in life in three ways: (1) the holy life, (2) Christian service, and (3) encounter with the forces of spiritual evil.

Throughout the whole of Christian history there has been a demand for the holy life fostered by the fellowship and demonstrated in the world. Let us take those phrases: *the holy life, fostered by the fellowship,* and *demonstrated in the world.* First the Christian community has always been called away from worldliness to habits of holiness, to moral standards, personal good will and spiritual exercises. True, many Christians have been accused of hypocrisy, but this charge is offensive to true Christians. The very fact that it is offensive shows that Christians disapprove of the hypocrisy itself as much as they dislike the accusation. Historically the Church has tried to meet the problem of members who fall short of the standards expected by means of the institution (using the word anthropologically) of *discipline.* That the churches have their patterns of discipline shows their concern about the maintenance of the way of the holy life. By *holy* I do not mean sanctimonious, for holiness is essentially humble. In my study of emerging churches I have not found a case of an individual or group suffering moral decline by following Christ, though from all periods of history transformations have come with conversion: individuals like John Newton, the slaver, who became a slavery reformer and hymn writer; or Ratu Cakobau, the cannibal king, who became a fervent Wesleyan; or whole societies like the headhunters of Tega in the Solomons, who have a fine organized church under national pastors today. There can be no doubt about the general flow of life from worldliness to holiness as an abiding feature of the conversion of people to Christ through history.

To live a moral life in an immoral world is part of "the earthly trial" of the Christian. History shows that humans have been strengthened in this endeavor by the existence of the Christian group, the "fellowship of believers." Here members share their spiritual enthusiasm, build each other up in the faith, are instructed in the Scriptures and meet for worship with psalms, hymns, prayers, preaching and usually the sacraments. To this point this is a universal feature; but when we come to look at the details—liturgical, linguistic, aesthetic, architectural, organizational and so on—we find no uniformity whatever. The structure of the ministry may vary from a hierarchy to a leaderless group where he leads who is called at any given moment. Even an institution like the Lord's Supper is celebrated in many different ways. Yet there has always been a Christian group, a fellowship, building up the faithful and helping them to lives "worthy of repentance." We now see that the *churches* always have a *cultural* structure but there is something *supra-cultural* about the *Church.* The former can change from land to land and from age to age and be modified to meet changing needs and situations. The latter is a constant. There always is a fellowship of believers—a worshipping and praying body, studying the Word of God. The cultural form may perish, but the fellowship group goes on and on. This we see in history. Beyond history, the Scriptures lead us to expect that this fellowship group will continue "until He comes."

So the Church through history has demanded the holy life of its members, disciplined them when they have fallen short, and provided the fellowship group with its various "means of grace" whereby they could "grow in grace" and holiness. This has been to the specific end that the righteous way might be *demonstrated in the world.* Holiness is not something to be shut up in the fellowship. This leads to Pharisaism for the participants and enclosure for the congregation. The life of the Church must flow out into the world. History shows that when the Church withdrew from the world two things happened: she lost her relevance in the world and she stopped growing. In those periods of history when, through religious revival, the Church has rediscovered herself, she has immediately become an outreaching body and made a Christian impact on the world about her.

The holy life, then is not the life shut off from the world, but the life that penetrates into the world making it a better place. The fellowship withdrawing from the world is, to put it anthropologically, a spiritual mechanism, to strengthen the thrust into the world. This impact of the Christian group on the world has recurred at different levels at many times and places, in many rural localities, in towns, in districts and sometimes whole nations have felt it as Bready's *England Before and After Wesley* (1938) shows. If you look at the full sweep of Christian history or if you probe with deeper research into some limited area, you find this to be a recurring phenomenon. The idea of the holy life is reflected through the Pastoral Epistles, in the early church manuals, in the writings of the Apologists and in the history of the expanding Church to our own times. Despite the deterioration of many congregations which manifest the disease of enclosure (not a few in our own day), the Church at large has always disapproved of this condition and "squirms" under the criticism, because it knows this behavior does not line up with either the biblical criteria or the experience of the Church through history. The idea of the holy life like a ray of light penetrating the darkness is an abiding belief of the Church. Christianity has to be applied to the world.

Also part of the *theme of application* is the concept of Christian *service.* The Gospel preaching of the love of God works out in love among mankind, a practical demonstration of meeting human needs. No church (Christian congregation) is worthy of the name without its social outreach. Any person who reads the documents of the Church through history—the essays, the apologies, the sermons, the catechisms—will discover a social message built in from the beginning. Here again we find variables due to social structure and cultural conditioning, but always there is again the same notion of the supra-cultural. There always has been some way for Christians to serve their fellow humans. There always has been some way of striving for human betterment. Conditioned by the different socio-political and cultural environments of history, wherever the Church has sprung up a social message has emerged, and usually reinforced with support, organized and controlled. Usually the service ministry is differentiated from the proclamation, that neither be neglected. This process emerged as early as Acts 6. From Tertullian we get a picture of organized almsgiving, support for teachers, widows, orphans, the sick, itinerant brethren, prisoners in the mines, the poor (unable to pay for burials, for example), the care of slaves, and a general stewardship program for the organization and activities of the Church itself. Harnack in his *Mission and Expansion of Christianity in the First Three Centuries* (1962) has a fifty page chapter on the service ministry which he found highly developed.

The service projects of the Church throughout history have varied because the human needs have varied in different regions of the world and periods of history. It is amazing how flexible the social programs of the Church have been whether helping the needy or fighting for social justice. The story of Christian missions in the Pacific over the last century comprised a series of fights for social justice, in which one social evil after another was confronted: participation in native wars, sexual permissiveness and the introduction of venereal disease, blackbirding and so forth—when the white missionaries were confronting their own race, for the protection of the islanders. Thus is the Church always involved in the world about her. Her faith and teaching are of little value unless *applied* in the world. She has been called to be the conscience of the world, and thus the great movements for education, for medical services, for labor reforms and such like at various points of history have usually come from outreaches of the Church and often in the wake of her spiritual awakenings, as Timothy L. Smith points out in *Revivalism and Social Reform* (1980).

The theme of *application,* of "working out one's salvation" in the world, either individually or communally conceptualized, has been frequently an *encounter with the organized forces of evil,* with demons and with organized paganism. We meet this in the New Testament, especially the Gospels and Acts. Jesus was especially concerned with demon possession. As the Gospel penetrated the world, this encounter became more and more significant: Justin, Tatian, Tertullian, and Origen speak of it. Tertullian stressed the role of exorcist. Origen also pressed that exorcism be "in the name of Jesus." The exorcist became a recognized role in the Church. These encounters were not merely with lowly or rural folk. Demon possession was in high places and especially penetrated the upper classes during the third century, as the greater cults broke down into sheer animism. When Constantine opened the way for the acceptance of Christianity in Rome, the great religion of that Empire was on the wane and polydaemonism was rampant. But whether Christianity was confronting demons or the great organized cults, a lively encounter with paganism was a continuing situation and a vital issue, as it still is on many mission fields. In our own big cities it may perhaps take the form of voodooism, spiritism, drug cults and astrology.

Down through history the conflict with paganism has been a major demonstration of an individual's Christianity. Several issues were at stake:

1. To what allegiance did the Christian bow? Who ruled his or her life? Who was Lord and Saviour?

2. Keeping free from pagan contamination was a supreme Christian duty. It was the negative aspect of confessing one's faith.

3. From the New Testament times (even to our present day) the battle is being fought against syncretism. The clash came here at the very beginning and frequently has resulted in persecution.

4. Because the Christians cut themselves off from some political and social indulgences they were branded as antisocial, and because they changed the old religion they were accused of atheism. The criticism that they were "destroyers of culture" needs to be qualified. They were rather agents of change within culture. They still spoke the same language, lived in the same economic structures and normally followed the same trades; but they had a new religion and a new ethic.

5. Their new supreme loyalty to Christ as Lord and Saviour led to social action against the Christians as individuals and as a community (the Church).

Christian apologists who lived through periods of persecution left us a picture of this adamant Christian resistance to paganism and its related practices. When resistance to paganism becomes a threat to its survival, paganism fights back with persecution. This is also true in modern missions. Thus is the Church permanently involved in the battle between Christ and Satan and the Christian engagement is part of the application of faith.

This is a continual battle. It did not end, for example, when Christianity was proclaimed the State religion with the Edict of Milan in 313 A.D. Neither did the persecutions end then. Only about one twentieth of the Empire became Christian and paganism was not prohibited. Pagan temples and Christian buildings were found side by side and both were beautiful and well cared for. Sunday was observed at court but not everywhere. Athenian temples were in use until the end of the century and some institutions until 529. In some regions (for example, the Peloponnesian mountains) peasants worshipped the mythical gods of animism for as long as five hundred years after Constantine. I do not think that the Church was ever promised any rest in the fight against paganism. The forms of the fight may vary in time and place, but the sovereignty of Christ is always the Christian's duty to defend. It may be an out and out conflict with paganism in the world or it may be inside the fellowship group itself as syncretism. It was so in New Testament times and we are concerned with it still.

THE AUTHORITY OF THE WORD

The abiding themes of the Church—faith, entity, mission and application—have been notions selected for discussion because as one explores the resources of the data bank of Christian history the material seems to fall into these four categories. Always there has been a variability due to environmental, cultural and historical factors, but always there has been something supracultural and suprahistorical. There is the notion of faith in the sovereignty of God and the Lordship of Christ; the notion of the fellowship group (the Church) as a reality and an entity, with awareness of its selfhood and its functional role in the world; there is the notion of the mission of the Church to convert individuals and incorporate them into the group and send them forth to witness; and there is the notion of the application of faith by demonstration in the world, through the holy life, the service of mankind and in encounter with paganism. These are the supra-cultural and supra-historical themes of the Church as I find them demonstrated in history.

Having established these points to my own satisfaction from history rather than from the Bible it seems appropriate that I should at least try to bring the Scriptures to bear on them, for the Bible itself is an historical collection of records about the people of God and their role in the world, and in our missiological definitions we have accepted its criteria. Theologically we regard Christianity as a *revealed* religion. Our information about that revelation is in the written Word of God. Thus we believe it has *authority*. At first I was disposed to include the notion of the authority of Scripture as one of the abiding themes of the Church, but more careful reflection reminded me that there have been some fine functioning congregations in history which have had no Bible in their own language and God has used other means of bringing individuals to Christ and revealing Himself to them. Furthermore, the Christian communities of the New Testament predating the formation of the canon depended on an oral message. God gave the New Testament to the Church within the structure of its own operations, meeting the felt needs of the Christian community in the world.

From that time the written Word has been handed down and translated into the languages of the world. It has been accepted by the Church as the criteria or rule for faith and practice. It has been the resource material of Christian preaching and instruction, and God has used the Scriptures time after time for bringing churches into being where no evangelist had ever been. The notion that the Bible is the Word of God and the rule of faith and practice for the Christian may be placed beside the abiding themes of the Church, which it reinforces and validates. It is true that in our day some liberal theologians and missiologists have rejected parts of the Bible and robbed it of authority by their selectivity, but their churches are nearly empty and their missions are static. Church growth case studies rather suggest that where the Church grows the authority of Scripture is not questioned.

Once Christians accept the authority of the written Word of God they are not confined to the purely historical experience for their knowledge of God and the faith. The Bible becomes an extremely valuable interpretive tool. Once they begin to develop a theological dimension in their thinking the Bible becomes the starting point for everything. This, however, is possible only because they first had an historical experience of the transformed life when they met Christ. When a number of people share this experience and meet together as a group, say, for Bible study, the capacity for discovery of spiritual truth is greatly increased—another reason why the group idea is necessary.

THE MODE OF COMMUNICATION

There is one other aspect of the activities of the Church which bears on its basic themes and to which history has something to say. I refer to the *mode of communication.* If I follow the same procedure and ask what features have persisted through the centuries, once again I find cultural and historical variables over against something that is supra-cultural and supra-historical.

In the first place there are always (if there is a written form of the language) two kinds of presentation: the written and the spoken. The former is the more endurable. It can be preserved, read and re-read, and recalled with greater accuracy. The written record may vary from simple pictographs imprinted on clay tablets, painted on walls, stenciled on cloth, or penned on vellum, to printed books and journals, microfilms and microfische. These variables are culturally and historically determined. The spoken communication likewise may vary from chants and sagas, songs and poems, recited laws and proverbs, to conversation, orations, lectures and sermons. Each age and culture developed the forms of expression of its own choice in its own manner and it was effective in that kind of society at that point of time. I have seen the Lord's Prayer printed in a hymn book by typography, typed on a wax sheet and duplicated, printed on vellum and illustrated with a brush, worked in silk and framed as a picture, in the microphotograph that could not be read without magnification, printed on Polynesian bark cloth. I have heard it recited after public prayer, chanted in both indigenous and foreign manner, sung as a solo, incorporated in catechisms and liturgies. I have known individuals to use it in trouble when they knew no other prayer. Jesus gave it originally as an "index prayer" or a model after the Jewish pattern. Yet despite all these diversified cultural forms of expression, the prayer itself, its *esse,* was a constant.

Allowing then for the various forms of writing and speaking, what basic modes of communication have been continually used by the Church through history? If there are abiding themes, are there abiding modes? I believe there are.

First, there is *proclamation,* by which I mean preaching after the prophetic manner: proclaiming what the Lord says to the people without any debate. Second, there has always been a place for *teaching,* which could be by instruction, dialogue or catechism. Third, there was the Christian *apology,* which might have been either spoken as a dialogue or debate, or a written discourse. The fourth form was personal *witness,* the distinctive feature of which was the personal statement of what the communicator had himself experienced, and was normally conversation or dialogue; or maybe a written letter.

The first and fourth seem to have been most used by God in winning converts from the world, the first and second for building up the inner strength of the Church. The third achieved the Church's recognition of the canon and authority of Scripture, and the Scripture itself has been a powerful communicator of Christian truth at all levels. It is interesting to note that while the technology of our day (radio and T.V.) tend to replace the public meeting and the printed book for many people, nevertheless the radio and T.V. presentations continue to use proclamation, teaching, apology and witness as the modes for communicating the message. The modes abide. The forms change.

What does all this say for missiology today? First, it identifies us with the historic stream of God's action in the Christian Church down through history. It puts us in the line of tradition where we belong and warns us against a "missiology" of syncretism or universalism. Second, it leads us from historical studies back to biblical roots and reminds us where the roots of mission lie. The authority of Scripture is a notion in tune with the abiding themes of the Church. This warns us against trying to build a so-called missiology on a fractured authority. Third, it helps us to distinguish between cultural and historical forms in which the Church must operate at any given location in time and place, and supra-cultural and supra-historical themes and modes; the former being subject to change and the latter being continuous. This is a valuable insight for Christian workers in times of crisis and rapid social change when church structures seem to be threatened. Fourth, it keeps before us the importance of the Christian group which has to grow and multiply and come to grips with the world. Finally, we see that the periods when the abiding themes of the Church are found to be most clearly articulated are also the periods of greatest church growth.

CHAPTER 19

"Contours of Reality" in the History of Mission

Today there is a lack of a general interest in the dynamic aspect of history by missiologists. Missiography is still dominated by the old formal classical models of "what history is," instead of catching the dynamics "that are really there." E.H. Carr asked the rhetorical question, "What is history?" and provided his own answer: "It is a continuous process of interaction between the historian and [the] facts, an unending dialogue between the present and the past" (1963: 34-35). Sevenster, in an article on "Why Study Church History?" formulated his definition of history as "the activity of man to find and choose among the facts of the past those meaningful to him" (1974: 82). The common element in those two definitions is the linkage between past and present. The purpose of this chapter is to explore that relationship in the historical process of Christian mission, the dynamic "contours of reality"[1] which pulls us out of the old classical models of dates, periods and ethnocentricism, and which the Post-colonial Age of Missions demands.

Let me enumerate some of those contours which I believe to constitute the reality of history.

THE CONTOUR OF CONTINUITY

All the historical books of the New Testament (i.e., those which provide the narrative of missionary foundations), the four Gospels and the

The original version of this chapter was published in *Missiology*, October 1975, Vol. III, No. 4, pp. 403-414. Gratitude is hereby expressed to the publisher for permission to include it here.

Acts, are open-ended. The great commission in Matthew reaches out to all ethnic groups, and does so "unto the end of the age" (Mt. 28: 20). The Markan commission is "unto all the world," "to every creature," with the promise of signs to follow, and leaves the apostles going forth and preaching everywhere (Mk. 16: 15,17,20). In Luke, the apostles "are witnesses of these things" and this they do "continually praising and blessing God" (Lk. 24: 48, 53). In John, Jesus says "As the Father hath sent me even so send I you" (20: 21) "into the world" (17: 18), the world which "could not contain the books" were they ever written (21: 25), which, as Sevenster points out, is not simply the events of our Lord's physical life on earth, but his Presence and deeds in the Church through history (1974: 82). And then the Book of Acts leaves Paul in his own hired house, ministering and preaching. It is an unfinished book. It tells us enough to reveal how the Spirit of God works with and through believers, and how we may expect Him to continue working through history.

Every historiographer has a chapter on continuity in his book, for "history has its origin in man's awareness of continuity" (Barzun & Graff 1962: 44). Christian mission is an historical or diachronic theme, because continuity was an inbuilt ingredient from the very start. God's mission to mankind must be a continuing proclamation "until He comes." What else needs to be said on the point?

THE CONTOUR OF CHANGE

The danger with continuities is that they sometimes become formalized stereotypes. In treasuring their ancient traditions people often institutionalize them so rigidly that they become mere archaeological artifacts. In some places this actually happens to the church. There is a way in which it can happen even to the Bible: when we treat the book as a legalistic rather than an experiential tool. This is a static view of the past as a closed record, and in reality is not a continuity at all. Those governed by such "a static view of society" and its cultural institution as Gustavson pointed out, "have no real awareness of the constant change" that is going on deep in society all the time (1955: 176). Furthermore, every culture has its inbuilt mechanisms for effecting change, for adapting to the situations it confronts, first, for survival sake, and second, for grasping the opportunities the change presents. A human society, a kinship group, or a Christian *koinonia,* does not demonstrate its continuity by survival "in a museum," but by its capacity for coming to grips with each new situation.

When the apostles were sent "into the world" with a commission which called for the continuity of mission, it was to a life of continual dynamic change, of confrontation; not to preach a creed or ethic which came from a first century cultural situation, but to bring individuals to relationship with a Person, who could save people, and inspire them to love one another and to live the life of holiness in terms of new cultures or life styles.

In a day when many of our sacred forms have become fetishes, when life styles are being challenged, when what we had taken to be continuities are found to be only cultural artifacts, we look to Christian historians to give us some light on the difference between static artifacts and ongoing living organisms.

THE CONTOUR OF ETHNOHISTORY

As soon as we confront the truth that our Lord sent the apostles out *into the world* we are involved in some kind of encounter with culture. They "were not of the world, as he was not of the world" (Jn. 17: 14, 16)—so presumably the sending implied that he was to transmit something supracultural through them. This was at least a "peace such as the world could not give" (Jn. 14: 27). It was of course *his* peace as he had "overcome the world" (Jn. 16: 33). But, nevertheless, the world was the scene of his mission, and throughout history, as the cultural scenes of changing generations and ethnic diffusion demonstrated the diversity of the world into which they were sent, the whole question of cross-cultural communication became inevitably part of Christian mission. The Lord committed his followers to cross-cultural proclamation and witness, and gave them gifts adequate for the task. They were bound to develop methods, strategies, and approaches as the Church expanded. Even in the Apostolic Age, the Church confronted ethnic problems, and learned to recognize the diversity of culture within the unity of the Body (for example, Acts 6: 1-7; 15: 22-32).

The careless use of the term *ethnohistory* by some missiologists, as if it were merely the sum of history and anthropology, calls for comment. History and anthropology are disciplines, but ethnohistory is a methodology. It recognizes its own system of values. It recognizes that historical and anthropological techniques have something to offer each other and correct each other's shortcomings. The methodology is symbiotic. I would even go further than this and suggest that it is syngenetic—in other words, something quite new is born through the union. Lynn T. White's article on "History and Horseshoe Nails" is a good example of this. He tells of how his discovery of Kroeber's method for reconstructing history from archaeological artifacts without the use of documents revolutionised his approach to the history of medieval technology (1970: 50). One of the features of the next generation of missiologists will certainly be the development of that currently vague area covered by terms like ethnohistory, ethnotheology, ethnolinguistics, ethnopsychology and ethnobiblical studies. If I am still alive at the end of the century I expect to see a large body of literature along these lines, and I think it will transform the character and quality of missiology in this Post-colonial Age. These methodologies are probing at the dimensions of missiological symbiosis, which pass unnoticed because of the overspecialization of the traditional disciplines. This, in turn, isolates the latter from the wholeness of human life and endeavor. If we do not develop these interdisciplinary methods missiology will perish and ecome no more than a historical experiment of the 1970s and 80s, an unsuccessful attempt to deal with the anomie of the 1960s.

THE CONTOUR OF METAHISTORY

The historian, Gottschalk, has raised the question of those forces which are not quite "historicable" because they are not verified by documents and cannot be measured, but which nevertheless do evidence some kind of human experience or some potent influence at work. They are real and part of history—*metahistory* he calls them (1969: 254-255). The ethnohistorian, Vansina, known for his historical reconstructions from African oral traditions, has discussed the weaknesses of the social sciences in this respect.

Social science is concerned with finding regularities by means of abstractions, but "every abstraction" he says "must be put back into reality." He illustrates this by the chemist seeking first to discover basic properties, and only thereafter turning to "the taste of the wine" and the perfume of the rose (1970: 240). Anthropology is still identifying variables and regularities, but there is poetry and sentiment in history which is part of its reality.

If one has to write his or her own life story certain moments would have to be included that defy scientific measurements and documentation— the metahistorical moments we might call them. There was a point in my life one Friday night in 1928, near the Victoria Market in Melbourne (I could take you to the precise place now) where I took the step of faith. My training had been Christian. I had not actually learned any more factual biblical knowledge that night. It was just that I was suddenly prompted to act on the faith I already knew to be true. From that moment my life was never the same again. There was another moment one night in Fiji, when I was imprisoned in an island house by a tropical downpour. An old Fijian pastor and I shared our inner lives with each other in one sacred hour, quite oblivious to our differences in color and culture, and thereafter neither of us was ever quite the same again. Although I cannot measure or document these events, no one will ever convince me they are not part of the reality of my personal history.

Likewise, there was that tremendous experience of the risen Lord that burst on the early Church (for example, Lk. 24: 32-35); that experience which pulled together a band of discouraged, and fearful disciples and sent them forth to proclaim the resurrection with power. Life was never quite the same for them again. As long as the lives of men and women are transformed by the conversion experience, which is difficult to document or measure, we need to allow for the metahistorical contour of reality.

THE CONTOUR OF CONVERGENCE

Anthropologists have a theory that a society has to be ready for change before new ideas offer a viable option for acceptance. Kroeber even speaks of situations in which "the time is not yet ripe" (1948: 366-367). He is thinking culturally, but there is also a religious factor which makes times propitious for innovation.

I believe it was Newman who used to speak of "the convergences of history." There are points in time when, in the divine economy, people and situations are brought together, and something new emerges in the confluence. In the New Testament we have the phrase "in the fullness of time" (Gal. 4: 4). Christ did indeed come at the precisely opportune time—when, for the first time, the world was unified by Roman rule and roads, a common language, and knowledge of the Greek translation of the Old Testament was widely diffused, and the old religion of Rome was being reformulated, and a new individualism was abroad through the Empire.

I remember in my own missionary researches into the diffusion of the faith throughout Oceania, how time and time again the entry of the Gospel was preceded by an amazing series of circumstances, which could only really be satisfactorily explained by means of a theocratic interpretation of history. The critical question is whether the convergences of history are accidents, or if there is a Power or a Will behind history. This is implied by the great commission. When the Lord sent forth His followers, told them to practice the way of prayer, promised them the guidance of the Comforter, and urged them to persevere until His return—was there not here an implied view of history? The contour of convergence in history, implies that God is Sovereign, and that those who go forth in mission, by prayer and obedience, should find themselves in "the stream of His will" as Brother Lawrence phrased it (1958). Many secular historians regard this position as simplistic, but for the Christian it stands firm as a faith position.

THE CONTOUR OF INTERPRETATION

If it is a faith position, then we must ask where we find the basis of our faith. Where do we discover the criteria for our evaluations when we interpret our data, especially when we study history in order "to understand our own place in history" (Sevenster 1974: 83)? I would argue that if the Scriptures themselves are the basis of our belief in the validity of the Christian mission in which we are engaged, then it should also provide our concept of history. To engage in Christian mission for biblical reasons, and yet not to accept either the biblical view of history, or the biblical statement of the Gospel message, or the biblical view of God, and so forth, would be an inconsistent use of the biblical tool. Scripture is its own interpreter (2 Tim. 3: 14-17).

The historian must by definition use the tools as "givens." You cannot abuse the integrity of the tool, or you might as well discard it altogether. This is why the doctrine of the resurrection, for example, must stand as stated if the rest of the New Testament is to be accepted. It may be metahistory, but its validity must stand if the tool stands. No historian is justified in making his or her "own measure of human credibility"—a tool for measuring the tool. This is merely to shift the criteria from the Word of God to the minds of humans, from something inspired to something incredible.

Let me illustrate from a secular example. Freud gave us a psycho-analytical study of Leonardo da Vinci's memory of a vulture, which came to him in his cradle, and became the key to his later fantasies. The historian, Hancock, points out that Freud leaned on a German translator. The bird was not a vulture but a kite, which has quite different associations in legend and myth. Hancock criticizes Freud for building "so large an edifice of interpretation" on a short, mistranslated sentence. He goes on to add that Freud

> conceived, and hotly pursued a bright idea, brushed aside all objection to it, and ended by persuading himself that the possibilities were probabilities, and the probabilities certainties (1968: 24-25).

In my humble opinion, this is precisely what the demythologizers have done with the narrative of the life of our Lord, and the fallacy, I believe, is methodological. The criterion which sends forth, must also tell us what to communicate. Once you fiddle with the tool, its measurements will no longer be true.

THE CONTOUR OF REVELATION

Is there then no human side to historical perception? Surely there is. When God reveals himself to a faithful historian, there has to be a response of some kind. The historian needs a capacity for appreciating the truth which God is showing in history. Perhaps we may describe it as *insight* rather than factual knowledge, for one may have mastery over the documented facts and still not perceive the dynamics. I believe that *revelation* does come to patient researchers. Revelation is a *two way process*. There is a sense in which it comes from God, but the historian also must have the eyes to see. History and science have this in common. The celebrated scientist, Sir Lawrence Bragg described this capacity for research insight in the following manner:

> When one has sought long for a clue to a secret of nature, and is rewarded by grasping some part of the answer, it comes as a blinding flash of revelation: it comes as something new, more simple and at the same time more anesthetically satisfying than anything one could have created in his own mind. This conviction is something revealed, and not something imagined.[2]

This is an experience. It is not just a "bright idea" in the imagination, for the proof of which subsequently the data has to be selected. It comes as a revelation, and it normally comes to people ready to respond to it.

Sometimes we do not perceive the whole truth at one time. We strain to understand what history is saying to us. We catch a facet of truth. We put it aside and ponder it from time to time.[3] Then suddenly the picture clears, and meaning comes out of the past, and it speaks to us in the present. If historians cannot see beyond dates, and periods, and dry facts, they are not likely to respond to a dynamic revelation, or to see what God really has done in history. One needs the eyes to see.

I recall one terrible trip I made on a six ton lugger in Fiji, peering through a dense haze of rain, looking for a peak which would mark the entrance to the reef, which we could not see either, though we heard the roar of the waves beating on it. Then suddenly the Chinese pilot, on whom my life depended, gave a shout: "It is there! I see it." He saw it. I never did, not until we were safely within the reef. Why did he see what I did not? He had experience on his side. He knew roughly where to look, precisely what he was looking for, and he had trained his eyes to penetrate the haze with expectation. And when he saw, he knew what he had to do. Missiography needs pilots with eyes that can penetrate the haze, who know what to look for, where to find it, and having seen, know how to make use of that perception in our present need.

THE CONTOUR OF RELEVANCE

It is not enough to have a well-written history of one's mission field, if it does not speak to the present situation. No branch of human study or research can really justify itself unless it offers some insight or know-how to people involved in the reality of living today. There is no revelation without the response of the sleeping eye and hearing ear either for the historian or the reader. And what is this perception without application? The historian, Stavrianos, complained that the discipline of history tended to be conditioned by a world which no longer exists, and that the majority of historians resist the application of "their academic interests to the urgencies of the present day." He argued from this presupposition that the integrity of the discipline of history is challenged when historians "fail to come to grips with the implications of the post-colonial situation" (1966: 4). Whether he be right or wrong about the involvement of his colleagues, he is certainly right in claiming that any study of the past must justify itself in application to the problems of the present.

All this brings us back to our starting point when we spoke of the continuities of history, and found our missiological origins in the open-ended historical books of the New Testament, and the implications of our Lord's sending his followers into the world, and demanding they remain there, involved, unto the end of the age—to the end of time as we now know it, and geographically to the ethnic extremities of the earth. The Lord's commission was inescapably diachronic and universal.

The history of how the Church has, or has not fulfilled this commission is full of examples of how we should, or should not do it. Similarly, the history of mission is replete with examples of how the Spirit of God (as promised by our Lord) has worked in the world through his faithful servants in times past, and will continue to do so in our midst today. We look at missions and missionaries in the past that we may know ourselves better in the present: both what we should and should not be. If history is a "continuous process of interaction between the historian and [the] facts, an unending dialogue between the present and the past" as was suggested at the beginning of this chapter, the very thought of mission in the Postcolonial Age requires the historical ingredient in missiology.

Notes:

1. The term "contours of reality" comes from Bergson, but I have it from Marc Bloch, who was arguing that reality cannot be measured by a clock or time line, but required a "variability of rhythm," "marginal zones" and "plasticity" (Bloch 1964: 189).

2. The passage comes from *Science and the Adventure of Living,* but I have it indirectly from Coulson's fine study on science and the Christian faith (1955: 99).

3. Historian Lynn T. White calls this "historical rumination" which he says "is a bit like making cheese; you shape it up, set it on a shelf in a cool place and after a time come back to see if it has matured properly" (1970: 61).

The original version of this chapter was published in *Missiology,* October 1975, Vol. III, No. 4, pp. 403-414. Gratitude is hereby expressed to the publisher for permission to include it here.

CHAPTER 20

Testing History by Church Growth Theory: People Movements of the Middle Ages

Recent church growth research has brought to light a great deal of important information about the nature of people movements from animism to Christianity. This research has a number of significant consequences for the Christian historian.

1. It calls for a reevaluation of the people movements of the Middle Ages, by means of which Europe became Christian.

2. Church growth research has penetrated further into the study of the character of the conversion experience from animism. Can affinities be established between the present day animism and the European forms? If so, what does church growth say to history, and vice versa?

3. Can it be established that people movements normally occur in periods known to be propitious for religious change? To what extent is this due to the breakdown or decay of animism? Is the ripeness for change demonstrated by the spread of other religions at the same time?

4. To what extent is the popular conception of the employment of pressure for conversion really accurate? What was the precise place of iconoclasm in stimulating these people movements, and why was the method employed? What meaning did the animist and missionary ascribe to this?

5.   What was the role of Christian education in the expansion of the
Church, both (a) as a cause of conversion, and (b) as a follow-up
of these people movements? Was the syncretism, which subsequently appeared in the pre-Reformation Church due to faulty
methods of conversion or to ineffective follow-up?

What I am suggesting in this essay is that much of the history of the
Middle Ages probably needs rewriting as a result of the church growth
case studies and the missiological theory based on this research. Even my
own research calls for this. *People Movements of Southern Polynesia*
(1971), contains four case studies of people movements based on a huge
amount of cited and uncited documentation and an essay on "The
Validity of the People Movement" based on that data. In *Solomon
Islands Christianity* (1967a), chapter seven, (and indeed everything on
the nativistic movements if you include the negative aspect) speaks to
these issues. "Religious Group Conversion in Non-western Society"
raises all kinds of questions for the historian of the Middle Ages. This
does not stand alone. McGavran was writing on this theme in India years
ago. His *Bridges of God* (1955) and his *Understanding Church Growth*
(1970), both have the people movement as a major theme. Pickett's
writing likewise: though we all began calling them mass movements, a
term we all ultimately rejected. I think the term *people movement* actually
came from McGavran. I read his *Bridges of God* in Fiji in 1958, and
there I found the term and accepted it for my own use. It is a fertile
concept. Every time we write about it we find some new aspect or
ramification; we find we need a more descriptive terminology (e.g. multi-
individual and multi-relational). Our church growth case studies build up
around the notion, and we become impressed by the wide distribution of
people movements in all parts of the world. Occasionally a thesis brings
out some new aspect, though mostly they use it as a kind of frame of
reference for their descriptions. In any case we do not have to battle any
more for the validity of the concept.

This recognition by the missionary oriented public of the fact that a
great deal of church planting has been as a result of people movements in
subrecent history and in current affairs has been one of the really great
achievements of Fuller Seminary's School of World Mission: not only the
idea itself but also the general acceptance of it. Up to this point we have
explored the concept synchronically in our own generation. Our time
depth has not been great. At best we have gone back to the planting of
modern Protestant missions a century or so; certainly no further back than
William Carey. This has been possible because of the superb documentation created by the great missionary societies: BMS, LMS, CMS, WMS
and ABCFM. In this essay I am arguing that what we have learned from
our study of recent people movements, together with our deeper
penetration into the nature of animism and the process of cross-cultural

religious conversion (though we still have to go much deeper yet) call for a reevaluation of the movements of the Middle Ages in Europe and Britain, particularly from the time of Constantine onwards.

Because of our biblical rootage we have already cast our thinking back to our Christian origins. McGavran gave a chapter to this concept in the New Testament Church in *Bridges of God*. More recently in *Church Growth and the Word of God* (1970a) I have insisted on the biblical validity of people movements in the workings of the Spirit of God. So we find our data at both ends of the Christian chronology, and I believe the time has come for us to probe more thoroughly some of the significant periods in the middle of that time line.

Actually, in 1954 McGavran pointed out that the people movements of Northern Europe had a place in our historical sequence of the expansion of the Church. The full scope of his book only permitted him two pages for the discussion. However, he suggested that our criticisms of the conversions after Constantine have been judgments by Western criteria of post-industrial revolution individualism. He also pointed out that the choice was never between a fourth-rate method of conversion by tribal discipling and a first-class individual one. "It was tribal conversions or nothing." In his more recent writing, although McGavran draws most of his illustrations from modern and especially contemporary missions, yet he occasionally does go back to the Middle Ages (for example, 1970:24-25) and when he does so he accepts the people movement as similar phenomena to those of the Bible and of our own day.

We have now enough documented and attested cases, which by the comparative method, have given us enough general hypotheses, and we have developed enough testing tools to warrant our taking a hard look at the medieval history of church planting.

TAKING A SECOND LOOK AT HISTORY

The middle ages covers a period of great migrations and general insecurity caused by the invasions and pressures of the mobile tribes. The degree to which the element of mobility itself, together with its resultant acculturation led to the breakdown of the old religious solidarity needs to be studied systematically. Latourette calls this period from 500 A.D. onwards "The Thousand Years of Uncertainty," but despite his masterly twenty page summary looking for causes and effects, I doubt if he really explores the cultural dynamics of the period. True, he allows for the "inward vitality" of expanding faiths, especially of Christianity, and he comes back to the idea of the "hidden springs of conduct" of the conquering faith, and admits that this may "carry us far beyond the domain to which the historian is supposed to be restricted. At the most he can only recognize the possible existence of realms into which the canons of his craft forbid him to venture" (1937; II:14).

This superb historical study lacks one thing—that element which Homer Barnett and Anthony Wallace could have given it. These men, the deep researchers who have pondered the nature of the innovative process and the stress situation, have revealed to us what we know of the dynamics of social and religious change in periods of stress and population mobility. When we have brought their work to bear on church growth data, we have greatly deepened our insights and developed our testing tools. My contention is that we should now turn these methods and criteria on to the data of church history at a greater time depth, and furthermore I regard this exercise as a legitimate part of the discipline of missiology. I disagree that these "hidden springs of conduct" are "beyond the domain of the historian." Is it right to leave Constantine and Boniface and Patrick to the formal historians, when we have anthropological and missiological tools which could be brought to play on the data? I do not think we will find much new data. There is none in this chapter. But we can bring it under a new focus.

The point I am trying to make is that as we have been studying history to see what it says to missiology and church growth, I think the time has come for reversing the process and bringing church growth dimensions to bear on history. C. J. Renier, in *History: Its Purpose and Method,* speaks of "new kinds of guidance" based on collective historical studies that demand that historians "retell the story from a new point of view." He speaks of looking more closely at aspects of the past which previous generations of investigators neglected. This "refocus"'in historical research "demands new investigation and gains greatly in accuracy as a result" (1965:25). Perhaps I may join to this something Huizinga said in an article on "Historical Conceptualization":

> Historical knowledge is dead and worthless that has not as its sounding-board and its measuring rod the historian's personal intellectual and spiritual life (Stern 1956:301).

He goes on to qualify this and point out its danger, but to me it says that the people movements of history should be historically evaluated by researchers who understand, psychologically and spiritually, what a people movement experience really is, and who have a positive attitude towards the phenomena.

RELIGIOUSLY INNOVATIVE PERIODS

An idea which church growth theory has taken from anthropology is the notion that great religious change tends to come when people are ready for it. The biblical figure is: when fields are white unto harvest. We have also made the point that when people are in the mood for religious change they are exposed to other options besides Christianity. In our own

day we have seen here in this country—drug cults, the peyote religion and
several forms of neo-animism spread by people movement patterns. Thus
we reject the idea of a secular age, and ask why these options have been
acceptable and not Christianity. We have seen that while Christianity was
spreading in the Roman world, Buddhism was spreading in the East; and
that while Scotland, France, England and Germany were being evan-
gelized, the older Christian world was being destroyed by Islam. These
were centuries of dramatic religious acceptance and rejection. Even
within the Roman Empire itself Christianity was by no means the only
serious option. The religion of Isis and the worship of Mithra were real
rivals. Traces of the Isis cult have been found as far afield as Britain,
polytheistic and immoral at the popular level, mystical and pantheistic for
its more educated adherents.

The origins of Mithraic sun worship were in Persia and, like the
Egyptian cult, it was spreading in the first century beside Christianity. In
the third century, according to Robinson (1917:32) at one time it
threatened to displace Christianity and even to become the religion of the
Empire. A Belgian scholar argues that the selection of December 25 for
Christmas Day was a deliberate attempt to displace the Mithraic worship
on that day. When we remember that Mithraism was spread by mobile
persons—Roman soldiers, traders and slaves, frequently the same kinds
of people who spread Christianity, and that the two religions offered
satisfactions for similar felt needs, that both had the symbolism of life out
of death, similar moral teachings, rites of baptism, meal of bread and
wine, and a belief in the resurrection of the body; I say when we remember
these similarities, we realize that the people movement potential of the
first few centuries was divided among several options. We have here a
general mood receptive for religious innovation. I think we might well go
back to this period of history and study it again in the light of our better
knowledge of people movement phenomena.

One of the main causes for the readiness to listen to the advocates of
these rival options was that the old animism was frequently unable to
fulfill its normal functions and meet the needs felt by societies undergoing
change. As early as 43 A.D. Druidism had been shocked by the arrival of
Roman legions. Aulus Plautius took four legions to Britain—48,000 men.
Suetonius Paulinus conquered Anglesey sixteen years later and slaughtered
the armies of Boadicea. This military conquest cut off the strength and
prestige of Druidism and reduced the British faith in it.

Lavisse in his *Historie de France* (1918) discusses how the Druidism
of Gaul was decadent when the Christian missionaries arrived. The
processes of Roman acculturation were already in operation. The prestige
and power of its hierarchy had been reduced by the Emperor Tiberius,
who had legislated against human sacrifice, thus interfering with basic
druidical rituals. Furthermore, the druid assemblies fell under the Roman
laws of "illicit associations." Under these destructive influences

Druidism had sought a syncretistic coexistence with the worship of the Roman gods and thus it was a very corrupted form of Druidism which survived in some places until the fourth century.

EUROPEAN ANIMISM

More and more I am convinced of the affinities between the animism of northern Europe and the forms current in our own day in Africa, Oceania and Indonesia. Two types of evidence suggest this: (1) the descriptions of the iconoclasm directed against the pagan sacred places and paraphernalia, and (2) the repeated pronouncements and sermons of the leaders of the Church against the paganism which threatened to invade the Church. Martin of Tours conducts an onslaught against groves, temples and idols. Columba cuts down the oaks on the shores of Loch Foyle and as a functional substitute builds a monastery. Columban over-throws the heathen altars on Lake Zurich and estabishes a mission. His iconoclasm against the sacred cauldrons of beer brewed for pagan sacrifice is typical. Boniface cuts down the sacred oak in an episode that is a staged encounter like that of Elijah and the prophets of Baal. Eligius, who trained as a goldsmith and left the royal mint to become a missionary exhorted his people against falling back into pagan practices—trust in amulets, soothsayers, diviners, auguries, the flight and singing of birds, omens for the journey, noctural revellry, worship of the earth or stars (Robinson 1917:326).

Beyond these things there were new forms of animism which grew up in the Church by the process of *syncretism,* which always was a tempta-tion to the convert from the beginning, being the way of compromise. Thus, for instance after the Council of Ephesus gave the virgin Mary the title *theotokos,* the virgin supplanted many local deities, which continued under the Christian "umbrella." In Sicily, for example, eight celebrated temples were dedicated to the Mother of God (Milman, Beugnot in Robinson 216). The same things happened with other pagan rites in the name of saints and martyrs. Nevertheless we should not overlook the fact that the sermons against these things that have survived are really numerous; and that a great many church assemblies did legislate against them. Some of these statements are in highly spiritual terms. For example, the British Bishop, Fastidius, writing between 420 and 450 put his warnings in strongly moral terms thus:

> It is the will of God that His people should be holy, and free from all stain of unrighteousness and iniquity, that they should be so righteous and so pious, so pure, so unspotted, so single-hearted, that the heathen should find in them no fault, but should say in wonder, Blessed is the nation whose God is the Lord and the people whom He hath chosen for His own inheritance (in Robinson, 96).

Early English Christianity at the popular level tended to be animistic in pattern. The Church preached against it for generations. They venerated trees, wells and stones, used spells, incantations and runes for magical purposes, burned grain to secure health for the living and burned a house after the death of the inmate. In time these gave way to holy water, relics of the saints and Christian prayers, because the world in which they lived was one of ogres, giants and ghouls who were at enmity against God. The hermit saints were remembered as those who fought the demons of the fen country. These things are described by Whitelock in *The Beginnings of English Society.* The greatest poem of Anglo-Saxon literature is the narrative of Beowulf, who spends his time releasing "human habitations from the ravages of supernatural creatures that inhabit the fens" (Whitelock 1964:25). This is precisely the animist world where much of our research is done today.

SOME EVENTS FOR EXAMINATION

We have long needed a careful and critical analysis of the conversion experience of Constantine and its significance for the Church. It is variously interpreted, and I know no theme in history that has been more subject to the opinions of the historians who look back from their own positions. Some judge his conversion as something positive for the Church, while others see it as a great calamity. Westcott in *The Two Empires* more fairly says:

> Slowly and painfully, moving ever towards the light, he seems to have seen . . . what the faith was which he first identified with. . . . Constantine is a figure of the passage from the old world to the new . . . if his worth be estimated he will rank second to few among the benefactors of humanity (1909:232).

The Church certainly did gain much by Constantine's conversion. The pagan world was never exactly the same afterwards. He was tolerant. He did not force people to become Christian. The influx was certainly great but it was not as great as is popularly imagined. Any fault that came with the Church in the following years seems to me to be traced to difficulties on the level of the incorporation of converts rather than their mode of conversion. This is the problem of Christian education. The Diocletian persecution which had immediately preceded this movement had deprived the Church of much recognized leadership. It had been specifically directed against the leadership and educational structures. The relationship of these factors needs to be explored.

My own church growth work directed to the popular claim that "you convert the chief and everybody follows" has led me to suspect this kind of claim. I think we could direct some of our testing tools to this aspect of earlier Christian history. I feel certain that all this can be examined within the frame of reference of my own model for studying the conversion process. Probably we would be hard pressed to get the statistical material to demonstrate the size of the people movement, although some idea of the strength of the Church can be obtained from records of the distribution and numbers of new bishoprics. A more recent book called *Constantine and the Conversion of Europe* (1962), by a British historian named Jones, has a chapter on Constantine's own conversion. He draws from Constantine's own correspondence and discusses how the populace saw him. He concludes that Constantine did have a religious experience although he will not call it a *spiritual* experience, because of his own (the historian's) value judgment of what spiritual experience is. Those of us who have lived closer to conversions from animism would have a completely different idea of what a spiritual experience is. It is just at this point that research needs to be done on the historical records of the middle ages by researchers who know what coming out of animism really means. Jones' account is a fair, objective, formal analysis, by competent Western standards. This is a matter calling for the canons, not of formal history, but of ethnohistory and the resources of the field of culture change.

Similarly, work needs to be done on the process of incorporating the new converts into the Church after Constantine. Without an adequate pastoral arm because of the persecutions, the problem of assimilation must have been serious. What leadership there was seems to have been divided between laxity and austerity, the former allowing an infusion of heathen material, the latter trying to preserve the original simplicity. Some effort had to be made at the organization of Christianity after the Edict of Toleration and, at least it seems to me, the Church ran into a period of organizational and ritual conflicts with no great emphasis on the idea of the Christian mission. Church growth studies have demonstrated that the best way of consolidating a people movement is to bring the converts quickly to a place where they themselves are live witnesses, seeking new converts. Nothing stabilizes a person's faith better than advocating it. The historian, Bliss (1897), has pointed out that this was an organizational period, but not a missionary one. To me this raises many questions. For example: to what extent was the emergence of the elaborate ritual of the Church the result of excessive concern with organization and the neglect of evangelism? This, like the lack of pastoral leadership, seem more likely to have been responsible for the degeneration of the Church than the nature of the conversion movement. I think that church growth research has much to say to this. This is our old problem of *consolidation*.

Again, faulty incorporation of converts is suggested by the fact that the animistic practices that came into the Church, though recognized as wrong (witness the many sermons and laws against them) were apparently not dealt with by careful personal instruction, so much as by occasional public utterance and legislation. When Theodosius came to the throne in 379 he determined on a vigorous extermination of paganism by means of legislation. It was aimed at idolatry and temple sacrifices. In 385 he legislated against divination. In 408 Honorius issued a decree secularizing temples and removing images. In 423 Theodosius II legislated against sacrificing to demons, and many came into the Church because they saw the writing on the wall. These were nominal conversions and as a result magic, divination and astrology were practiced in submerged activity long after the passing of the laws against them.

In 1954 I wrote a long monograph called *The Christian: Fiji—1835-67* in which I devoted some pages to the conversion of the Fijian Chief, Cakobau, and especially to the conferences he held with various groups where he had significant status: family, lineage, kingdom. I was trying to break down what I then wrongly called a *mass movement* into its component parts. I was struggling with ideas which we have much more clearly articulated now—the multi-individual, multi-relational people movements. Here again I believe we can go back and take a fresh look at the planting of the Church in northern Europe. I think immediately of chapter 13 in *Bede's Ecclesiastical History* (1963). Paulinus has just convinced King Edwin to become a Christian. He has made a personal decision, but wants to "confer about it with his principal friends and counsellors" so that if they are convinced they may go through the ceremonies together. Here we have the participation of these persons. They discuss the old religion, and Coifi, the chief priest, gives his opinion on the emptiness of the old faith. The elders also participate until everyone is aware that a consensus has been reached. Then ultimately it is the chief priest who proposes the burning of the temples and destroying of the altars. When the question is asked who will undertake this iconoclasm, he replies, "I, for who can more properly than myself destroy those things which I worshipped through ignorance, for an example to all others . . . ?" He profanes the temple and his companions set fire to it. Thus we have evidence of a group conversion.

Pope Gregory's instructions to missionaries in 601 recommended the conversion of pagan temples into Christian churches "in order that the people may the more familiarly resort to the places to which they have been accustomed." However, in practice the temple was usually destroyed and frequently the converts themselves wanted it this way. The few cases I know of apostasy were places where the sacred places or paraphernalia were not destroyed when the old gods were rejected.

Let me refresh you on the narrative of Patrick lighting the fire in Ireland. The high festival of Rach was the occasion of "walking in darkness" and the hour was consecrated to the prince of darkness. Every fire in the province had to be extinguished, ultimately to be relit from the ceremonial bonfire. Patrick did an unprecedented thing by lighting that fire and Laoghaire, the king was angry at this presumption. A Druid magician reminded the king of an old prophecy "Unless yonder fire be this night extinguished, he who lighted it, together with his followers, will reign over the whole island." There was indeed also another prediction which ran like this:

One shall arrive here,
Having his head shaven in a circle,
Bearing a crooked staff,
And his table in the eastern part of the house.
His people shall stand behind him,
And he shall sing forth wickedness from his table
All his household shall answer
So be it: So be it.!

And this man when he cometh
Shall destroy our gods
Overturn their temples and altars,
And subdue the kings that resist him. . . .
And his doctrine shall rain for ever and ever.

Eventually, when Patrick was brought before the king the latter had taken the magical precautions against the enchantments of Patrick. The king, satisfied that Patrick had no designs against his kingdom, gave him leave to preach publically before the assembly of Irish princes. This has a culturally valid ring about it and pagan prophecies have certainly played a great part in modern mission field acceptances of the Gospel. The question I raise is whether perhaps we have not been too ready to dismiss valuable historical data as mere legend. Perhaps we should take another look at some of these things where data seems to be culturally relevant and where modern people movements among animist people run parallel courses. If we are to write the history of animist people we have to assure ourselves that valid records are not dismissed as legend because we peer at them through ethnocentric spectacles.

Boniface is best known for the dramatic encounter in which he cut down the sacred oak at Geissmar. What is less known is that each individual convert had to make a public renunciation of his idol worship, tree worship, practice of auguries and so forth. These were measured in terms of the devil: so that this was the struggle between Christ and Satan. Each convert had to answer these questions:

Q.   Dost thou forsake the devil?
A.   I forsake the devil.

Q.   And all the devil's wage?

A.   And I forsake all the devil's wage.

Q. And all the devil's works?
A. And I forsake all the devil's works and words, Thunor and Woden and Saxnote, and all the fiends that are their companions.

Q. Doest thou believe in God the Father Almighty?
A. I believe in God the Father Almighty.

Q. Dost thou believe in Christ the Son of God?
A. I believe in Christ the Son of God.

Q. Dost thou believe in the Holy Ghost?
A. I believe in the Holy Ghost.

Thus at their conversion converts had to answer these questions of their simple belief in public and take their stand with the people of God.

This philosophy of regarding the Christian mission as an encounter of the Lord with devils was common also in England, whence the missionaries had come. They were ethnically related. Whitelock records the words of a Christian poet:

Woden wrought idols;
The Almighty, that is the powerful God,
The true King himself,
The Saviour of souls,
Wrought glory, the spacious heavens (1964:23, rearranged).

This chapter has been no more than a flight through the Middle Ages, glimpsing here and there at people movements associated with such names as Constantine, Boniface and Patrick. Enough descriptive data of this type exists for a dissertation research. The purpose of this chapter is not to show the wealth of material available, but to suggest that church growth theory, being based on similar modern movements, can shed light on the interpretation of the people movements of the Middle Ages, to a greater degree than the historians have ventured.

European animism is found to compare with extant forms. History is found to have religiously innovative periods, like the present day. Tendencies to syncretism have to be watched. Faulty perfection growth is often blamed on people movement conversions, whereas the fault more likely lies with problems of incorporation and nuture. Importance is attached to the destruction of religious places and paraphernalia. Myths may play an important part in acceptance of religious change. The concept of the Christ-Satan encounter is frequent. Church growth theory speaks to all these aspects.

We agree with Renier that a "new kind of guidance" is needed to interpret the people movements of the Middle Ages; the "story needs retelling from a new point of view." In other words we badly need a church growth history of the Middle Ages. As the Australian historian,

Hancock, says, events of the human-historical world have outside and inside, matter and mind, deed and thought. The historian has to get *inside the act*. It seems to me that this kind of process for missionary history requires that the researcher possess a certain missionary empathy, a knowledge of animism, an awareness of the conversion processes themselves if he or she is to get inside the act. I think that this kind of writing will have to come from the discipline of missiology rather than secular history, for missiology is the symbiosis of theology, anthropology and history, not the mere sum of the three, but the new autonomous entity achieved by their interaction and maturation.

CHAPTER 21

A Statement on the
Use of Documents:
The Complexity of the
Conversion of the Tahitians

The purpose of this brief chapter is to show the real danger of the worldview of the particular ethnohistorian influencing his or her use and interpretation of the historical facts and documents. I cite here three different examples of reporting a single event, followed by an analysis.

EXAMPLE 1: THE ANTHROPOLOGIST

The first missionaries had very little success in the conversion of the people, though the material goods they brought were much appreciated. The missionaries were opposed, and many of them left the island in despair. When a fresh set of missionaries arrived some years later, Pomare was in a more chastened frame of mind. He had been defeated in battle and had taken refuge on the neighboring island of Mo'orea. The missionaries accompanied him there and began to make headway with him. Pomare had begun to distrust his gods because of his lack of success against his enemies. He began to flirt with the missionaries, in the hope that their god was more powerful than his own and would bring him the military success he wanted. At the same time he was chary of abandoning his own gods entirely. Thus, though the missionaries had hopes of converting Pomare, they could not get him to abandon his gods publicly. In view of the prospects, however, the missionaries ranged themselves on the side of Pomare and regarded his enemies as "heathen." In 1815, Pomare's enemies on the island of Tahiti invited

The original version of this chapter was published in *People Movements in Southern Polynesia* (Chicago: Moody Press, 1971), pp. 221-226, under the title, "Appendix A: The Complexity of the Conversion of the Tahitians." Gratitude is hereby expressed to the publisher for permission to include it here.

him to attend a conference with them. Pomare, accompanied by his supporters and some of the missionaries, sailed over to Tahiti and, on a Sunday morning, he and his people attended a service conducted by the missionaries. During the service, the enemy was observed advancing with a large armed force, evidently to attack. The congregation became alarmed and the missionaries were prepared to break off the service. Pomare, however, ordered the service to be continued to its proper ending and stated that the enemy could be attended to afterwards. The missionary writer, Rev. W. Ellis, had praised Pomare's piety and faith in the face of the enemy. The truth is that any religious ritual that was broken off was regarded by the Polynesians as an ill omen for future success. The gods being invoked for assistance turned against their worshippers if the ritual was not properly completed. It was not Christian piety that induced Pomare and his followers to go on with the service but the fear of a broken ritual. At the end of the service both Pomare and his followers had plucked up courage in the hope that the Christian god would assist them in gaining the victory.

From the outset of the battle which ensued, fortune smiled on Pomare. The opposing leader, whose rank was immeasurably superior to that of Pomare, was killed with a musket-ball. On the death of their leader, the enemy retired and victory lay with Pomare and with the Christian god who had supported him. The power of Jehovah having been demonstrated, Christianity was accepted by the whole island of Tahiti, and Pomare became king of the group. Pomare handed over the material symbols of his native gods to the missionaries to be sent to England to show the people of that country what fools the Tahitians had been. A lucky shot had done more than seventeen years of preaching had been able to accomplish (Buck 1939:65-67).

EXAMPLE 2: THE MISSIONARY HISTORIAN

Pomare II walked in his [father's] footsteps ["fickle and brutal, offered thousands of human sacrifices to his gods"] until the missionary outlook became as dark as possible.

Prompted by the grave reports received from the field, a special meeting was called in London in July 1812, to pray for Pomare's conversion, and in that very month he gave up his idols and asked for baptism. This was the turning point of the work in Tahiti. Idolatry was completely overthrown, the king sent for a printing press to prepare Bibles and hymn books for his people, and at his own expense he built a huge church, where, in the presence of four thousand of his subjects he was baptized. The light spread not only over all Tahiti, but also from island to island and other groups, through the efforts of the Tahitian Christians as well as from the missionaries and Tahiti will ever be known as the seed-plot from which the gospel was scattered far and wide over Oceania (Glover 1960:437-438).

EXAMPLE 3: THE MISSIONARY THEORETICIAN

After the missionaries had been laboring through a long night of
fruitless toil lasting for years, the king made known his wish to be
baptized. If after so many years of disappointed expectation the missionaries had been eagerly ready to grant the desire of the royal applicant it
would not have been surprising, but for four years he was kept back
until more satisfactory proof was given of his knowledge of the Gospel.
The earliest missionaries were the children of the revival of the
Eighteenth Century, and they took with them to their work standards
which united Puritan severity and evangelical spirituality, and they
looked for and were not satisfied until they thought they had found
evidence of a radical change of heart (King 1902:378).

ANALYSIS

At first it must be difficult for the reader to see that these three
passages are each records of the conversion of Tahiti. Each at one point is
sound and at other points quite wrong. Not one can be documented as it
stands. All are faulty with respect to time depth, dynamic factors, and the
total configuration. The historical reconstruction of both anthropologist
and missionary historian is appalling. They create quite wrong impressions,
and all suffer from oversimplification.

Each writer naturally has a different motive. There is no harm in this,
nor in the selectivity this may involve, provided the integrity of the context
is not distorted thereby. In this respect the anthropologist's manipulation
of his source material is shocking.

The anthropologist is concerned with showing the acceptance of
Christianity to have been a simple matter, almost an accident, the matter
of a lucky shot. He would presumably argue also that the great war of
1914-18 was entirely *caused* by the shooting of an Austrian archduke. To
arrive at his conclusion he has to deliberately omit a great body of facts
that hold together firmly within the very sources he uses.

The motive of the historian was to write a world survey. World
surveys are, by nature, unreliable because they have to reduce complexities to simplicities and in doing so lose sight of patterns. By compressing
a field of history worthy of a whole volume into a paragraph, both focus
and time depth are wrong. They give the impression of something that just
never happened. The one contribution is an allowance for the divine
element. This is missing from the others.

The theoretician is concerned with an issue of missionary technique
and cites the incident out of its context to illustrate his theoretical point.
This is a common procedure; but it throws the responsibility on the writer,
either to verify or document his source for the historical information on
which the theory stands. Many of the myths of history are the supports of

all kinds of theory. The third writer is quite correct in pointing out the slowness of L.M.S. baptisms, and the fact he stresses seriously undermines the other two impressions; but not only is his own legalistic picture quite devoid of a dynamism that was certainly in the historic events, but he is careless about his figures. Whether Pomare II was kept waiting four or seven years does not injure his argument, as it happens, but this figure is the very support of his theory, and he happens to be wrong.

The anthropologist did contribute an interesting cultural point that was not in the historical sources. It came from his special knowledge in his Polynesian background, he being a Maori. But that same background has given Buck a mental set against the taking of Polynesian gods to England to show what fools the people were, and the iconoclasm of destroying ancient Polynesian sites, which we know from other writings also of this man. We see him in his own specific class — a salvage anthropologist[1] — with a certain cynicism which militates against his capacity for objective analysis when the question of missions is involved. Buck is denying missionary value judgments any validity (yet he is categorical in his own), drawing his own opinions of Pomare II, distorting the evidence of those who knew him face to face, and getting away with it because of his own Polynesian connections. He was, in the majority of his work, a good anthropologist, and because of this his opinions of Pomare II have been widely cited by other anthropologists as beyond dispute (for example, Howells 1948:256-257). Yet his personal grievance against the Tahiti Christian teachers has been so vocal in other writings that we ought to be warned at this point. After all, if an anthropologist appeals to history, he or she is obligated to respect the canons and criteria of historical method. If out of the anthropologist's special knowledge, something interpretive can be added this is good; but facts cannot be selected, omitted, and distorted as set down in the documents. The anthropologist may disagree with them, but they must be stated and dealt with.

Glover and Kane give us the impression that the reason for the whole train of events lies in a certain prayer meeting held in London in 1812. It gives an impression of the complete overthrow of paganism because of Pomare II's conversion, and that the Bibles came from the press he sent for and that he was baptized in a great newly built church, and so on, one sweeping sequence of events in a limited space of time. All this was incorrect. The picture eliminates all the dynamics of the local events. Pomare II ate the turtle alone. He was kept seven years for baptism. No serious biblical translation work was done for another twenty years. As far as prayers were concerned, the evidence is that those of Tahiti were far more fervent than those in Britain. I have no doubt about the value of prayer, but to pin it to one particular meeting in Britain in 1812 is far too facile.

A brief analysis of the chronology of Pomare II's quest for baptism from sources that were public and not difficult for any of the writers to obtain will expose the weaknesses of each description.

> Pomare first asked for baptism after a conversation with Nott, who did not disclose it to the brethren at the time, lest they build hope on a vain boast (Lovett 1899:1:196-197).

> Either he must have feared disagreement on the matter among the missionaries or he himself was unsatisfied. Some time later Pomare pressed his claim again, but during the interim he had been trying to win the support of some of his relations of status [Tamaloa, his father-in-law, and Tapoa, both high chiefs of nearby islands] but had failed.[2]

Seven missionaries had written to London about this. Pomare's words to the missionaries were, "You do not know the thought of my heart, nor I yours, but God does." This in itself is a simple statement of faith, which was worthy of support. He was told that two things were customary: first, instruction in the Christian way, and then a period during which his walking in the way would be observed and tested. That was all before July 1812. It shows Pomare II's leaning to Christianity and requests for acceptance long before the battle described in the first report, and before the London prayer meeting. At the beginning of 1815, three years after the prayer meeting, the situation was still the same. Some two hundred of Pomare II's people had been received before him by this time, as we have seen in the movement of the *praying people.* Pomare II was still being instructed and observed. At this time the missionaries wrote:

> The case of Pomare grieves and perplexes us. He wishes to be baptized . . . but we are far, very far from being satisfied that he is a proper subject. He has extensive knowledge of the doctrines of the Gospel, but is a slave to drinking.[3]

After the battle of Bunaauia, when Tahiti had actually become nominally Christian it was another four years before Pomare was eventually baptized—May 16, 1819.[4] This makes the report of the 1812 prayer meeting look rather foolish. And Buck said Pomare II was chary about leaving his own gods, and drops the story of his eating the turtle from the source where he gleaned his other facts. Yet the documents are quite clear that he strove with the missionaries for baptism for at least seven, possibly eight years.

These passages have been arranged side by side to show the importance of critical testing and the folly of oversimplification like trying to reduce conversion to a single factor. We are dealing with highly complex configurations that build up over a period of time. While we are never certain of having observed all the factors, we can and must observe all the factors in the available sources. The three writers have given us cartoons, exaggerating one feature at the expense of the others to the distortion of the general effect. This is not good enough in anthropology, or history, or theory.

On the other hand, if only the published sources are examined carefully, it will be quite apparent that *structurally* there were several configurations of conversion movement operating in Tahiti and the neighboring islands. There were "praying people" building up into a small Christian fellowship. There was a large segment of Pomare II's family connections, both by blood and marriage, which he himself set out to win, and he was so engaged over a long period of time. Others were impressed by the idol burnings started by Patii. Only the rebel units came over after the battle, and only indirectly as a result of it—it was the post-victory policy of Pomare II ("Spare the rebels but destroy their religion"), not merely a "lucky" shot. All this is found in the data in the printed works of the missionaries and the officially published history, although none have worked out the patterns. Church growth research assembles such data and seeks out the patterns, because knowledge of those patterns is of tremendous importance to all engaged in church planting today.

Notes:

1. A salvage anthropologist is one whose main concern is to salvage cultural items.

2. Letter of the seven missionaries dated October 21, 1812, cited in Lovett: 1899; 1:198.

3. Letter of January 14, 1815, cited in several sources, including Lovett (205).

4. Account of the event written three days later and cited in Lovett (219-20). All these references are here shown to have appeared in the official published L.M.S. centenary volume, so that there could be no doubt about their availability to the three writers.

CHAPTER 22

Contemporary Departures from Traditional Christianity in Cross-Cultural Situations: A Melanesian Ethnohistorical Case Study

No topic has generated more enthusiasm for research in Melanesia than the study of its Nativism, by which I mean the large homogeneous ethnic units, sometimes whole lineages, breaking away from the traditional Christianity which emerged in the era of colonial missions.[1] It has been argued that these movements are the result of stress situations which arise when two very different cultures clash or come into acculturative contact. The clash is said to derive from: (1) the inherent cultural differences, (2) the conflicting values and attitudes of the two societies, (3) the precise nature of the dominance/submission situation, and (4) the effect of forces which emerged with World War II in the Pacific, with the G.I. in particular as the catalyst.[2]

The movement may be resistive or reformative, perpetuative or accommodating, aggressive or passive.[3] It may seek to reintegrate the whole subject society, or merely some subordinate homogeneous unit within it; either by the rejection of alien elements in it, or the modification of new elements (i.e. by accepting the forms but ascribing their own meanings to them), or a syncretism of basic ingredients from the two cultures. The literature on the subject is tremendous[4] and the typologies are numerous.[5] In the literature the movements may be viewed negatively as ("nativistic movements" or "Cargo Cults") or positively (as "people movements" or "revitalization." [These two are distinguished by the possibility of a foreigner, or outgroup person being the catalyst in the people movements, whereas revitalization may be stimulated only by an ingroup person.]) Figure 16 illustrates some of the various approaches in the literature.

270

FIGURE 16
Approaches to the Analysis of Nativism

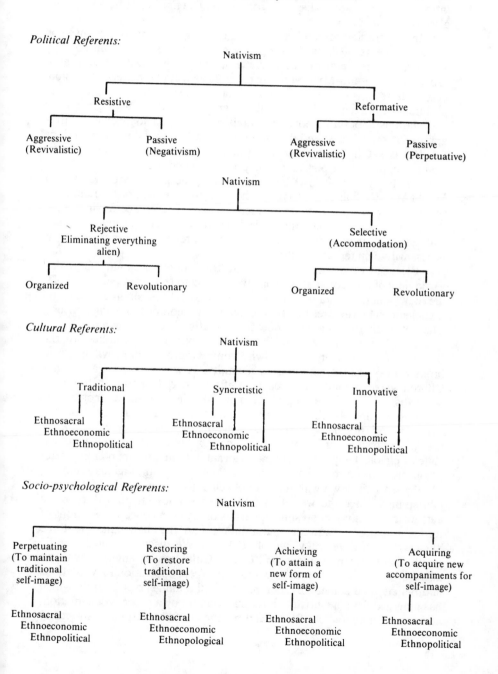

Political Referents:

Nativism

Resistive / Reformative

Aggressive (Revivalistic) — Passive (Negativism) — Aggressive (Revivalistic) — Passive (Perpetuative)

Nativism

Rejective Eliminating everything alien) / Selective (Accommodation)

Organized — Revolutionary — Organized — Revolutionary

Cultural Referents:

Nativism

Traditional — Syncretistic — Innovative

Ethnosacral Ethnoeconomic Ethnopolitical — Ethnosacral Ethnoeconomic Ethnopolitical — Ethnosacral Ethnoeconomic Ethnopolitical

Socio-psychological Referents:

Nativism

Perpetuating (To maintain traditional self-image) — Restoring (To restore traditional self-image) — Achieving (To attain a new form of self-image) — Acquiring (To acquire new accompaniments for self-image)

Ethnosacral Ethnoeconomic Ethnopolitical — Ethnosacral Ethnoeconomic Ethnopological — Ethnosacral Ethnoeconomic Ethnopolitical — Ethnosacral Ethnoeconomic Ethnopolitical

This chapter is focused on Melanesia as far as the data base is concerned (although there is even more data for Africa, which would also introduce us to concepts like "Negritude").[6] The findings, I believe, apply also to Africa.[7]

In Melanesian research most of the investigation has been focused on the components of the nativistic movement or Cargo Cult, pin-pointing such features as messianism or millenarianism in the eschatology, its anti-Government or anti-Mission motivation; its aspect of counter-conversion, and endless speculations as to the real causes of the defection from traditional Christianity. We have also been weighed down with generalized speculations about a "theory of Nativism." This is a somewhat negative approach which has suited the mood of the cultural relativists, who since the 1930s set themselves up as "judges over Israel." I think a more positive approach to our subject is possible when we ask, not what was lost (or thought to be lost) but what really emerged in Melanesia after World War II. This is not to reject the existing research, or the numerous typologies, which all provide different frames of reference for investigation, and certainly aid our ethnological description. But a positive approach will certainly save us from the error of interpreting these movements as necessarily disintegrate or chaotic.[8]

We need to see that, although the traditional missionary Christian worldview of the Colonial Age has been rejected (either in part or whole) the new emergent state is not one of chaos. It is an integrated and homogeneous structure, functioning as an autonomous ongoing concern. The notion that change has to be disintegrative is entirely wrong.

In 1964 I was sent by the World Council of Churches to the Solomon Islands to investigate why some twenty or more villages had broken away from traditional Christianity. It was a breakaway from a Church whose members had received fifty years of Christian instruction.[9] My Western and some Anglo Solomon Islander informants mostly saw the whole thing as chaotic and disintegrative.[10] But however tacit a Christian missionary may consider the heresy which emerged in the breakaway of these tribal groups, one cannot honestly say they were in a state of chaos. They were dynamic, vibrant with life, self-expressive, with a cohesive structure and a programmed daily life and religious routine.

When I sit down with the data of religious innovation in Melanesian Christianity since the war, I find the case studies fall into three basic categories. I am not analysing on a basis of my own conceptualizations of forms, function or attitude, but rather I find the data falls into three "heaps," with different views of selfhood. We discover: (1) the cultic group, nativistic movement or "Cargo Cult" which emerges with an aggressive, syncretistic theology and is in direct opposition to regulations and beliefs, and sometimes its morals; (2) the indigenous Church, which has emerged from a Christian mission structure by a process of evolution, and retains a character of faith and practice (and sometimes a structure) indigenized, but very little different from the mission prototype; and (3) the Independent Church, which breaks away on a revolutionary principle, has often assumed folk elements in the process, and demonstrates its autonomy by featuring strongly those elements which were either paternalistically controlled or neglected altogether—say, a healing ministry.

The African data which has come my way will fit the same three categories. How does it come about that the same set of causative factors suggested above can lead to three quite different but equally autonomous solutions? Furthermore, how is it that in no case do we find the breakdown of traditional Christianity leads to anything resembling a state of chaos? For better or for worse we are dealing with dynamic, functioning, autonomous living organisms.

Most of the missionary churches of Melanesia and Polynesia were planted as the result of people movements, which I have described elsewhere at length,[11] and mostly these were power encounter situations in which the old animistic divinities or their shrines were formally (i.e. ceremonially) rejected by the groups concerned by means of an ocular demonstration in which the responsible official (headman of the village, chief of the lineage, priest of the temple or head of the household) destroyed or abused the mana repository or symbolic locus of power (skull houses, ceremonial skulls, fetishes, idols, monoliths, sacred groves or taboo totem animals.) The mode of destruction was by burning, burial, drowning or devouring according to the local conception of mana disposal.[12]

These people movements usually led to the planting of Christianity as a functional substitute for the original animistic religious structure; and although they took from one to ten years to run through the sometimes scattered tribal unit, from subunit to subunit, they resulted in reasonably total substitutions.

These Christian churches have continued in some parts of Melanesia since about 1840. Most parts (except for the New Guinea Highlands) had a time depth of more than half a century of Christian history by the beginning of World War II in the Pacific, which means they had survived the first generation of Christian converts from animism.[13] Quite apart from the psychological effect the war had on them, Melanesian Christians of the postwar period were mostly persons who had been born to Christian parents in traditional missionary island Christianity. They had never themselves rejected animism, burned their fetishes, buried their mana skulls, destroyed their idols or cut down their sacred groves. That is, they had never experienced a power encounter deliverance from the old life; and frequently (but not always) they had been quite cut off from the animistic worldview and mental set by mission education.

Historically the period following World War II was not only one of rapid social change due to acculturation, but the changes in technology and electronics going on in the West itself, were also being felt in the islands. These changes were social and political as well as religious and I think we are wrong if we assume we can really study the religious change in isolation; politics, medicine, economics, electronics are all part of the picture, and the religious life suffered no more than any other of these configurations, or "integral institutions" as Malinowski calls them.[14] I make the point, not because I want to discuss it here, but because it is often overlooked, and this chapter is really not a complete study without this dimension.

The experience of the war introduced the Pacific islanders to resources far greater than anything they had ever dreamed of—the number of warships, the power of their armament, the quantities of canned food in the cargo ships, the aircraft in the sky—the islanders were completely bewildered by such resources of power and quantity. Added to this was the vocal anticolonialism of the average G.I., who saw a good deal of the people in his off-duty time.[15] We do not wonder that many of the innovative reactions to traditional Christianity and Colonial Government grasped on "cargo," and "airplanes" and "ships" as their symbolic reference points,[16] as they also did of the American military system itself,[17] and the notion of administrative authority.[18]

Recognizing that this capacity for group movement with some symbolic reference point was inherent in the Melanesian situation anyway, whenever some prophetic or charismatic leader emerged to grasp control of it, it is not difficult to see how the war first, followed by technological and electronic change, led parts of Melanesia into periods of innovative religious movements.[19] Melanesia began (if she had not already thought of it before) to see herself as deprived of her "place in the sun." Sometimes she felt she had lost something from her past by culture contact. Her old religion was gone. Had the white colonial administrators and missionaries robbed her of her birthright: her cultural heritage, authority, wealth and religious power? Were these to be regained by totally rejecting the Government and the Missions? Sometimes she felt she had something valuable in traditional Christianity which she should not cast lightly away. How could she master it, deal with it and use it in her own way, as something indigenous rather than foreign, autonomous rather than paternalistic? Soon after the war many missionaries were found working towards this end, especially from about 1945 to 1946, and indigenous churches began to emerge.[20] Where this did not happen many ethnic groups broke away and established independent churches or, better called perhaps, "folk churches," which though they claimed to be Christian, were inclined to be syncretistic or biliomythical.

Using then an ethnohistorical referent I find that these three types of innovative movement have characterized the Post-colonial Period: the Nativistic Cult, the Indigenous Church and the Independent Folk Church. The character of Melanesia as a missionary field has thus been completely transformed since the war. The old paternalistic type of traditional Christianity has been greatly reduced. I do not intend reconstructing in this chapter the nature of the old missionary traditional Christianity, except indirectly by way of comment in the following descriptions. It was too uneven to describe here. Let it suffice to say that it ranged on the scale from pathetically paternalistic to remarkable indigenous; and I do not need to do more than point out that traditional Christianity at the former pole tended to suffer after the war from nativistic cults, while those at the latter pole passed from Mission to Church with little serious culture shock. Let me now turn briefly to the three types one by one.

THE NATIVISTIC CULT

This type of movement, commonly called a "Cargo Cult" (although in reality not all such forms of nativism feature cargo) utilizes the term cargo to focus on a concept of wealth. It came out of the war, when white man wealth came to be envisioned in cases of canned meat, such as were seen in the army supplies. A whole mythology developed about it and described how the white man had stolen the islanders' heritage and wealth back in primeval times.[21] These myths may be collected in hundreds, and they have been interwoven in the origin tales. This, in itself, is a return to pre-Christian values and aesthetic forms and is a rebellion against Christianity and a claim that something was lost at culture contact. The army stores of food and arms revolutionized the islanders' conception of the meaning of plenty as unlimited, and it was natural for them to latch on to this symbol. This mental set is found in the Church especially along the north coast of New Guinea, where the missionaries of today call it the "cargo mentality."

Wealth in canned goods became an element of a new eschatology. It promised a new day which was about to dawn for the islanders when they would regain all they had lost—lands, authority, wealth—and which were rightly theirs from the beginning of time. This conception of Melanesian paradise was soon formulated into an apocalyptic belief structure, for which the model was sometimes the New Jerusalem in the New Testament, and new villages might even be given biblical names. When this Golden Age is articulated we speak of the movement as millenarian.[22]

The millenarian element is often accompanied by the emergence of a prophetic or charismatic figure around whom the group rallies (though all prophetic movements are not millenarian). The interesting factor, in my experience at least, is that this leader usually turns out to be one who has previously been trained in some white man institution in a role of subordinate leadership: a teacher, a policeman, an orderly in the army or a catechist. The man has had authority under authority, and has Melanesianized the white authority pattern in his nativistic cult.[23]

Most nativistic cults are highly structured after the nature of a church organization, an educational complex, an administrative system or a military organization. They may include such features as drill parades, marching formation round a flagpole, with commissioned and noncommissioned officers and men, or an administrator in control behind a desk. The white man's authority, like his wealth, must be returned to the Melanesian in the Golden Age.

The key personality of the movement has a prophetic character. He is not always a natural orator, but gains power by his authoritative utterances in the specific situation of crisis—he is a man for the hour. The movement depends on him. It may be economic, political or religious, depending on the nature of the situational crisis; and by the same criteria the role of the charismatic figure will be seen. It does not follow that a nativistic cult has to be religious. If the crisis is purely political, as in the case of Marching Rule, there may be no religious aspect. A number of Christian pastors actually held office in this particular movement, for example.[24]

However, it may well be that the movement is entirely religious, or religious and economic, as with the John Frum movement.[25] A religious (sacrosyncretic) cult will develop a religious doctrine of some kind, and perhaps a verbal creed and a liturgy. A collection of hymns emerges, usually quite heretical from the biblical standpoint. The institution of hymn singing will be regarded as an essential functional substitute for its Christian counterpart, and (in the absence of a printing press) there may be a handwritten hymnbook, which each member copies by hand as part of the reception into membership ritual.[26] Likewise we may expect an organized prayer system, and perhaps a few written prayers for worship.[27] The doctrine of the movement will be found in the hymns and liturgies, and may even be the composition of the charismatic leader himself. I found this myself in a Solomon Island case. The theology reflects a syncretism of biblical ideas and elements from the ancient myths—either truly remembered or imagined.

Quite frequently this role of the prophet is extended as more and more extravagant claims are made of him. He becomes the promised one of imagined ancient myths. This type of situation acquires the descriptor "messianic."[28] Once the figure becomes messianic the movement usually becomes millenarian; and in extreme cases (one known to me personally) the messiah goes beyond this to deification. We now have on our hands a fully developed sacrosyncretic nativistic cult (in terms of cultural referents), and a sacrorestorative cult (in terms of socio-psychological referents) if the movement purports to restore the faith of the ancient heritage, as the act of deification may well do. In still another classificatory frame of reference we may say we have a revolutionary selective accommodation; in other words, a breakaway from traditional Christianity which selects its desirable elements for modification in terms of the pre-Christian past and validation by means of myth.

We must remember that no two movements are exactly alike and any classificatory system is not only merely approximate, but is indeed in the mind of the observer as his or her own abstraction. As long as we have the large number of variables—cultural values, historical antecedents, complexities of the crisis situation, and different responses to the movement beginnings by the local authorities—we will never find two exactly alike. Neither will two be the same to two different observers. So within these limitations, and using my own ethnohistorical referent, let me identify the normal characteristics of a cultic nativistic breakaway from traditional Christianity as having the following features:

1. a new, accommodating mythology,
2. a symbolic locus of power transfer,
3. a new eschatology,
4. a syncretistic belief system,
5. a speculative reconstruction of pre-Christian values, and
6. a mythologization of the worship structure.

All these are dynamic and evolving factors. The extent of their development will depend on the impact they make on the community and the reaction of the civil authorities and Church, or any other against whom they may be directed. In the above features I have omitted the immoral dimension because it is not a constant, but when it appears it is usually the major factor, as in the case of the Hahalis Welfare Society, in which the Baby Garden was to provide the society ultimately with the birth of the messiah.

THE INDIGENOUS CHURCH

We should not imagine that the entire world of Melanesian traditional Christianity has dissolved into revolutionary nativistic cults. Statistically they represent only a small percentage of the island world population. Possibly the biggest of them would be covering twenty or so villages. Over against this we have numerous churches of 200,000 practising members. The process whereby these strong indigenous churches have emerged is clearly evolutionary rather than revolutionary or rebellious.[29] These churches conduct their own business, social and religious affairs on the village, national and international level; and where they still have white workers (fraternal workers rather than missionaries) they are under the authority and discipline of the island churches. These island churches manage their own property, administer their own finances, pastor their

own churches, train their own leaders (except perhaps at the highest level
for which they may be sent overseas), and integrate their own evangelistic
efforts, publication programs, social service projects, and in every way
represent the voice of the Church in the community. Furthermore they
belong to the new world of our day and interact with the representatives of
other churches in international conferences.

Yet although they have retained many of the traditional church
structures they differ from their prototypes in many ways. They maintain
a basic continuity especially in their theological foundations. They study
the Bible in groups all over the country and regard it as their norm for faith
and practice. They retain many features of the old preaching pattern,
although this had already assumed some indigenous features in former
times. Their hymnologies are well developed and theologically biblical,
and many of the hymns are their own composition for island hymnwriters
are very creative when given the opportunity. They will have no dealings
with any attempt to speculate on, or seek to recover anything of the pre-
Christian mythology, and are quick to detect and oppose syncretism with
old myths. They are vocal in opposition to anything approaching a
nativistic movement, and if one arises in a small group or village they
immediately discipline the offender as "backsliders" who have "fallen
from grace."

On the other hand, they differ from the pre-war missionary church
structures at a number of significant points. The white foreign missionary
has no longer any authority over them. Where they have fraternal
workers, they have been invited to be there by the island church bodies
and have been stationed by them through the regular elective and
appointive mechanisms, which deal also with indigenous appointments.

I remember myself once being assigned a clerical task by my Fijian
colleagues somewhere about thirty years ago. Two of us had to eliminate
the adjectives "European" and "Native" from the Fijian lawbook, which
was in their language. A Fijian-controlled synod had appointed and
instructed us in our assignment, and told us to bring a revised script for
discussion and ratification at the following synod. If I remember correctly
the Fijian to Australian ratio of that legislative body was about 15 to 1.
When I first went down to Fiji before the war the most critical issues were
determined by a European synod which was the highest court of appeal in
the island church. It was comprised entirely of missionaries. About the
end of the war I was involved in the procedures which disposed of their
synod. It could only be done by the Europeans of the synod organizing
their own demise. The matter was discussed over a series of conferences
by the composition of the text of a new constitution, which was then
submitted to the Fijians who discussed it for some days on their own. And
suddenly the European synod had gone, and with it a century of white
missionary authority. Fijians and missionaries alike were now "pastors,"
'catechists," "teachers" and so on without adjectival descriptors. About a

dozen white workers found themselves in the midst of 160 Fijians. They had no longer the power of autonomy. They were a minority voice. Thereafter the Fijians determined our appointments.

At the World Methodist Conference in 1956 I presented a paper on these developments, and I identified three highly developed configurations in the island world:

1. an increasing responsibility in leadership roles on the level of local church activities,

2. constitutional developments constructively moving in the direction of indigeous government and autonomy, and

3. the emergence of new and indigenous forms of evangelism.[30]

As far as Fiji was concerned this stage lasted for seventeen years. Over this time as the European missionaries retired one by one they were frequently replaced by indigenous nominees. Theological training was strengthened, select people were groomed for responsible positions, and a bilateral curriculum for ten transitional years to provide indigenous ministers for the very different rural and urban (and academic) ministries.[31] Some cooperative beginnings were launched to bring Fijian, Tongan and Samoan programs into step as a move towards the standardization of entrance requirements for a hoped-for central theological seminary in the South Pacific where a divinity degree might be obtained. Eventually after the T.E.F. Consultation on Theological Training in the South Pacific this dream materialized.[32] The Pacific Churches now have both university and seminary resources in Fiji.

Today the Fijian Church, over 200,000 strong, is completely indigenous, and by its own choice has affiliated with the Australasian General Conference as a full status and equal body with Australian and Island Conference on an international level. I have used the Fijian Methodists because I knew them best and have served under them, but this is only one of many examples I might have cited for an indigenous church.

The indigenous church is the diametric opposite of the nativistic cult, both at the theological level and at the level of harmonious working with the mother church. In both these respects one rebels and the other develops, one is revolutionary the other evolutionary. Both have in a way withdrawn from the parent body. Both have undergone dramatic change in the process, but one is reactionary, the other cooperative.

Before passing on to the third type I should point out that the attitude of the white missionaries undoubtedly was one of the crucial factors in each case. In the former they were authoritarian, unbending and paternalistic. In the latter they recognized that the traditional missionary churches had to change with the changing times: that the church was a dynamic organism and could not be treated as a static organization. They accepted the notion of change as appropriate. The task was not always easy. It was like navigating a banana raft on a flooded river and trying to keep in the current without upsetting the craft. The missionaries recognized this and let the current carry the raft, working themselves with their poling, not to increase momentum but to keep them facing in the right direction.

INDEPENDENT CHURCHES

The question now arises: What happens when the people do not desire to return to pre-Christian mythology, and when the Christian faith meets their needs, but the missionaries continue to be paternalistic and resistant to change?

The natural thing is for them to break away from the missionary church and to form an independent church of their own. To this extent they are revolutionary, and they may be quite anti-white; but they keep nearer to Christian scripture, are strongly evangelistic, and their new theological emphases are bible-based. Often these are indigenous elaborations of some biblical ingredient which had been neglected in the missionaries' training program, may be, say, the doctrine of the Spirit or the rites of healing, and there are some elaborate developments of baptism. Africa can supply us with hundreds of documented examples of this, but we do meet them also in Oceania. Another strong element is catharsis.[33]

They are often prophetic or charismatic, strongly liturgical, and present us with an abundance of functional substitutes for the Christian vestments, rituals and sacred paraphernalia. They have less syncretism than the nativistic movements but some are borderline cases. Their main difference is that the independent movements are clearly Christian. They have not rejected the Christian religion of the white man and his sacred book. Rather they want to claim it for themselves and they want to be able to achieve status beyond what they can in the white church, and to express themselves indigenously in participant roles. They do not strive to recapture the ancient animism from which their fathers departed.

The probability with this revolutionary departure from traditional Christianity is that it leads to a rapid institutionalization of the breakaway movement that ultimately becomes quite rigid. The forms become set. They do not have the internal flexibility of the indigenous churches mentioned above, or their intellectual exchange from outside contacts, or the quality of their theological training. Most cases that I know or have read about have manifested these shortcomings, and I think it probably natural because whereas in the indigenous church, missionary controls have been phased out slowly over a period of time in a smooth evolutionary manner; in the other, the revolutionary cutoff has demanded a whole complex of institutions "over night" and the new officials have not been properly trained for it.[34]

Usually such an independent church will be forced to work out its constitution to get public recognition and if it has day schools they will be at a much lower educational level.[35]

Sometimes we meet with borderline cases between the Nativistic Cult and the Independent Church. The borderline marks not so much the degree of syncretism, as to whether or not it is consciously and deliberately intended to go back to native values which predate the white man's presence, or whether it is a failure of a theologically unsophisticated prophet to discriminate between what is Christian and what is not. It may well be that the prophet believes he is biblical and claims the right to his own interpretation.[36] Such men have often argued that as each denomination interprets Scripture in its own way, why should not a Melanesian also do so.[37]

However, the common point between the Nativistic Cult and the Independent Church is the revolutionary character of the breakaway, as opposed to the evolutionary character of the passage from Mission to Church in the case of the Indigenous Church.

The common point between the Indigenous and Independent Churches is the manifest intention to retain their Christianity, as against the intentional rejection of Christianity by the Nativistic Cult.

The tragedy of the Independent Church is that in all probability it need not have happened that way had the mission policy been different. The same may be argued of the Nativistic Cult. The number of Western features retained by all three types of movement demonstrates the Melanesian readiness for cultural borrowing from the West. Unless there are factors I have not identified we are left with the following residue:

1. A process of change under the rapid acculturation and end of insularity was inevitable.

2. Ultimate resistance against Western paternalism and overloading authority had to come sooner or later.

3. The Melanesians inevitably had to develop a new self image adequate for the new day.

4. World War II provided the crisis situation for the emergence of Melanesian prophets, and saviors.

These were common factors for all three new and nontraditional forms of religiosity we have discussed. The Melanesians found three different ways of reacting to these factors and to some extent at least it may be argued that the manifest operations of the white traders, settlers, and especially the public servants, administrators and missionaries influenced the precise form of the Melanesian reaction.

Notes:

1. The phenomenon is not peculiar to Christianity, to the Post-colonial Age, or to Oceania. History is replete with accounts of such movements in Africa, Asia and America; but in Africa and Oceania especially they have increased by hundreds since World War II.

2. Nativistic movements frequently follow in the aftermath of wars. One of the best studies of this theme is Wallace's investigation of the relation between war and religious group movement in the history of the Delaware Indians (1956:1-21).

3. The passive type, such as the Gandhi resistance in India, does not appear frequently in Melanesia. There have been a few minor strikes among students on mission compounds (see Crocombe 1954:6-21) but Melanesian movements are notably aggressive, the aggression rising or falling according to the way in which the Administration or Mission handles the disturbance.

4. See the bibliographies in Worsley's *The Trumpet Shall Sound* (1957:277-283), Lawrence's *Road Belong Cargo* (1964:276-280), Kamma's *Korari* (1972:300-319), and Leeson.

5. Typologies for nativism were developed by Linton (1943:230-240), Kobben (1960:117-164), Clemhout (1964:14-15), Worsley (1957), Turner (1974), and many others.

6. The concept of "Negritude" was used to describe the resurgence of Bantu paganism, and the exaltation of the African past (Steenberghen 1959:287-288).

7. The Christian church in Africa was made widely aware of this phenomena by a growing body of literature on such movements which appeared about 1948. The most notable work was Sundkler's *Bantu Prophets in South Africa*, published in 1948 and updated in 1961. But there are many others, Welbourne (1961) Barrett (1968) and Baeta (1962) and by Comparative Religionists like Lanternari (1963) and many others.

8. Early writers on "culture contact" used the term "culture clash" which was subsequently discarded because it gave the impression of a powerful culture destroying a passive or static one. Later anthropologists pointed out that the less powerful one was not disintegrating, but that sooner or later, after the initial culture shock it would reformulate its structures and continue as an ongoing organism. Culture contact is a two-way process of interaction.

9. For the report of the research see *Solomon Islands Christianity* (1967a) and in particular pp. 212-214, 217-266.

10. Somewhere in the same source is a report of an interview on this subject with an Anglo Solomoner. An Anglo Solomon Islander is an acculturated or Westernized native. In this case, despite his acculturation he still subconsciously cherished his tradition.

11. *People Movements in Southern Polynesia* (1971) is entirely devoted to this subject. See also *Solomon Islands Christianity* (1967a:42-43, 60).

12. This is discussed at length in my "Research in Progress Paper #11" (1967c). Examples also abound in the two sources mentioned above in reference 11. For an indepth analysis of power encounter see ch. 25, below, "Problems of Power Encounter."

13. Christianity entered Fiji in 1835. for a record of its diffusion in statistically large movements see *The Christian: Fiji 1835-67* (1954).

14. This concept developed in a most important essay on "The Functional Theory of Culture" found in *The Dynamics of Culture Change* (1961:41-51). He also describes these institutions as "systems" and as "instrumental imperatives" (p.46).

15. In my own field research on the Eto Movement I repeatedly had expressions of this opinion from my Solomon Islander informants.

16. Many movements had secret clearings in the forest with a model of an airplane, for example, set up as a symbol. One example of this was the John Frum Movement. The symbol is illustrated in Attenborough's *Quest in Paradise,* facing p.154.

17. The Marching Rule Movement in Malaita was structured on the model of the U.S. Army. For a description see *Solomon Islands Christianity* (1967a:204-209).

18. The classical example of the symbolization of administration was a wartime movement in Ysabel (Solomon Islands) which spread through Gela, Savo and San Cristoval, which related to native representation on the Advisory Council. The Melanesians raised a flag together with a wooden chair and a wooden rule. They also agitated for higher wages. As an outcome of this movement plans were initiated for Native Courts (see Belshaw 1950).

19. This was certainly so in the Paliau Movement in the Admiralty islands, researched by Margaret Mead (1961) and Schwartz (1962). (For Mead's reference to electronics see 1961:141 and 1970:xvii-xviii, 58).

20. This was discussed in a lecture I delivered in Melbourne, Australia in 1947. It was subsequently printed under the title, "Fiji's Tomorrow" (1947).

21. A useful aid in identifying the self-image of the movement is to ascertain whether it builds its ritual around a collection of hymns or myths. One might at least start from this position. This would place Etoism as an Independent Church, in spite of its heavy syncretism with pre-Christian elements.

22. Millenial visions and apocalyptic aspects of these movements featured in Linton's original essay (1943) but he did not include them in the classification descriptors in his typology.

23. Of the leaders of the Solomon Islands movements of which I gathered data, Silas Eto was a mission catechist, Paukubatu a teacher, Taosin trained as a teacher also but failed to graduate, Pekokoqore was a discharged policeman, and Timothy George had witnessed the Sydney dock strike in 1913 (1967a:201).

24. Fifteen percent of the leadership of Marching Rule was said to have been borrowed from the Christian churches (Allen 1950:41). See also Fox's autobiographical account (1962:127-135, especially p. 134).

25. This movement sought to rid the land of the taint of European money, of European trade, of immigrant natives, and to return to the old customs prescribed by the theocratic Presbyterian Church, as Belshaw puts it (1950). It was both anti-Western economic and anti-Church. See also the writings of Guiart (n.d.; 1956:ix, 5, etc.).

26. The Eto document did this. When I was living in Wanawana I procured such a collection of hymns. It became a major source for *Solomon Islands Christianity*, (253-264).

27. The pietism of the Eto Movement prayer pattern was highly institutionalized. Members recorded the score of their prayers by inserting the midrib of a palm frond in the hair. These tallies marked the building up of merit (see *Solomon Islands Christianity*, p.233).

28. There is always a key personality in any group movement, either to or from Christianity. Even in communal groups where new group norms are sought the momentum begins with an individual, (see *People Movements of Southern Polynesia*, pp. 199-214).

29. For my own historical account of the evolutionary emergence of an indigenous church see "A Church is Built" which was the feature article of the inauguration program of the autonomous Methodist Conference in Fiji (1964).

30. This was published in the *Transactions & Proceedings of the World Methodist Conference* held at Lake Junaluska, N.C., in 1956, under the title "Methodism in the Southwest Pacific."

31. A full account of the emergence of theological education in Fiji was multigraphed and distributed to delegates at the T.E.F. "Consultation on Theological Education in the Pacific" in 1961. See also the report (Dearing 1961:65-68) for a synopsis of the same.

32. The Pacific Theological College at Suva Point, Fiji.

33. The catharsis relates to the struggle with sin and may be violent. It may recur, and reduce in intensity each time. It is seen as a power encounter with Satan. It may well be stimulated by some kind of rhythmic beating, tapping or clapping. It may have strong similarities to Voodoo and may lead to possession (cf. "Problems of Power Encounter," ch. 25, below).

34. A schismatic indigenous church which breaks away from the main body (which retains the institutions and more sophisticated pastors) may be confronted with this same problem as it was the last century in Tonga.

35. In 1967 I pointed this out in the case of Etoism (1967a:225). I understand that since then they have been forced to secure a constitution to gain their recognition, and even be permitted to run schools.

36. For example, Silas Eto argued that the Bible was a reference book which he would cite when needed. It was not for the people to read.

37. For example, the Hauhau Movement which followed the Mauri Wars was established on this attitude to Scripture.

CHAPTER 23

Ethnic Cohesion and Acceptance of Cultural Change: An Indonesian Ethnohistorical Case Study

THEORETICAL PREAMBLE

Data for this study was collected from Indonesia. It has been assembled in such a way as to enable us to explore the notion of acceptance in cultural change *within its context.* This has been approached from many angles by many writers, and, like the apostle Paul, I am a "debtor to both the Greek and the Barbarian," yet I have called no one my master and I hold no authority responsible for having been my model. The theoretical position taken in this paper has evolved mainly in a field similar to Indonesia in many ways and with the stimulus of certain anthropological writers. It is not a theory formulated and then proved by selected cases: it was itself an attempt to explain collected data. Thus, for the writer, this chapter is an examination of another locality in the light of the theory. The writer has not visited Indonesia, though he has had interviews with people from that archipelago, so that most of the material herein has been collected from library reading and the research of other people. There is always danger in using the research of others for developing cultural theory.

H.G. Barnett (1953:17) has pointed out that in their attitude to innovation people fall into two categories, those who consider mankind as complacent and as having to be shocked into the acceptance of new ideas, and those who believe mankind to be fundamentally creative. This dichotomy effects all types of people, including anthropologists, so that while one emphasizes innovativeness, imitation, exploration or progress, another will dwell on stability in culture, themes and attitudes that persist and resist change. Yet clearly, if we emphasize one of these aspects at the expense of the other, we have slipped into unreality; for if there is anything at all in this life that is real, it is this dichotomy—that individuals reject and accept, that at one time a person is stable and resistant and at another the same person is responsive and innovative. Furthermore, as with individuals so too with ethnic groups, social cliques, religious communities, political parties and even nations. If we accept the notion that these aggregates of persons are not possessed of a group mind, but are multi-individual complexes (which view allows for the interaction of individuals within the groups as the group mind concept does not) then we are bound at some point to answer certain problems that arise from such a notion.

The first of these is—what gives the group its wholeness? The mere imitation of one innovative person is not an adequate explanation though it may apply in many cases. There is a *cohesion* that is real. It is this that has led some to speak of "stability in culture" and others of "the group mind," though when this is done, it is often at the expense of the individual role within the group.

The second problem is equally significant; viz., why does a group, adamant in resistance to change for years, perhaps centuries, suddenly, without warning as it were, become an acceptor of all that it has resisted for so long? That societies actually do this, (and in particular, kin groups) behaving like individuals, who change their mind and are open to conversion, has been a powerful argument for the group mind concept. Such situations are at the heart of what has become known as "people movements." It is, of course, an allegory, a powerful one, but we must not lose sight of what it really is.

The third problem is why does the group so seldom accept new ideas as they are presented for acceptance by the advocates of acceptance without some modification? This may be acceptance of form without the essence, or of the essence without the form, or part of either. This signifies rejection in part and acceptance in part, so that the group itself, whether viewed as a consensus or as multi-individual or as a consolidated unit, does discriminate: the *group* discriminates.

Arising from these three we are faced with the problem of the integration of the component parts of this cohesive entity. What is their involvement in each other? Can culture change be accepted when one configuration within the total configuration is "ripe," or does an interacting configuration, which is "unripe," cause the whole to reject the change? Is this the reason why administrators, missionaries and technical advisors get so disgusted with the "unprogressiveness" of the people they serve? Is this the cause of rejection by ethnic groups?

Is there in culture a counterpart of what Sapir found in language "a shifting about without loss of pattern"? (1949:182). He says this is the most important tendency in the history of speech sounds. Change is acceptable as long as it fits the pattern, but if it upsets the morphological balances there is resistance.

In the face of these problems then let us examine the theoretical proposition.

I define *ethnic cohesion* as an endemic force which represents to a given ethnic group its entity, its solidarity and its security in the face of the outside world, and its physical, mental and spiritual satisfaction within itself. I believe this is the dominant factor which determines acceptance or rejection of innovative change. Society is disposed to accept new ideas if they are in alignment with ethnic cohesion, but disposed to reject when they threaten it. The fact that people are ready to accept modified proposals indicates a willingness to change.

Arising from the problems stated above we propose that there are four attributes (there may be more, but there are at least four) of ethnic cohesion. They are:

1.   The ethnic group has a wholeness with a drive to keep that entity permanent.

2.   The ethnic group has the capacity to change its "attitude" at an appropriate moment.

3.   The ethnic group has a power to "discriminate" between aspects of proposed innovation, "selecting" and/or "discarding" in the light of its entity, solidarity and security and satisfaction.

4.   The cohesion of the ethnic group depends on intra-configurational relationships, which are involved in each other. Their orientation must be culturally approved.

By giving the ethnic group attitudes and powers of discriminating, selecting and discarding, I do not mean to imply personality, which would bring me back to the group mind. I recognize that culture is an abstraction, but it is my abstraction of something that is there as a force, and I think that force manifests itself within the collective behavior of the group concerned.

We accept the notion that an ethnic group is multi-individual, and that many changes are cases of imitation, but even these cases must align themselves correctly. However there are many nonimitative cases, and particularly so in Indonesia, which indicate that there is something in the cultural matrix which is not explained by imitation of some innovative individual or change agent. I shall call this the *reservoir of tension*. It is a built-up communal experience which only requires a spark to explode it.

Over a period of time an ethnic group interacts within itself and in relationship with its environment. From time to time would-be dominant factors are imposed on it, it encounters conflicting and sympathetic forces, it may even be confronted by direct advocates of change, but it goes on its own sweet way oblivious of all these forces around it. Yet it is not unaffected. In reality the ethnic group is testing, watching, being impressed or unimpressed, as the case may be. Even though it vigorously rejects these new ideas it is building up an attitude, an ethnic group attitude, fixing its reference points. There may be gradual approval, or increasing hostility, desire, resentment, sense of need. It may be an intellectual, emotional, or spiritual buildup, or a complex of them all. This reservoir of tension may be a feeling of expectancy or an intense passion for emancipation. Then suddenly into this ethnic group is injected a new factor that releases the tension. It may be a person—a mad prophet, an idealist poet, a political agitator—or it may be an invention—writing, firearms—or the Koran or the Bible. From this new factor flows a whole flood of new innovations. A whole culture pattern seems to turn over and find a new level. The innovations are spontaneous unpremeditated, but when the ethnic group recovers from its initial shock and finds its equilibrium again in a new direction, we are amazed to find the ethnic cohesion still applies and the intra-configurational involvements are still the same. There has been terrific change but something lives on—at least as far as we can test it in historic periods.

In those innovative moments which follow the bursting of the reservoir of tension things may work out for good or for bad, especially if two ethnic groups are in conflict at the outburst. It depends on which group produces leadership or initiative to come first out of the state of unbalance.

The fact that these outbursts are people movements (we decline to use the term "mass movement") demonstrates how basic is this sense of ethnic cohesion, which resists disintegration and even through cataclysm persists until it re-establishes its equilibrium. An authority already cited speaks of these crises as "unstructured situations" which present "the need for some kind of solution to bring order out of fluidity." He is following Sherif, who points out that "when a group of individuals faces a new, unstable situation . . . the result is not chaos; a new norm arises, and the situation is structured in relation to the common norm" (Barnett 1953:117).

If it is true, as Barnett says that these are "propitious circumstances for innovation because they provoke destructuralized situations that demand a reformulation," and I take this position, but wonder if the point has been sufficiently pressed that under such circumstances, especially when the explosion has been at the end of a long period of accumulating tension, the restructuralizing is achieved in terms of desires, passions, ideals and motives that were being dammed up in that reservoir of tension—awaiting (consciously or unconsciously) such a time as this. The Biblical writers had a concept like this when they thought of history building up to a point of crisis. They spoke of it in the phrase "in the fullness of time," and our calendar reflects it in the distinction between B.C. and A.D.

Having stated the problems and the theoretical proposition we turn for a moment to examine its bearing on Indonesia before assembling our data for examination.

Indonesia offers good opportunity for the study of this kind of phenomena. Its history reveals several phases of widespread idealogical and religious change—invasion, penetration and revolution on the one hand, and Hindu, Islamic and Christian impositions on the basic Animism on the other. We have abundant examples of the working out of the four attributes of ethnic cohesion described above. They reveal its persistence as an active force. It involves real action and this is why it is so often personified in literature. (Most British speak of their nation as "She," thinking of Britannia. In the United States one hears much of Uncle Sam. The Greeks defied Athena).

In all countries where there is tension between two ethnic units that tension can be traced to either a threat or a fear of a threat to this difficult to define force of ethnic or cohesive entity or solidarity. This is why we get nativistic movements. They are a negative expression of ethnic cohesive entity against what is taken to threaten solidarity or satisfaction. Nativistic movements are not the direct result of processes of acculturation. If they concern acculturation process or foreign impositions it is at the point where their cohesive entity is threatened. Indonesia offers examples for examination.

In this apparent paradox—stability and change—we find our focus. Would it be better perhaps to speak of stability in change? In Indonesia, as elsewhere, we see that sometimes the material artifact is discarded but the function or essence is retained; and likewise sometimes the function is completely modified to meet new ideals but the form is retained. These aspects may be illuminated by examination of the patterns of the great religions as practised in Indonesia. What is important is to see that there are no vacuums. As plowed land that is not planted by the farmer grows a crop of weeds; so you cannot remove cultural elements and leave nothing. Ethnic cohesion will not permit it. It represents a threat, a danger and an opening for a divisive force. Purely negative regulations, prohibitions, often fall into disfavor at this point. Particularly administrative lawmakers, but also reformers and medical personnel, need to remember that negative correctives, which leave a vacuum are not likely to be accepted by an ethnic group.

The ease with which we return to this anthropomorphic idea of group acceptance and rejection in the explanation of our own theory is not foreign to Indonesia and indeed to all south Asia. In recent years the personification of the ethnic group has been reflected in the speeches and writing of the South Asian Christian philosophers (and I feel sure it is not confined to them) under the term "Selfhood" (Ghana 1958:23). Under this personal concept it is easy to visualize the configuration of the whole as the interrelating parts of the body—interdependent, an entity. As we proceed to analyze our data we will discover that this ethnic entity has a total configuration, which is a complex of lesser configurations, which interact like the parts of a body, each having significance for the other in the body process of maturation. A change to any part involves all other parts. Therefore it may be resisted until all parts are ready for that change, then it will be accepted as an act, not of one part, but of the ethnic whole.

There is much room for further study at this point of culture change—the intra-configurational involvement of one part with another. Indonesia offers scope for this study.

This raises a matter of supreme importance to all areas of rapid change. The more change that comes upon Indonesia—and it must be admitted she is living in most formative days—all subsequent appraisals will have to be made beside the pre-revolution appraisals. Comparative anthropology becomes more deeply significant. Records of administrators and articles in missionary journals become important. Many of them are crammed with facts: what bias they have can be allowed for with little trouble. In almost every area of Oceania the best linguistic work has been done by missionaries, and much of it is ethnological treasure beyond price.

In the data now to be assembled it will need to conform to certain requirements if we are study processes of change.

1.   It will need to be historically oriented.

2.   It will have to deal more with behavior and spoken word than with material culture.

3.   Where material culture can be used it must have some observable sequence of change.

This means we will be far more concerned with conceptual data. Our theme more or less forces us into this position, but I believe that it applies equally on all levels.

Obviously some limit will need to be set on the field of testing. As a result, I will limit the discussion to the acceptance of Christianity by certain ethnic blocks in Sumatra among the Batak people, this being my field of special interest. Enough data is available to repeat this form of treatment among the Dyaks of Borneo, the Toradja of Celebes, the Dani, Uhuduni and Kapauku of Irian, and the Tagalogs of the Philippines, but the quantity of material available would have made a whole book.

ADVOCATES AND ACCEPTORS IN BATAKLAND

Historical Note:

Two Englishmen, Ward and Burton (1820), and two Americans, Lyman and Munson (1834), proved ineffective advocates of Christianity to the Bataks. The former were ineffective because an Islamic invasion drove them out, the latter were killed and eaten. A Dutchman, Van Asselt, worked in the south (1856) but was also unsuccessful because of the spread of Muslim propaganda after the invasion (Warneck 1911:20).

However, it must not be assumed that the area was Muslim. Though Islam had been in Sumatra since the thirteenth century, it had never won the Bataks. The early missionaries insisted that neither had Hinduism penetrated this area—it was thoroughly animistic. If this be so religiously, at least the title "Rajah" had been accepted. There is reason to believe that the known invasion of the eighteen-twenties was stimulated by the arrival of the British missionaries. By 1834 an Islamic veneer had at least been imposed on some of the area. Davis' estimates a century later classified 200,000 as remaining Muslim, and 600,000 as completely Animist (1938:26). The 400,000 Christian converts by this time had been won largely from Animism and there had been considerable population growth over the century, I think we may safely assume that the Muslim veneer in Batakland did not extend very far. The fact that the figures just given fell also into a regional pattern supports this view.

In 1861 the Rhenish Missionary Society established a base in a purely Animistic area further north. Their earliest converts were a few individuals who won their own family units. These small cohesive units grew into groups of families by independent advocacy. They were viewed as outcasts for breaking with tradition, and insulting their ancestors upon whose good will the prosperity of the group was thought to depend. Because of this they had to suffer abuse and some persecution. Yet Christianity made sufficient difference to their lives to enable them endure the abuse and demonstrate a new behavior pattern in their lives. This pattern became a factor in the advocacy of their new faith in the community, and weakened disapproval and the strength of rejection of Christianity by the whole body. Another factor which strengthened the advocacy of Christianity was the manner in which these small Christian family units continued to function and prosper without the aid of the ancestor's guardianship. Thus the rank and file came to accept the idea of the presence of Christian families, if they did not accept Christianity itself. They realized that the presence of Christians did not bring danger upon them. Slowly over a period of twenty years one family and then another would become Christian,[1] and then suddenly the whole province of Si Lindung with 20,000 inhabitants, opened its doors (Warneck: 20-22). Whole villages accepted Christianity, even into a locality which had been closed and savage. In one year with no change in advocacy, after 20 years of strong resistance the whole region virtually became Christian. Before the effect was fully realized the same thing happened among the northern neighbors around the Toba Sea, which had been completely closed to all foreign forces for centuries. The course was the same—a few individuals, who became advocates to the family, which in turn became witness advocates to the community and a regular people movement resulted.

In the absence of any change of method of advocacy we are here confronted with one of our basic problems in this investigation: what broke down the 20 years resistance and achieved widespread acceptance? Tentatively we suggest that a reservoir of tension had been created, possibly because the demonstration of Christianity by a few families revealed that the family structure did not disintegrate, that the Christians were good members of society, that their "atheism" did not injure the group, that *adat* still meant something to them, and that there were some superior points about the Christian way of life, and that it was religious. To the Batak, custom, law, morals, social and family life was built on a foundation of religion, which is a subject in itself.[2] The probability is that the animistic Bataks came to see the Christian Bataks were also deeply religious and came to set the two religions beside each other of their own accord. The reservoir of tension, then, would include a growing conviction that the new religion was better. There is room for further research at this point. Do people movements come when the people concerned realize that the new innovation is not atheistic but religious? It seems to be a factor, at least one of them, but does not guarantee acceptance. However, it has bearing often on the mental set of the animist that leads to acceptance, or makes acceptance possible.

Another factor which was injected into the situation was the policy of the Dutch Government in opening up road construction works and their forceful subjection of certain customs like headhunting and cannibalism. Christianity followed the new roads with amazing rapidity, and though thousands still remained Animist, within two or three years a strong, compact area of Christianity had been established in Toba. From this solid nucleus it spread beyond the Toba Sea until it reached areas of Moslem influence. When Warneck produced his survey in 1911 it had been advancing in ethnic bursts for 30 years in solidly Animist areas where Islamic influence was quite unknown. There was a Christian Batak community of 114,728 out of an estimated total Batak population at that time of 600,000 to 700,000 (1911:22).

The outstanding feature of the acceptance of Christianity is the strong place of group action. Groups rejected and groups accepted: families first, then extended families or regional localities, or villages; but always socially related groups. Individual conviction of the rightness of Christianity does not usually bring much action until some socially cohesive entity has built up a reservoir of tension that reaches a breaking point, at which point the whole flood comes at once. This is demonstrated all over Oceania also.[3] The factor has been ignored by many historical writers.

The damming up of this reservoir of tension is a natural and an inherent process. It is inevitable. Many critics of missions fail to allow for this—that in the next "so many" years hundreds of thousands of Animists are going to become something. We cannot stop this. All we can do is to see that the right forces are at hand to channel the flood when the dam bursts.[4] The opening up of countries by means of roads is important for the development of the places concerned that the population may be fed and educated for the coming years. The subjection of cannibalism and headhunting is necessary for obvious reasons. A Government has to attend to these things, but in all this they are building up factors that increase the reservoir of tension. What is often missed by critics of "missionaries who convert the heathen" is that they are really offering a new orientation that will be more adequate in their opinion to meet the inevitable bursting of the reservoir of tension. They may be right or wrong in the way they channel it, and here they may stand for criticism. The destruction of cannibalism and headhunting, which are tied with the whole intra-configurational network of society through the prayer and sacrificial strands has serious consequences. Pull one thread from the fabric and many others are unravelled or set free from their former linkages. An administrative policy of reform at the point of human sacrifice affects the entire religious orientation; and this is a threat to solidarity and to security. This is a major crisis. Once Animists see that their faith is misplaced they discard their fetish and make another (Wallis 1939:34), but if this happens to be faith in their ancestors this is a shattering discovery. This is the most vital and vulnerable point in Animism. A shock at this point is always a dominant factor in bringing a reservoir of tension to the breaking point.

The ancestor is not the spirit of an individual; but the collective spirit who belongs to the tribe as the tribe belongs to it. This is why individual conversions count for little at this state in animistic society, and why tribal, or family conversion is so significant—it is a communal discarding of faith in the communal spirit. This opens the whole question as to whether this accounts for the difference in effectiveness of missionary advocacy to pure Animist and Islamized-Animist subjects. The latter has perhaps been channeled away from the point of greatest vulnerability into a belief in Allah.

Here also we see the reason for ethnic group cohesion—the common ancestor, is not only the spirit protector of the whole ethnic unit; but the social, domestic and economic pattern is built round this—even to the planting and reaping of crops, marriage and inter-responsibilities of people within the clan. After the rejection of ancestor worship the social patterns continue and cannot be ignored by administrators and missionaries but they are less tightly held and as the young people of subsequent generations drift to the towns they may even disappear altogether. This is why at one stage, when certain missionaries tried to make one Batak Church, regardless of linguistic and social groups within the Batak configuration, they struck trouble, and their universalism only stimulated a drift from one area to the city.

One more point arises from our reference to the Dutch Government. To build roads is to invite travel. There is no such thing as a road *to* a village as far as the local people are concerned, it is always a road *from* a village. Roads break self-contained enclosures, encourage migration, threaten cohesive entity. When families increase and land is fragmented, roads suggest migration. Roads are powerful advocates of change. Either the road itself must be integrated into the pattern or it becomes a threat.

The Christian Bataks accepted the idea of the road because they could incorporate it into their pattern and use it to retain their ethnic cohesion. They became a missionary Church—their new patterns of economics and religion integrated effectively.

At one point in the theoretical preamble I spoke of the ethnic group's capacity to discriminate, by analysing the innovation advocated and determining to select part and reject other parts. This is well illustrated in this historical note. The advocates did not achieve all they desired, they had themselves to accept modifications of their proposals. The Church as they would have had it was Patriarchal—the missionary being the "father." For the first twenty years this had been practical. However the sudden influx of 20,000 "children" in a few months rather dislocated the role of "fatherhood." This led to a reduction of the time demanded for catechetical instruction prior to baptism, a leaning far more on indigenous workers, with the result that the Church became far more indigenous than it might otherwise have been (Warneck 1911:23). To meet, what seemed to be, the shortcomings of the new converts the missionaries were forced into policy changes. A special place had to be given to missionary linguists, who worked on Scripture translation, the preparation of pre- and post-baptismal tracts, etc. This vernacular literature was quickly and effectively accepted and absorbed into the indigenous pattern, without any need of advocacy, the need itself being adequate and as a result the Christians from this movement were far more thoroughly Christians than the Muslims were Muslims. The pattern of Christian learning interrelated with the school organization and with educational literature, and thus the Batak Christians were oriented for an educational program and for independent thinking which was to be significant later on in the history of their race.

Thus it will be seen that the roles of indigenous worker and missionary changed considerably between 1881 and 1911—three significant decades when the Christian movement grew from nothing to 103,528. The missionary became, not the "father" of the congregation he knew personally, but a director of a large area, a supplier of advice for leaders, and a producer of vernacular literature; and the pastoral role was assumed by an indigene, who was very much nearer the popular level in intellectual outlook and not foreign.

I have attempted to schematize this situation in Figure 17. Missionaries were wise enough to see their dependence on indigenous agents on the popular level and modified their own role to suit the needs. They restructuralized the situation to make themselves trainers of indigenous leaders. This demonstrates an interesting factor in advocacy and acceptance. An advocacy can itself be deflected from its course by striking a nonresponsive or an obstructive situational matrix. To have pressed advocacy at this point would have meant to confine themselves to a single small mission station, and the flood of released energy would possibly have turned to a nativistic cult or movement; which is exactly what happened in Papua when a mission, unwilling to restructuralize its own role to absorb a movement, left it to pass through and beyond its area in the form of the Taro Cult.[5]

FIGURE 17
Missionaries and Advocacy

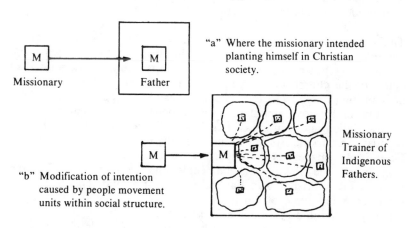

"a" Where the missionary intended planting himself in Christian society.

Missionary   Father

Missionary Trainer of Indigenous Fathers.

"b" Modification of intention caused by people movement units within social structure.

The indigenes were ordained as elders and ordained in office and their duties were laid down (Warneck 1911:24). This was a status innovation to meet the complications of the situational matrix. As a result of this the missionary was also fixed into the pattern with a modified status role, and this was continued until the rising tide of nationalism built up another reservoir of tension from a different set of forces.

The situation was fluid. It was apparent also that the chiefs had to be given a role in the Church when they became Christian, if the Church was to be identified with society. Ethnic cohesion demanded it and out of the crisis came, not chaos, but a restructuralizing. Ethnic entity was retained, but there had been dramatic rejections and acceptances.

Warneck (1911:25) may be cited at this point, having been himself in this field for 14 years in its early stages:

> Having in view the influence of the family among the Bataks, the missionaries took pain not only to influence and win chiefs, as heads of the families and tribes, but to give them a place in the organization of the

Church corresponding to their position. As heathen, these men ranked as the priests of the people in the worship of ancestors, which constitutes the kernel of the Indonesian religion . . . they were invested with responsibility in matters of church government and church discipline, and the settling of quarrels among Christians, in the fixing of church rates, and the erection of church buildings. The elders and the chiefs—the latter, of course, only in so far as they are real Christians—are thus the chief pillars in the organization of the Batak Church.

This illustrates what I have pressed, that there may be dramatic rejections and acceptances—modifications of the initial advocacy—and yet the ethnic entity and cohesion be retained. In fact, I believe that it was to retain this entity that the modifications were acceptable. Christianity though not endemic, was indigenous.

We have noted also that the missionaries accepted a literary role. This was a necessary aspect of the work but could not be handed over to the indigenes at such an early stage. The time was to come when they asked to take this over, and were given the management and journalistic duties of the church newspaper, but that was part of the rising tide of nationalism (Davis 1938:16). The paper had been appearing from 1891.

One of the most significant literary productions at the early stage was the translation and printing of *The Pilgrim's Progress,* which I mention because, next to the Bible, this has been the most influential book in all Oceania. Its imagery is thoroughly Oceanic and the use of names with meanings fits the thinking of island people. I have known Pacific Islanders to argue that Christian and Faithful were real people. This book is the most common source of illustration in native sermons and was unconsciously substituted by converts for their pagan mythology.

Thus the missionaries established a pattern of bible classes, devotional meetings, groups for young men, young women, and for elders—but they had to depend on indigenes to run them. So the foreign literature and machinery was accepted because it was indigenously transmitted, the indigenes responsible having come from the same background as the acceptors. No principle has operated more effectively in advocating Christianity in the whole Pacific—advocacy by advocates themselves acceptors from the same environment. Bursting reservoirs of tension inevitably throw foreign missionaries back on the native agency. The patterns that settle are often quite different from those originally advocated.

Most innovations, as conceived, are impossibly simple because we tend to think in terms of wholes that are ethnocentrically conditioned. Christianity, as known in the West, is often offered in simple exchange for Animism. The schematization infra of Figure 18 is still far too much of a simplification but I think it is sufficient to illustrate the point. This is what happened in the case of the Batak Church before 1911.

FIGURE 18
Ethnocentrically Conditioned Over-Simplification: (Substitution)

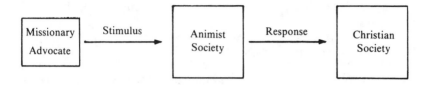

      Out of this thoroughly innovative situation a virile Church developed. The experimentation applied to the earlier period, and once the pattern settled it developed as a living organism in the environment. By 1911 there was an army of 432 trained teacher-preachers, who had received a four year training course, and an indigenous ministry of 33 who had received a further two years in the institutions. The Church on the village level was quite indigenous, and an education pattern had evolved that was to play its part in rousing the spirit of nationalism. Deaconesses had been introduced by the missionary society to attend to female education, and a school system was built up with Government aid. Out of this there arose a concept of responsibility—the people pay for their religion and the State pays for education, even though the two be attended to together and by the same persons. Church buildings were financed by the people who ceremonially donated a portion of their rice crop at the end of the harvest in line with pre-Christian custom. The Batak natural love of music had been directed into hymn singing and interschool competitions were organized. The organization of the Church developed and solidified. This had been possible because only one society was working the area (Warneck 1911:25-29).

      Kraemer's survey of statistics in 1938, and Davis' in the same year, provide us with another reference point in the study of the growth of this movement. We are fortunate to have these at a point immediately prior to the war. They reveal two facts which must be seen together here in our present study. (1) The process I have described above continued up to the war. Growth was by development rather than by innovation. There was a constant expansion into Islamic areas but what innovations there were to organization were slight. In the 25 years from 1911 to the 1936 census the Christian Batak community expanded from 103,528 to 381,677. It more than tripled in 25 years, and this was considerably more than biological growth. Davis (1938:20,31) showed concern that some of that growth had been too rapid, and pinpointed the period of the Great War as one time when standards of admission were lowered, however he seemed satisfied that the 20,000 a year additions in the thirties were healthy enough. (2) It seems also that although there was great growth in numbers both of converts and indigenous staff, that no real scope was given for indigenes to take over the higher supervisory and administrative posts held by missionaries. In 25 years with the levels this mission had achieved, some higher level indigenous leadership should have been discovered.

We are therefore not surprised that towards the end of this period the tide of nationalism should express itself in this Church. Even in the year of that conference there were drastic reductions in Government grants-in-aid because of the financial crisis. Many normal schools were closed and village schools also were cut. In numerous places the village people, determined not to be without education, undertook to provide and finance their own, and as a result the Government granted a larger degree of liberty in school organization and curriculum (*International Review of Mission* [I.R.M.] 1938:28). However in 1939 apparently under some pressure, the Government stopped Batak missionary work in North Sumatra (as it did East Javan work in Bali) where it was being carried on by Christian settlers (I.R.M. 1939:20). Then came the war.

On May 10, 1940, the German missionaries were interned. There were 64 in Indonesia at the time, 28 of them among the Batak (I.R.M. 1941:114). At the same time 500 schools were withdrawn and placed under Government control. The weakness of the Patriarchal pattern on the administrative level was now apparent. There were only six Bataks of administrative level. Furthermore, with the withdrawal of the missionaries all the teacher-preachers became government servants. The Bataks and the Nias (there was a strong Christian Church also run by the Rhenish missionaries among them) were allocated three Dutch missionaries. A Synod was called and the Batak Christians revealed a strong desire to complete independence. It is quite apparent that the removal of the German missionaries was the removal of an obstruction to complete independence.

A Batak pastor was chosen as first Chairman. An Independent Church was established: the three Dutch missionaries were given the status of "church visitors," defined to mean "they have admission to all our meetings, our homes and our churches." (There was already a proto-type for this in East Java. To what extent did this prototype become the prototype for Indonesian independence?) Thus the Europeans completely lost both the central role and control (I.R.M. 1941:26-27). This was spoken of overseas in missionary circles as great "blows on the Batak Church." Clearly the Bataks were ready for independence. The next year it was reported:

> The evident pressure for greater autonomy and independence, which ... found expression when the political crisis arose in 1940, has not been without its reflection in the churches (I.R.M. 1942:20).

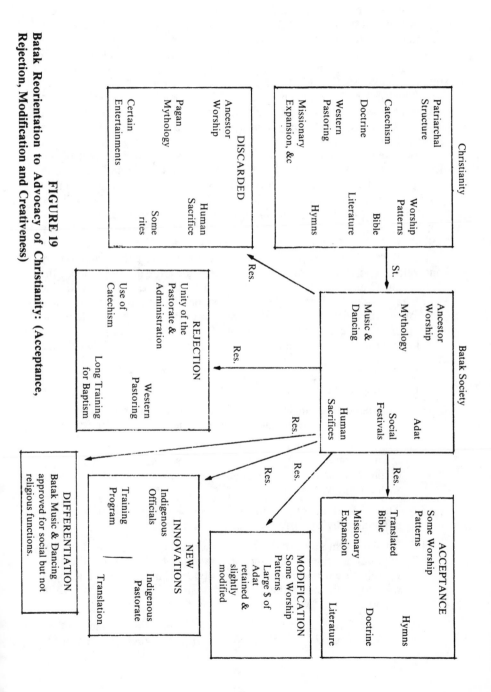

FIGURE 19

Batak Reorientation to Advocacy of Christianity: (Acceptance, Rejection, Modification and Creativeness)

Christianity

Patriarchal Structure	
Catechism	Worship Patterns
Doctrine	Bible
Western Pastoring	Literature
Missionary Expansion, &c	Hymns

Batak Society

Ancestor Worship	
Mythology	Adat
Music & Dancing	Social Festivals
	Human Sacrifices

DISCARDED

Ancestor Worship	
Pagan Mythology	Human Sacrifice
Certain Entertainments	Some rites

REJECTION

Unity of the Pastorate & Administration	
Use of Catechism	Western Pastoring
	Long Training for Baptism

ACCEPTANCE

Some Worship Patterns	
Translated Bible	Hymns
Missionary Expansion	Doctrine
	Literature

MODIFICATION

| Some Worship Patterns | |
| Large $ of Adat retained & slightly modified | Indigenous Pastorate |

NEW INNOVATIONS

| Indigenous Officials | |
| Training Program | Translation |

DIFFERENTIATION

Batak Music & Dancing approved for social but not religious functions.

St.

Res.

299

Although at the time of the internment of the German missionaries most critics doubted the ability of the Batak people to carry their Church in the manner they felt confident they could, within two years competent observers regarded their new system of administration as "surpassing all expectation" and were amazed at the way in which it "removed the financial anxiety" (I.R.M. 1942:21).

Then came the Japanese but the Church leadership stood the test remarkably well and missionary administrators began to wonder what sort of a situation would develop when the war was over and the missionaries returned (I.R.M. 1945:18), for reports from Indonesia revealed "a complete revitalization of the Church" and initiative on the part of the Batak Christian leaders (I.R.M. 1945:70). Yet the Church suffered during that period of the war in all parts of Indonesia. A hundred missionaries died of starvation or murder (I.R.M. 1945:n.p.). Some of the political parties were strongly anti-Christian. However the Christians were themselves deeply involved in the nationalist ferment. Yet there had been threats to exterminate them in 1945. Many Indonesian Christians died, but the Batak Christians proved a competent ability to administer welfare and relief. The Rhenish Mission admitted, that after the first shock, the life of the Church went on "hardly interrupted by the absence of the European workers." Nor did the Indonesians lose control when the war was over—they defined evangelism as the responsibility of Indonesian Christians and were prepared to allow for missionary collaboration in theological training, preparation of literature and medical services (I.R.M. 1947:20 ff.).

That situation is a complex of varied factors, but it seems to me that the determinants were mainly:

1. A reservoir of tension was built up because a people obviously ready for high level leadership was denied the opportunity.

2. That what would earlier have been a calamity (the removal of all the missionary staff without warning at one time) caused the dammed tension to burst, terminating a long period of development without innovation.

3. That the advocacy for independence was both stimulating and stimulated by the drive for national independence.

4. That the Christian party was so thoroughly behind the drive for national independence and so essential to its efforts that the Islamic threat had little popular support. This shows the Church was so indigenous that it could stand with or without white support.

We can go further than this. After the crisis of 1940 the mood of the Batak Church on certain levels was so anti-white that there was a move to remove all the hymns which were of German composition from the hymnbook, however the Batak leaders had no intention of supporting fanaticism (Gramberg 1942:322-328).

Some of the missionaries had sensed this nationalism before the war. Some had written of it, of the restlessness of the young people who were "critical, negative and anti-white" for whom the "nation becomes highest value," a "feeling that Christianity was foreign." This had been met by a drive in youth organizations and the establishment of a youth department with its own director (Verwiebe 1938:208-211).

The indigenous spirit had also manifested itself in a revival of Indonesian musical entertainment which had not been used for 50 years. The old significance had completely gone and now they wanted to present their ceremonial gifts in a ceremonial way. There was division. The missionaries did not take sides. They saw the people had to decide for themselves—the Christian nationalists were demanding a national expression for a national Church (Granberg: 322-328).

There is abundant evidence of this type to show the mood of the Batak Church when the reservoir of tension burst leaving the way open for independence. The manifest success of the creation of an independent Church is the fact that since independence it has added another 250,000 adherents to its strength. Yet the advocate for an independent Church was not mere political nationalism. To some extent nationalism was itself a child of the Church. The Batak Church was still aggressively missionary. It had long boasted as its war cry "The Christianizing of Sumatra by Sumatran Christians!" (Warneck 1911:26). The concept of Selfhood can be the most powerful of all advocates on all levels, material or spiritual.

Notes:

1. This is a common pattern right across the Pacific. In by far the majority of cases the Church has spread by people movements after a period of 3 or 4 to 20 years of individual converts, advocates to the family, and so on. Usually 10 or 11 years would apply. 20 years is a long period of resistance.

2. Cf. Warneck (1954) who devotes over 100 pages to a study of the character of Batak Animism.

3. Cakobau of Bau, Tamai Vunisa of Bua, and others were convinced of the truth of Christianity long before they felt free to accept it, because they knew that they could not rule their kingdoms, with their heathen convictions, if they tried to rule as Christians.

4. A literacy campaign often causes a dam to burst. The successful advocate is not the body which teaches reading, but the body which supplies the books to read. Witness—Communist tracts in Africa.

5. This statement is based on work I have done in that connection relating anthropological work of F.E. Williams with records of that mission, I have charted the course of the Taro Cult.

The Practical Dimension: A Cluster of Missiological Problems

The Practical Dimension: A Cluster of Missiological Problems

No body of theory has any material value unless it can be applied and works within precise practical situations. To this point we have seen missiology as a body of concepts with theological, anthropological and historical dimensions, interacting in a kind of symbiotic relationship. The question now arises: does this work in the practical dimension of the field situation?

Manifestly the field situation is not a constant, and there are numerous ways of classifying it: rural and urban, institutional and itinerant, foreign and indigenous, monocultural and multicultural, first generation and second and so forth. If one chose to arrange the material under the division of first and subsequent generations, there would be a need to distinguish between new missions (church planting) and older established ones (church growth or nongrowth).

The chapters in this section which relate to pioneering missions concern a selection of basic missionary problems: How does a missionary bring an emerging congregation to an adequate "meaning" of the Gospel and not obstruct qualitative growth? What are the dynamics of a confrontation between the religion of the pagans and the religion of the missionary in a power encounter? How does one go about the complex task of evangelism among animistic people? What is the place of polygamy in the social system and what does it mean for the convert?

With second generation situations we assume the existence of churches, yet churches which are not without problems. In the chapter on "Shifting Attitudes to Sex and Marriage: An Example from Fiji," we look at how later generations of Christians often need new ways of addressing issues which once were adequately handled by the people before they became Christian, but which need to be addressed in different ways for succeeding Christian generations. In the chapters on "Membership Shrinkage" and "Static Churches" we examine some of the causes of nongrowth.

Increasingly today, Christian churches, especially in urban situations, are needing to confront the problem of bicultural and even multicultural church situations, a problem addressed in "The Dynamics of the Bicultural Church." In like manner, the question of indigeneity is currently a hotly debated topic and one which we attempt to find some answers in "Indigenous Principles and Mission Today."

Another very practical area involves the role of the missionary in this day and age. Questions arise in the minds of the missionaries and in the minds of the national Christians: Are missionaries still needed or is the national church better off without missionaries? Should the missionaries indeed go home?

This section in no way exhausts the problem issues of the practical field situation, but the articles selected show how the theological, anthropological and historical dimensions are "bound up together in the bundle of life" for the missiologist. None of these were written specially for this book. They all came into being to bear down on precise situations, which had to be discussed and evaluated in the missionary encounter. They were not "cooked up" problems. They were, and continue to be, real issues demanding attention.

CHAPTER 24

The Missionary
Problem of "Meaning"

Assuming that the missionary is commissioned to proclaim a Gospel of salvation unto acceptance, to the end that a church or fellowship may be planted (1 Jn. 1:1-3), there are several ways in which we may fail to bring the emergent congregation to an adequate meaning of the Gospel and thereby obstruct qualitative growth.

This missionary problem explains why a national evangelist is normally more effective than a foreign missionary. My categories are neither exclusive nor exhaustive, but are presented merely for purposes of description and analysis. My contention is that *meaning may be obscured* by (1) the advocate's self-image, (2) the advocate's comprehension of his or her message, (3) the advocate's communication of his message, (4) the acceptor's receptivity, or (5) the cultural conditioning. I use the anthropological terminology from studies in innovation, acceptance and rejection, speaking of the missionary as the *advocate* and the convert(s) as the acceptor(s) (Barnett 1953).

THE ADVOCATE'S SELF-IMAGE

How do the advocates conceptualize their roles? The variety of viewpoints is confusing. Take, for example, the missionary teacher. Missionary teachers in one field known to the writer, and in one denomination, have conceptualized themselves in three different *roles* over three

The original version of this chapter was published in *Church Growth Bulletin*, January 1968, Vol. IV, No. 3, pp. 273-275. Gratitude is hereby expressed to the publisher for permission to include it here.

periods of history. Once they were "training-masters" rejecting the title "teacher" and insisting they were merely developing what was already latent. At another time, they were evangelists, providing mental equipment for Bible study and facilities for religious instruction. Currently they are educators, teaching secular facts and often oblivious to the significant fact that they are supposedly *missionary* teachers. Their self-image is reflected in both their methods and results, and transmitted to those whom they teach.

In the period when the first missionaries in Tahiti were pushing the policy of *"civilizing in order to evanqelize,"* they unintentionally created the impression that industry for profit was the essential Christian virtue. This operated against the general acceptance of the Gospel, because pre-Christian Tahitians had *a different concept of work.*

THE ADVOCATE'S COMPREHENSION OF HIS MESSAGE

How do the advocates comprehend the message they proclaim? If they assume a brand of liberal theology which places their evaluative faculty within their own judgments, they will comprehend their message in terms of their own thinking and bend Scriptures to suit their purposes. Even if they accept the Bible as their rule for faith and practice, they may yet present it in a Western manner—denominationally, for instance. Such interpretations militate against a healthy use of the Bible at this point of *meaning.*

The early New Zealand nativistic Hauhau movement used the Bible to its own neo-pagan ends, justifying it on the score that if Anglican, Wesleyan and Roman Catholic interpretations were justified, so was a Maori one. They accepted the Bible as the Word of God and norm for faith and practice, but the missionary advocates' denominational comprehension out of foreign religious controversy led the converts into heretical syncretism based on Maori mythology.

THE ADVOCATE'S COMMUNICATION

The effectiveness of the missionary's proclamation depends on their capacity to communicate cross-culturally. This is more than reasoning ability, vocabulary and grammar. They do not really communicate until they think in the language, using idiom, symbolism, indigenous logic (which may flow counter to Western logic) and values other than their own. They must conceptualize the problem and reason towards a solution in the indigenous manner. This is more than linguistic proficiency. It is feeling, recognizing the need, not as they themselves envisage it, but as the national feels it. It requires the evangelist's own self: in areas of personal life, witness, and empathy. I knew a missionary who spoke the vernacular superbly. He was a good man and preached a fine sermon. Nationals went to him for all kinds of help, but I never heard of his winning a convert. They said he "was not one of them." His children were not allowed to run in the village. His concept of time and administration were foreign. For all his linguistic skill he did not communicate because he did not identify.

THE ACCEPTOR'S RECEPTION

The innovator is the acceptor, not the advocate. The innovation (here the conversion) assumes a meaning the *acceptor assigns* to it. To be certain converts really understand the Gospel message, is often a serious problem to the missionary. Acceptors reject paganism and demonstrate a real change of life, but their baptism is delayed because they cannot testify in Western terms. The convert never really understands the Western Gospel, nor the missionary the nature of the convert's conversion experience. Conversion from animism demonstrates a non-Western pattern: first, conversion from paganism as a system, bringing converts under instruction, and subsequently a consummating experience of deep conviction. Both are real works of grace through the Holy Spirit—first a change of lordship from the power of demons to the power of Christ, and second, a conviction of sin and acceptance of grace. Strong indigenous churches have grown by this process. Unless missionaries think in terms of indigenous experiences, they face a real problem of meaning.

CULTURAL CONDITIONING

Missionaries and social workers often see their people's needs in terms of their own perceptions. They strive after what *they* consider best. That "best" is determined by cultural conditioning and values, and sometimes scientific or theological generalizations without any context at all. We teach agriculture and sanitation and organize churches in a Western manner.

Anthropologists speak of *felt needs*. But they mean the needs *felt by the people*, not what the reformer thinks ought to be felt. The changes we advocate may mean something quite different to the acceptors, and may be accepted for different motivation than we believe. We misunderstand the acceptance if we ignore its cultural conditioning and values.

The problem of meaning shows up the importance of striving toward the indigenous church, where the advocates are the people themselves, proclaiming a meaningful Gospel. But, meantime, while God calls us to cross-cultural mission, let us safeguard against a Western orientation which obscures the meaning of our proclamation. As advocates our obligation is to make the message as meaningful as possible.

CHAPTER 25

 Problems of Power Encounter

MANA AND TABOO

A missionary from the area narrates a series of events associated with the cutting down of a taboo banyan tree. Tradition held that any person breaking this taboo would surely die. A Christian teacher with about thirty axmen set about removing the forbidden monster after public declaration of their intention to engage in this encounter. A great crowd assembled in an atmosphere of tension. "They will die! They will die!" some cried. "Let me be the first to die then!" the teacher declared, driving his ax first into the tree. Some hid their faces in their hands, but the tree was cut down, though a week was required to reduce it to firewood. The teacher and his friends suffered no harm. They erected a cross on the sacred place and held a Christian worship service there. For a long time a few diehards refused to go near the terrible place, but for the majority of the people it lost its fears.

Every reader of Church history is familiar with this type of incident, and no one can dispute that the Church grew mightily in this manner. However, those who know the facts are by no means of one mind in their interpretation of them. The missionary in question writes:

> I personally was delighted to hear that the banyan tree was going to be chopped down. When the natives responsible for its felling suffered no ill effects, the villagers would have to accept the evidence of their own eyes. The pernicious doctrine of *tapu* would be revealed in all its stupidity.

The original version of this chapter was published in *Solomon Islands Christianity*, (London: Lutterworth Press, 1967), pp. 100-118. Reprinted in 1975 by William Carey Library, 1705 N. Sierra Bonita Avenue, Pasadena, CA 91104. Gratitude is hereby expressed to the publisher for permission to include it here.

> Unscrupulous witch doctors would no longer be able to terrify the credulous native with such flagrant absurdity. If men could ignore the formidable *tapu* of the banyan tree and still live, then all other *tapus* were demonstrably innocuous.

And again:

> The evil symbol was methodically razed to the ground, but nobody was bewitched and nobody died as a result. The *tapu* was a fake.

Whether one agrees or not with the personal opinion of this missionary, whose name I withhold, is not the point so much as the bunch of fallacies in its logic, and its failure to allow for Melanesian logic. The doctrine of *tapu* or taboo[1] is prejudged as pernicious—a generalization which will not stand testing, because many taboos in Melanesia are protective and operate as a form of law to protect personal and communal rights, persons and property. The "witch doctors" are prejudged as unscrupulous, although the term is not defined and the missionary concerned does not distinguish between sorcerers and medicine men. Terms like "all its stupidity" and "such flagrant absurdity" reveal a personal disposition to impatience on the part of the missionary which will not help in understanding the basic problems. That all taboos are "demonstrably innocuous" because one is found false does not follow, even in Western logic. The assumption that the deliberate breaking of a taboo would cause one to be bewitched shows a misunderstanding of terms and processes. Finally, because a taboo fails, it does not necessarily mean it was a fake. It may be so but it is not proved.

This raises a great many problems which are basic to any appreciation of Melanesian thought and action. The missionary tells us the taboo was created so long ago that no one really knew much about it. A powerful chief had put the taboo on the tree but the circumstances regarding the inauguration of the prohibition were forgotten. We do not appear to be concerned with sorcerers and medicine men. The tree is sacred because of its *mana*. It is the *mana* which kills. The taboo is the prohibition. *Mana* is quantitative. Its supply has been built up. There are many ways of doing this. Sometimes skulls were placed in banyan trees. Sacrifices were made at banyan trees. Often snake cults were associated with them. All through Melanesia from New Guinea to Fiji we meet this kind of thing. Quite apart from the fact that banyan trees themselves are widely regarded as sacred, *mana* by means of sacred rituals is a basic presupposition for animists.

The incident under discussion would not be taken to mean the taboo was a fake. The taboo failed because the *mana* had failed, just as with us a law of prohibition fails when the police cannot enforce it. The Melanesian would ask why had the *mana* failed, and to this question there would be found one of two answers. Either (1) the sacred tree had lost its *mana* because, for a long time, the rites had been neglected, no sacrificial rituals had been performed, and the traditions had become vague and half forgotten, or (2) the *mana* of the sacred tree had been overcome by a greater *mana*. The teacher and the young axemen would in this case be seen by the animists to possess a Christian *mana* that was all powerful. Two things ought to be noted: (a) they claimed victory in the name of Christ, and (b) they erected a cross, which, in the eyes of the villagers became a functional substitute for the tree, the symbol of a power which claimed their allegiance.

Whether or not the Western missionary personally rejects this philosophy is to beg the question. The missionary is working in a Melanesian world, facing a Melanesian philosophy, and will have to learn to understand Melanesian thought forms, and fight for Christianity on Melanesian levels. Actually this is a relevant encounter and a real victory, with many scriptural precedents. Western missions might do well to face up to the statistical evidence that animists are being won today by a Bible of power encounter, not a demythologized edition. I am not introducing the rights and wrongs of the latter, but merely the statistical facts of conversion figures.

To return to the quotation—the "evil symbol" of the taboo was said to be able to "bewitch" the axmen. We ought to clarify our concepts. A taboo is a prohibition, sacred or legal, valid only if it has enough *mana* behind it to enforce it. The *mana* is quiescent as long as people observe the taboo. The *mana* is activated by the offender who voluntarily or involuntarily stimulates it. Sorcery is activated by another party with malignant intent, to cause sickness, death or some other harm. The missionary cited did not distinguish between a penalty brought on oneself by breaking a prohibition and a sickness caused by a malevolent second party. The missionary needs to be aware of these distinctions because of the differences in communal attitude towards these various forces. If the missionary fails to appreciate the attitudes and motivation in the Melanesian power complex, he or she will certainly not understand Melanesian reactions to victory in Christ, which are matters of real encounter, not merely a proof that one Melanesian institution was a fake.

If the missionary is to be effective across cultural barriers, an atmosphere of sympathy, even of empathy, must be transmitted. To make prejudgements that things are absurdities and fakes is not the way to win converts. If a mission operates in an atmosphere of *mana* and taboo, the missionary should at least be aware that the Gospel will have some different implications in this mental climate from those with which the missionary is familiar in the West.

POWER ENCOUNTER IN CONVERSION

In conversion, power encounter and people movements go together. I purpose recording as cases two movements described originally by persons who were involved in them, ad using these as a basis for discussion. We will take the case of Florida, which was recorded at length by Alfred Penny (1888:ch. 9), the missionary who baptized hundreds of the converts; and the case of Ulawa as recorded by Clement Marau (Codrington 1894:ch. 5), the Melanesian teacher involved in the movement.

Case Study One: Florida (Gaeta)

The growth of the Church in Florida began with Charles Sapibuana, whom Bishop Patteson had taken to Norfolk Island as a boy of twelve. In 1877, at twenty-three, he settled on his own island at Gaeta, as a Christian teacher, against considerable opposition. Working within the kin structure he first won his own family, then that of his brother, and then the relatives of his brother's wife. These were baptized as a group in 1878 and marked the beginning of the Church. Sapibuana established classes for Christian instruction.

The witness and stability of this group led to many enquiries, and within a year the classes for enquirers were crowded with persons who had virtually resolved to give up heathenism. Penny, who knew them, said:

> They let go their old superstition, and faced danger in the strength of a new religion, refusing to attend sacrifices, treading on forbidden ground where sickness once was found through fear, and doing things which once brought death (1888:185).

There is no reason to doubt the contemporary vigor of the heathenism of Florida, as the *Sandfly* murders of that time show. By 1882 Penny had 100 adult baptisms, and Sapibuana was ordained as a deacon.

In the following year Florida witnessed a *debacle* among the spirit-shrines *(tindalo)*.[2] It began at Gaeta, when chief Kalekona (who had been obstructive hitherto) and some of his people suddenly appeared at Sapibuana's school one evening and announced that they had destroyed their charms and relics and now wished to be taught. By this time about 250 adults had been baptized on Florida, all having registered their decision for Christ by giving up their *tindalo* and their paraphernalia. These events had led to much discussion in the chiefly and priestly circles, and Kalekona had now made his own decision. News of his rejection of his *tindalo* spread rapidly and, as usual, all forms of calamity were predicted, but nothing happened. Heathen opinion began to swing to the view that the new religion at Gaeta was one of great power. The heathen argued that this power was confined to Gaeta, but let Kalekona come outside its orbit and see what his new power stood for outside!

This opinion led Kalekona to undertake an encounter with Rogani, who owed him a debt and apparently had no intention of adjusting his accounts. Custom provided a legitimate mechanism known as *dunning* for the recovery of debt. Kalekona, acting within his just rights, dunned the debt, making sure that the pigs he seized in settlement were actually taboo pigs, and at the same time smashing the *tindalo*. None of his party suffered any ill effects through this venturesome act.

As a result of this general deflation of *tindalo mana,* much sacred ground was now thrown open for garden use, taboo anchorages were opened to the public, sacrifices were dropped, sacred objects were either destroyed, or given to the missionary, or traded as curios, and many pagan priests either retired or began enquiring about Christianity.

The *tindalo* which lost their power in this movement comprised ancient war clubs, clamshell rings up to nine inches in diameter, and armlets made from stalactites from a sacred cave. Hitherto all had been concealed within taboo houses. There was also prehistoric taboo money kept in sacred baskets, each new basket made receiving the remains of its predecessor so that no human hands need touch the sacred money. The remains of twenty-five baskets in one case suggested this particular *tindalo* had been served for two to three hundred years. Kalekona's own tutelary *tindalo* was a lemon-shaped stone with a rude human face. To this he had prayed regularly for a personal supply of *mana*. He alone knew its secret place, which had been revealed to him by his father.

This movement expanded into an almost complete conquest, with but a few limits. In some localities intimidation and fear remained to oppose the new religion. Any accident or misfortune to a Christian was declared to be the work of some offended *tindalo,* but such reactions were brief and soon gave way to Christian advance. The Gaeta movement required about three years for the intake of converts. Each convert was given about a year of instruction before baptism, and Penny recorded adult baptisms as about 200 in the first year, 200 more in the second, and 283 in the third. No infants were baptized until after their parents. This represented the winning of a total social unit, and was typical of the movement which continued spreading through Florida.

In his last year in the Solomons, Penny saw a similar "spiritual upheaval" at Honga. It began with the baptism of twenty adults with "the same tokens of power working in the hearts of the people in a remarkable manner." He described the changed character of the chief, Tambukoru, who was afterwards baptized with fifty-six others by the bishop. Actually this movement at Honga was a *planned* evangelistic thrust organized from Gaeta. The new Christian community had developed a concept of outreach from the start.

Case Study Two: Ulawa

Clement Marau was sent to Ulawa. It was not his own home and he had no kin connections there. He had met Ulawa boys at Norfolk Island but had yet to learn their language. After three years of failure he asked the bishop to remove him. The bishop prayed with him and left him for another year. Marau worked on a young man of his own age, convinced him of the truth of Christianity and sent him to win his parents. The youth met with hot opposition, but Marau followed up his work. He started a little class for gospel narratives. Before long the mother of the youth came to the class and in time the father also. They were the first couple in Ulawa to "put on the cloth" as the symbol of changed hearts. As a family they met with much opposition, but they stood together as a family and endured. Their nearest neighbor was impressed by their witness and changed lives, and shortly he and his family joined the group. Marau himself had convinced another youthful neighbor, and together these comprised a Christian cell of eight persons on a basis of locality and two family units. They formed a compact unit, building each other up in prayer and faith in the face of persecution.

The question now arose in their discussion: could the cell remain firm if Marau were taken away from them? Although they had formed a real bond of fellowship, yet Marau knew that there were still things in their houses that would undermine their strength in the face of danger. He felt the time had come to challenge them on the point. "If you are sincere, let me see a proof in you!" he demanded, and went on to speak of "things belonging to deceiving spirits—holy stones and money sacred to deceiving spirits, and things used in sacrifices." They accepted this challenge and handed over the sacred paraphernalia to Marau. Together they took them out to sea and formally threw them overboard. This was a regular Melanesian pattern for disposing of things supposedly charged with *mana,* salt water being as effective as fire or burial. As sacred objects they no longer existed. The Christian cell had rejected its ancient traditions.

There was at Ulawa, near their locality, a sacred grove. A revengeful snake, supposed to dwell there, afflicted men with ulcers. The Christian group now decided on a bold stroke. The iconoclasm up to this time had applied only to their personal and household fetishes. They now determined to involve the non-Christian community and made a public challenge. It was a wedding occasion when folk had gathered from far and wide. They declared they would burn the grove and destroy it to prove that they no longer had fear of the spirits, and to demonstrate the power of the True Spirit.

As good as their boast, the father of the first family cut the sacred vines and together they pulled down the fence. They took the holy stone from its place of honor and set it in the path to be trodden on by men. They took females of the group to the place which was forbidden to their sex. They did away with the skulls and bones venerated there for ages.

They cooked and ate the sacred yams which were for the spirits alone, and transformed the sacred enclosure into a food garden. The astonished pagans adopted a "wait and see" attitude, predicting calamity. The spirits were powerless and the pagans now declared that the missionary ship had driven away the *mana* of the place.[3] In time, some were angry and wanted to kill the Christians, but the latter were not intimidated. They felt that things in Ulawa would never be happy until all the people came to the truth and took the same stand. After a long description of these events Clement Marau added:

> This was the beginning made in their new religion . . . when I sought a proof whether they would let it slip or not. . . . Now there are already sixty-two of us. When anyone wishes to enter the school he asks that he may be thought of in prayer; and on the day that he comes in as a hearer he declares that he entirely gives up all that he has to do with ghosts of the dead or the spirits that he has worshipped. . . . He begs me to teach him a little prayer, that he may pray to God to protect him from the anger of those spirits . . . he prays and he has no more fears.

For a time the movement in Ulawa had a family structure, passing in small units from family to family. Eventually it became a full-scale people movement on a community level. In the center of the island was a large public building where dwelt the ghost of greatest power and where arms and war regalia were deposited. Groups from all round Ulawa sacrificed here where a regular priesthood was established. Marau won the priest in charge for Christ.

It was now incumbent on the priestly convert to demonstrate the sincerity of his decision. He issued a public statement that he was about to be baptized as a Christian, that all his life he had been concerned with holy things, but that he was now turning from the ancient forms of holiness to Him who was the Holy One, who gave him power to overcome the spirits which had hitherto impoverished him. Having made this announcement in terms appropriate to their thinking, he set to work destroying the sacred place of his old faith. As a result of this demonstration a new public attitude emerged, for this priest, Marita, now knew the True Spirit. Was he not there, with his son and heir, smashing the skulls and bones they had all feared for generations? They knew he had the truth. Clement Marau gave himself for Ulawa, ministering there until his death. He married a girl of the island, built a church of coral blocks, and gave his son to enter the Christian priesthood.

Discussion

Christian missions have been criticized for their iconoclasm, especially by the salvage anthropologists. The criticisms have been mainly against two points: the loss of material of cultural and archaeological value, and the imposition of one religion on the people of another by force rather than reason. Neither criticism is quite fair, because missions and missionaries have very seldom done this. Of the hundreds of cases I have investigated, I know only two (possibly three) in which a missionary was foolish enough to initiate any iconoclasm, though objects were frequently handed over to missionaries for disposal. There is logic in this. Iconoclasm was the indigenous symbol of the rejection of a *mana* repository. Throughout Polynesia and Melanesia this is the indigenous conceptualization of power encounter. I remember once seeing a fine Melanesian spear dance which ended with every dancer shouting and smashing his spear across his knee. This was a great loss of cultural material and a waste of fine craftsmanship; but the termination of the dance was a symbolic act representing the end of war and the beginning of a new day of change. It was thoroughly meaningful and appreciated by the large audience. So the iconoclasm must be seen for what it is—a cultural mechanism within a social pattern, the proof of sincerity in a time of major decision making. Again, it was always a voluntary act undertaken by the approved authority within the structure, or a challenge of proof by contest within a specific frame of reference. When done by a large group it was preceded by much discussion and agreement—i.e. by multi-individual decision—the approved authority of the group thereafter taking the initiative with the support of the group.

To pass from these generalizations to specific points in the two cases outlined, one of the first things which strikes me is *the place of the social structure in power encounter.* The patterns of this type of movement are not uniform everywhere but the differences can often be accounted for by social structure. In the case of Sapibuana, the man was set down within his own kin unit, but in the face of communal opposition. He wisely set out to win first the nuclear family to which he belonged, and then extended family followed by those related by marriage. It was out of this that the Church grew. He started with the smallest cohesive group, expanding until their very solidarity began to win folk from the wider community.

In the case of Marau, who had no kin connections and had inadequate language for proper communication, the evangelist was faced with a more serious barrier. But Marau was a shrewd observer and had the courage to discard any method which did not work. As he said afterwards, he made the mistake of speaking to the pagan community at large. Considerable crowds gave him a hearing but there was no response. Fortunately he recorded his reason for changing his tactics. He had observed the cohesive units of pre-Christian religious life in Ulawa were the independent families:

> these Ulawa people, *every family,* having its own spirit, every man sacrificing without fail, and sacrificing without exception about everything ... in every place there is a place or object of sacrifice, *according to the family.... In every family* a pig is set apart for the spirit and kept so. ...

It is a long passage and Marau went on to ponder the phases of family life to which these sacrifices applied.

With this in mind Marau strove to win his friends—the appeal of youth to youth—and through him, his family. Each family was urged to seek to win its neighbor. This was possible because the families were independent decision making units. Marau had, by his own testimony, found his prototype for family action in the Old Testament Hebrews, and he himself conceptualized his task as leading them from their family sacrifices to the One True Sacrifice. He was impressed by the place of sacrificing and praying in their lives, and felt that if only they could come to know the Scriptures they would attain to a superior knowledge in these things.

By the time a number of families had become Christian, Marau considered the wider community with the same astuteness. He identified the key figure of communal affairs in the chief priest of the central shrine, and directed his attention to this person. This man, more than any other, could have been his enemy and obstructor. Marau, having won him for Christ, demanded evidence of his sincerity, and the resultant demonstration, devised by the priest himself, became itself the stimulus of a community movement. Marau might have won scores of lesser persons, priests among them; but nothing was as effective as winning the competent authority for affairs at the central grove. It was an important victory. The public statement made by Marita shows how deeply Marau's teaching had gone and how clearly Marita himself had thought out the consequences of his symbolic actions.

Another form of public encounter set out above is *encounter by challenge*. This was often used by island evangelists who found it difficult to break through social obstructions. Its biblical prototype was the contest between Elijah and Baal on Mount Carmel; and as with all societies which employ mechanisms of contest for proof or ordeal, it is assumed that the result is not merely the personal strengths of the contestants but the power of the God or spirit on whom the contestants call. "The God who answers by fire, let him be God!" (1 Kgs. 18:24).

When a chief came with a group of people and announced that they had destroyed their paraphernalia and were ready for instruction, as Kalekona did, it may be quite certain that a long period of discussion had preceded this act. Some missionaries avoid this kind of behavior, wrongly considering it mass action without individual conviction. Invariably it is the result of long debate and often complete unanimity is required before any group action. When Dr. Welchman ascended 1,800 feet to Juleka to start a Christian cause there and gave a brief exposition of the faith to those who gathered to meet him, he asked for assurance that they were definite about wanting to be Christian. Two or three said together, "If we had not made up our minds, should we have been here today?" It had been well discussed. Frequently the multi-individual decision included not only the decision to become Christian but also the specific ocular demonstration to be employed as a power encounter to prove the validity of the new faith.

One question which arises from this is whether or not such a demonstration is adequate proof of faith to permit baptism or whether further instruction should be demanded. The question is whether an individual should be *baptized on the basis of an act of faith* or *an understanding of the faith.* Baulee, an old high priest and a powerful magic man of the Belaga district, forced this issue. He wanted baptism there and then without any delay of a year. He pointed out that he had let go his hold on all those resources of power on which he had relied all his life, and he wanted the full resources of the new life. His old sacrificial role had been completely discarded, and he now wanted to partake of the means of grace of Christian fellowship. Confronted with a definite conviction and demand, missionary Penny felt constrained to grant his wish and baptized him immediately on this expression of faith (1888:207-208). But not all the missionaries would have agreed with him. On what basis is an individual baptized when he or she comes out of paganism—an act of faith or on knowledge of the faith?[4] In the eyes of the Melanesian the symbolic act is conclusive.

There is another reason for pressing for some ocular demonstration of effective encounter. A second generation Christian who knows his New Testament might put it thus: You cannot escape from Satan; he will never leave you alone; you can only deal with him by facing him and defeating him. Penny felt that few, if any, Melanesians came to understand that those spirit forces in which they had once believed never really existed at all. They were powers which had been defeated in Christ, and would still hold people who were not Christ's. That this dynamic experience should be conceptualized in terms of personalized or spiritualized encounter, is perhaps a better way of formulating these vital and determinative experiences, than our modern, sophisticated, disbelieving explanations in terms of chemicals, mathematics and gastric juices—which, be it well noted, in the final analysis have to be described in symbols themselves. In simplest terms we are confronted with changed lives: in mental set, in behavior patterns and in spiritual satisfactions. It is a change from fear to triumph. If the Melanesian chooses to demonstrate this by dismembering or burning his *tindalo* or *tingono-na,* or burying the skull of an ancestor, we ought to accept this at its face value—an act of faith and a symbol of victory. Whether we ourselves believe those ghostly forces were real or not, for this convert from animism they were real. The convert has met the ghost face to face and defeated him. He or she has struggled with Satan and won. If the convert does not have this victory, then Satan is bound to return. First generation Christians who lapsed back into paganism were very few, but in those cases where evidence is available they usually seem to be people, who, for some reason or other, failed to demonstrate their faith by an act of power encounter. I have never found a case of pagan resurgence—individual, family or community—without an accompanying recovery of the spirit shrine, or a rebuilding of the altar, or a restoration of the sacred grove. If the shrine had actually been destroyed, a new symbol or fetish would have to be created. We need not wonder at this—it was the regular pattern in pre-captivity times in the Old Testament. (In a third or fourth generation, more remote from the animistic original state, there can be a lapse into materialism under the influence of acculturation, but we are not discussing that here.)

With people who have just come out of animism there is a *continuity of temptation when paraphernalia are not destroyed*. This is demonstrated by the case of a shaman, Siama, of Barasaka, who had given up his practice and for some time had been attending Christian prayers. He had, however, made no public demonstration of his apparently quite genuine change of heart. In the end he went to Dr. Welchman for baptism and took his paraphernalia with him—a bag of leaf prepared in scented oil (*manuni*) and a tin box with some scented beans. He confessed that though he had been attending prayers and this was well known, and he had not performed his rituals for some time, yet people continued plaguing him to perform them on behalf of their sick. Because he only did good in trying to help the sick and because he made no sacrifice to ghosts, he had apparently voided any demonstration of encounter. But not until he made his confession and handed over his equipment to the missionary and accepted baptism did the community accept his devotions as sincere and stop plaguing him for his shamanistic services (Wilson 1935:95-97).

If the act of destruction is not a public challenge or ordeal, it is expected that it *be performed by the approved authority*—the individual himself for a personal charm, the head of the family for some family relic, and a priest if the sacred object has wider significance. It must be the priest of that particular shrine. This is another reason why the mission should not be the perpetrator of the act. An indigenous preacher can also run into trouble at this point unless his act is accepted by the public as a challenge or ordeal. Abraham Faidangi allowed his Christian enthusiasm to run away with him in San Cristoval. He collected the carved sharks of Lomahui, which were skull repositories, and threw them away as if they were nothing. Abraham found that heathen authority still counted for something and he was compelled to replace them in the devil-house. In time, however, his work was effective and the same elders determined to become Christian, whereupon they themselves discarded the skulls and sacred paraphernalia. The right of disposal could be transferred by a timid authority provided he himself took the responsibility of giving it away. This was interpreted as regarding it now as a mere thing of no value, despised like the household gods of Laban that could be hidden by a woman sitting upon them (Gen. 31:34). In the museum at Munda is a piece of prehistoric clamshell filigree work (*barava*) carved from material extracted from an uplifted reef by some obsolete technique. The little figures of dancing men and rings are supposedly the work of the gods. This sacred object brought death to a Lauru bushman, and the people, terrified by its *mana,* wanted to dispose of it. By community decision two Christians, Simon Peter and Mulakana, were allowed to take it away and present it to the missionary. The approval was legitimate, the Christians took the risk, and the actual disposal was left to the missionary. This was frequent in the Western Solomons, effective but not nearly as realistic. Goldie wrote in a 1917 District Report:

> Our mission house verandah is lumbered up with gods—gods of all shapes and sizes—the one time objects of veneration and worship of our people, who offered sacrifices and prayers to them continually.

With the South Sea Evangelicals also the onus for destruction and disposal was often left to the missionary. In *Dr. Deck's Letter,* written in 1914, is given an account of the opening of the church at Tanaha. The people asked him to remove their *adaros.* Deck and his party dismantled the charms and sacred objects, took them away and cast them into the sea.[5] If the people were not even prepared to dismantle the sacred objects themselves and bring them to the missionary, their Christian commitment was not very deep.

In the case of the filigree removed by the two Christians, the people of the village concerned were still heathen, and were afraid of the sacred object because it had killed a man. The two Christians gained very much respect for their bravery, and as a result gained a hearing. We are not surprised then that before long they were able to bring the whole group into Christianity. This Christian fearlessness of sacred objects and taboos was part of the power encounter complex. Sometimes a taboo, such as a prohibition against climbing a sacred mountain, would be discussed in a village. Such conversations were frequently a source of inspiration to dynamic Christians open for challenge. Solomon Damausoe was one such who accepted a challenge at Zonga to climb Mount Sambe, which rises from the lagoon by dangerous precipices. The climb was quite a physical test in any case and local tradition declared that anyone attempting it should surely die. Damausoe and a small party of Christians accomplished the feat without fear or ill effects. The achievement gave Damausoe a hearing and shortly afterwards as a result of his advocacy the Zonga people accepted Christianity.[6]

All the cases cited in this chapter on power encounter are fairly typical. Many others could be narrated but they would be redundant. The unit shows *the importance of specific decision in coming to Christ and the public demonstration of that decision* within the thought forms and behavioral forms of the cultural structure. The power encounter for the new convert is both a symbolic act and a step of faith. However, this is not the end of the road, but rather the beginning. A growth in faith and knowledge and grace has to follow. The power encounter experience has to be consummated. Evangelism always requires effective follow up. Conversion growth requires consolidation in quality growth. McGavran speaks of these two processes as *discipling* and *perfecting*—the former the rejection of the pagan gods and spirits and the enthronement of Christ, making disciples, and the latter "teaching them to observe all things I have commanded" (1955:13-15).

I realize that some readers may not accept the intellectual orientation of this chapter on power encounter, but I must insist on two things: (1) unless they are aware of it, they cannot think Melanesian and (2) unless they can put themselves in this position, at least conceptually, any acceptance of the Gospel they achieve will have a different meaning to the acceptors from what they intend.

Notes:

1. *Tapu* is the Polynesian form of the word which appears as "taboo" in the Oxford Dictionary. The more common Melanesian form is *tabu,* remembering that the "b" sometimes has the value of the English "mb." The "t" is sometimes dropped, so that another form is "ambu." In the passages cited the missionary used the Polynesian form. There are many Polynesian communities in Melanesia.

2. Penny seems to use the term *tindalo* either for the *shrine* or for the spirit for whom it was the vehicle. They are related, of course, for to destroy the shrine is a symbolic disposal of the *mana* of the spirit in that repository.

3. Note that they did not say the sacred things were fakes, but that they had been deprived of *mana.* This is Melanesian reporting.

4. Since the completion of this manuscript a report has come to hand from the W.C.C. Consultation on Evangelism in West Africa. I note they discussed this very point, with the following result: "It is essential that baptism be seen as a manifestation of the grace of God in Jesus Christ, and as the point of departure for the new life in which the convert will step by step discover what the God who loves him asks of him. On no account may baptism be made to appear as a kind of diploma attesting that the convert knows all about God and the practice of his faith" (p. 5).

5. *Dr. Deck's Letter* was a quarterly letter of Norman Deck published by this South Seas Evangelical Mission representative in the Solomons for about twenty years from c. 1907.

6. *Solomon Damusoe* is an unpublished manuscript of John F. Metcalfe.

CHAPTER 26

The Evangelization of Animists

The title of this chapter seems to imply the existence of a concrete religious system, called *Animism*—something which might be set over against, say Hinduism or Buddhism, not only for purposes of description and study but also as a subject requiring a strategy for evangelistic approach. Because the greatest number of currently open doors for the Gospel are among animist people, the inclusion of the topic in an *Introduction to Missiology* is certainly appropriate, in spite of any intellectual problems the title raises. Therefore, to avoid using too much space in debating semantics, this preamble seems desirable.

ANIMISM

Some scholars prefer to subdivide Animism and to deal with the subunits—Shamanism, Fetishism, Ancestor Worship, and so on—treating each as a religion in its own right, thus avoiding the term "Animism" altogether. This may have some descriptive advantages, until one discovers that the subunits are not discrete: several may be found interwoven together, and their practitioners may have multifunctional roles. These "religious systems" are thus found to be merely functional distinctions within what certainly looks like a general religious system, with no more diversity than Hinduism or Buddhism; and now we are back again to the notion of Animism.

The original version of this chapter was published in *Let the Earth Hear His Voice,* J.D. Douglas (ed.), (Minneapolis: World Wide Publications, 1975), pp. 844-857. Gratitude is hereby expressed to the publisher for permission to include it here.

The term "Animism" is certainly to be preferred to *Tribal Religion(s),* because Animism is active in great cities like Los Angeles, New Orleans, or Sao Paulo, and has many nontribal aspects. It is preferable also to *Primitive Religion(s),* as it is neither chronologically nor conceptually primitive; indeed, it is currently much alive, and frequently quite sophisticated. Nevertheless, we should recognize that we are using the word as a term of convenience to provide a frame of reference for our discussions, presupposing that Animism is a discrete enough philosophical "system" among the religions to warrant our consideration of an evangelistic strategy for winning its followers to Christ. This is precisely the same position the members of our other groups will find themselves in, for Hinduism, Islam and Buddhism may also be manifested in a great diversity of systematic forms.

The popular use of the term "Animism" comes down to us from E.B. Tylor (1871). He did not give it the technical meaning it acquired from the comparative religionists, of a "kind of religion," but used it to signify "the deep-lying doctrine of Spiritual Beings, which embodies the very essence of Spiritualistic as opposed to Materialistic philosophy." It was, for him, a "minimum definition of religion" which saw the animistic way of life as accepting the reality of spiritual force(s) and beings, over against the materialist outlook on life. "In its full development," Tylor agreed, it formulated concrete beliefs in such notions as the soul(s), the future state, controlling deities and subordinate spirits, especially when these beliefs result in "some kind of active worship" (1871; I:425).

I believe this is a realistic approach, because it permits us to talk about animism and biblical religion in the same philosophical or conceptual structure, and to weigh one over against the other; and therefore to understand the meaning of commitment when a present-day animist comes to the "moment of truth" and makes a decision for Christ. Thus the very term "evangelizing animists" puts us into an identifiable category of communication and response. We are not dealing with secularists or scientific agnostics, whom we would need to approach by means of a different path in order to witness. But Animists and Christians have one thing in common: they accept the spiritual view of life. They do not need to be convinced of the existence of the supernatural. This opens many ways for dialogue; even though, at the same time, it exposes us to many problems and dangers, which we shall examine in a moment.

In spite of the wide range of categories, forms, and functions that may be identified in the study of animistic communities, and which compel us to admit that perhaps every animist community is different from every other one, I firmly believe that Animism can be examined as a cohesive thing, and that enough universals can be identified to permit us to discuss the evangelization of this kind of community in general terms. I believe we should be able to deal with tribes in the forests of Africa, in the highlands of New Guinea, or in the hogans on the mesas of New Mexico under this head—and to a large extent also the drug cults of Hollywood. My purpose, therefore, is to generalize as far as I can, and to delineate some common problem areas for discussion, rather than diversify one form of Animism as over against another. But I hope the diversity will be apparent in our discussions.

Whether evangelists be from an old or a young church, if they are witnessing cross-culturally they will be hoping to leave some kind of an indigenous church behind them. The fellowship group will have to be the Body of Christ ministering the mind, touch and heart of Christ in its cultural and animist world; for evangelism is not merely the winning of individuals, but also their incorporation into relevant local fellowship groups. Therefore, before I enumerate my common problem areas, I must examine the biblical data base from which I operate.

THE BIBLICAL THEOLOGY OF ANIMISM

From the biblical point of view there is really no such thing as a taxonomy of religions for comparative study. Not even Hinduism or Buddhism has any biblical standing as a religion. For the people of God there is only one God, and all those who do not serve Him are grouped together in a single category. Although there is sufficient data in the biblical narrative for a whole textbook on Animism, the common practice of classifying religions, with Animism at one end and Christianity at the other, as if in an evolutionary scale of development, is not in tune either with Scripture or with the anthropological data.

Of course, I may turn to the Scriptures and read about the deities with whom the people of God came into contact from time to time on their pilgrimage—of Dagon, of Chemosh, of Molech, of Tammuz, and of Bel. I also learn of their confrontations with fertility cults, of heathen sacrifices and libations, of ceremonial inhumanity like infanticide, of making cakes to the Queen of Heaven, and of worshiping the smooth round stones of the valley. We have everything—from individual and domestic ritual acts to national assemblies and the worship of national war gods—rites performed in the fields, by the wayside, in groves and high places, and in great temples. We have divination, necromancy, and sorcery, and numerous other ideas covered by the biblical word "idolatry." We could break down the whole animistic system of the biblical world into categories for study, but in the last analysis the Bible disposes of them *as a single category* in the first two commandments (Ex. 20:2-6)—anything that would usurp the Lord's place in the life of his people and set itself in God's place is grouped together as "over against Him" and idolatrous.

Nevertheless, when we consider the world of biblical times—the first two millennia before Christ and the first Christian century afterwards—we find it very similar to that of our own. The people of God stood over against all the forms we meet in Christian mission today, on all the various levels: private individual, domestic, peasant, and national. The characteristics of each of these levels recur through history with the kind of lives people live on those respective levels, and do not fit into a chronological evolutionary scale from the simple to the sophisticated. The Bible deals with both tribal and great religions, with both simple and complex, with both oral and written religious traditions—and it treats them all under one rubric both in the Old and New Testaments (Ex. 20:2-6; Rom. 1:19-25).

In the same way Walter Freytag had argued for the notion of the *people of God,* a biblical concept, as set over against the biblical counter-concept of the *Gentiles*—the "not-people-of-God"—because they are nations serving other gods, and have not yet come to the life of faith that makes people new creations and permits them to belong to the community of faith. This lines up with the concept coming from the Old Testament where "Gentiles" or "heathen" is *goyim* (the plural), for which the Septuagint adopted ethnos in many places—ethnos being the original root of the word "heathen" (again "ta ethne," plural). Canaan was occupied by heathen nations, but was to become the possession of the seed of Abraham, through whom all the *goyim* of the earth would be blessed. The heathen would come to seek the Messiah (Isa. 11:10), who would minister judgment to them (Isa. 42:1), and offer light and salvation to the end of the earth (Isa. 49:6). In the New Testament also, "ta ethne" is used of the nations who are over against the Lord (Mt. 24:9; 25:32, etc.) and as the object of evangelization (Mt. 28:19; Lk. 24:47; Rom. 16:26; Rev. 18:3; etc.).

The people of God are the Chosen Ones. But they always have a *responsibility* to the Gentiles. The latter were not excluded from Israel. Even in the Old Testament times they had their rights as resident strangers under the Law. The doctrine of the rights of the resident stranger in Israel is expressed in the Deuteronomic source and in the narrative of the book of Ruth, which is a practical demonstration of the Deuteronomic Laws: Deut. 1:16; 10:9; 14:21; 24:17, etc., and Ruth 2:2f; 2:8-10, etc. But in the New Testament, when the notion of the people of God is separated from the historical people, and we meet the new Israel, we also see the universal purpose of God for the whole human race. The possibility of incorporation into the New Humanity is there, but the Gentiles, or heathen, are still not yet incorporated (Eph. 2:11-22), because they are still living in opposition to God, worshiping "not-gods" (Gal. 4:8), defying themselves, and they are classified as under the realm of the prince of this world (Eph. 2:1-3; 1 Cor. 10:19-21). This is why the Christian mission must continue "until the end of the age" as the Great Commission indicates.

In this chapter I wish to speak of evangelization in a somewhat wider sense than just bringing individuals to an act of "decision for Christ." It is this, of course—but more. It involves both a step of commitment and an experience of consummation, in which the Spirit witnesses with the convert's spirit that the convert is now a son or daughter of the Father, and if a son or daughter, then an heir through Christ (Gal. 4:6-7)—that the blessing of Abraham might come to the Gentiles, or heathen through Christ, receiving the promise of the Spirit through faith (Gal. 3:14). This is a process, bringing folk out of heathenism—here defined by Paul as "worshiping not-gods" (Gal. 4:8). The picture we have here of conversion from heathenism, illustrated in Figure 20, is that of a *process* — an *ongoing experience.*

FIGURE 20
The Process of Conversion

From the "not-people-of-God" . . . to . . . the People of God.

Adoption into the household of God brings the convert into a *group experience.* Some kind of incorporation into the fellowship group is always part of the evangelization process. This comes out clearly in the opening verses of 1 John, where witness (vv. 1-2) leads up to joining in the fellowship (v. 3), and from that verse on, John is dealing not with an individual in isolation, but one in context, in a state of fellowship (vv. 6-7).

Now, as we consider the evangelization of animists, it should be remembered that we are not dealing with individuals in isolation, but with people brought from death unto life—life *within a fellowship group.* We cannot escape the truth, that to give an individual the Gospel of personal salvation demands incorporation into a fellowship group as a concomitant. Evangelization implies the existence of, or planting of, a church.

THE EVANGELIZATION OF ANIMISTS

The conversion of animists and their incorporation into fellowship groups involves us in each of the following problems, which I have conceptualized anthropologically because I think that such a treatment best opens up the subject for our discussions. I am reminded of the question of Henri Maurier, "Does not every theology have to be accompanied, in counterpoint, by as concrete an anthropology as possible? It is not enough for the apostle to learn what God has said; he also has to understand the men to whom he is bringing the Word" (1968:268).

1. Pay Attention to the Problem of Encounter

Animists cannot just *drift* into the Christian faith. True, they may attach themselves to the fringe of some congregation as interested spectators, and maybe even become what we sometimes call "sympathizers," and it may well be that by so doing they will fall under the influence of the Spirit of God and be brought to vigorous commitment; but the passage from heathenism to the Christian faith is a definite and clear-cut act, a specific change of life, a "coming out of something" and an "entry into something quite different," a change of loyalty—or in the biblical analogy, a change of citizenship (Eph. 2:12-13).

The notion of making a definite act of commitment to the Lord is a biblical concept in both the Old and New Testaments, and was normally accompanied by some kind of ocular demonstration of the commitment. The book of Joshua ends with such an episode (24:14-15): "Choose you this day whom you will serve; whether the gods your fathers served in the region beyond the river, or the gods of the Amorites in whose land you dwell; but as for me and my house, we will serve the Lord." Here, there is a definite encounter of religions. There are three options: the ancestral animism, or the current environmental animism of the land, or the Lord God. Then, after the public discussion (for no pressure is brought to bear on them) the decision is made, and Joshua then demands a demonstration of that decision. "Then, *put away* the foreign gods and incline your hearts to the Lord" (v. 23). A covenant is made at Shechem (v. 25), and a stone is set up as a *witness* to the act of commitment (vv. 26-27).

Was it not the same in the days of New Testament Ephesus? The people movement among the workers of magic led to the public burning of their magical literature—and so large a bonfire it was that the value of the books burned was recorded as 50,000 pieces of silver (Acts 19:18-19). Be it noted that this demonstration was both an *act of commitment* and an *act of rejection,* a spiritual encounter. Indeed, the anthropologist Van Gennep (1960), would have called it a *rite of separation,* because it marked a precise cutoff from an old life and status, before entering into a new one. Was it not to these same Ephesians that Paul so articulated it? Put off the old self (4:22), and put on the new self (4:24)—"put off" and "put on," as one changing clothes.

The biblical evidence of this demand for commitment to Christ in some form of dramatic encounter shows the converts demonstrating that the old way no longer has power over them, and henceforth he or she is "God's person" (the collective, "people of God"). Thus Paul, seeking to encourage the young man Timothy, addresses him, "O man of God," committed now to fight the good fight of faith, and to strive for Christian perfection (1 Tim. 6:11; 2 Tim. 3:17).

In the animist world today the public demonstration, or *rite of separation*, varies with the cultural climate—fetish burning, burial of ancestral skulls, casting the sacred paraphernalia into the sea or river, eating the forbidden totem fish or animal, according to the pattern of their animism. These are cultural equivalents of Joshua setting up the stone of witness, and the Ephesian magicians burning their books. This is symbolism, but more than symbolism. Psychologically, people are strengthened to keep their covenant by having made a public confession and having done it as a *company of converts*. "Let the redeemed of the Lord say so!" said the Psalmist (107:2).

The symbolic rejection of the old way not only involves a religious encounter, but thereafter it serves as a continual reminder of the act of rejection that alone can save the convert from syncretism or polytheism. It was just at this point that Paul had trouble with the Corinthian Christians, who found it easier to incorporate Christ into their heathen pantheon, than reject that pantheon for Christ. "No way!" says Paul, "Ye cannot drink the cup of the Lord and the cup of devils" (1 Cor. 10:21). And it is precisely at this same point that the modern mission among animists is really Christian or just another kind of Animism.

Pay Attention to the Problem of Motivation

Animists may be interested in Christianity for many and varied reasons—some good, others bad. Many factors may bring a field to ripen unto harvest. Of course, we are interested in all enquirers, but problems are bound to arise if the evangelist accepts all such inquiry at its face value without really evaluating the basic motivation; which may be for as materialistic a reason, for example, as the fact that the power of Western armies and navies in war surely makes the religion of these powerful foreigners better to have on your side than against you.

Many supposed converts misunderstand both Christianity itself and the salvation it proclaims. They misunderstand their own needs also. The book of Acts (Ch. 8) supplies us with a good example of the problem. On the surface, the conversion of Simon, the sorcerer, at Samaria was quite genuine when he came to Philip (vv. 9-13) and believed. However, shortly afterwards, when confronted with Peter's ministry and the gift of the Spirit, it is immediately apparent that Simon had a complete misunderstanding of the nature of the Gospel, due to his wrong motivation: he thought he could buy the gift of God with money (vv. 18-24).

Animists sometimes respond because the Christian mission offers a ministry of healing which seems to be more effective than that of their own shamans and medicine men. Animist chiefs have even invited missionaries to live in their midst in order to have a trade store in their community—this meaning a regular supply of steel knives, fishhooks, nails, and ax heads, all of which are not only utilitarian, but are also symbols of wealth and status for both this chief among other chiefs, and this tribe among other tribes.

The motivations for accepting Christianity naturally affects their view of Christianity, the character of the Gospel, the nature of their Christian ethics, and their concept of Christian responsibility.

Let me give you an example of the problem as I met it repeatedly in Papua, New Guinea. One of the real problems there is that of the Cargo Cult. It even occurs where there have been prolonged prebaptismal training programs. Indeed, perhaps the unduly long period of training has itself made baptism appear as a goal rather than an entry into an experience of nurture and growth. It gives the impression that converts "have arrived," as it were. They came enthusiastically in the first place, but now they want to "back out" in syncretistic cults which deny much that they have been taught. I met a young New Guinean who put it this way to me, "A few years ago I became a Christian because I wanted to achieve the white man's status and wealth. I wanted a good job, with a good wage and a house like the white men have. I worked hard in mission educational institutions, and I was baptized. But now it is all empty and worth nothing." This young man was thoroughly disillusioned with Christianity because his motivation had been wrong in the first place. His spiritual advisers had not detected this. They had interpreted his industry as a behavior change due to conversion, and now he is a potential troublemaker.

I also picked up a report from a missionary who had shared his all with a New Guinea colleague—a national pastor—whom he trusted implicitly. After many years, the pastor, recognizing this missionary's openness, asked, "Now we have shared everything, won't you tell me the secrets Jesus gave you?" The missionary was staggered to discover that even his pastoral colleague had what they call "the cargo mentality," which must have been there in his mind from the very motivation of his first attraction to Christianity. One major cause of Cargo Cults is the wrong expectation converts have had of Christianity.

I do not want to give the impression that all conversions from Animism are like this—that would not be true. There are thousands and thousands of wonderful warm-hearted Christians who really know Jesus as Lord. But, nevertheless, it remains quite true that we have never really faced up to the problem of motivation when the convert first comes for instruction. We ought to be asking the question—what is the role of the pastoral counselor when the would-be convert first moves forward to respond to the Gospel?

3. Pay Attention to the Problem of Meaning

Paul and Barnabas cured the cripple at Lystra in the name of the Gospel after proclaiming the Word, thinking thereby that the name of God would be praised. The people took the incident to mean that the two evangelists were the Greek gods, Mercury and Jupiter, anthropomorphized; and they brought forth their approved religious paraphernalia and the sacrifice, to worship them—the very last things Paul and Barnabas wanted (Acts 14:8-13)—and, indeed, the people could hardly be restrained from this intention (v. 18). Here we are confronted with the problem of meaning. The proclamation, no doubt, was faithfully given, but alas, quite misunderstood.

Anthropology has a number of suggestions to offer the evangelist in this area of communication—at least to indicate why this kind of thing can happen. Let me enumerate a few, for purposes of discussion.

The biblical case I have just cited represented a confusion which arose from the *worldview of the listeners*. Seeing the miracle, which was beyond the normal powers of science as they knew it, and therefore had to be due to supernatural factors, they interpreted it in terms of their own mythology. Every cross-cultural missionary runs into this problem sooner or later. It is the problem of translation and of Scripture interpretation. Every word selected—the word for God, for the Spirit, for the Son of God, for sin, for love, for pray, for forgive—comes from a nonbiblical worldview, and is a potential for misunderstood meaning. If it is a problem for the evangelist who speaks in the language of his or her listeners it is doubly so for the evangelist who does not learn the language, but uses a third party to come between the evangelist and the audience.

The meaning of the message can be distorted also by *the image of the evangelist* in the eyes of the audience. It was for this reason that Western missionaries to China before the Communist days, were often heard as imperialists and capitalists, even though they did not think of themselves in that way. As one scholar put it, they became essential to the Revolution, so that Christianity could be rejected. I know the documents of one place where missionaries worked for sixteen years without a convert, living devout, industrious lives, and by their very industry giving the impression that salvation was merely a Gospel of hard work and trade—the very last thing they desired to do.

Then again the *evangelist's conceptualization of the message* can condition the meaning ascribed to it. Is he or she proclaiming a faith prophetically, or a teaching philosophically? Does the teaching of Scripture come through in a foreign or denominational garment? Is it presented as a moral, legal code, or oriented to the joy of the Lord and the glory of God? Is it directed to the problems of the evangelist, or to the felt needs of the listeners? The animists have come from a world of power encounter and presumably they therefore need a God who speaks and demonstrates with power. The preaching of a purely ethical Gospel is hardly likely to inspire such a people; but a life transformed by a God of power will lead to a new ethic. Why do the charismatic figures of so many nativistic movements retain the use of the Bible in their cultic practices? Several prophets have spoken on the point. Recognizing the power of the Word, they have pointed out that the missionaries of each denomination interpret the Word in their own way, and asked, "Why cannot we do it in our way?" And this they then do—in terms of their mythology.

Thus there are three points where the message of the Word may be blurred in communication: (1) *at the "advocate end"* (evangelist), (2) *at the "acceptor end"* (convert), and (3) *in the message itself* (the theological emphasis of the evangelist). We can no longer run the risk of sending out missionaries (Westerners or nationals) without some cross-cultural training, and, of course, it follows also that they should be competent interpreters of the Word.

4. Pay Attention to the Problem of Social Structure

At first thought we may wonder what social structure has to do with evangelization. This is because many of us are individualists, and we assume that everyone should do things the way we do. But the peoples of the world do not have identical social behavior patterns, and this creates problems when evangelization is cross-cultural. The people to whom the evangelist goes may organize their daily life very differently from the evangelist and he or she should remember that the process of evangelization should lead to the formation of fellowship groups; and that these should be indigenous and not foreign in structure. At least the evangelist ought to be aware of social structure, and reckon on the Holy Spirit being able to use ways of life different from his or her own. Let me cite two examples of the importance of social structure for evangelization.

(1) Most animist societies are communally orientated: i.e., they tend to operate in homogeneous groups. These groups, of course, do not ignore the individual; but he or she is always an individual within a group context. Groups are multi-individual. Discussions of important issues for decision go on and on until a *consensus* is reached. This may take a long time but it eliminates the problem created by "majority decision" which denies some of the rights of the minority that is outvoted. These communal societies have a high degree of social responsibility, and often the individualistic foreign evangelist has trouble with group decision making. Groups exist at different levels of social organization, and authority for decision may lie at different levels—for example, decision making in domestic affairs, agriculture, religion, politics, and war may be the responsibility of household, extended family, village, or clan. It is important for the evangelist to identify these because the manifest behavior of the multi-individual group in turning from heathenism to Christ will have the appearance of *group movements:* households, villages, age grades, extended families or clans, according to their normal social organization. Unless it is so, it will not be meaningful to the people.

There is nothing strange or unbiblical about this. The apostles found that the rural villages and townships of Palestine often "turned to the Lord" as whole communities, like Sharon and Lydda (Acts 9:35), whereas in other cases, like that of the centurion at Philippi (Acts 16:30-34) and Crispus, the chief of the synagogue at Corinth (Acts 18:8), the groups became Christian as households. They were acting within the regular operative social mechanisms of daily life.

(2) In the same way, those who respond in these group movements have to be formed into fellowship groups or churches; and the operating character of these should either reflect or, at least, be compatible with their familiar structures. This applies especially to any leadership patterns introduced. For example, a common blunder in church planting across cultures has been to appoint a young Christian leader (on the grounds that he can read and has had some education) over a new Christian community in a gerontocratic society, normally led by a council of elders, where the basic values are maturity, experience, and grey hairs. In this way the evangelization of these people brings an unfortunate and unnecessary bone of contention.

These two illustrations, at the levels of decision making and leadership, will serve to make the point that effective evangelization requires a church indigenous from the beginning; and the more foreign organizational structures imposed on a church planting situation the more problems will be created for the subsequent generation which has to find the passage "from mission to church," which can be a painful experience.

5. Pay Attention to the Problem of Incorporation

One of the tests of valid biblical evangelism is the provision of a way for incorporating converts into the fellowship of believers. The Bible demonstrates this in several ways. First, there are passages, like the introduction of John's first letter, wherein the notion of *witness* (vv. 1-2) is associated with that of fellowship (v. 3); and the Great Commission itself, which does not end with "Go and make disciples," but continues "baptize and teach." For the purpose of study, we take these texts separately, but in reality they are wholes. The analysis must be adjusted by synthesis, or our evangelization is only partial.

Second, the notion of the fellowship is crucial in biblical argument. True, we can speak of evangelism as bringing individuals face to face with Christ, but we cannot leave it there, because the New Testament did not leave it there. Christ is, of course, the Ultimate, and in that sense we need no more than to be with him. But for this present point of time in which he or she has been born, the convert has to be incorporated into some precise fellowship group, the Church, which is Christ's Body. In the records of the early Church (Acts) and the letters which tell us so much of its inner life, the configuration which holds it all together structurally is the church—be it theologically the Church Universal, or practically the local church.

Remove that concept from the New Testament and look for a disembodied collection of isolated people who had met Christ, and you will soon be disillusioned. Christian activity and theology are always spoken of in collective figures: Christians are "fellow citizens," "members of the household of God," a "priesthood," a "nation," a "flock," a "fellowship," the "members of the Body," or "the church which is at . . ."

Fellowship forming or church planting is thus part of evangelization. Right at the beginning of Acts (1:13-14), we have a fellowship group in prayer, and immediately a worshiping, witnessing, growing body (Acts 2:46-47), meeting for instruction, fellowship, breaking of bread and prayer (v. 42). Thus is the Church his Body, fulfilling his ministry in this world in this day, and if evangelization does not mean that, it is defective.

To pass from this biblical base to the situation in the animist world, where people are being won to Christ in communities completely different in both social life and values perhaps from that to which the evangelist belongs, the latter has to consider what converts from animism need to find in the fellowship group into which they are incorporated. How do they get their new experience of Christian *belonging,* so that they become participating, worshiping, witnessing, and serving members of the Body of Christ *in their own kind of world?* I hope for a profitable discussion of this issue, not only to provide us with some worthwhile directions for ministry in such situations, but also to help cross-cultural evangelists at large to appreciate a problem which many of them have never thought about at all.

6. Pay Attention to the Problem of the Cultural Void

Over the last ten years I have been able to visit a great many young churches whose members have come to Christ out of animist backgrounds. Apart from their wide range of cultural differences, there are also manifest spiritual differences. Some of them, though quite strange to me culturally and linguistically, have nevertheless been obviously vibrant with life, creative in their worship, using their own indigenous forms of music and art with enthusiasm, and performing significant service ministries in the animist world about them. On the other hand, others have been the very opposite. They have tried to worship according to patterns more familiar in the West, and sing hymns in Western music and to have many quite obvious accouterments of European denominationalism. These churches have been misfits in their own worlds. They limp along as if almost ready to die; as if trying to be what they really are not. In some cases they are even led entirely by a foreigner, and there is little, if any, congregational participation; and financially their work is possible only with the aid of foreign funds. If they have a national pastor, he is a little replica of the foreign missionary. How is this church ever going to see itself as the Body of Christ, ministering the mind and heart and Word of Christ to the animist world outside? In a hundred years of history it has no more than a hundred members, and is currently static. The truth remains that the

Christian programs of evangelization used over the last century of Christian missions produced these two kinds of churches. And I believe that in each case their characters were, more often than not, formed in the early periods when the first fellowship groups were being formulated. I believe that the majority (I did not say all) of our second generation problems have their roots in faulty follow up of the original religious awakenings. In church growth parlance we say, "The people movement has to be effectively consummated."

One of the problems of following up a great movement of the Spirit of God in bringing many persons to Christ, is not just to incorporate them into a Christian group, but to be sure that it is an indigenously structured and meaningful group, in which they can participate in their own way. Thus, for example, a New Guinea convert should not have to become American or Australian to be a Christian; linguistically and culturally he or she should be a *New Guinea* Christian. Likewise the fellowship group should be New Guinean. The members' participation, praying, worship, and service ministry should be New Guinean. A gifted New Guinean animist musician, on becoming Christian, should be a *New Guinean* Christian musician—and so on.

If we get into this kind of a situation where evangelists dispose of all cultural values and creative arts on the presupposition that they are all incompatible with Christianity because they have been used previously for heathen purposes (as many evangelists do argue), we find ourselves with creative people who can no longer create, and would-be participators who become nonparticipant, and before long the cultural voids we have created begin to be felt. Cargo Cults are only partly due to foreign domination; they are also due to cultural voids. Those who believe they are called to evangelism should remember that evangelization does not take place in a vacuum.

The problem of *maintenance* (as the anthropologist, F.E. Williams, 1951, called the preservation of traditional techniques and values in a situation of changing culture), of course, involves a value judgment: can this or that element be preserved and be made truly Christian? Or will its maintenance involve the church in syncretism? The New Testament warns us that we are bound to meet this problem and that it must be faced squarely. This is why I began this statement with "The Problem of Encounter." But, even so, when the basic commitment to Christ has been effectively faced, there will yet remain an indigenous way of life which is also worth winning for Christ. It should be possible for a tribal person from, say, Africa or New Guinea, to be a Christian without having to reject his or her tribe. It must be so or we could hardly hope for the "great multitude which no one can number of all nations, and kindreds, and peoples and tongues (standing) before the throne and before the Lamb" in that day.

I asked a tribal man whose people had come into Christianity from animism, but whose Christian life was largely innocuous and foreign, making little impact on its surrounding world, "What happened to your tribal skills?" He told me sadly that they had "melted away" and that life was empty because of it. He was feeling the cultural void. Something within him was crying out to be creative. He had discovered another Christian church in his country which utilized the indigenous arts and crafts to the glory of God, and he felt his own tribe had been robbed of something precious. A basic question recurs: What does it mean to a Christian convert from animism to be a Christian in an animist world, and to be a participating member in a fellowship group of converted animists? This applies to more than arts and crafts. How does the converted animist meet the physical and spiritual needs that spring from the tribal way of life—problems of danger, of death, of sickness, or sorcery—and how does one discover the will of God for that person?

Evangelization does not end with an offer of the Gospel, or with the conversion of an individual, but with the coming into being of an ongoing fellowship, which is the Body of Christ in that kind of world.

CHAPTER 27

Polygamy as a Missionary Problem: The Anthropological Issues

In communal societies marriage, whatever its organizational form, is undertaken on the assumption that it will endure. The idea of *perpetuity* is just as strong with the family as with the tribe itself. This means that when missionaries interfere with the marriage pattern they threaten something that is tied to all the social life of the community, its economic stability and its personal relationships. Right or wrong, a change of this kind in marriage relationships is a socially disruptive process, which like marriage itself "is not to be undertaken lightly." Therefore, for this chapter I shall try to rise above my subjective views and be objective. Without suggesting that a thing is good or bad I shall simply say that polygamy works this way or that and indicate what that means for the Church.

THE MISSIONARY AS AN AGENT OF CHANGE

A human society comprises individuals organized into groups of persons in specific relationships, for cooperation and interaction in and through the institutions of that society. The missionary, as an agent of change, must allow for each of those elements. Change itself is not a bad thing. It is going on all the time. Societies can change without falling into chaos. The teacher, the doctor, the sanitation officer and the missionary are directing change all the time. This is part of progress. But such

The original version of this chapter was published in *Church Growth Bulletin,* March 1969, Vol. V, No. 4, pp. 351-354. Gratitude is hereby expressed to the publisher for permission to include it here.

directed change involves tremendous responsibility. Some changes are more simple to effect than others, as for instance when the total group is more congenially disposed to it, or socially ready for it. Other kinds of change are extremely difficult. Sometimes an advocate offers something attractive, but does so in a kind of "package deal." Christianity has often been offered as a Western or denominational "package deal," and this accounts for some of the obstructions its advocates have met. Thus, for example, we might ask if the missionary demand for monogamous marriage is really one of the essential marks of a true believer, or is it part of the Western trimmings of a "package deal" Christianity?

Change which threatens existing institutions which serve the function of maintaining tribal perpetuity is always subject to obstruction. One of these institutions is the family. Family structure is built to endure. It is a configuration within the larger configuration of the tribal entity itself. Its influences and operations ramify throughout the whole of society. When an agent of change interferes with the structure of the family that agent is involved in culture change in every aspect of society, and is therefore responsible for economic factors and personal problems at a very deep level. Some things in a society can be changed with ease, but the family is not one of them. The missionary is therefore faced with the following question: Does this demand for basic structural modifications in the family pattern either warrant or justify one's subsequent involvement in solving the resultant problems, and what does this responsibility actually imply? It would seem then that either the missionary is not justified in changing the family structure at all, or if this is done the missionary is committed also to involvement at a score of other social focal points.

THE COHESION OF THE POLYGAMOUS SYSTEM

Let me give an example of the implications of the demand for monogamy for converts from polygamous societies. Tanner (1967) has written of this in the Sukuma tribe (Tanzania), showing how difficult it is to break a polygamous marriage in a society where a religious reason is not adequate to break a contract entered into under customary law, even if the bride wealth obligations and economic complications are adjusted. To be baptized, the husband has to send away his additional wives, but customary law does not permit him to divorce them, so he still has to maintain them. Therefore he has "one household in which he will cohabit and one or more households which he has to maintain socially and economically without cohabiting. He is married to these other women, so they can still claim support in court or informally through their families" (95-96). The husband still has to visit these households for purposes of cultivation and to contribute time and labor. Tanner points out that this continued relationship increases his emotional problems. Socially he is still father of the children born before his conversion, but religiously they are illegitimate. These "wives" are denied physical contact, so that these women, who are socially mothers of the children, are no longer physically wives. If there is still some affection the "mother" may even commit "adultery" with the "husband" and in the requisite discipline of the "monogamous" husband the Church is involved in "detective work."

Thus, in a society without adequate mechanisms for divorce it is quite difficult to change over from polygamy to monogamy. On the other hand, if a way of divorce does exist and the Church resorts to this means of solving the problem of polygamy, she has to justify her support of divorce as a legitimate social institution. This cannot be done on a basis of scriptural exegesis and therefore she has to argue or rationalize her position. Here we get involved in many problems. Is divorce Christian? Is a marriage contract honestly entered into between two parties (regardless of what their religion was at the time) a matter in which they are honor bound? Is a man, for the sake of Christian baptism, justified in putting away his wives, with whom he has entered into such a contract in good faith, when they desire to continue in the agreed state of wedlock? If the Bible does not supply us with adequate guidance in these matters, on what kind of criteria can the case be reasoned? In point of fact we discover the polygamous system extremely cohesive and this cohesiveness is part of the strength of the society itself. If we are to be social iconoclasts we had better know well just what we are doing.

THE INTERRELATEDNESS OF SOCIAL INSTITUTIONS

The polygamous family is not an institutional isolate. Take for example a society which practices levirate marriage, and there are scores of them among the currently responsive animistic societies of the mission field. Thus, through the death of his brother, a man (who already has a wife and family) may suddenly find himself with an additional one. Even though he may have become a Christian as the husband of one wife, he is now confronted with the problem of accepting his family responsibilities, which were the basic assumptions of both the individuals and the families involved when the pre-Christian marriage was first contracted. When the new Christian structure forbids the levirate marriage, there emerges in that Christian society a new set of social problems not known previously— the ramifying problems of the widow and the orphan. Christianity has destroyed the social mechanisms which previously provided for the welfare of these persons, and unless some special functional substitute is introduced, these unfortunate people are just not provided for at all. One does not have to travel far through the mission fields of the world to realize the tragic truth of this. What I am really saying then, is that polygamous human societies normally have a network of interrelated institutions functionally responsible for preserving the perpetuity of the extended family, and the personal security of each individual in them.

In a chapter of this length I cannot outline all the social and personal functions of polygamy. Luzbetak (1963:247) listed eleven of them. Many of these work out for the benefit of the women, all of them in some way for the benefit of the total group. Whether they concern social security, work programs or group protection, if polygamy is prohibited every one of those social functions has to be met in some way or other. When missionaries offer the Gospel in a "package deal" which demands the giving up of polygamy they are also morally bound to propose some adequate solution to each of the new social problems they create. Otherwise these will be the unmet social needs of the next generation, and they will have been responsible.

POLYGAMY AS AN ISSUE BEFORE THE CHURCH

Whereas the current processes of acculturation would suggest that it is only a matter of time before polygamy disappears, nevertheless, for the time being it is very much a live issue for missionaries winning converts from polygamous societies. It emerges as an obstructive factor where animist converts are confronted with an option between Christianity and Islam, for Muslim advocates are prone to argue the validity of their religion for Africans for the very reason that it allows polygamy—which Christianity supposedly forbids. This raises the basic question which Christians have never really faced at all: just how "pagan" is a society because it is polygamous? Can an extended family, which preserves every individual and cares for the widow and orphan, which distributes work and protection, so that no individual loses their rights or has an excessive burden to bear, be called "pagan"? Have we perhaps here a social ethic which could be won for Christ? Many missionaries have begun to ask the question: Could not polygamy be accepted as a "given" of the social structure within which they are called to work? Should not the missionary be offering Christ to the people, and allowing the Christ-life to work itself out in the structure of polygamous society as it is?

This complex of problems comes into focus at the point of Christian baptism. Frequently abandonment of polygamy has become the test of sincerity for baptism. Yet the Church has a multitude of attitudes to this problem. One can recall at least six different attitudes on the different mission fields of the world:

1. Baptize the women and children but not the men.

2. Baptize none at all if they have anything to do with polygamy.

3. Baptize all on a testimony of faith—polygamists or not.

4. Let the husband retain the first wife and divorce the rest.

5. Let him divorce all but the preferred one.

6. For the first generation, baptize on a profession of faith, but demand monogamy thereafter.

To set out these attitudes in tabular form demonstrates the seriousness of the problem and its inconsistency. Some of these attitudes are hardly Christian at all and leave many injustices.

In communal society it is appropriate that people should become Christian in extended family groups. To win the whole groups the elders must be won and these are most likely to be the polygamists. Therefore, the whole matter of the baptism of polygamists currently calls for much thought and prayer. This chapter purports to delineate some of the problems so that they may be the more intelligently discussed. The current situation is urgent.

CHAPTER 28

Shifting Attitudes to Sex and Marriage: An Example from Fiji

A bold step was taken at the Methodist pre-synod retreat in Fiji years ago to stimulate frank discussion on certain issues which the church had hitherto refrained from discussing, among them sex education and the marriage pattern.

It had been usual at such retreats to introduce group discussion by means of factual surveys or Biblical studies aimed at bringing the vital issues into focus for the subsequent discussion. In this case, however, it was felt that too forthright a factual survey might defeat the object by stimulating defense mechanisms. So we took a page from the book of Marguerite d'Angouleme, who introduced the new learning into the court by means of her tales or plays, deliberately provocative, to be followed by conversation. We would hardly consider her tales as worthy for moral teaching as they stand; but, of course, she did not prepare them for standing alone. They were "scandal" for a particular group and a particular situation, a vehicle to precipitate evangelical discussion and instruction.

To this end also the students of the Theological Institution at Davuilevu presented their plays or conversation pieces: episodes imagined to have taken place in a pastor's house. The pastor was facing problems on the village level. In reality these problems are often not faced on that

The original version of this chapter was published in *Practical Anthropology*, 1965, Vol. 12, No. 2, pp. 85-91, under the title, "Shifting Attitudes to Sex and Marriage in Fiji." Gratitude is hereby expressed to the publisher for permission to include it here.

level. That was *our* problem. How could we get discussion without it being thought that we were criticizing?

These problems have their counterparts in every culture or society, but in many of the young churches they have peculiar cultural twists, resulting from war-stimulated accentuation of the acculturation processes. Our people in Fiji, after a century of slow acculturation, without too serious a dislocation of the basic culture pattern itself, have suddenly discovered that the money economy of the West has been substituted for the subsistence economy without the establishment of adequate safeguards for the transition. Migration to industrial areas has wrecked their status society and the loss of status controls has upset the whole pattern of standards and procedures, as, for example, in the pattern of courtship. This dramatic modification of the whole cultural milieu has revealed some weaknesses and neglects in our religious attitudes and pastoral behavior over the years of slow acculturation.

The use of the "play" or dialogue instead of the factual survey had the indirect motive of casting the problem into the pastoral setting without giving the impression that the indigenous ministry was under criticism. It was hoped that each observer (all indigenous ministers and lay leaders, save for a half dozen missionaries) would register in his or her own mind (without being told directly) that such problems were properly faced in the pastor's house, and that the playwriter had merely assumed this as normal. The result was that the members accepted the position that we were facing a problem together and seeking the answer. They all looked objectively at the drama and a good many took part freely, and I thought, with good profit to all.

SEX EDUCATION

The first play showed a broken-hearted couple coming to the pastor and telling him how, in spite of their efforts to keep their daughter in the way, she had gone astray and brought disgrace on them all. In a personal and sympathetic scene the facts came out. The girl's sex education had been neglected. The parents themselves had disagreed about its necessity and about how it could be done.

The pastor pointed out how in pre-Christian times there had been both male and female initiation rites and a socially approved pattern of sex education with specific persons responsible for the instruction and a set of taboos to be observed. Now, under Christianity, these things had gone, but the sex education still had to be attended to. The parents agreed that this seemed true, but felt themselves unable to provide it. What about the younger children they had coming on? Could the minister help them? Was there something printed by the church? (There was not and this was an indirect motive in the play.) The play ended leaving all these issues in focus but unanswered. The discussion that followed concerned the responsibilities of parents, school, and pastor, and the value of literature, if any.

At the end of the discussion, members registered their opinions by voluntary ballot. Of the 37 who chose to do so, 32 were Fijians. Eventually the discussion narrowed itself down to the following:

1. Should village pastors and their wives be running groups for sex education at the appropriate age level?

2. Should the subject be handed as human biology in the schools?

3. Where the parents in each home responsible?

4. Was it time for the church to publish vernacular literature on the subject, and if so, what kind?

These questions would be taken for granted by the average Westerner, but in an island society in a process of transition, they are highly significant.

It is interesting to note that only one person registered a negative vote on all counts. I took it to mean that for him the whole subject was still taboo. No doubt, had the discussion taken place on a lower level in the church, he would have had more supporters. That only one leader should take this position of conservatism represents a remarkable shift of opinion in a period of five or six years. Six years earlier I had been engaged in a program of vernacular publication and had explored the possibilities of such literature only to discover a dominant negative attitude from church leaders.

This may mean they had really moved forward in their thinking or it may indicate sudden alarm at the social situation and realization that something had to be done. No one seemed inclined to dispute the suggestion that neglect of sex education was *a* (if not *the*) basic cause of the girl's moral lapse in the play. There was agreement that some education was needed and that something was wrong somewhere.

DIFFERING SUGGESTIONS

They differed considerably in their ideas of the character of that education. One favored strong teaching from the pastors on the "sacredness of the body" — an attempt to avoid the biological education. I imagine this view would have considerable support from the church at large. Another thought the place to begin was in the theological institution as a subject on the curriculum for ministerial trainees. This was my province at the time and strengthened my hand, though it left me with the feeling that some thought the matter one for pastoral and not parental correction. Still another thought it ought to be dealt with in the regular youth camps (a very live and spiritual feature of Fijian Christianity). Another sought refuge in the law. Do this! Don't do that! Punish the wrongdoer!

Two young leaders, who had been overseas, had seen Christian educational material on this matter and pressed for something in the vernacular; one thought for the young people, the other thought for the parents only. The character of certain sex literature being sold by some booksellers in the colony gives us a good deal of trouble and some feel the church should provide a clean and educative substitute for Christian young people.

One senior minister, who supported this view, also confessed that the really new thing to him in the whole discussion was the idea of "parental responsibility."

Another felt that biological education in the schools would lead to further sinning by exposing or secularizing a sacred matter. It was quite obvious that though there was a general readiness for better education there was no uniformity as to the precise nature of that education. Some saw it as biological, some as moral, some as both.

There is nothing new to a Westerner in this, but that such a free discussion could take place among Fijian church leaders was something entirely new.

The voting showed that about two-thirds of the synod members felt that the pastor's duty did include sex education, either moral or biological or both. Approximately the same percentage favored a serious attack on the problem in the schools, though several desired to apply restrictions at this point (that the teacher be one of mature Christian experience).

In view of the fact it had been stated voluntarily that the notion of parental responsibility was new, it is interesting to note that only four votes were registered against it. My impression was that this strong affirmative vote was an outcome of the discussion itself.

The need for literature was felt by more than three-quarters of the members, but their voting showed numerous qualifications. There was a strong feeling that any biological education should be accompanied by strong warning. There was a fear of straight biology without Christian bias. One even specified the person he thought should prepare the literature, another described the kind of person. There was a difference of opinion as to whether the literature should be for parents only, for young people, or for both.

This dramatic change of attitude from my enquiry of six years earlier confirms the principle stressed by anthropology that change should not be forced on people of another culture until that *cultural moment* when the people are psychologically ready for change. To have forced such things six years ago would have done damage. But clearly Fiji is fast moving to the crest of the wave. The church will have to take this at the flood or miss her opportunities. Before the war the Fijian church was static. The tempo increased during the war and continues.

Anthropologically I should also point out that this emerging cultural moment is a God-given moment for the church to amend an error made in the early days. These people moved into Christianity in great people movements. The discarded initiation rites did have an educative function. The rites were dispensed with and sex education with them. This left a void where there should have been a functional substitute. It has taken nearly a century to break down the Western taboo about sex education that was imposed on them. It was one of the very few mistakes this particular body of missionary pioneers made. Most of their follow-up of the people movements was superb.

THE MARRIAGE PATTERN

The second dialogue was between the pastor and a young man who faced approaching marriage. He found himself in a dilemma that is quite common in Fiji today. He was about to be married within the culture pattern to a girl who had been chosen for him by his father. He himself had been absent from the village, working in the town, and there had learned to choose his own company. He felt he belonged to the new day, that the future lay ahead of him, and that the life of the past in which his parents were still rooted was really behind him. He wanted to go forward choosing his own life partner.

On the other hand he knew he was still tied to the old tradition in many ways, and that there would inevitably be times when he would still have to draw on tribal resources and securities. He would have to leave open the way for his periodic return from the town to his tribal lands and people, even if he married against the will of his people. He knew his only real economic security was in the village, not in the town. His employment was to be in an itinerant occupation, and although it would take him away from communal duties for much of his life, he would have to return to his home in the end. Above all, he respected his parents and desired to avoid offense. Indeed, it was mainly at this point of divided loyalty that his tensions arose. Family loyalty is an ingrained quality of Fijian life. I have known cases where it means more than truth.

What often happens today (as in the play) is that when the father hears or suspects that his son is paying particular attention to some girl in town, he immediately arranges a marriage for his son and sends a message to his son that the marriage has been arranged. As like as not (as in this case) the young man has asked the town girl to marry him—the result of attending the cinema (which is the pattern of Western courtship continually placed before them). Back home the ancient ceremonials have already bound together two families in ties that are themselves as strong as those of the marriage contract itself.

The father, in the play, precipitated a crisis in the boy's life. He was forced to choose between his traditions and his true affection. He knew that to decide against tradition was to involve two families back home as well as the girl in town. It could cause a family split in his village. It could divide the village congregation. I should really like to know how many splits in church congregations have been caused by this factor. The father did this with honest intent that sprang from his concept of family honor and security, from his desire to preserve the clan and his fear of disgrace. It is very seldom a desire to preserve paternal authority.

It is to the great credit of the young men of Fiji that they feel so intensely the tension of such situations. Two of the comrades of the young men presenting this play in my institution were in this position at the time and I knew what it cost them. Normally they went to their own indigenous ministers on this matter. The number who came to me over those same years of dramatic change, suggested to me the tide had turned and they were seeking Western advice rather than traditional. It had no bearing on any lack of confidence in their own ministers. They wanted to act outside the pattern without offense. The only way I could help them was by setting in motion a traditional sequence of events—a way of atonement— which I could do through a senior indigenous minister if there was one connected with their extended family. But I was reluctant to do this and they knew it. I insisted that the only way to escape traditional ties was by the traditional mechanisms of escape.

MARRIAGE PATTERN IN DANGER

The discussion which followed the play opened with a frank, general admission of the reality of the problem and a genuine concern that the whole pattern of marriage planning was in grave danger. The first speaker, one of the younger leaders, pointed out that they had well-nigh lost the pattern altogether. He stressed the fact that the church must give guidance to the young people. Marriages should not be allowed just to happen. If the old pattern was inadequate, then a new one must be worked out and approved.

Another felt that the old way was dying slowly of its own accord. It should be left to die in its own way, but the new way had many difficulties and would have to be worked out over a period of time—a kind of Fijian natural evolutionist.

Still another Fijian, whose leadership is highly valued by both his own people and the missionaries, pressed the view that the Fijian life was a dichotomy today and clearly two marriage patterns were required for this transition period. The old way could not yet be dispensed with. Many villagers would not take initiative except through traditional patterns, which provided the natural, approved mechanisms for proposal within the safeguards of family rights, land ownership, and interfamily involvements. It was a good protective device, both in making a suitable choice and in protecting the marriage thereafter. At the same time he felt the needs and rights of the class of young men and women who had been educated for

nonvillage roles, or at least itinerant roles—teachers, ministers, magis-
trates, doctors, agricultural advisers, and so on—who were more competent
to know the kind of wives required for their various occupations. He
approved their making their own choice of wife. Clearly Fiji needs two
patterns, but there should be approved patterns in both cases.

The most interesting thing about this useful contribution was that
there was no Western individualism in the second point, though with the
young men themselves this was strong. To the speaker, the marriage
pattern on both levels was socially functional. The kind of life to be lived
in the new, approved role was the norm, not the personal desire. In one
case, the young man needed his father's guidance; in the second, the
father could not give it. Marriage to him was a social instrument to enable
a man to fulfill in life the role which God has planned for him. If the new
day required new roles, they would need new patterns. This speech,
completely indigenous, was of a high spiritual tone throughout.

Now let us turn to the young man whose father determines he shall
marry in the traditional pattern, but who declines to do so because of the
girl of his choice. He marries her in town. The family cannot attend. They
are already traditionally bound by rites to another family. To support the
marriage when they have contracted another within approved patterns
would be a grave breach of custom and lead to strife and loss of status. I
have seen how this can tear at a father's heart. If the young man marries
the town girl, or any other girl, against tradition, he has sinned culturally
and only he can make good the situation. He cannot return to the village
again without making the traditional atonement.

Henry IV is reported to have said that Paris was worth a mass and
many young Fijians have said free choice of marriage is worth an
atonement. But it is not an ideal solution. It is roundabout and it is hurtful
to all parties, but in the last 20 years it has become a regular escape
pattern rather than the exception. Let it be noted that the majority of
Fijian divorces come from this type of marriage. If statistics prove
anything at all, they prove the superiority of the traditional pattern for
holding a marriage together. With the young people, atonement is only
formal, only a face-saver. Undercurrents remain and often emerge in
other ways.

MUTUAL SHARING NEEDED

One of the lay leaders pressed the point that whatever the pattern
followed, there should be a sharing between father and son. If the son was
wrong in acting against the father's wish, so was the father wrong in
forcing the marriage on his son. There ought to be a mutual understanding.
The layman's comments represent another interesting shift of attitude,
because hitherto everything has rested in the father's hands and the
possibility of the father having to present an atonement under these

circumstances is unthinkable. Yet apparently the layman thought the son had his rights in the case and was inclined to bring the focus on the marriage itself rather than on the father's wish.

The general impression left by the whole discussion was that the leaders of the Fijian church, on the whole, had a good deal of sympathy with young folk facing this problem. They were alert to current acculturation and not unaware of the dangers involved and were ready to make cultural adaptations where they felt them necessary. There was just a little apprehensiveness lest the adaptations be too rapidly accelerated. In some cases their auto-defensive mechanisms were slightly over-alert. This is understandable because of the long period of rigid status control from above that was terminated with the abolition of the European Synod at the end of the war and the voluntary acceptance of a Fijian absolute majority by the Australian missionaries. Sex education and the marriage pattern are only two of many configurations of the total pattern that are currently being rapidly modified. The indigenous ministry of this young church has a major task before it and is making a realistic and valiant effort. Many of the basic problems will have to be met on the level of the pastorate. But it is not so much the need for planning for tomorrow that is the vital point. Rather it is maintaining balance and direction as the local church directs its course in this dangerous period of rapid change she faces today.

Dangerous because all periods of greatest opportunity are dangerous. There is life and momentum in the young church. It reminds me of a Fiji bamboo banana raft on a flooded river. The speed seems too fast to be safe but there is no alternative. The craft is in the current. The task therefore is one of navigation, not of propulsion; keeping the head in the right direction, avoiding the rocks, keeping out of whirlpools that spin the craft and imperil freight. But all the time there is power and momentum in the current which cannot be resisted. We are in such a time as this.

Perhaps the call of Abram from sedentary life in Ur to the nomadic life of faith with nought to follow but a voice and a conviction that it is of God, is being lived again. This time it is not for a man but for a young church.

This study is offered to readers in the hope that it will be suggestive to missionaries facing similar problems of acculturation and to point out a few aspects of anthropological significance in this type of situation.

1. There is the missionary problem of getting the indigenous church to admit and discuss the reality of these local problems. In this case this was tackled by a pattern of group dynamics on the basis of observation and participation.

2. Local participation in problem solving is a potent mechanism for alerting local leaders to the reality of problems and stimulating their own thought towards solution. But it requires the confidence of the missionaries in indigenous judgement.

3. It is also important that the cultural moment for action be recognized. Harvests ripen. Act too soon and you meet with resistance. Leave it too late and decisions tend to be radical. But situations, static for decades, are ripening overnight.

4. Missionaries should learn to respond to suddenly emergent situations, not on the basis of the static past, but on the advice of mature indigenous leadership. By maturity I do not mean "years" or "status" but mature perception into the life of the people. I am convinced God does not leave young churches without such individuals.

5. Where people normally think and act communally, new ways should not be allowed to "just happen," but should be established as recognized and approved patterns by the group (in this case, the church). Guard against Hollywood impressions being taken as accepted Western patterns.

6. Changes made by communal approval are more stable than those fought on a basis of individual rights. Innovations are easier to make when groups first move into Christianity; but if not made then, the cultural moment has to be awaited, to avoid resistance. On the other hand, to ignore a cultural moment for change can be dangerous. This is a basis of nativistic movements, Cargo Cults, etc.

CHAPTER 29

Static Churches

When we say that a church on the mission field is *growing,* what do we mean? Perhaps the general statistics of the field show a steady rise year after year, and yet this may be accounted for by a phenomenal rise of interest in the Gospel in one newly opened locality. This growth hides the painful fact that in numerous localities of longer occupation the church is quite static. Only a careful analysis of independent village congregations can provide the data needed to reconstruct the true situation.

This chapter looks at a few of the relatively common static village congregations on the mission field and raises a few basic questions for consideration. It is based on village depth studies undertaken by the writer personally in Melanesia and, though the names of the villages are not disclosed, each village mentioned is an actual place where the writer lived in a leaf house for six weeks or more. These types are by no means peculiar to Melanesia.

When we ask if a church is growing, whether we think of growth in *quantitative* terms of evangelical expansion, or *qualitative* internal growth in grace within the fellowship, or in terms of *organic* growth in the emergence of an organized indigenous church, it is *on the level of the village congregation* that the verdict of growth or nongrowth must be given. Annual reports and decisions of synods, assemblies and boards may express ideals, desires and programs, but only at the grass roots level

The original version of this chapter was published in *World Vision Magazine,* February 1966, pp. 12-13, 28, under the title, "Church Growth or Else!" Gratitude is hereby expressed to the publisher for permission to include it here.

of the village congregation can growth or nongrowth be really studied. The central committee may modify its official terminology from "mission" to "church" orientation; but if there is no corresponding change towards indigeneity in the village congregation, the new terms are mere verbiage.

QUANTITATIVELY STATIC

One problem of area "M" is that the quantitative growth of the church has ceased. It has ceased before the winning of all the pagans of the region. This was a difficult field in many ways, but for some decades the various denominations working in the area have enjoyed a steady intake from paganism until they number roughly 20,000 today. Now the growth has dropped to a mere trickle with some 20 percent of the total population still unreached for Christ.

Religious life in these Christian villages is well organized with some pastoral leadership and regular means of grace. The congregations are well fed. They are recipients of the ministrations of the pastorate but not themselves actively evangelistic. They recognize the need for evangelism. They desire their church to have outreach. They have set aside some of their number to go far afield as missionaries among tribes on the fringe of their island world. They have local prayer groups which engage in prayer daily for their selected evangelists. They have accepted this position and the mission pays for it. They see their own burden bearing in terms of prayer. Yet all around them are pagan pockets. Many villages are half-Christian and half-pagan. Here there are no evangelists. The members of the local congregations, who pray for their evangelists further afield, are oblivious to the cry for evangelism at their door. They have settled down to Christian-pagan coexistence and quantitative growth has ceased.

These Christians mix with the pagans in communal work projects, in trade exchanges and fishing drives. They obtain their water from the same communal sources and meet together there. They are jointly organized for civil and festival functions. Yet they are quite unaware of these opportunities for evangelism at their door, because they have settled down to a state of coexistence. Nothing will terminate quantitative growth from paganism quicker than indifferent resignation to the presence of that paganism near at hand. The churches in "M" are static.

QUALITATIVELY STATIC

Another depth study conducted in the village of "R", a second generation Christian community, permitted appraisal of the quality growth within the church. The members of the congregation were classified for our purposes along an axis from *nuclear* Christians at one pole to *nominals* at the other. The former comprised the devotional and active core of the church. The nominals were Christians in name only, and next to them were the *marginals,* the fringe of the congregation, which attended occasionally. Records kept over a period of time revealed a slow drift of average members to marginality and of marginals to nominality. It was an active drift and the church was quite unaware of it, because the nuclear core was constant and the same persons were involved in everything. Average and marginal members had no opportunity of active participation and tended to drift slowly towards mere nominality. This congregation was considered to be strong, but it was qualitatively static. It badly needed a revival to bring the average and marginal members face to face with Christ. Unless a congregation makes a conscious effort at moving its members towards the nuclear pole, they will slowly drift in the opposite direction to nominality. This is a common problem with second generation congregations on the mission field. We must continually keep in mind that each new generation must be won for Christ.

ORGANICALLY STATIC

Island "W" is some distance from the mission station, but the life of the village in which I stayed was largely directed from the mission station. The folk were economically established and paganism had vanished from the area. Yet, organically, the congregation had no desire to become a church. It was crippled by its own resignation to mission paternalism. They had put a little cross in the church. The missionary had suggested it, but the people told me he had *decided* the matter. The mission was represented in that village by a catechist and a teacher, both in mission pay. They decided most of the church business and led most of the meetings, organized any programs, trained the choir for any special singing, and represented the congregation at conferences held in other places.

The natural capacity of the congregation was untapped. When I suggested the place needed a Sunday school—meaning they already had the competent personnel in the congregation to staff the school—they simply said, "Yes: The Mission should appoint us another teacher." Stewardship was choked because the mission plantations provided for so much of the district revenue and permitted the local congregation to avoid the financial obligations which were well within its economic capacity.

This village community had the potential, in education, personnel and physical resources, for achieving the indigenous goal—self-support, self-determination and self-propagation—but it was thoroughly resigned to a state of dependence on a paternally orientated mission. This mission is anxious to stimulate the growth of indigenous churches, and has changed its official terminology to suggest this; but at the village level things are still organically static.

THE WINDS OF CHANGE

The three cases that have been outlined indicate something of the type of problem that has emerged for missions in this post-war period. They are not new problems, but the speeding up of change in our day had brought them more into focus. Although the Church grows rapidly in many places, once we break down our statistics we become painfully aware that it is static in others. It can be quantitatively, qualitatively or organically static. Yet in any of these respects it could be growing, even in these days of change.

Anthropological research in religious change indicates that local Christian communities of the second generation mission fields are frequently faced with three possible alternatives:

1. The local congregation remains subordinate to the paternalistic mission, everything being done by the paid mission agent or directed from the station through him. *This possibility is static,* but it cannot remain so indefinitely.

2. The local congregation emerges from paternalism as the Church in the local situation, coming into encounter with the problems at its doors, making its own decisions, looking into its own financial responsibilities, and becoming aware of its own selfhood. *This possibility is dynamic* and full of opportunity.

3. Frequently a local group, aware of its own selfhood, but unable to break free from mission paternalism or control, reinforces its selfhood with neo-pagan dimensions and becomes a Christopagan breakaway movement. *This possibility is revolutionary.* Sometimes an independent church emerges but more often it is destructive or heretical or secular when the revolution ultimately crystallizes into something permanent. In any case it represents a serious loss to missionary effort and devotion.

Missions are in this type of confrontation today and all who are involved should be aware of these possibilities. The Church of Jesus Christ can only really grow properly in the second or dynamic situation. The first means ultimate rejection of the mission. A mission has to learn to die that a church may grow. The third is beset with dangers and uncertainties. Let us note that when local prophets arise and lead these breakaways they win social segments, and time after time those very units they win have been total village Christian congregations. When a congregation stops growing—is underfed within, loses its evangelical outreach and fails to emerge organically—it is most vulnerable.

WHAT CAN BE DONE ABOUT IT?

We have seen that these processes take place at the grass roots level. It may well be asked, what can missionaries do at that level? There are at least two things they can do, although how they do them will depend on the pattern of the field in which they labor.

The most active agents in change are the village leaders, both the elders and indigenous pastors. In that the missionaries have responsibility for pastoral and lay leadership training, they ought to see that such leaders are trained to meet this type of confrontation. It is more important that they should be trained for encounter in their local environment than in involved theological issues of the Western academic world. Missionaries entrusted with this training need to establish themselves in indigenous thought, identifying themselves culturally and itinerating through the areas where their graduates are eventually to be stationed. This is important when missionaries are set in sedentary institutional posts.

When the missionary has the general supervision of an area and is responsible for directing village pastors, he or she needs to stress continually that village congregations have to be won and rewon for Christ with each generation. The imagery of "fields white unto harvest" not only means harvesting today, but also a *sequence* of harvests. No generation can live on the experience of its predecessor. Many of our second-generation problems arise from this erroneous assumption. The congregational outreach into paganism, the spiritual growth within the fellowship, and the organic growth of the structure and leadership of the young Church all depend on this winning of each generation. What farmer would buy a field with the intention of harvesting only a single crop?

My own in-depth studies in Melanesia (1967a) revealed need for action in both these respects. This will probably apply to other areas, too. The most urgent need among second generation congregations is the stimulation of church growth in all its forms. Renewed growth among the thousands of second generation congregations will determine the character of the young Churches for the next decade or more possibly the most crucial decade to date in Christian world mission.

CHAPTER 30

Membership Shrinkage

Some time ago I read a book by a Korean missionary with a chapter headed "Shrinkage." The writer, if I remember correctly, had stayed in an inn in a town where, to his knowledge, the Gospel had not been preached previously. He was surprised to meet an isolated Christian, forgotten and without a congregation to which to belong. The man had become a Christian in some other place and had migrated outside the Christian orbit. The missionary fell to meditating on the members who were lost to the Church by this kind of migration out into the world without their discovery of a Christian fellowship. Many church statistics reflect the effect of this *membership shrinkage,* which is surely both a quantitative and a qualitative decline.

In recent years, I have observed this process in two completely different situations which I have researched.

1. In certain rural communities in the Solomon Islands a large number of people are absent from their villages for a number of years. They may be in the growing town of the group or perhaps on a coconut plantation, where work for wages is available for contract labor. The nature and effect of this village absenteeism I have discussed in another place (1967a:178-180, 341-345).

The original version of this chapter was published in *Church Growth Bulletin,* March 1968, Vol. IV, No. 4, pp. 284-286. Gratitude is hereby expressed to the publisher for permission to include it here.

2. In researching the problem of nongrowth for a Mission to a certain community of American Indians, I became acutely aware at the statistical level that somewhere the process of membership shrinkage was going on. I found that I was able to measure this both with respect to the baptized children and the adult communicant members. Therefore, the cause had to apply both to adults and children, so this suggested some physical factor.

These two situations are quite different. Nevertheless, they have some common points. Both were mission churches in the context of rapid acculturation, where the people were beginning to explore foreign economic resources. Both offered jobs with a cash return for labor in collective concentrations. The precise situations varied—plantation, industrial, closer settlement, irrigation, urban; but in all cases the people had temporarily broken from the ties of family and/or village structures and had come to live in impermanent, emerging structures with new authority patterns. Sometimes the migrants took up existing housing. Sometimes they squatted, building a temporary home, pending development. If they failed in one location they might migrate to another. If the authorities decided to move out the squatters, they were on the move again.

In this state of insecure mobility there was frequently no organized Christian congregation, neither had these new "mushroom" communities been assigned to the pastoral care of the existing missions; the work loads of the missionaries at their stations tied them down to administrative tasks. It was thus inevitable that the names of these people gradually disappeared from the records. If they remained, they were marked "Inactive," "Scattered" or "Whereabouts unknown." Sometimes they married persons of other religious persuasion.

THE PHYSICAL RECORD

The following chart (Figure 21) shows the somewhat static membership graph of one Indian mission over a period of seven years (Line "b"). Without allowing for deaths, which would have been few, that line should have been cumulative (Line "a"). We have here what the physical record actually showed ("b") against what it should have been ("a"). In this case, in a period of seven years, 164 baptized persons had been lost track of, a shrinkage of 33 percent of the total number of baptized persons in the constituency of that denomination.

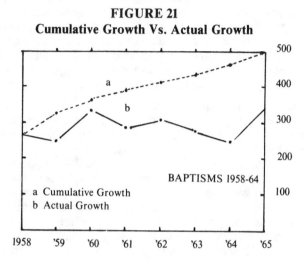

FIGURE 21
Cumulative Growth Vs. Actual Growth

In this graph we are measuring something that is more than quantitative. It is internal qualitative growth (or nongrowth) we are measuring, otherwise known as "perfection growth" (McGavran 1955:15). The line "a" is the state of affairs to be expected when members are "taught to observe all things which the Lord commanded." With effective education and pastoral care baptized members are expected to remain in the congregation. But the official records indicate not "a" but "b". If these records are accurately kept, they should measure something real, namely, persons actually receiving pastoral care and Christian education.

The 1960 and 1965 figures both show rises in excess of the number of baptisms for those years. This must have one of two possible explanations. Either (1) intensified pastoral visitation has sought out and brought back some of the wanderers, or (2) migrations have come into the area from some other congregation or parish where they had previously been baptized. Missionaries, when they see this kind of pattern on their graph should ask the reason and probe their pastoral records. The purpose of the pastoral records is not to glory in statistics, but to understand what is going on in one's pastorate.

THE THEOLOGICAL RECORD

We have seen that the true function of church statistics is pastoral. Statistical presentations like this remind us that we are not Christian *isolates,* but that we belong to a *corporate group.* The Church is a fellowship, and from earliest times the Lord "added to this daily." Individuals getting lost out in the world are separated from the fellowship. They need to be in that fellowship to grow. We witness to this end that converts may be incorporated into the fellowship (1 Jn. 1:3). No matter how much Christian service is to be done out in the world, one needs roots in the fellowship.

Christians who become isolates in the world when they migrate away from their home group are spiritually vulnerable in many ways. Sometimes, without witness and involvement they rationalize a theory of "Christian presence." Sometimes they surrender their distinctiveness to the world in conformity. In either case, they are lost in the records, to the fellowship, and to the abundance of spiritual resources that come from participation in the life of the Body of Christ.

A Fijian medical student, cut off from home and the congregation he knew, struggling with social and academic problems in an urban setting, once asked me if he could be a Christian by himself, provided he read his Bible and said his prayers. I had to tell him he would read his Bible with more understanding and say his prayers with more meaning and be a much better Christian if he was involved in the fellowship. He needed to be part of the Body to share its life. Furthermore, the Body needed him. Without his physical presence it was deprived of an organ. As he was a medical student, I was able to say to him that I did not think he could be an isolate in terms of the body and its organs.

More and more we are involved in the problem of the migrating members, with the acceleration of urbanization. We need clear teaching on this. Members migrating to the city need a letter or certificate of membership so they can establish themselves in a Christian fellowship in their new place of abode. We ought to be big enough to say that if our denomination is not operating in the new locality that the migrants should nevertheless join the fellowship which is there, for what they need is not a denomination, but a *Church*—and the Church in that locality needs *them*.

CHAPTER 31

The Dynamics
of the Bicultural Church

Two streams of thought which appear to be flowing in opposite directions are found in the New Testament. On the one hand, the apostle Paul could say to "the children of God by faith in Christ Jesus" that "there is neither Jew nor Greek, there is neither bond nor free, there is neither male nor female; for ye are all one in Christ Jesus" (Gal. 3:26, 28). Yet even as he wrote these words he knew well that in point of fact he was either bond or free, and either male or female. It was impossible for him to be human without being either one or the other. Far from denying the validity of anthropological, biological and social differences, he acknowledged his indebtedness to both the Greeks and the Barbarians (Rom. 1:14). In other passages these ethnic differences are most clearly articulated: groups retaining their national character, their social patterns and their languages. Revelation 7:9, 10 is an example of a great multitude of people comprising discrete ethnic segments, yet they are united in worship before the one Lord. So, whatever we mean by being "one in Christ," it certainly cannot mean denying one's ethnic entity. Indeed the more one reads the New Testament the more it seems that the Church was called into being precisely to minister with the multi-racial situation.

Many of the churches of the New Testament provide us with internal scriptural evidence of their multi-racial character. Scan the names of folk mentioned by Paul in the last chapter of his letter to Rome. Here we meet Greek, Roman and Jewish names. Consider the narratives of the church at Philippi—a Jewish proselyte business woman, a Roman centurion, and a Greek slave girl (Acts 16:14-40). Remember the cities which lay at the junctions of the trade and shipping routes—Corinth, Ephesus, Laodicea— and the ethnic interaction of these market communities and the danger of syncretism which confronted the young churches there. Nor are we surprised when we find such references as that in Acts 16:1 to the young man Timotheus, "son of a certain woman who was a Jewess, and a believer; but whose father was a Greek." So the New Testament church had its counterpart of the mestizo, or latino or Euronesian. Not only was there a place for this kind of person in the Church, but he played an active participating role in the ministry of the Church. Indeed, two intensely practical and down-to-earth letters in the New Testament were addressed to him.

Furthermore, the Church had not gone far into its history before it was confronted by that problem of Christian procedure about which we still dispute to this day—the service program that claims so much attention that the proclamation of the Word is neglected. The first time the Church met that issue, the argument had an interracial base: "there arose a murmuring of the Grecians against the Hebrews" (Acts 6:1). How well we are aware of this sad truth: our disputes seem all the more vicious when they have an ethnic division at their roots. Yet if the Church is to minister to all, if we are to be "one in Christ" we cannot achieve this by denying that our differences exist. In some way we must recognize the groups involved, and discover that *in spite of* these differences He is *Lord of all.* There must be "one flock and one Shepherd" though many sheep may belong to "other folds" (Jn. 10:16). The recognition of diversity within unity is clearly stated in Scripture.

Now to return to the episode in Acts 6, we have here a good example of how the early Church dealt with this kind of a problem—a practical and theological dispute, made all the more disturbing because it attached itself to the racial divisions in the congregation. The problem was solved by congregational action. They realistically examined the issues at stake. They recognized the basic importance of both sides of the dispute. They saw the need for differentiation of function and the creation of new roles. They took the initiative to deal with the problem and those chosen for the new functional role were not all taken from one social group, one at least being a proselyte from Antioch. Either he must have been an outstanding individual or he represented a group of Antiocheans in Jerusalem at the time. In any case, they faced the problem, talked over a practical solution and did something specific about it. As a result we are told, the Church grew and many priests (Jews) were won to the faith (v. 7).

The Jewish and Grecian Christians frequently clashed and again in Acts 15 we have a specific attempt to deal with their disagreements on an intensely practical level. Here is the principle of *conference and representation.* The apostles and elders debated the matter. The key point seems to have been the gift of the Holy Spirit. Peter pointed out that the Holy Spirit had been given to the Gentiles (vv. 7ff.) and in point of fact the real criterion was not a person's birth but his or her faith. Paul and Barnabas supported him (v. 12). Then came James, who was apparently the chairman

(vv. 13ff.) with the verdict (v. 19). The congregation would receive Greek converts as long as they believed. They did not have to cross an ethnic barrier and become Jews. Despite these ethnic differences, and their maintenance of racial integrity, yet they were one in Christ. They were warned against syncretism but allowed to be themselves and to worship God in their own way. This termination of the debate pleased the apostles, elders and congregation, and they sent representatives, greetings and letters to Antioch, Syria and Cilicia (vv. 22-23) localities which were particularly interested in the issue. We have ten or twelve verses on how they went about circulating this information. The Church is becoming a network of congregations and this is a matter which concerns more than one congregation.

We have here virtually the same process as we met in Acts 6. First, the Church recognized the existence of the problem. Second, they faced up to it and talked the matter out in an orderly way. Third, they reached a consensus under God, and this was a common sense and practical solution. Finally, as a result, the Church grew. Indeed it was on the basis of this decision (that to be a Christian a Greek did not have to become a Jew, but that Jew and Greek could be one in Christ and yet be truly themselves) that the Christian mission began to take on a specific form: the missionary journeys of Paul and Barnabus came out of this.

Now, as we turn to the precise missionary situation before us; as we see the Church in which we are involved today; I believe the Bible speaks to us in these three ways:

1. The Bible does not despise the ethnic groups, but rather recognizes them. It recognizes ethnic rights and entity. It recognizes them as units which can and should be won for Christ, and which should be free, each one to worship Christ in its own way.

2. The Bible recognizes that the Church has to grow in a multi-ethnic context. This situation, as far as we are concerned, is a *given*. Our duty lies in accepting the world situation of our day and asking ourselves how we can serve God in it. How can we be the Body of Christ ministering the mind and the word of Christ and demonstrating His love in it?

3. However, although we recognize the existence of ethnic units within society, and the right of each to its entity, we should strive to help their unity in Christ, and should so organize the life of the Church in our day that we may understand the meaning of the distinction of *the fold* and *the flock,* which we have from the lips of Jesus himself.

Therefore, in studying the dynamics of the interracial Church I believe the Bible speaks to three things as we engage in the ministry and mission of the Church today. It recongnizes the ethnic unit, it recognizes the multi-ethnic context in which we operate, and it recognizes the desirability of multi-ethnic unity in Christ. I believe it is a safe generalization that these biblical guidelines produce goodwill and growth where they are tried today and that the churches in which one meets with exclusive enclosure and prejudice are usually those where the congregation is not prepared to put the guidelines to the test.

RECOGNIZE THE ETHNIC UNITS

We saw in the case of the New Testament Church that the first thing in reaching a satisfactory solution to their problems was to recognize the nature of the problem before them. In many ways the problems of the pioneering Church and the transitional Church are the same. New issues are arising, many of them with some element of cultural clash as the cause of misunderstanding. Let's examine some of the modern day problems of the bicultural church with reference to the example of Hispanics in Los Angeles.

Today Spanish-speaking people from Mexico, Cuba and Puerto Rico are pouring into American cities. The second generation tends to be English-speaking, yet retains a great deal of its basic Spanish culture. This applies also in many of the agricultural areas of the South and California. In Guatemala I met with congregations where Spanish-speaking Latinos and Maya Indians faced each other in a state of potential tension. I found the same thing in Mexico. In the United States the tension of Caucasian and African traditions is a continual potential, despite the fact that English is spoken by both. Virtually the same problem arises in some of the American Indian communities, for instance, in Navaholand. So frequently the dispute, which seems on the surface to be economic, or political or theological, is found to have a racial base. The Church is continually confronted with these problem situations. Every minister who serves a bi- or multi-racial congregation knows how this affects the church structure, leadership, participation, and even the worship.

I am convinced that the only solution is the New Testament one. The problem must be recongnized, and the congregation must sit down together and seek a consensus under God. Clearly when people do this conscientiously, the Lord blesses their deliberation.

Again, we notice that the New Testament shows that, when the Church did this, some kind of organic growth of the Church resulted. New participant roles were created. Missionary programs were undertaken. More effective witness was demonstrated. The groups in the congregation were not denied their right of existence. The Greeks were not forced to assume Jewish cultural aspects. They were received as Greeks and given representation. The New Testament answer to cultural differences was not absorption into something noncultural, but to recognize the diversity and to captivate it for greater interaction and participation. Indeed the congregation of the consummation is depicted as a multi-ethnic multitude (Rev. 7:9).

A church congregation is an extremely diversified assembly. If it includes people of all races, all those races should be considered in the internal programs of the church life and in the external witness and ministry of the Church as the Body of Christ in the world. Quite apart from the bi- or multicultural elements, the diversity covers many other cultural features. There are the age groups, for example. It is possible for one congregation to care for and use the old people and ignore the youth; or it is equally possible for the reverse to apply. I have known both. A congregation must grow organically in such a way as to minister to and to use the ministry of every social segment—the English-speakers and the Spanish-speakers, the young and the old. Any group which is "neglected in the ministrations" or denied its right to express itself will start complaining and discord will result. The best way to maintain a happy multicultural congregation is to see that everyone in need is cared for and everyone is kept busy in the service of the Lord. If disputes arise, face up to them squarely, recognize the problem, and honestly seek an answer under God, and then have the courage to act on the decision reached. I have never known people to do this without some growth resulting.

The recognition of the problem and the arrival at an adequate solution, then, means first the identification of each group within the fellowship and second the incorporation of that group within the program of the congregation so that they may be participators and not mere spectators. This means that where nurture is needed, their precise needs must be considered and where programs are undertaken, they must be given a participant role. If the problems arise with respect to the bilingual structure of the congregation, that fellowship is bound to provide facilities and opportunities. The transitional churches, being brought into existence because of migration of people, say, from Mexico, and speaking Spanish, into a community where the language of economic advancement is English, such as in Los Angeles, are bound to provide a bilingual ministry. This element of complexity must be recognized and there must be planning to make use of it. This is the peculiar character of the task to which God calls those in bilingual ministries.

Furthermore, it will be more than bilingual, it will be bicultural; there will be both traditionalists and progressives; and all of these diverse cultural subgroups will have to be dealt with just as if they were different age groups. The complexity of society means the complexity of the Church. This character is certain to be reflected in the internal shape of the fellowship of believers. This is to be expected and should not be regarded as a bad thing. It is the natural environment of the transitional Church. Furthermore, it is a glorious opportunity. Who, but bilingual Christians, can give this bilingual witness in the growing bilingual metropolitan communities of today's world, like Los Angeles. As long as there are unchurched Spanish-speakers migrating into Los Angeles, there is a ministry both on the levels of proclamation and service for evangelical speakers of Spanish.

I wish we had a full narrative of the planting of the first Christian congregations in the city of Rome. It must have been very similar to the situation facing Christians today in Los Angeles. I think the New Testament provides the models needed for church planting and culture. The first point then is to recognize the need to have to deal with groups of people who differ in culture and language, and also in their stage of transition from one way of life to another. Having recognized their existence and their rights, it is necessary to see that they are all provided for, both with respect to the resources of the fellowship on which they draw, and the opportunities of the outgoing ministry in which they participate. No ethnic, linguistic or social group can be ignored, even though it means modifying the structure of the congregation or providing new participant roles. Acts 6 is the model.

RECOGNIZE THE MULTI-ETHNIC CONTEXT

I have already suggested that we must go further than just recognize the different ethnic units. We need to realize that we live in a multi-ethnic world. This is our context. It may be that many of the historical factors which produced the kind of world we live in were bad and we live under the grim shadow of the injustices of the past, but for us, this is the world into which we have been born. This is our environment: our context. The world in which we perform our ministry is manifestly multi-ethnic. If Christian responsibility means anything at all, God will not hold *us* responsible for what happened a century ago, *our* judgment will concern what we do with the present. As Charles Wesley recognized, his calling did not operate in a vacuum:

To serve the present age,
  My calling to fulfill:
O may it all my powers engage
To do my Master's will!

Our "present age" is multi-ethnic. A multi-ethnic witness is certainly required. If your fellowship of believers which meets under your pastoral guidance is multi-ethnic, then you have both opportunity and responsibility to "serve your present age" and "do your Master's will." What can you— you as a congregation, not just as individual Christians, but as a corporate Body—do in your multi-ethnic context? How can you be the Body of Christ there, ministering the word and mind of Christ and demonstrating his love? How can you *proclaim* his message in that multi-ethnic context.?

Let me give you an example from my own experience. The world of the Fiji Islands is quite different from that of Los Angeles, except that it provides a great opportunity for a multi-ethnic witness and ministry. I was in charge of a Fijian institution, an educational center with a large campus and several schools, one of which was interracial and coeducational. In the country round about were Fijian villages and many Indian peasant farmers, a small mill town across the river and a large mission complex, similar to my own but serving the Indian people, lay between us and the town. This gave us a truly mixed complex as the context of our ministry. Both the Indian mission and my own had heavy institutional programs and it would have been quite easy for us to have become so involved that we overlooked the obligation we had as Christian units in a multi-ethnic context. We felt that there were two points at which the multi-ethnic ministry needed demonstration: (1) within the fellowship of believers, and (2) within the community operating as the Body of Christ. We tried to meet the former by means of a monthly combined worship service where the various groups from round about met in the largest building, where they were recognized as groups, sitting as groups, and yet sharing together, often with group musical contributions, and with the sermon rotating among the preachers of the various congregations involved. These were deeply meaningful services, and a regular element in our program. We also got together from time to time for the social and festival events that emerged in the religious life of our community. We patronized each other's public functions and money raising efforts; we shared each others preachers and teachers; and social events like weddings were quite multi-ethnic. Thus in the fellowship of believers, although our organizations were distinct and we retired into Fijian, Hindustani or English at many points, yet we were always glad for the events we shared as a multi-ethnic community, whether these were conducted in English or were multi-lingual. I remember one wonderful dawn communion service which was conducted in six languages.

On the level of the Church as the Body of Christ proclaiming the word of Christ to the outside world, we sought to demonstrate that the Gospel was adequate to incorporate all races, that it was not confined to one language, and to present an appeal outside the church building as a corporate appeal, by public meetings held in the theatre in the mill town or in the open air market. Sometimes we had religious films. Always we had specially prepared items contributed by the various ethnic groups partici-pating—songs and choruses, instrumental numbers, puppets and various visual aids. We switched from one language to another, for most of us were bilingual, and we who were involved were manifestly recognizable as belonging to different races. I cannot say that this approach directly won many converts, but it did open up scores of contacts for personal witness through which people were actually won. But quite apart from this presentation of multi-ethnic concern in the community at large, it did something to us and clarified our vision of how the fellowship of believers can also be the Body of Christ, and the multi-ethnic circumstances need not in any way destroy this. The various elements which made up these gatherings were, if viewed as independent units, quite ethnic, but they were woven together in a multicolored fabric. Naturally, the Fijian items meant more to the Fijians and those in Hindustani were more meaningful to the Indians, but as time went on both groups began to appreciate more the choices and values of the others, and they accepted the idea of living in a multi-ethnic world as a *given*. I see no hope for the redemption of multi-ethnic society without first the acceptance of the fact that it is indeed multi-ethnic. Once we accept that fact, then we can get to work on the relationships between the groups. I do not mean that we merely recognize the existence of these groups and that we are satisfied with some kind of coexistence. I mean an interrelating multi-ethnic existence. We are "bound up together in the bundle of life with the Lord." This brings me to the question of what we really mean by being "one in Christ."

RECOGNIZE MULTI-ETHNIC UNITY IN CHRIST

In the example of multi-ethnic fellowship and witness I cited above, it was apparent that not only were the ethnic entities recognized, but they were also working together with their hearts beating as one heart. The diversity was within a unity. I venture to say these people were "one in Christ" in spite of their differences. They were well aware of the fact that they belonged to different *folds,* yet were also one *flock* under one Shepherd.

If I may illustrate again from Fiji, I might add that this philosophy is built in to the constitution of the indigenous Church there. In the city of Suva, for example, one has a choice of worship in a large Fijian church, in the Fijian language, with unaccompanied Fijian music, with Fijian procedure and leadership and called by the beat of a Fijian drum; or secondly, worship in Hindustani in a building of distinctly Indian architecture and expressed in the singing of bhajans; or in the third place, one may worship in English in a lively evangelical service with gospel songs and testimonies. This last is not a foreign service, though many foreigners would be happy in it. It is the worship service of the part-European community. These three groups exist in sufficiently large numbers to support their own congregational patterns in the cultural atmosphere and language in which they can best draw near to God. That is, they recognize the ethnic unit and its validity. If it ended there this would be segregation. However, they all recognize that they belong to a multi-ethnic context and periodically they get together so that they may remember and the world may know of their unity in Christ. They have their conferences where they have a great deal of autonomy, but once a year they send their representatives to a United Synod. Here they discuss the matters which concern the Church at large, matters of basic belief, programs for united mission in proclamation of the Gospel to the world outside, church literature and publications and many other things. At the time of the Annual Synod, many public meetings will be held giving opportunity for them to worship and witness together—instructional, social, religious. They include a Youth Rally, a Combined Communion Service, the Ordination Service and other gatherings. It is a kind of festival occasion. Once a year all over Fiji the various ethnic units unite for what is known as the Week of Witness, which usually includes a procession when the Christians of different racial units march together.

This is the way one Church meets the problem. I do not say it is the only way, or even the best way. But at least I do say that this Church both meets the needs of the ethnic units and makes a united witness. Here I am using the word "church" of the Church at large, a complex of congregations loosely tied together as in a denomination. When the congregations are ethnic, special effort and vigilance are required to make the oneness in Christ manifest. This will apply also to places like Los Angeles if circumstances call for Spanish-speaking and English-speaking congregations as discrete entities. Likewise, where a denomination has both black and white congregations meeting separately to permit more freedom of expression in worship patterns, it is obligated to see they get together frequently to cultivate and demonstrate their oneness in Christ on the levels of both worship and witness to the world. The danger of establishing our congregations as *folds* is that it is easy to forget the *flock*. The implication of the Lord's allegory is surely that if there is an appropriate time for the sheep to be in the folds, there is also an appropriate time when they should go about as the flock, the one flock under the one Shepherd, and when this should be manifest.

There are some brave congregations which set out to symbolize the flock rather than the fold. In this case the danger lies in the opposite direction, that they will fail to recognize the ethnic and social units of which the congregation is comprised. For this reason they frequently fail to meet the needs of all the members and have many lonely and unincorporated people. It is surely not by accident that so often the church which attracts people through its front door because of its apparent unity, has also a heavy traffic out through the back door, as its staic statistics demonstrate. I attended such a church for some years, a white congregation which welcomed black members. In my time I saw some twenty or thirty fine Blacks come into membership with anticipation and be presented to the congregation. There was no problem of different economic levels or education, yet the new members never felt they belonged. They stayed for a month or two and tried to integrate, but left at about the same rate as they came. They had not been rejected, but it had been a nebulous "take-it-or-leave-it" kind of acceptance. They had never been shown that the congregation needed them badly, that there was indeed a job in that community that only they could do, and other jobs which could only be done by black and white together. The dream of unity in this congregation was based on the equation of the ideas of unity and uniformity. You cannot establish a flock by elimination of the folds. If the folds are there, they have to be taken into account.

Then the question arises: is the allegory of our Lord realistic? Can we have a congregation which is truly the flock but also recognizes and utilizes the folds? Not only is this theologically sound, but it is also good anthropology. Anthropology demonstrates the importance of recognizing the social segments during the process of social change. I shall demonstrate this again with a concrete example, the case of the Church of All Nations in Melbourne, Australia. This church has a realistic way of meeting a complex and changing situation by winning highly divergent ethnic groups and manifesting a positive drive for the unity which is possible in Christ alone. This is seen to be possible only because the church recognizes and provides for the divergent groups.

The church stands in an inner suburb of Melbourne. Originally it was a residential area. As the city grew, the inner suburbs became industrial and the inhabitants moved to the outer suburbs. The church became the old type of rescue mission. I remember it as such in my university days before the war. Attendance grew smaller and smaller and as a congregation it virtually ceased to exist. After the war Australia received two million refugees and settlers from Europe. They crowded into the cities of Melbourne and Sydney. Before long they had occupied the inner suburbs and began building huge apartment houses, an innovation on the Australian landscape. These new residents were European in culture and if they had religion it was more Roman Catholic. They changed the environment. The old congregation no longer existed, but a good set of buildings remained. This is now the Church of All Nations. The congregation comprises several clearly differentiated ethnic entities. One is English, one Hungarian, another Armenian and still another Spanish. A Greek unit is moving in at present. These people have been welded together as a flock. The preacher at the worship service sees in the old gallery at the back of the church a set of booths. From each of these a man follows his service and sermon, translating everything into Hungarian, Arabic, Spanish and so forth. Down below those in the center listen to the preacher as he speaks in English. The others have earphones and each person turns on the particular channel he or she desires. However, a glance at their physical appearance shows they actually sit in ethnic clusters. Sometimes one of the groups will make a contribution. The Sunday I preached to this multi-ethnic congregation, the Spanish group supplied some special music. For prayer meetings and devotionals the groups could meet as ethnic units, arranging their own times. One group, the Hungarian, if I remember rightly, had been in the community far longer than the others, and they had intimated their readiness to accept the worship in English, in which language they had now become proficient, in order to vacate their channel for the use of Greek. One does not wonder that the old empty church has now a large, growing congregation with extensive participation. Here is a congregation which has taken the multi-ethnic context and directed its resourcefulness to this very fact, asking themselves how they could use this precise set of circumstances to fill again the pews of the empty set of buildings they had inherited. There is something about the Church of All Nations which suggests that we face a new day in church planting and a new kind of church structure. In any case, were they not following Him who said,

> Other sheep I have, which are not of this fold: them also I must bring, and they shall hear my voice; and there shall be one flock and one Shepherd? (Jn. 10:16)

By recognizing the existence of the divergent folds they saw before them the opportunity of bringing together the flock. Would anyone dare to say that these people are not "one in Christ"?

CHAPTER 32

Indigenous Principles
in Mission Today

It was my joy and blessing to spend my term of missionary service in a field where, over a period of twenty years, an independent Church was emerging and step by step discarding the trimmings of nineteenth-century missions. This was possible because of the progressive approach to mission which had allowed for development from the start, and the periodic restructuring which is a feature of its history. Here is a Church which has grown qualitatively and organically as it grew numerically, a large indigenous ministry, where the words "missionary" and "native" have been removed from its law book, with thousands of lay preachers and female class leaders, with catechists to help the ministers and a number of approved prayer leaders in each congregation. Here is a Church which determines its own affairs and appoints any "missionaries" as it desires. The local pastorates are self-supporting and pay their own ministers. The central theological seminary and the Bible school are both supported by the local Church (Tippett 1967a). Since my retirement from that field I have been able to inspect many other fields of a different character. I do not want to set one field against another, except perhaps where they are very similar culturally, because I know that every field is unique. That is a principle we have to keep in mind when we make church growth comparisons. However, I believe that we have a universal need, both for missions now being planted and for missions struggling with the transition to independency, for a straightforward statement on what we

The original version of this chapter was published in *Verdict Theology in Missionary Theory,* second edition, (Pasadena: William Carey Library, 1973), pp. 126-141. Gratitude is hereby expressed to the publisher, William Carey Library, 1705 N. Sierra Bonita Avenue, Pasadena, CA 91104, for permission to include it here.

really mean by the *indigenous principles*. Clearly there is a great deal of confusion about it, with some very unhappy results.

In this chapter, therefore, I purpose addressing myself to four basic questions: How does an indigenous Church grow? How does a mission station become an indigenous Church? What are the marks of a truly indigenous Church? What does this mean to the sending Churches?

HOW DOES AN INDIGENOUS CHURCH GROW?

An indigenous Church must grow, as any other, in three dimensions—quantitatively, qualitatively, and organically. There should be a certain balance in this growth. If one outstrips the other, we get distortions of growth—monstrosities—to which I will return when I have defined the terms.

1. Quantitative Growth

A Church must grow numerically. If a human being does not grow, we send him or her to the doctor and ask why. The Body is the biblical figure for the Church. With each generation there should be *biological* growth. Children born to Christian parents should be brought to an experience of commitment. This must be accomplished with each generation. But the Church is committed to outreach, bringing in converts from the world round about, from paganism or secularism as the case may be. This is sheer increase. Care has to be taken to combat *membership shrinkage* (see Chapter 30, above) by watching transfers and migration, but quite apart from avoiding these losses, there must be numerical gains from the world. If a Church has no evangelical outreach, it is also likely to neglect its service outreach unless it uses this as a substitute for evangelism. In the former case a congregation becomes enclosed and shut off from the world; in the latter it becomes distorted in its impact. So quantitative growth is spiritually essential for every Christian congregation. Having won people by conversion, the Church has to incorporate them into the fellowship (1 Jn. 1:3).

2. Qualitative Growth

McGavran used the term perfection growth. We have tended to use the term "qualitative" because of the common but quite unfair criticism of quantitative growth under the cliche "not quantity but quality," in order to show that these are not two opposite poles but two quite different axes. Just as there is a desirable and an undesirable quantitative growth, the same may be said of quality, which can be seen as selfless love shared in humility at one pole, and legalistic perfection at the other. The former is outreaching, the latter inclusive. The mechanisms whereby this growth is achieved are Christian education, Bible study, worship, fellowship (within the group), and by witness and service (without). As Scripture tells us, we are to "grow in grace." The incorporation of large numbers of converts without provision for their spiritual nurture has never been allowed in church growth theory. Indeed, we have always insisted that "a people movement has to be brought to consummation."

3. *Organic Growth*

The moment a group or society comes into being some form of organization, however simple, is required. Thus from the very start of church planting the Church is viewed as an organism. Organic growth includes the participation and roles of persons designated for group action, the structure within which they operate, their inner relationships and outside contacts, so that the Church may be a living organism within an environment. This has to grow continually and in such a way that fulfills its function within its environment. It must not be allowed to grow in a foreign form but in a form suitable to the world in which it lives.

With respect to these three dimensions, two things need to be said. First, the growth should be *continuous*. Second, growth should be *in equilibrium*. Occasionally a church growth analysis reveals that missionaries have deliberately stopped taking in converts because they have not enough pastors to shepherd them. To stop a people movement is to seal it off. Even when this is done to "consolidate" gains, the movement is not likely to start again after a few years of "consolidation" have produced more leaders. When the Spirit of God indicates the flood tide, that tide should be used to the full. Church growth takes a vigorous attitude against these so-called breaks for consolidation (Clark 1933:7; McGavran, Huegel and Taylor 1963:96, 133; McGavran 1959:19-20; Tippett 1967a:132, 364). Clark developed this concept under the figure of a tree. Its growth must be continuous. If it stops to consolidate, it dies. You cannot "turn off" quantitative growth, while you "turn on" organic growth. In living things there must be an equilibrium in growth. Like the tree, the Body has to develop organically and in bulk together.

If one dimension of the Church develops at the expense of another, we get a monstrosity—paternalistic structures, foreign patterns, monolithic excesses, home church domination, enclosed congregations—all are different forms of distorted growth, because one feature has grown at the expense of the others. To seek quantity without attending to quality is to neglect the teaching clause of the Great Commission. To seek quality without quantity neglects the scope of the Great Commission. Without organic growth the "going," the "teaching," and the "incorporation through baptism" cannot be effectively put into effect. The first decades of this century left us a great legacy of problems in this respect. It is largely because of these distortions in missions that the church growth emphasis has been stressed. We do not believe, as some of our critics seem to believe, that the idea of the Church is dispensable. We are aware that through the human shortcomings of the Christian people, the Church has often presented a distorted image to the world, and this has often hindered her acceptance and growth. Nevertheless, time after time, through history we have seen the divine corrective work of the Holy Spirit first rebuke and then restore her. Furthermore, we believe that in the great consummation she will be presented as the Bride of Christ. With this presence of the Bride in the last chapter of the Bible, we ignore those critics who think church growth is the Church fighting for survival. The ultimate is not in our hands. What is in our hands is the present, here in this world, this confined area of time and space into which we have been born and appointed as stewards and workmen, where we will be held accountable for using all the resources at our disposal. Church growth theory and method relate to this orbit of a Christian's responsibility in our day and generation.

HOW DOES A MISSION STATION BECOME AN INDIGENOUS CHURCH?

It is much easier to start a Church on indigenous principles than it is to change over from a long established, paternalistic, enclosed, mission station congregation. In the decade before the war the missionary strategist Clark was pointing out this truth and urging that the missionary policymakers pay attention to it. Since then it has passed on into church growth theory, but it was Clark who provided the basic concepts of *Construction and Reconstruction* (1928:16-18). It is interesting to note that Clark saw the latter in virtually the same terms as F.E. Williams, who listed criteria for directed change though he merely stated the principles and left them undeveloped. He said:

> Reconstruction involves three things. The first, the scrapping of whatever is useless, having served its purpose; the second, the reshaping of whatever has still some power of service; and the third, the adding of whatever is required of the new to make the instrument with which we work efficient for its purposes today (1928:17).

Those were vital days when we still had a choice in China. Clark was asking for more and more church growth research, for a willingness to act on the basis of their findings, to ascertain by testing "what to rectify in the old, what to avoid in the new." He found in China "a new spirit moving among the people" and called for reconstruction in the new (1928:18). He urged the planting of indigenous churches. Where indigenous principles were applied, there was people movement growth (Peill and Rowlands 1930; Rowlands 1931), but on the whole Clark was a voice crying in the wilderness. This was a quarter of a century before David Paton's *Christian Missions and the Judgement of God* (1953). As we look back now we can see how, as Clark said, the doors of opportunity were open, but the "new spirit moving among the people" was captured by another ideology. The opportunity was lost, and for my part I believe that it was lost because of an unreadiness on the part of the Christian agents of change—foreigners and nationals who were part of the foreign system by status or economic dependence—to come to terms with the situation that formed their environmental world. Paton, in the above mentioned book, had something of a church growth attitude. "When a disaster has occurred," he said, "nothing is really wise, or even kind, save ruthless examination of the causes." You don't "fob this off," he goes on, "when early recourse to the surgeon may save your life." You may have cancer, but yet have also good lungs and feet. Thus he recognizes much faithful work in a critical chapter about missions (1953:34).

The work in China stands as an example of foreign structured missions that, because of their reluctance to give up their foreignness, thereby resisted indigeneity. We shall probably never be able to measure the extent to which this threw the populace into the arms of Communism, but if the archival data were open to us, I believe we would find this a major factor.

In other parts of the world the same factors have led to breakaway movements, schisms, the emergence of independent churches and Cargo Cults. Where the foreign mission has refused to yield to the emerging indigeneity, these disturbances have come, and hundreds of thousands of Christians have been lost, and many who might have been won for Christ have responded to other advocacy. Barrett has examined six thousand of these movements in Africa alone (1968). The point I am trying to make is that these movements towards selfhood represent a right idea, and church growth should be so directed from the start, that in the "fullness of time" the transmission from mission to Church should be smooth and simple without repercussions.

I well remember the time in my own mission when our mission leader, an older man, was retiring after ten years in the chair. He had done much for the Church and people, but had always been somewhat paternal. Frequently he had suppressed the desire for a contrary decision by using soft words. "We are here to guide you," he would say. We younger members felt the rising tide against this domination from the chair. Then a younger man was appointed to take his place, and the senior pastor rose to welcome him as he took office. He expressed their pleasure at the appointment but added, "There is one thing we would request as you assume authority over us. We feel that your job is not to tell us what you think is best for us, but to show us how to get what we want." The young man was wise enough to take these words seriously, and a new form of partnership began from that hour. From this point the growth of the Church was rapid in the direction of indigeneity. One by one the positions held by foreigners were handed over to nationals, and eventually the day came when the Church was functioning under a national president. In the emergence of the indigenous Church we may expect such "convergences of history" when "battles" are won or lost. Surely it is the Lord who brings the Church to such an hour. These convergences of history have to be recognized by both missionaries and nationals. They have to be seen as God-given opportunities which can be lost or won.

I wish I could impress on every missionary theorist that when a Church emerges in this way, the partnership will continue. If missionary paternalism is resistant, the time will come when the takeover or the breakaway will be more violent, and it may well be that partnership is never possible at all. We have seen this in the political development of colonies. Some have evolved gently into independence, others have come by way of revolution. The former is to be preferred, because it leaves the way more open for a wholesome partnership and preserves better human relationships.

Frequently I am asked if I can put in a single guiding principle the key to the passage from mission station to indigenous Church. With the qualification that only God can really do this, I can do no more than venture an opinion. Yet it is an opinion based on a great many church growth case studies in which I believe the Spirit of God has been at work. It seems to me that the key principle is to recognize the psychological moment for the changeover, to accept this as God's moment, the "fullness of time" as it were, the time when by the activity of His Spirit in the situation He has brought everything to a state of "ripeness." It is as if God is taking the situation out of our hands for a moment, to give it back as something new. I believe we have to recognize that moment. It is not the moment when *we think* we should force indigeneity upon the nationals and bemoan the slowness of their desire to take over. It is not the moment when the home board or sending church feels it is time their financial aid was removed elsewhere. It is a feeling, an experience of ripeness, when the voice of God speaks saying, "Now is the time." Then the missionary must know when to bend his or her will to God's and support every move that opens toward indigeneity. There will be several features of the fraternal gatherings in those days. One will be a general tendency on the part of the nationals to accept every offer extended by the missionaries. They may even initiate the moves and hope the missionaries will agree. An unresponsiveness from the nationals shows the time is not ripe. A resistance from the missionaries shows their excessive paternalism and unreadiness to go forward in true faith that, after all, God is in control of this situation. By nationals here I mean the people of the Church, not the national pastors, unless they are already in the pay of the people. National pastors in mission pay tend to be the most conservative of all the resisters of change. They have to learn the same lessons as the missionaries.

It is folly to force indigeneity on a Church that is not ready. The only way to deal with this situation is to educate the people for indigeneity, and this has to be accepted at the congregational level. The strength and state of an indigenous Church is measured always at the local village level, not in the superstructure, although the superstructure tends to have more significance with increased acculturation.

In handing over to the local Church the missionaries involved will soon see the importance of equilibrium in growth. Any degree of imbalance will make the transfer more difficult. If you find a young Church which can carry itself devotionally but not financially, you may recognize here the effect of qualitative growth at the expense of organic growth in missionary policy. There are a surprisingly large number of mission field churches in precisely this position. We need to realize that this is the fault of missionary policy. It may be that indigeneity should be developed in the area of strength slowly, and education for it in the area of weakness pressed with more vigor. In the above case this would be education in stewardship. One thing that must not be done is to suddenly withdraw all support in a moment of time, when the state of dependence itself has been the result of years of paternal policy by the home body. Some missions have effectively distributed the withdrawal of support over a period of years balancing each withdrawal with some increase of autonomy in some form or other. But every situation is unique. It is fatal to generalize.

The problems of transferring missionary churches to an indigenous Church highlight the importance of planting indigenous principles from the very start. Converts should be given responsibility for numerical, qualitative, and organic growth from the very beginning so they grow to maturity with these Christian dimensions in proportion.

WHAT ARE THE MARKS OF
A TRULY INDIGENOUS CHURCH?

The idea of the indigenous church came to us in its original form from the greatest missionary theoriest of the last century, Henry Venn. The idea was based on the concept of *Selfhood,* and was always accompanied by its sister doctrine of *Euthanasia.* Thus the emergence of the Church and the dying of the Mission in the foreign land were conceptualized as part of a single process. Under Venn's influence the object of the Church Missionary Society became:

> . . . the development of Native Churches, with a view to their ultimate settlement upon a self-supporting, self-governing and self-extending system. When this settlement has been effected, the Mission will have attained its euthanasia, and the missionary and all missionary agency can be transferred to the regions beyond.

This is cited from an official paper on "Native Church Organization" published by Venn's society. Venn's development and use of this theory over his long period of office is the subject for a book. I hope that some day someone, who is able to bring out an appreciation of the real value of his work, will write such a book. In the meantime, I mention Venn merely to show that the idea came from him and to comment on the fact that for over a century the missionary world has had this basic theory of mission before it. Because God spoke to the missionary world through Venn's writings, we have no one to blame but ourselves for our preference for paternalistic and foreign missions and the problems that have emerged from our policy.

In many ways we could claim Venn as an early church growth writer. Many of the things he emphasized by insight we now know to be true on a basis of church growth studies. In the principles of selfhood that he stated both quantitative and organic growth are well provided for, and qualitative growth is clearly implied, if not directly stated.

However, it seems to me that in our present exigency we need a modern restatement of the doctrine of selfhood, and this I shall attempt under the head, "The Marks of an Indigenous Church." This is necessary because of the current lack of clarity about what the indigenous church is. To many it is conceptualized entirely in terms of self-support, which is quite wrong and has sometimes led to tragic mistakes in policy.

In the first place, *selfhood is a total entity.* Even if you see it in terms of the "three selfs," which being only part of the whole in any case are not to be seen in isolation. They are interrelating features, not discrete compartments. As I have said before, the Church must grow in equilibrium, otherwise the Body is a monstrosity. Therefore, if I proceed to analyze these aspects of selfhood, it must be clearly understood that this is purely an abstraction for purposes of consideration, that we may meditate upon the constituent features. They are not discrete and cannot stand alone. They are different ways of looking at a whole Church. In this case we are considering a Church which is indigenous to some given mission field. It may or may not have been planted by foreigners, but it is not a foreign Church.

First Mark: Self-Image

The first mark of an indigenous Church is its self-image. Does it see itself as *the* Church of Jesus Christ in its own local situation, mediating the work, the mind, the word, and the ministry of Christ in its own environment. How does the Church operate in times of emergency? Do the leaders run off to the missionary for guidance and financial help? Or do they meet together and face the crisis that has come upon them and ask themselves how they can deal with it? Does the Church see that crisis and catastrophe in their community is their opportunity to minister to the need about them? Do they see themselves as the Body of Christ there? Have they such a self-image? Or are they still seeing themselves as children under the fatherly mission?

Second Mark: Self-Function

The second mark of an indigenous Church is that it is self-functioning. If the Church sees itself as the Church, as the Body of Christ, presumably the Body will have its parts and these parts will have their different functions, for "all the members have not the same office." However, the parts as isolated organs do not make a body unless they all perform their respective functions and interact with each other. A body is a self-functioning organic whole. Only by effective internal growth in grace within a developing organic structure, where members interact and cooperate and fulfill their natural functions, can the Body be healthy and perform its appointed role in the world. A mission field community is not likely to emerge as a Church until it has developed into an entity with parts that permit the differentiation of function, yet a participation of the parts as they function in interdependence for the good of the whole. A body which is dependent on one leader is not likely to stand on its own feet. The more people who are involved in a ministry of participation, the nearer the society comes to being a Church, and if those members are nationals, then it is an indigenous Church, at least in this respect. When such a group can provide for its own worship services, Bible study groups, prayer meetings, and classes for Christian education, and the participation in these things is active, then the quality growth of this community is assured. But if this or that group meets only when a mission-paid catechist calls them together, then such a group is far from indigeneity, because it is not self-functioning.

Third Mark: Self-Determination

The third mark of an indigenous Church relates to its self-determining capacity. Is the group an autonomous body, facing its own affairs as they relate both to the group and the group's outside relations? Have they some kind of decision making mechanism? Is this in their own hands and not in the hands of the missionary? Does its structure fit the decision making patterns of the social structure, or is it foreign? Two elements are important here. Let me reiterate. The decision must be with the people themselves or their approved representative, not with any external authority like a mission or missionary. The only authority a missionary retains in a truly indigenous Church is the authority of the office to which the nationals appoint him or her. Then, the decision making should be carried out within a structure which is culturally appropriate. It should reflect in some way the accepted decision making mechanisms of the tribe; that is, it should be something they can feel is their own. The greatest threat to an indigenous Church is the denominational character of Christian missions. We tend to plant denominational structures. Every missionary organization should be ready to fit the culture.

The mission has to die for the Church to be born, as Venn saw it. I well remember the intense emotional feeling that we all shared in my mission field Church when we realized that this had been accomplished. We had given away our authority and sat in the ministerial stationing session knowing that for the first time we were overwhelmingly outvoted. A motion was before the chair. A certain missionary was recommended for a particular post. A national moved an amendment, and when the vote was taken, the amendment was carried. The nationals had apppointed a missionary where they wanted him. It was a great moment, when the emerging Church saw itself as a self-determining body for the first time.

Fourth Mark: Self-Support

The fourth mark of an indigenous Church is its self-supporting nature. This is the mark of stewardship. It has two aspects which may be covered by the questions: (1) Does the Church carry its own financial burdens? and (2) Does it adequately finance its own service projects?

It is never easy to convince a "Church" which has been carried by mission funds that those funds should be withdrawn. It is frequently interpreted to mean "The Mission no longer loves us." I have even known cases of transfer of allegiance to some other denomination because of it. These are signs that education in stewardship is sadly needed, and mission policy over the years is to be held responsible for the attitude. A paternalistic Mission raises paternally expectant children. Training in stewardship should begin with the very planting of a Church. It should be a Church from the beginning. Another reason for the difficulty of the passage from paternal funding to stewardship is the high costs of the kind of work missions have established and expect the national Church to take over. Had this been related to the economic levels and cultural patterns from the beginning, there would have been no problems for us today. However, as we have the problem, we must find some way of dealing with it. The attitude has to be corrected by education. The old program should be phased out and the new one phased in. Some additional rights should be given with each reduction of outside funds. New funds established by the indigenous Church which is being born should be administered by that same body. Everything should be done in relation to the specific situation, not by general rules. Remember, we are correcting our own mistakes.

The second aspect of stewardship lies in the local service projects. This can be hindered by overseas funding of the home Church or board. A truly indigenous Church regards the social problems of its environment as its own concern and should be doing more than distributing foreign aid. I do not mean to the exclusion of foreign aid, but the initiative should come from the young Church itself. This has an important bearing on the Church's image in the community as being on the one hand the Body of Christ in the situation, or on the other hand an agent of foreign aid. Sometimes one progressive congregation may be encouraged to experiment with self-support, hoping to inspire others to emulation. I have described such a case elsewhere (Tippett 1967a:363).

Fifth Mark: Self-Propagation

The fifth mark of the truly indigenous Church is its self-propagating fervor. Does the young Church see itself as being directly addressed by the words of the Great Commission? Is the matter of quantitative church growth from the pagan regions beyond of real concern to the young Church? This was a matter in which the young Churches of the South Pacific excelled. From Tahiti and Tonga, from Samoa, Rotuma and Fiji, national missionaries moved out into the west. It was thus that the Gospel spread as far as Papua and New Guinea. The president of the Fijian Church wears a beautiful presidential stole during his term of office. The stole is ornamented by two symbols, on the one side the cross to signify the Gospel of salvation to be proclaimed, and on the other a Fijian canoe, signifying that this is an outgoing Church. And few Churches there be anywhere which have sent out more missionaries in the same proportion to its members. Furthermore, the Pentecostal offerings of every Fijian village are devoted to the outreaching proclamation.

Sixth Mark: Self-Giving

The sixth mark of the indigenous Church is its devotion to self-giving. This is the mark of service. Does a young Church have its own service program? Does it exercise itself with facing and alleviating the social needs and problems of the local world in which it lives? I know a young Church which shares the service burden among its members in numerous ways. For instance, after the morning worship service, when the full members meet for their regular class meeting, one man and one woman each Sunday are excused to visit the sick in the village. They give a brief outline of the preacher's message, read the lesson, and lead in prayer so no one need miss his or her share of the blessing because of sickness. This is a service rendered by the congregation to members of the congregation. Other service programs reach out into the wider secular world.

Now it may be said that these things are marks of the Church anywhere, and this is quite true. But they are the marks of an indigenous Church when the young Church undertakes them of its own volition, when they are spontaneously done, by indigenes and within their own pattern of life. When the indigenous people of a community think of the Lord as their own, not a foreign Christ; when they do things as unto the Lord, meeting the cultural needs around them, worshiping in patterns they understand; when their congregations function in participation in a body, which is structurally indigenous; then you have an *indigenous* Church.

It is possible for a Church to reach out toward indigeneity in one direction and yet to be deficient in another. In view of the imbalance of much mission policy over the years, many emerging Churches will reflect the consequences of that imbalance. This can only be corrected through time by education and sympathy. The truly indigenous Church is an ideal for which we strive—something truly a Church and truly indigenous.

WHAT DOES THIS MEAN TO THE
SENDING CHURCHES AND BOARDS?

Unfortunately, we cannot wipe the slate clear and start again. We have to proceed from the existential situation. For example, the tragic division of the missionary world among the denominations cannot be ignored, much as we would like to change it. The existing resources of people and money flow along these channels. At least we must start there and recognize the fact. There are many ways in which we may draw together by planned action and directed change, but we cannot just scrap everything and begin again. History does not allow that. Meanwhile, home Churches and sending boards are asking: if the young Churches are to be indigenous, are we still needed? Should our people and money be directed to other channels? If missionaries are still required, what kind of individuals should they be and how trained? In what way does the "drama" of mission differ for us in the days immediately ahead?

1. Spreading the Church Is Still Our Concern
The spread of the Church throughout all the world in the terms of the Great Commission is still our concern. As Bishop Pickett put it, "The Church has no authority to revise the mandate to preach, teach, and propagate the gospel, to change its message about God and man, or to limit the company of those to whom it is presented" (1962:34). This has not been changed by the social and political changes of our day. Indeed, we are called to new dimensions of mission. This does not mean that the day of mission has passed, but it does mean that the exterior forms of mission may need reformulation to meet the changes of the day. I have always been impressed by the fact that the great age of modern missions that is now coming to an end was itself ushered in by dramatic changes. It was an age of experiment and innovation, of adventure and new patterns of navigation, of industrial expansion, agricultural changes, social disturbances, and so forth. Yet these very events, including the voyages of Cook and the discovery of the Pacific world, new races, languages, and cultures, drove Carey to see in these a new field of opportunity and a new meaning of the Great Commission for his own day. There is no doubt that the opportunities for mission in the next century will be vastly different from those of the last, but there is also no doubt that God is still calling His people in mission. We Westerners may have to learn that the Churches planted in foreign lands belong to the people and not to us. If God calls us to such a situation, we have to recognize that we are called out of our own culture and be ready to leave it behind us. Likewise it may be that we will have to part with our denominationalism and see the Church where we serve as God's and not ours. The idea of the mission field still continues, and young Churches must be planted. The mission field still demands the concern, interest, and prayers of the sending

Churches and their financial support, but more and more the latter has to be directed away from paternal nurture to specific projects that will help the young Churches to stand on their own feet. There are still hundreds of places where pioneering missions are called for. More funding should be directed to these, but it has to be differently administered than it was in the last century. This leads me to the second point.

2. People and Money Are Still Needed

Because we are still involved in mission, even though the material forms may be new, people and money are still needed. I suppose there are more openings today for "missionaries" than there ever were—on all levels, as advisers, colleagues, and servants of the indigenous Churches. Today we have many new functional roles in Christian mission, we have many more nationals ready to train in the roles we are handing over. In pioneering areas we still need individuals who can break through the cultural barriers and establish themselves as empathetics, and communicate effectively.

However, new attitudes are required. A new type of missionary training is required. Whether a person goes as a preacher, teacher, or technician, he or she needs an adequate training in cross-cultural communication. The Church can no longer send out individuals without adequate training in anthropology. Missionaries have to learn how to face culture shock and identify in spite of it.

Such a program cannot be provided by the sending Churches without their involvement in considerable stewardship responsibility. Money is needed as much as ever, and our administrators still have to learn much about its distribution. It has to be strategically located so that it will help the young Churches to emerge with selfhood, without doing for them what they can and ought to do for themselves. Money which slows up self-support on the field is unwisely spent. Money expended in such a way as it helps the indigenous Church to assume responsibility more quickly is wisely spent. This brings me to the third point.

3. Sending Churches Need an Improved Understanding of Mission

The sending Churches, or contributing congregations, need improved education in what mission is all about. People like to know how their gifts are being used. They want facts. They want to know how the world mission of the Church is getting on. There is a good deal of fuzzy thinking about this in our day. We need to be definite in asserting that the Christian mission is still going on, that it is still concerned with bringing people out of darkness into light, with introducing people to Christ. We have to show the Christian people at home who support our efforts with their contributions and prayers that this effort is specifically directed to giving people a real option of accepting Christ, even though the forms by which this is presented may be quite new. The Church at home, having educated its members on the nature and scope of the Church's mission in the regions beyond, should then provide ways and means by which its own members have the option of responding to the call of God to mission themselves.

I do not mean to imply by this that the Church has no other mission, such as that at its own door in the outside world. This is most certainly mission and most certainly urgent. The only difference is that the latter is performed in the cultural forms known by the Church in the locality; the mission to the regions beyond is cross-cultural and the forms are strange and the language often quite difficult. Missionaries need special dimensions in their training to have any real idea of how to cope with their responsibilities.

I believe the sending Church has the responsibility for seeing the missionaries are properly equipped for their cross-cultural work. When they come home on furlough, they should be given adequate refresher courses, and if they are able to engage in any research project, their home Church should provide them with the necessary scholarship for the venture, for they are indeed the home Church's representative on the field. They should keep them supplied with books and technical journals, because isolation on the field denies missionaries these resources.

Many mistakes which older missionaries made were honest mistakes made in true zeal for the Lord. Missions today, however, can no longer afford to make these. No missionaries should be sent to the field without anthropological training. A certain type of literature, critical of the mistakes of the past, has pointed out what had been done in the name of the Church. This criticism had to be made, but anthropology is not merely a negative study. There is a positive side which speaks to the Christian mission, and this is open to us. Anthropology has given us new tools for understanding cross-cultural situations, tools for observing and testing and interviewing, tools for comparison. Anthropology has taught us much about cultural patterns, the wholeness of situations, and the importance of interrelationships. Anthropology has given us new and useful models and frames of reference for arranging and testing data. In conjunction with history, anthropology has given us the ethnohistorical methods which are so important in church growth studies. In communication, anthropology shows us the importance of lines of structure and relationships within the society, along which it is most natural for the Gospel to be transmitted by the indigenous people themselves and bring forth the utmost participation. Anthropology shows us the significance of the actual field situation in which we work. It is here that the Gospel must be advocated, accepted, consummated, and propagated. What really counts in the end is not theory but achievement at the local level. Anthropology shows us much about cultural incorporation, about how things are diffused, how ideas become indigenous, the significance of meaning, and how we have to fit *into* a situation and not *over* it. There is no end to the service anthropology can render to the missionary. There is no excuse for missionary training programs to ignore the availability of this discipline for inclusion in their training courses. Anthropology stands to missionary work in much the same relationship as reading and writing. Furthermore, if the young Churches are to be indigenous and not foreign, an appreciation of anthropology is indispensable to missionaries or fraternal workers who have to see their roles functionally in a cultural structure foreign to their own.

The person who does go out to missionary service as what we call the *professional missionary,* who is still needed in world mission, if I may borrow Scherer's six points, needs to have the following qualifications: (1) apostolic mentality, (2) superb intellectual equipment, (3) the gift for communicating the Christian faith and sharing the Christian life, (4) life commitment, (5) spiritual depth, and (6) costly identification. Scherer sees these as missionary *charismata* (1964:70-72). He develops these points in their spiritual, personal, and cultural dimensions. Besides theology and knowledge of the Scriptures, for instance, in (2) he asks for a knowledge of "cultural relations in the country of service and a penetrating knowledge of its religion"; in (3) he asks for "thorough language preparation" and an aptitude for work in the social structures; and in (6) he asks for "sharing life to the full with another people." Thus, while the biblical and devotional training of missionaries should help to give them the right motivations, they are not likely to forget their Westernness and to be really empathetic without a knowledge of the culture and people to whom they are to minister and the environment in which they live. The fact that many missionaries have failed at this point has led some nationals to cry, "Missionary, go home!" Now there are still many areas in the world where the missionary is needed today. It is our responsibility to see that those we send are persons who not only have the call from God but can adjust themselves cross-culturally for His sake. The missionary has to undergo *self-emptying* to enter this world which is foreign to him or her culturally, as did our Lord when He came to this earth as a human. This does not necessarily mean wearing a pigtail or some national garment. It means rather being with the other people in their situation, seeing their point of view and problems, with them in their burden bearing, for them in advocacy, appreciating their non-Western values—that is, empathizing. Such a person has a right to speak of Christ and share the riches of His Word, but both Christ and the Word will have to be presented in indigenous garments.

We conclude this study of the indigenous Church by saying that the sending Church has to send missionaries or fraternal workers who are culturally ready for self-emptying of their Westernism, for the "drama" of church planting and of church growth has to be "played" in "acts" and "scenes" radically different from the dramas of the past hundred years. The door is no longer open for the ethnocentric or foreign missionary. Although every situation is unique, the one common feature, the "given" of every situation, is that the Church in its planting or its growing should be a "thing of the soil." This means the indigenizing of the missionaries must be a major feature of their training. The genuineness of their *kenosis* should be the humble and continuous prayer of missionaries.

CHAPTER 33

Missionary Go Home?

For three decades now the missionary has been carrying on in the face of the cry, "Missionary go home!" Some anthropologists have added fuel to the fire, which was possible because they convinced themselves that they were objective observers. But now things have taken a turn, and all the social sciences are being asked to justify their existence by applying their disciplines for the betterment of mankind. A large body of anthropologists is now concerned with directing culture change and some of them are beginning to understand the missionary better. And now we hear the cry, "Anthropologist go home!"

This arises partly from the basic fact of new nations emerging, and new ideas of independence, but there is another reason not so frequently pinpointed. There is a *new national competence,* not the old traditional skills they always had, but competence in the proficiencies of the West. This new competence in competition with the West is emerging in every aspect of human progress. Christian mission began to feel it when bright young converts were sent abroad for biblical degrees. White paternalism is now dispensable.

PHASING-IN AND PHASING-OUT

At a recent "round table exchange" between American Indians and professional anthropologists one Indian anthropologist asked, "Is anthro-

The original version of this chapter was published in *Church Growth Bulletin,* July 1971, Vol. VII, No. 6, pp. 7-9, under the title, "An Anthropologist Looks at Mission-Church Transition." Gratitude is hereby expressed to the publisher for permission to include it here.

pology dead?" and went on to answer, "If you only want to use us as a
research laboratory, yes. If you want to work side by side with us for the
betterment of our ethnic development, no. But then you will have to follow
our directives."

At a Fijian church synod during the war a young missionary was
appointed to replace an old one. The senior Fijian pastor, in welcoming
him, said, "It is not your job to tell us what we need, but to show us how to
get what we want." The young Chairman "got the message." His period
of office was one of rich experiment in new patterns of mission, with new
relationships between nationals and expatriates. Out of this new partnership came many innovations, which neither nationals nor expatriates
could have achieved alone.

Had the old pastor said, "Missionary, go home!" the Church would
have been the loser. As it was new concepts of mission emerged by the
interrelationship. For example, the Fijians saw their responsibility not
only in the internal workings of the Church, but also in the evangelization
of the Fiji Indians. Not long before this another Fijian pastor said to me,
"You people brought the Indians to this land, you evangelize them."[1] I
lived to hear him speak for the motion when the Fijian-controlled synod
appointed a Fijian to the task of Indian evangelism.

I see now that the ongoing mission of the Church was saved by the
change in missionary-national relationships, not by withdrawing missionaries altogether. The success of the Mission-Church transition in Fiji was
due to the pattern of *planned phasing-out and phasing-in* over twenty
years. Had the political development been faster than that of the Church
we may not have had twenty years. Now I look back on them—years of
real organic church growth, as I worked first *over,* then *beside,* and
eventually under Fijian colleagues. I saw Henry Venn's dream[2] of
euthanasia enacted. A mission died and a Church was born.

A NEW AUTONOMOUS ENTITY

There are good spiritual reasons why you do not achieve an indigenous
Church by sending all the missionaries home at one point of time. I have
found a recurring comment in scores of mission records, "We work
towards an indigenous Church—but the time is not yet." Before missionaries leave they must demonstrate their sincerity about these words. They
ought to show the nationals that they believe the time has come, that they
rejoice because of it, and that, if required, they will work as subordinates
under it. They have to demonstrate the role of colleague instead of master,
indeed, even of servant. A mission which departs without that demonstration has presented a defective Gospel. The indigenous Church needs a
period of sharing in which the old missionary-national roles are reversed.

Anthropologically this period of transition, when the young Church is
feeling its new responsibilities, but while the expatriate is still present, is a

dynamic process. Malinowski (1938) used a phrase *"a new autonomous entity"* for what I am describing: a state wherein expatriate and national experience new, interacting and interpenetrating relationships.

In such a Church something of the old ethnic values and forms will tarry, something of the contact institution will be incorporated, the undesirable and obsolete elements of tradition will be purged as also the foreignness and formalism of the contact institution. But the interpenetration of the pure Gospel with purified tradition should lead the participants, not into syncretism, but a new kind of indigenous entity, a unique complex of interactions—a process of church maturation. Here we have a formula:

> Sanctified tarriance and Gospel incorporation, interpenetrating in the sharing process, should lead to indigenous church maturation.

Without some such process I do not see how either (1) the foreignized mission churches can survive (let alone grow), or (2) the reactionary indigenous churches can adequately confront the current dynamic world situation. The formula is not a theory of hypothesis for testing, but an interpretation of observed facts in cross-cultural mission, which I have witnessed and participated in. My own faith, biblical understanding and theology have been enriched by this experience of *new level* interaction with Fijian and Indian fellow Christians.

OTHER SITUATIONS—OTHER PATTERNS

Although the formula is sound, even as a generalization, the pattern of phasing-in and phasing-out is not the only viable way of demonstrating the experience. We must allow for the multiplicity of variant situations where the Mission-Church transition must be effected.

Another possibility is the policy of *Mission-Church Coexistence.* The mission continues to operate as a contact institution, forming new fellowship groups by conversions from the world, organizing them into churches and establishing them as autonomous entities as they come to spiritual and organizational maturity. With each new church unit established the mission moves on further penetrating beyond its present frontier, maybe using the same language, until the whole related large unit is won. Here interaction is between two organizations—Mission and Church—rather than missionary and national within one organization. This offers scope for Mission-Church cooperating in evangelistic thrust. The policy is discussed and evaluated in Read (1965:60-62, 84, 116) where it is called *The Brazil Plan.*

Another possibility for speeding up indigenity, at least on the level of leadership and self-support, is the *pilot project.* An unusually large degree of autonomy is extended to one spiritually innovative village congregation in, say, a large valley of villages. If the efforts of this primary village lead to effective self-sufficiency, the case is bound to become a model for other villages to emulate (Tippett: 1967a:131, 363 n. 12). I am sure there are many other patterns, but their common point is that they are all *processes through time*. They do not permit total missionary withdrawal *at a point of time*.

OBSTRUCTIONS TO INDIGENITY

The movement towards indigenity is obstructed by methodological factors in the policy of the parent mission, and are therefore correctable— but only *through time*. Sudden home decision to force indigenity on a young Church shows up thus:

1. A failure to develop an adequate evangel in the young Church, so that the removal of the missionary terminates missionary outreach.

2. A failure to develop an adequate operating leadership structure that will survive after missionary withdrawal, so that internal affairs drift and the community impact is innocuous.

3. A failure to develop stewardship dimensions adequate for local Christian action within and without the Church.

These weaknesses can only be avoided by a period of planned education (instruction and participation) *on the level of village congregations*. No Church can realize its selfhood without a sense of mission, leadership, stewardship and community responsibility. These are "learned by doing." The virility of some folk churches demonstrates there is no lack of capacity. These "marks of the Church" are prerequisites of autonomy and should be *explored in partnership* by nationals and expatriates in the period of phasing-in and phasing-out.

A period of mission paternalism terminated suddenly by withdrawing funds and personnel brings a familiar cry, "The Mission no longer loves us." Education for autonomy brings a new set of experiences to both parties. If the expatriate is still a foreigner he or she is nevertheless "*our* foreigner." That individual is "one of us"—a designation in Fiji which a foreigner really has to earn. Society gives the foreigner an approved role. He or she is part of the new autonomous entity.

Except where the ax has already fallen to the root of the tree, hope surely lies in this direction. But this new kind of expatriate-national relationship is an individual matter which no home board can determine. Expatriates have to prove themselves and establish their own rapport (which is why training in anthropology is so essential). A person does not achieve this by wearing a pigtail or buying a native garment. It requires a demonstrated and felt empathy, as between two mature adult persons, a respect for the indigenous cultural values, a familiarity with the language, a sharing of the national biases, indeed one must be ready to laugh and shed a tear, and this without affectation. Any trace of insincerity is an obstruction.

THE PRESENT NEED

Clearly the role of the missionary has changed. The old way that was so tied to Colonialism has had its day. It performed many services in spite of its mistakes. Sure, this person has to go home. But the missionary role continues, modified to suit a new day—with the same Gospel message but new ways of communicating it, and new personal relationships involved in the process. To be part of the new autonomous entity requires a real dedication. The opportunity to share in the education and experiment that develops true indigenous autonomy will probably only remain open for a few decades. So much yet remains to be done—and apparently so little time to do it. But for those who can cut themselves off from home and friends and Western values it is exciting as one discovers new spiritual dimensions in cross-cultural adventure under God.

The most urgent need for the immediate present then is not that missionaries should "go home," but that they should look critically at the situation they face and ask themselves if they *dare* go home without responsibly terminating their work. If they have completed plowing and can honestly now take their hands from the plow, maybe they will find another field in the valley beyond.

Notes:

1. Introduced by the Government for cane field labor from 1879. They are now more numerous than the Fijians and somewhat at cross-purposes.

2. Secretary of the Church Missionary Society. He was pressing this idea 130 years ago. See Stock's *History of the Church Missionary Society* (1899).

PART V

Retrospect and Prospect

Retrospect and Prospect

There is something sad about having to write concluding last chapters. It suggests that something is finished, and yet the pilgrimage is far from over. I felt that way when I left the mission field two decades ago. I find myself more involved in mission than ever, for indeed I have shifted from the microcosm to the macrocosm. I recognize the tremendous changes going on in mission—both in its essential theory and in the field situation. Never before was there such interaction, for example, between anthropology and mission; and I wonder if the church at large has ever been so ignorant of what is really going on. Both anthropology and Christian mission are dynamic. They are two balls bouncing against each other, but each itself a complex of bouncing particles.

Every chapter in this *Introduction to Missiology* has been a vignette of my own experience. I now intend to bring it all to a close by looking, in a very personal retrospect, at my own life and how I was influenced by and how I have influenced others in the various dimensions of missiological theory described throughout this book; and by looking forward in propsect of what I believe has to be the role of missiology in our day.

CHAPTER 34

Retrospect:
A Personal Narrative

It took me twenty-five years to become an anthropologist: the hard way. This essential dimension of the missionary preparation was denied me, both unintentionally and deliberately: unintentionally in that it was absent from the curriculum at the theological institution and not taught at the nearby university, and deliberately in that my mission board secretary refused to allow me to correct the shortcoming, either on my way to the field or on my first furlough. On the latter occasion I was told that I had already knowledge of the field and knew the language and that was enough. So what I got in anthropology had to come by the hard way of self-education on a remote island field where there was no library but my own. Anything in the way of books had to be bought from the married missionary's stipend. During my training when money was even scarcer, I had acquired a number of secondhand books by the older anthropologists, which involved me in the controversies of Frazer, McLennan and Lang. I had a little material on the Pacific, but during the war the Americans bought every book on the islands they could lay their hands on and it cost me all the spending money I had for a quarter to get a copy of Mariner's *Tonga* (1827). Because the resources I had were dated, my anthropology tended to follow the historic line through unilinear evolution (which was the base of Comparative Religion at the time I was in training) to diffusionism, and in time to functionalism. I researched in folklore and speculated in interpretation, after the nature of my models, and was especially concerned with the problem of origins, using methods which had already become obsolete. I tried to be systematic and kept careful notes and tried a little writing. Recently, in looking back through, it I was amazed to discover the trail I had blazed for myself through those years. I developed a number of data collecting techniques of my own out of the exigencies of the situations I met, and many of these I still use. They stood up well to the criteria of the university course on research method, which I was denied until 1962.

The significance of the social group, the falsity of trying to deal with an individual isolated from the group, the interrelationship of person and institution, and the general emphases of functionalism, I believe I discovered for myself. I was so close in thought to Malinowski that when I first read him in 1955 he struck me as saying nothing new. The Fijians themselves did something for me. I began to draw new values from the Fijian way of life. In particular the Old Testament became charged with new meaning for me. This was an anthropological discovery as well as a religious experience.

These changes in my anthropological orientation were reflected in my missionary life. I found my way into ethnolinguistics, long before I had met the term. Before I had ever seen an article on the subject I had worked through four or five editions of the Fijian hymnbook and could indicate the linguistic and theological changes and date them. I had traced a dozen or so Fijian word changes through the various editions of the vernacular Scriptures and I could identify a number of early Fijian preachers by their favorite phrases and idioms. I had made a collection of Fijian proverbs and classified them as indigenous or acculturative. I bought a new Fijian dictionary and had it inter-leaved. This has a few hundred words which are not in any other dictionary. Normally I spoke Bauan, but could understand table talk in the dialects of Kadavu and Nadroga and later wrote down some vocabulary and grammatical peculiarities of the Ra dialect. I never did have any training in technical linguistics, but I can point out the errors in the Ph.D. dissertations I have seen on the Fijian language. I always dealt with my informants in their own language and learned to make a note of the indigenous terms for artifacts, institutions and cultural concepts. I do not remember ever being told to do this. I just did it. It seemed to be the right thing to do. I had reason to be thankful for this when I came to write my dissertation some years later.

In 1955 I discovered Edward Sapir. He revolutionized my ideas of diffusion by showing me the pattern in linguistic change. I saw things hanging together in clusters, and change in one aspect being resisted by the others until the whole cluster could change as a totality. This triggered off a whole world of cultural material in my collected but as yet uninterpreted data bank. I began to see the potential of this for interpreting acceptance and rejection in Christian mission. It was a real breakthrough on my missiological journey.

The academic year, 1955-56, had opened up resources for my studying in America for the full calendar year, including the summer. Although my study had to be done under the head of history, I minored in social anthropology and did more coursework in anthropology than in history. This experience not only introduced me to Sapir, but also showed me where I stood in the history of anthropology. A most cooperative professor worked out a summer reading course especially to fill in the gaps in my anthropology. I met a new breed of men: Boas, Kroeber, Linton, Kluckhohn, Radin, Lowie and others. I discovered that anthropology was not an additive science but a reinterpreting one; that each phase in the course of its history has made some real contribution, but has needed a subsequent reinterpretation. (Thus, let me add now, the diffusionist, the salvage anthropologist and the cultural relativist were all essential as marks along the way, but none represents the ultimate goal for the anthropological or missiological adventure.) We simply *must* go by those points if we want to reach the ultimate goal, but we *must not* "bog down" there.

Although my board had paid my traveling expenses and given my wife a furlough allowance, for which I was very thankful, the experience left me very critical of the home Church and board for not providing missionaries with education in anthropology in the first place. My research fellowship was in history (more particularly archival research) and I certainly had to manipulate my program to drag in the anthropological dimension as I did. The section on the anthropological dimension in this book really began with that experience.

Another thing that year did for me was to demonstrate the artificiality of curriculum analysis, which segregates our academic disciplines. I came to the conclusion that one of the greatest offerings of American graduate education was the willingness to explore the interdisciplinary fields. I explored a little in ethnolinguistics and ethnopsychology (as they are now called) with great personal profit. As I look back now on my Fijian anthropological writing, I find a large part of it to have been ethnohistory, although I had not then consciously thought of this as a field of research and its methodology had not been developed.

When I returned again to serve in my missionary field I had all kinds of new dimensions to explore. I was no longer in the village situation, but had been put in charge of theological training. This confronted me with the question of the relevance of the training program for the rural and urban situation where the graduates would serve. The Fijians and not the missionaries had appointed me and set the goals. Then they gave me a free hand to innovate.

I was convinced that the old approach had to go. Our theology was related to historical controversies in the west. I tried to relate it to such things as confronting the Fiji Hindu, who found the incarnation in a mythical poem rather than a historic event, for example. Our ethics confused Western and Christian ethics. Our mission history was missionary centered and classified data. I highlighted the national evangelists and pastors and tried to make it dynamic, a dimension in which I had previously experimented in the Bible School and it had involved me in organized archival research. This removed the old promotional distortion of the secondary sources written for home supporters. A number of long standing courses were discarded and new ones which related to the island world were substituted, including one on anthropology. As long as I was there and afterwards until the supplies of my lecture notes ran out, the indigenized curriculum was continued.

A functional curriculum which demanded relevance at every point meant rejecting many old concepts of mission. A missiological approach (as distinct from a home church one) was emerging through the demands of the situation itself. The missionaries had handed over their power to the nationals and the latter were disposed to demand new things. They knew the socioreligious situation and saw the need of speaking to all aspects of its diversity. This is an aim of the interdisciplinary approach, and in this case the new discipline is missiology. I shared my business with those who had assigned me to it. At synod time, the students prepared a display of projects and demonstrations for the benefit of the older ministers at the synod. There was material to hand out, such as they could themselves use. For my last five years they supported the new approach. They gave me everything I asked for. We began to build a library such as had not been there before. The whole thing was financed from local funds. At this time all my most intimate friends were Fijians. I so learned to worship in Fijian that I have never been comfortable in English since. If I went on to write down all those things which had brought me close to the Fijians and opened the way for sharing on the most confidential level, and those moments when we had together drawn nearest to God, the page would be colored with anthropological dimensions. I do not mean to say that an individual is saved by anthropology, but if God communicates to humans through humans and the humans involved are of different cultures, one at least will have to make some adjustments for that message to get across. Then, after twenty years, I found I had more power than was good for me and the realization frightened me. For years I had advocated the authority of the indigene and the subordinate role of the missionary, and to be consistent I had to admit my day was done.

Should I go home to a pastorate, or transfer to another field, or do some further study or write. Eventually, the way to the wider world mission opened. I teamed up with Donald McGavran. We had been working on similar problems from way back in the early fifties, especially the place of the people movement in conversion. We have a number of points of fundamental agreement and regard each other as fellow church growth missiologists.[1] Our differences would be in presuppositions, methodology and presentation. After ten years, hundreds of missionaries and many nationals from scores of countries and denominations have studied with us. Thousands have been contacted in conferences and seminars, both in America and overseas. I have studied churches and peoples in other lands, like the Solomon Islands, Mexico, Ethiopia, Kenya and Guatemala, and worked on mission records in archives and libraries in Hawaii, Fiji, Australia, New Zealand, as well as in this country, always with the reinforcement of this dual conviction: that on the one hand we have the cultural diversity of human societies, and on the other the commonality of their problems.[2] The church growth case studies (which are the data base of church growth theory) have pinpointed both these features in such a way as to show their significance for the Christian mission. So the research program, first at Oregon and now at Pasadena, has played a formative role in exploring new dimensions of missiology.[3] Some of the early studies at Oregon helped to pinpoint really significant principles for the new discipline of missiology.

The three years I spent in Oregon placed me in a juxtaposition of two very different worlds: the anthropological world of the university and the missionary realm of McGavran, who was in his own Disciples of Christ stronghold. I lived in a state of intense psychological tension at many levels. However, several things came out of the experience. If I did anything for church growth and for missiology, it was to validate it in terms of anthropology. At the university I undertook a heavy reading program in addition to coursework. The most transforming concept I found was Homer Barnett's *recombination theory*, which is the basis of his *Innovation: The Basis of Cultural Change* (1953). Once again, I already had all the data. Everything fell into place. The same book led me to a few good sources, one of them Sherif (1936), the psychologist. Wallace's revitalization thesis (1956) and van Gennep's rites of passage (1960), to mention just a couple, were structures which helped me to say what I was trying to articulate across the road. Barnett himself was a tremendous person and I took every course I could under him. I went further in such studies as religion and magic and in anthropological theory, and found myself reacting one way to White and another way to Bidney. This was a mind stretching experience. For comprehensives I had to read much from those aspects of anthropology which say little to Christian mission, but perhaps that was a good discipline and a necessary hurdle *en route* to the degree. I came out of it with a firm conviction that the missiology needed for the Christian mission in the world of tomorrow could not be articulated without the conceptual structures of social and theoretical anthropology; and what is more, that missiology itself is a form of applied anthropology, as my colleague Charles Kraft calls it now—ethnotheology.

Having taken out my degree at Oregon, McGavran's Institute offered me a permanent position. I undertook a field research study in the Solomon Islands. I also had two other invitations in America and one in the islands, although my heart was to teach missions in Australia—a door which never did open, though I tried my best to open it. I wanted to be sure the islands were not still too strong in my blood before saying "yes" to a permanent church growth assignment. The Solomons disillusioned me. I would not have believed the same Colonial Office could have handled two island situations so differently, or my own Church have so differently served such similar fields. I now became aware of the temporal element in mission history and the variant theological weightage (Lowie's word) of periods in the same Church and the significance of this in the pioneering thrust. This led me to reconsider the differences between the Fijian and Indian Churches in Fiji, a thing that had always puzzled me. I developed this idea later under the term *time perspective*. I lived in a leaf house in the Solomons and collected material enough for three or four books. The actual report, though I cut it down considerably, was published as *Solomon Islands Christianity* (1967a), and was very well reviewed, both in England and America. This was encouraging because it showed that critical persons were ready to look at Christian mission as a missiological study with a strong anthropological dimension.

The Solomon Islands project introduced a new dimension into my own researches. In Fiji I was operating as a missionary. I had a certain inside information, a status and an authority. I was provided with living quarters and was well-known in the community. In the Solomons I operated as an anthropologist, lived in leaf houses, and although I was known to be a Christian, in the west my missionary connections were not disclosed and in the east the missions were different denominations from my own. This experience convinced me of two things: (1) the missionary cannot do without the anthropologist and (2) the anthropologist cannot do without the missionary. They observe through different doors and neither sees the whole without the other. Somehow this bifocality has to be injected into missiology.

The other thing that came out of the Solomon Islands project was the possibility of observing a town emerging where a few years ago there was merely an airstrip. Here in microcosm were all the principles of population mobility, urbanization, settlement formation that are basic in the current missionary context in this changing world. More concentrated research into this kind of development should help us pinpoint significant trends and values for new kinds of mission.

Missiology differs from the old study of missions in that it is dynamic, not static. It has to be observed in motion. As long as we are concerned with such dynamic situations we need never feel we have come to the end of the adventure. Like the Navaho weaver, who for fear of finality leaves an unfinished unit in the design or a path of escape, we weave our missiology by bringing together a multitude of threads from many sources with new colors and ideas. As long as anthropology is dynamic, missiology, which borrows from it, will also be dynamic. Only the base on the loom is constant or continuous, and this it seems to me is the biblical concept of mission itself.

Every new project widens the missiological vista. There was the trip to Mexico with the CGRILA team. These men were to research over the whole of Latin America and this was a two week trial, concentrating on interviewing techniques and programming. We were to investigate the kind of approaches to use, the type of responses to expect and the situations to avoid. Although instructional and experimental, it did provide me with two weeks of good data collecting and permitted my working out some standard, structured interview patterns and schedules. I realized the importance of instructing missionaries in data collecting methods, if they were to be engaged in church growth surveys. As I watched the CGRILA program in operation, though I had only a remote connection with it, I found it a learning experience. Not a quarter of the collected data got into the final report, and the complex editorial process eliminated some essential qualifying statements, and we had a lot to learn about project controls. I discovered the difference between individual and team projects. My own Mexican data has never been written up as a study, but a great many episodes and small research items have been used for illustration in lectures and seminars.

Mexico introduced me to the low flying small aircraft as a useful means for observation from a convenient height. It is amazing how the processes of human activity can be observed in this manner. You see how people live, how settlements develop, how agricultural patterns change. It helps one to fix in his mind the scope of cultural change going on. I had the same experience again in Ethiopia and have described it at length in the book *Peoples of Southwest Ethiopia* (1970b).

The Ethiopian visit was to survey the tribal situations where the Presbyterians have recently commenced work. It represents an aspect of missiology in the early stage of a mission before there have been any responses to the Gospel. It was a quick survey of the basic anthropology of the region which resulted in a written description with suggestions as to what kind of problems might be anticipated when the people begin responding to the Christian mission. Its motive was partly to prevent mistakes.

For the Episcopalians several visits have been made to Navaho country: sometimes to look at specific problems and sometimes for a general report, or maybe a consultation of some kind. I had a trip to Guatemala for a Maya Indian pastors' conference, where one had to "shift gears" and speak to nationals rather than missionaries. This, of course, called for vastly different subject matter and I found myself back in "Fiji" again in the evangelical and pastoral situation. I made no attempt to talk the missionary idiom, although a good number of them were present. I had the opportunity of visiting a couple of country gatherings and doing a little anthropological research which permits some comparisons with other Indian groups I have studied a little.

Another feature of missiological activity we meet in Pasadena is the opportunity to attend conferences, consultations, lectures and seminars and to contribute to them: all this quite apart from the regular course work of the School of World Mission.

I have concentrated on the place of anthropology in my personal narrative of adventure in missiology, as this was where my specific concern lay as Professor of Missionary Anthropology, but my second string is history, and academically I "piggy-backed" into anthropology on history. A great deal of the writing I did in Fiji for my own pleasure and for the benefit of the Fijian people themselves was an ethnohistorical approach to Christian mission. History played a major role in establishing the young independent Church in Fiji. With independence came a series of significant centenaries, for which I had to provide the basic data. I found it possible to reconstruct the events from the archives throwing the focus on the role of the nationals at many points. This was received with great enthusiasm and did much in consolidating the newly independent Church. Many articles I wrote in the Fijian language, and some were reprinted as brochures for distribution at the centenary celebrations. I discovered how precious is tradition to a traditional society. The sooner they have a body of local church history of their own the sooner they rise above their old pre-Christian mythology. I would that all pioneer missionaries would record the story of their converts rather than the history of a foreign mission.

Missiology, to recapture the true dimensions of the earlier periods, needs to be aware of the primary sources. Many of these are in the family possessions of the later generations. Many are forgotten. There needs to be a large scale drive to collect old journals and records for proper preservation. Miss Loomis' splendid book on the first decade of the Hawaiian mission (1966), so essential for the correction of Michener's unfortunate novel (1959), was the result of an almost accidental discovery of the old journal of her ancestor who was in this missionary party as the printer.

Recently I did a survey of the resources of the archives and libraries of my area: Fiji, Hawaii, Australia and New Zealand. In any one of these locations one could settle down for a lifetime of historical research. Record after record throws light on how churches were planted and what happened to them at all periods of history. These are records of live people. We see the missionaries in encounter with whalers, sandalwooders and sea captains. You suddenly discover why things happened as they did, and therefore how the churches developed in the forms they now manifest. And so often these discoveries speak out of history to present situations and policies.

I suppose the greatest discovery of the recent trip was the increased accessibility of historical documents. With the passing of colonial restrictions records are now open for inspection. A book has recently been written in Fiji on the vexed question of Fiji lands. It is almost entirely documented from Lands Commission Reports, hitherto so secret that one could not in any way break through the barrier. This research throws a great deal of new light on the subject, but it can never be anything but a biased account until the mission records also are made available. This is the kind of material missiologists must root out and classify and evaluate in order that historians be not misguided by one non-mission repository of documents. The tendency has been to dismiss mission documents as biased. Of course they are. So is every other documentary source. The art of using documents is to discover the bias, allow for it and distinguish between the bias and the recorded facts.

The shift from mission to Church, from missionary to national, from dependency to indigenity, the general change of temper in our post-war mission world, with new features each decade, demands a rewriting of mission history—not because it was wrong but because it was partial, intended only to meet the stresses of the day gone by, never to return. The real stuff of history, that has to be recovered from the past in our day, and research must speak to the new world in such a way that the new can discover that it has real roots in the past, and that it may "inherit the promises." This kind of material cannot be had from the secondary sources, for they were written for other requirements. Our missiologists have to go back into the primary sources and discover for themselves what the documents say for our day and generation. What do the church planters of history have to say to us today? Can the old dynamism be rediscovered in historical research and applied to the new trends in missionary technique?

The church growth case study is a diachronic exercise. It has to be reconstructed from the records, statistics, minutes and journals. It has to be reliably researched at many points of time. Church growth case studies are the data base of the church growth theory. One case study may prove nothing; but when twenty or thirty of them present a similar combination of facts and responses, then the historical research has indicated at least a trend or tendency. You cannot study long-range processes through time without developing historical methods, criteria and values. We cannot set up control experiments today to study a hundred years of growth in artificial situations where the variables have been eliminated. We can only get a century of data by going back into the past, after the event. Not only are we dependent on historical methods for the true facts, but we need enough cases for comparison. If we get enough cases and they all indicate the same thing that will be hard to disprove. Furthermore, there is always something artificial about the control experiment. It has great value for certain kinds of study, but the longer the time of the experiment the more difficult to control. Church growth calls for long-range analysis. Long-range culture change studies after the event are not artificial, depending on the skill of the experimenter to eliminate or control factors. They are a real thing that happened that way. All the factors are in the situation. If twenty cases manifesting the same general combination of factors produce the same kind of statistical response that is about all we can expect. If the historical researching is accurate, history has done her duty.

I do not agree with those who underrate historical research because it is reconstructed after the event and cannot be tested by experiment, as for example the evaluation: "unfortunately there is no clinically controlled evidence for successful (people) movements in virgin situations where good rather than bad methods were applied."[4] Without decrying the control experiment method of research, which I think could well be more used for church growth studies, especially at the perfecting level, the experimental and historical methods should not be confused or set one against the other. If there is something to be gained in one case by experimentally controlling variables, there is something in the other in knowing you are dealing with a total thing without a manipulating experimenter. I have never yet found an experimenter who has been able to control the operation of the Holy Spirit. Furthermore, we can produce cases where the same missionary society, using the same patterns, with missionaries trained in the same theology, under the same salary and employment pattern, and supported by the same praying people and working among remarkably similar ethnic groups, have yet experienced different rates of organic growth in indigenity. Historical research has revealed only one difference: namely, an operating policy difference on the level of missionary paternalism. This is reflected numerically in the graphs of organic and perfection growth and the instability of the adherent figures. Much can be demonstrated by historical methods. True, it cannot always be turned on to order, but it is amazing what the archives do preserve.

I have never yet spent a day in any of the archives I have frequented without finding some valuable data demonstrating some key church growth principles. The case I have just cited, which demonstrated the effect of missionary paternalism as a retarder of the development of indigenous leadership, and an instability among the fringe members, was originally prepared in the form of comparative graphs for examination at the Consultation on Church Growth at Iberville, Canada. I have also presented it in the form of comparative tables showing the ratios of lay preachers, leadership roles and ministers to the congregational member-ship in the two indigenous churches concerned.[5] When the W.C.C. invited McGavran, Pickett and myself to that Consultation they assigned us each some specific task. I was asked to prepare a set of statistical presentations, one of which was to show a long-range picture in which a long period of nongrowth was changed into a growing situation at a point of deliberate policy change in missionary methods. I had no difficulty in providing this and used a type of graph that made it so obvious that not a single question was asked.[6]

To use the historical method for this kind of verification implies one or two prerequisites: (1) The researcher must have set out to master the history of the church being examined. You do not just pull these tricks out of the hat. They are not just illustrative snippets from your reading. They are the result of solid research and testing. (2) Neither do you normally get them from secondary historical studies. You have to know your way about the primary sources. That means you have already devoted many hours to verifying facts which others consider a waste of time. I have held up a publication for as many as six years to find the data for the verification of a single paragraph—sometimes to the chagrin of those who have wanted the text. (3) This kind of research presupposes that the church concerned did make records (statistics, minute books, membership rolls, annual reports, etc.,) or that the missionaries wrote letters home, or kept journals, or wrote reports. It also presupposes that you can obtain access to them. (4) Arising from the last point of accessibility of documents, this presupposes that you are willing to seek them out. These are not fruit on trees for plucking. There may be archives of the mission where you can start, but not everybody is this fortunate. One has to be as relentless as the "Hound of Heaven" in the search for documents. (5) A really good study of the "personality" and growth of a church takes many years to write. Most of our church growth studies have been done in a year or two. This means that they are all "research in progress." They are "hypotheses, suggested by the limited data, and now up for testing." The majority of the findings will stand the test, but every new piece of research on the same or an allied theme may mean we have to update our own. Or a newly discovered resource from a non-missionary authority may introduce a value you had not allowed for, and may call for the insertion of a paragraph or footnote. The historical method as we need to use it in missiology is a relentless, exacting, time consuming task, but there is nothing more satisfying than the confidence you have in the ultimate result.

The more one pursues the missionary document the more one is astonished at the quantity of material that awaits discovery. Some day I hope to write a biography of a Fijian missionary named Lorimer Fison. For some years I have been building up a checklist of his manuscript and published material, noting where it is preserved, copying and microfilming when possible. My current list comprises 140 items in four different countries, in official, government, missionary, university and private collections, and every one of these documents says something to the Christian mission although they were not all written with that intention. These concern one Fijian missionary. How many must exist over a century and a third?

I can produce Fiji data for, say, the statistical decline of church leadership in the seventies of the last century due to the measles epidemic, because I know my way through the documents. I can produce three independent archival sources to check against each other.

I have just classified the subject matter of some sermons from A.B.C.F.M. officials and Hawaiian missionaries between 1820 and 1850 so I can evaluate the miserable distortion of James Michener's fictional sermon in the novel *Hawaii*. I learned a great deal about the structure and content of the Calvinist congregational preaching that I did not know before, and now I know how Michener capitalized on a current twentieth century image of puritanism and projected it back in a manner I consider most unscrupulous. What I am saying here is that the material was available, if I had the time and patience to search it out just to prove a point, though in this particular case my search took me to Hawaii and to Yale before I found it.

The historical dimension of missiology has some fantastic possibilities for the patient and critical researcher. When I am too old for the work of a field anthropologist I shall gladly retire to the archives and search out the glorious data of God in action in missionary endeavor that has hitherto escaped my notice. In the meantime I would point out that while we are trying to cover a number of fields for some degree of specialized reading, I have always felt that a missiologist ought to get really immersed in one region and master it thoroughly—and which one better than that in which he can speak the language and show empathy with the cultural values.

That is a suitable place to end the personal narrative. Let me now turn to sum up my feelings with respect to missiology in general and the direction I believe it should take in the years which lie immediately ahead. I recognize that my basic concern is in Oceania, and that this area I have set out to understand is but a small part of the world and has a minute portion of its population. My colleagues speak for India, China, Korea, Latin America and Africa. So let the vision be widened a little.

Notes:

1. We have strong points of agreement in such things as the biblical base of the Christian mission, the place of the Church in the mission of God, the nature of people movement conversions, the great number of present day opportunities for mission and their urgency, the Christian responsibility for good stewardship, the significance of church statistics (not to be gloried in, not an end in themselves, but a useful tool for measuring the state of the church) and many other principles of the church growth viewpoint.

2. This idea has been developed by Goldschmidt (1966:30-31) in his study of comparative functionalism. While recognizing the validity of the methods of functional analysis and statistical comparisons, nevertheless he wants to go further beyond the institutions to the social problems with which they deal, and to study the solutions from society to society.

3. The method has been criticized by some who ask for control experiments rather than after-the-event studies. However, the church growth studies have revealed commonalities, which when acted on in static situations have led to growth. The proof of the pudding is in the eating.

4. Cf. James A. Scherer's review article of McGavran's *Understanding Church Growth* (1970:130). I think he misuses the term "clinical" in any case.

5. Used in a lecture on "The Relationship of Social and Religious Change and the Missionary Role in it" published in *Verdict Theology in Missionary Theory* (1973a:108).

6. The twelve graphic presentations I prepared are now found in the bound manuscript *The Acceptance and Rejection of Christianity* (1964b).

CHAPTER 35

Prospect:
The Relevance of Missiology

Quite apart from the relevance of mission to the Christian because of the mandate of Our Lord, recorded in Scripture, and the purpose of the Father to save mankind, which cannot be rejected or bypassed without rejecting or bypassing Scripture itself, there are very good practical reasons for the scientific study of mission—i.e. missiology. Mankind has been described as "incurably religious." We have already discussed the integrative function of religion in society. In doing this we have seen that in some special way religion has to make itself relevant in a multitude of quite different forms of society. It has to be part of the cultural process. It has to relate to a particular world—or to many different particular worlds. We have here a complex or configuration for religion which demonstrates both a *universality* and a *particularity*. Missiology in our day has this precise business of finding the ways and means of applying the universality of the Great Commission to the multitudinous particularities of human society.

As Edward Sapir said:

Religion (said Edward Sapir) in some sense is everywhere present. . . . Religion is man's never-ceasing attempt to discover a road to spiritual serenity across the perplexities and dangers of daily life. . . . Where the need for such serenity is passionately felt, we have a religious yearning; where it is absent religious behaviour is . . . a socially sanctioned form. . . . What constitutes serenity must be answered afresh for every culture and for every community—in the last analysis, for every individual. Culture defines for every society, the world in which it lives (1949b:346-347).

In that same work, Sapir continues to speak of the expectations in any given society as having a religion that will "awaken and overcome the feelings of danger, of individual helplessness, that is *proper to that particular world. . . .*" (emphasis mine). If we take Sapir's insight with respect to religion *per se,* and apply it to Christian missiology, I think the anthropologist says two things: (1) everywhere mankind has a real interest and concern about religion, and (2) individuals are entitled to a religion which speaks to their needs and is meaningful within their particular cultural world. Sapir does not discuss any such thing as a universal religion, but the universality of religion. He is not talking about Christianity, but I am asking what his concept means by implication to those of us who say that Christ is the Savior of the World. He implies just this: that we cannot claim any universality for the Christian religion without also demonstrating its particularity. If there is to be a Christian mission to the world, there has to be a scientific missiology to discover and demonstrate the ways and means of communicating and relating meaningfully in cultural forms very different from those of the West. The function of missiology in our day and generation, then, is to show that *Christianity can be universal by being particular.*

It has to be theological because its message is theological. It has to be anthropological because it deals with mankind, the wide world over. It has to be historical because it concerns divine action in and through time. It also has to explore other disciplines if they bear on Christian mission in any way: for example, conversion is a psychological process, and cross-cultural conversion badly needs researching. It has to explore many of the interdisciplinary areas—ethnolinguistics, ethnohistory, ethnopsychology and ethnotheology. If you stand back and look at this in perspective it becomes perfectly clear that missiology is now a precise discipline by its own rights, and I do not see how the Christian mission can face the new era in mission without recognizing this fact.

Another feature of mission in the new era will simply have to be a greater recognition of the significance of the *human group.* The period of modern missions has been dominated by the concept of individualism, and yet if you examine the localities where the Church has grown and where strong indigenous Churches have emerged it has been *growth by group* that has been most used by the Holy Spirit. Not until, confronted by this, you return to the Scriptures and go into the matter carefully, do you discover that the Church grew that way from the beginning. Another function of missiology, then, is to take a good look at the way groups of people have been brought into the Faith, and revived the Faith. History gives us much material for study and anthropology has given us tools and concepts for research. Concepts like Barnett's recombination theory, van Gennep's rites of passage and Wallace's revitalization study have indicated a real positive value of anthropology for our research and discipline. I do not see how there can ever be a missiology without this kind of theoretical base.

Over the twenty years of our own institutional history at the School of World Mission we have explored some of these dimensions ourselves. I believe we have done some original work that will stand the test of time, especially in the areas of description, classification and culture change. In the latter we have analysed at some depth the nature of the people movement and smaller group movements, and have taken a good look at the functional substitute as a means of transition from the old way to an abiding new way. In these group studies special attention has been paid to the role of the individual, with the result that we start the new era in mission with a different kind of individual. We have discarded the *individual in isolation* and made him the *individual in context.* This makes all the difference between a *static* and *dynamic* view of group movements. The old view of the individual made the group movement a "mass movement." We now recognize it as multi-individual.

In the "road to survival" for mankind at any level the hope has to be seen in the idea of *group entity.* There is plenty of room for individuals in this, but an individual who operates as an isolate is an iconoclast. Both in anthropology and in history we discover humans as religious creatures in a dynamic, diachronic, social context. As a social creature he or she activates and is activated in one or more multi-individual group situations. These multi-individual groups in turn interact in still larger multi-group contexts, whose relationships are in a continual state of change, through which, while accepting change, they nevertheless strive for the perpetuity of the group entity. Each group is unique or particular, despite the commonalities of the personalities who comprise them; but the personalities cannot be extracted from their unique cultural contexts. If the Christian mission is to be vital and make a relevant witness in these multi-individual and multi-group contexts, relating to the social patterns in which the people operate and satisfying their felt needs, missiology will have to set its course in this direction.

This should not be difficult because the whole idea of Church is based on the same concept of corporality. Our Lord set out to establish a small community of followers, who remained after his physical departure, and to whom he gave the commission to world mission. I believe we are committed to "teach them to observe all things whatsoever I have commanded you," which would have included our Lord's references to them as a flock—a corporate body. The parable of the lost sheep indicates the seriousness of the loss of even a single member of the flock, and therefore the importance of the preservation of its entity; and the Last Supper reference to the "little flock" suggests its ultimate destiny. This agrees with the general tenor of the New Testament, which leads us to expect the necessity of the Church going on "until he comes." The Church as a corporate, witnessing, serving body in the world must go on. As the Gospel spreads across ethnic barriers, it follows that new fellowships must emerge. Churches must be planted. Persons brought to Christ must be incorporated into fellowships. The Church must be there in the situation. To be culturally relevant its form will differ from place to place; but there must be a fellowship there—a Church, which is the Body of Christ, ministering the love and mind and word of Christ in that place in a culturally meaningful manner. Because in our day we are responsible for effective witness to our own day and generation, we need a science of missiology to bring into relationship our scriptural mandate and our anthropological resources. This is part of our being good stewards in the service of the Lord. A good steward is one who is responsible in the use of special knowledge and skills in the service of a master. This is a biblical concept, and we might well ask what the Lord expects of his anthropologist-steward.

Social anthropology takes a holistic view of society. It sees people and groups integrated by sets of relationships based on roles, functions and values. Action is going on through these relationships. At the same time the total complex is undergoing change (due to both external and internal factors). The functional operation and interplay of roles are part of the decision making process by which the society can bring about changes within itself without destroying itself. Thus the theoretical model we have from social anthropology is dynamic, not static. The study of a new movement of religious change (say, the conversion of a tribal group from animism to Christianity) is thus a perfectly valid subject for anthropological enquiry. Although the anthropologist and missionary are approaching this study from different standpoints they are concerned with the same data and processes, and they should be able to share resources and information.

When we structuralize a culture pattern, we have a static, abstracted, idealized form. In collecting data we discover that, although informants validate the *ideal* pattern they admit many aberrations in the *real* behavior. The study of deviation from the ideal pattern is extremely important for the missiologist, who has to interpret the effectiveness or ineffectiveness of the Christian mission for the missionary. The interconnected, interdependent microsystem we call the culture pattern reflects certain traditional values. To find ourselves in a moral system different from our own makes us aware of more than merely formal differences. The more we enter into cross-cultural studies at depth, the more we realize that we are dealing with the people of another microsystem and see that we are ourselves ethnocentric and possibly paternalistic also. Until we have felt the shock of this discovery we are not ready to start with missiological research. This is the first thing that anthropology can do for us.

To this end it has provided us with many valuable tools and methods, so that most of our data collecting and research is strongly conditioned by anthropology. It has also given us a technical vocabulary, which I believe will more and more become the terminology of missiology, because unless we master it we cannot draw on the full resources of anthropology. Anthropology itself has some strong values which need to be transmitted to the missiologist (I do not mean just the theories and frames of reference which I have already mentioned), values which are the result of observed situations. For example, there is the fact of cultural diversity. How often one reads an article from some mission theorist appealing for unity, confusing unity for uniformity, and indeed a divisive rather than a unifying word, because it refuses to recognize the diversity of human groups within the larger whole. Or again, there is the notion of the basic orderliness of the human group, that mankind likes to operate within patterns, so that even the most "primitive" people may have the most elaborate and orderly kinship and marriage patterns. I suppose one could work out a table of a dozen or so of these basic notions. We might call them *the axioms of missiology*. At base they are anthropological observations.

We must follow by this route, yet we must not stop here or we will all end up cultural relativists. It is true that human groups are extremely diverse and that in some way these groups should all be able to be themselves. But if that is the end of the journey there is little hope for the minority group in the modern world. The applied anthropologist fully recognizes this. The post-war world has impressed us with the inevitability of culture change—whether directed or otherwise. The society with a static model is doomed before acculturation. The function of applied anthropology in this situation is to discover mechanisms whereby these societies can change, modify, adapt, without disintegrating. Anthropological research seeks out information about the decision making roles, group acceptances and rejections, innovation and so forth. By adding the dimension of ethnohistory the anthropologist recaptures models which worked in crisis periods in history; discovering humans constructing and reconstructing their own systems to meet the changing situations and crises of their experiences. So the new set of questions that emerge from anthropological research are usually precisely the same as interrogate us in missiology. How do societies change? How are decisions made? How are situations redefined? How do people respond to conflicting situations? How are new ventures or modifications proposed, tested, rejected or accepted? How do new roles develop to meet changing relationships? In other words, anthropology is concerned with the processes of culture and culture change. It also investigates how much of that change is inherent in the organization itself, how much is imposed from outside, (1) by directed change, (2) by historic accident, (3) by cultural borrowing; and whether the acceptances have the same meaning they had to the advocate.

Therefore, the post-war situation has brought home to us in both anthropology and missiology two dimensions that the older anthropologists (the cultural relativists) did not recognize. First, there is the recognition of the inevitability of change. The world shrinkage due to the speeding up of communication and facilities for travel and interaction has led to rapid acculturation, and technological advance has led to modernization. Second, there is the incompatibility of traditional society and the modern world. The idea emerges clearly that group survival depends on the utilization of the forces of acculturation. It is a case of acceptance or extinction. If you cannot resist the stream you learn to navigate through it. Urbanization, industrialization, the money economy and Western education, to mention a few of many, are factors which have to be utilized for survival. In such a world cultural relativism is unrealistic. The little island that wants to live its own life in the Solomon Group, can do this only at the price of extinction. The best it can do is to forego its own human rights and come in with the larger islands which will ultimately become the nation. The only freedom it has is the freedom to sell its soul to survive.

Yet anthropology had to come into the present by way of cultural relativism, because it was only thus it could escape its own ethnocentricism, and speak for the minority groups. By coming this route anthropology can say now: "Sure, to survive in the modern world, you will have to accept the modern world—but we'll see that in the process of modernization forced on you, that nothing will be taken from you that can be preserved, and we shall do all in our power to see that your entity is preserved." The anthropologist today has a mighty heavy responsibility before God at this point; because, having come this route, none knows better the awful alternatives of acceptance or extinction for the small traditional society.

Now, what does this mean for missiology? It means two things—maybe more. First, the missiologist must start with the anthropologist by passing through what Goldschmidt calls "the relativistic phase" and for the reason he gives "to relieve us of the habit of evaluating cultures in terms of our own culturally determined predilections." Then he adds that having done this we must "divest ourselves of too rigid a cultural relativism" (1966:138-139). To this motive of self-correction I would add the need to see positively what real values there are in the other culture. In the School of World Mission we have used F.E. Williams' ideas for directing change, which differentiate between things to discard, things to preserve, and things to modify (1951). Before I had read Williams I had used this identical pattern, using a biblical allegory, for presenting a program of change to the chiefs of Bau, Fiji. They responded well because the proposal was reformative but not iconoclastic. Another reason why the anthropologists have been turning away from cultural relativism lies in the current exigency, the state of the world and the desire for universal criteria and values. Without doubt the anthropologist and missiologist are exploring the same fields.

Second, the reader will recall that I have cited half a dozen anthropologists who have worked on the subject of religion and its place as integrator or governor in the social organization. These have provided me with some useful integrative models which adequately interpreted the material I had collected and documented—and, more importantly, the religious field situations of my face to face encounters. Furthermore, I elaborated some of them diagrammatically, to permit them to interpret dynamic situations. The current mood among the younger anthropologists is against the old static models. They seek for models to describe culture changes, flexibility of choice, decision making process, etc. (Smith and Fischer 1970:35). Once again we are seen to be travelling in the same direction and searching for similar tools. Once again, however, I must add, that the models I have found useful for depicting religious change could never have been created had I not come first by the route of the static model of societal integration. An individual has to see a society as an integrated thing at a hypothetical static moment, before he or she can study it in a time sequence and discover just what is going on in the process of culture change. Thus I can (and do) give a lecture entitled "Church Growth as Process." I do not see how you can describe a process without a static model of a system from which to start. Thus our theoretical problems and our processing analyses in anthropology and missiology are interpreting the same kind of phenomenological data. Once again the study of the conversion of a tribe of animists to Christianity is a legitimate project for anthropological research.

In a study of this type we would use the standard anthropological data collecting methods, storing and classifying our material after approved patterns. We would test our data against other material in the data bank and the library resources, and farm some things out for feedback and re-evaluation. We would consult the resources of other disciplines. Ours is a problem solving program, which starts with identifying the problem and finishes with recommendations for the modification of missionary policy. For cross-cultural problems, no discipline can help us better in these respects than anthropology.

Now that applied anthropology, like other branches of science, is professionally committed to the betterment of society, the notion of directed change has become respectable. Under various terms—technical aid, development, technical advice, education, medical aid, agricultural development, rehabilitation programs and humanization programs—under all kinds of sponsorship, deliberate and programmed changes are brought about in the name of social betterment and "progress." This current outpouring of conscience on the part of the affluent nations toward their poorer, less fortunate and "underdeveloped" brothers and sisters has been possible because of the shift from cultural relativism. Mankind has realized the change which has to be made in traditional societies if they are to survive in our world. Anthropology has considered this situation and has laid down some criteria for operation. The situation is recognized as inevitable. This inevitability demands directed change, and this carries ethical responsibility. Many things have to be safeguarded. Goal change must not be allowed to throw the society into dysequilibrium. Those in control must not override the people of the society. Good advice may be

---

more likely in team operations. The target group must be the ultimate decision maker. Directed change should not be attempted from a distance: it requires contact and rapport, and is based on field work. Theoretical reports are related to the ongoing program, with advocate-innovator feedback. Data is collected by interviewing, observation, schedules, questionnaires and systematic sampling—the regular methods, and the data is put at the service of the people concerned. The difference between this procedure and the normal anthropological research is that here the society being researched is not an object for investigation, but has a participant role and has access to the results of the investigation in a way that helps its decision making.

Missiological research is heading in this same direction in the sense that reports are made available and frequently discussed by groups of national leaders and missionaries or committees of newly independent churches, but we still have a long way to go. One thing is clear, however, namely, that the changed tempo and conditions under which the mission of God goes forward in our time, calls for a great deal of research of a new and participant character.

Most of the published material from the anthropological side is quite silent about missions. Not long ago anthropologists made a scapegoat of the whole missionary image. In their research they visited mission stations and got access to records and tapped the experiences of the resident missionary, they used mission-trained translators, and when they learned the language they used vocabulary or dictionaries prepared by the missionaries, they asked the missionaries to open doors to resources and persons. Some acknowledged their debt. Others built the missionary into their lectures as the scapegoat. The missionary has been the victim of barbed wit and all sorts of unscientific generalization. The anthropologist who talks this way today is dated. I believe that one reason for this is that the emergence of the science of applied anthropology has led to a realization that even an anthropological training does not provide all the answers and that the most valuable thing in developing a sound theory is actual prolonged field experience. Many applied anthropologists have met all kinds of technical defeat—from building dams to convincing people to plant a new kind of corn. The destruction of the missionary image is left now to the novelist, the undergraduate and the anthropological small fry. So my hope is that the old day of the salvage anthropologists has gone by.

In the meantime many missionaries have emerged with anthropological training. There has been a healthier criticism—healthier because it has come from within. The missionary has not always been self-defensive. Thousands have exposed themselves to criticism for the sake of better methodology. The most valuable missionary literature of today is intensely self-critical and anthropologically orientated. Several practical journals have emerged that bring anthropology to bear on mission. But all these things come from within the missionary world itself.

Anthropology, although it opens its conferences to us and makes way for any who will contribute papers, never has become reconciled to the idea of helping the missionary. Applied anthropology will help the agriculturalist, the health worker, the veterinarian, the educator and the Peace Corps, but it is still "touchy" about mentioning the missionary. Yet the creed of the missionary is no more philosophically loaded than that of the doctor or the educator, and no more disturbing to the traditional social structures and values. Most of the doctors I have met in cross-cultural situations and a good many of the teachers cannot speak the local language, and one wonders how the former can share an emotional experience with the patient and how the latter can be sure the meaning communicated is the one intended. Yet one must presuppose the labors of the former in hygiene and healing are an improvement on those of the shaman (psychologically I am not so sure), and those of the latter will speed the country to maturity (maturity being perhaps something related to the outside world, rather than internal relevance). Again are we to assume that to score an economic gain that makes it easier for people to pay the foreign thing called tax, certain crops should be cultivated because they will provide a surplus, regardless of the effect on other cultural configurations. Now, the anthropologist comes into the picture so that the disruptive effect of these problems may be avoided. Otherwise the doctor, teacher and agriculturalist should be trained in anthropology before entering such cross-cultural employment. My question is, then: does not the validation of these programs also validate the Christian mission?

This is an anthropological question (not missiological). All three examples mentioned above destroy the local religion. Unless a functional substitute is found a void is created, and this is step number one towards a subsequent nativistic movement. It is anthropologically irresponsible to leave a communal society without a religion. Again, if we consider the native anthropology of most tribal peoples we discover they conceptualized mankind, as most of us do, in terms of body, mind and spirit (or soul). They have a precise creed for each domain, but the creeds integrate and interact. They form a *cultural cluster,* and you cannot change one without involving another. Together they resist change: together they change. I have followed up this cohesion of conceptual anthropology with about a dozen different tribes, and I am satisfied that it is anthropologically irresponsible to set out programs to meet the needs of two dimensions and to deny the needs of the third. Furthermore, the anthropologist, who, say, because he is an agnostic himself, denies the tribal person his or her tripartite conceptual anthropology, is as egocentric and ethnocentric as any missionary I know; and if he goes so far as to raise the question of the separation of Church and State, or the supposed irrelevance of religion, or the supposed scientific assumption of its approaching demise, I must also add that his manifest ethnocentricity is most deplorable for an anthropologist. Yet there are such anthropologists. No! For anthropology to be consistent within itself, if there is such a legitimate thing as *applied* anthropology we must allow its application to the Christian mission.

I have been pursuing a purely anthropological argument, namely that these forms of human betterment must stand as a cultural cluster. When a people becomes culturally ready for change the whole cluster is disposed to change in cohesion. Everywhere throughout the tribal world today acculturation and human betterment programs are associated with religious change—to Christianity, to Islam, to Communism (phenomenologically religious) or to a drastically modified Neo-paganism. This is a manifest fact of current history, and I find it quite irresponsible that medical and educational change should be stimulated but religious change obstructed. The anthropological argument does not stand alone.

One could trace the record of conversion to Christianity through history. Or in recent times, for which the documentation is more superior, one could consider the great revivals, like Timothy L. Smith (1980) and J. Edwin Orr (1975, for example) have done. Time and time again we find spiritual revival accompanied by social reforms. Some of these, like the Wesleyan Revival, had such effects that started new dimensions of progress that are still going on. Only the other day I read two reviews of sociological studies which reached the same findings of this interrelationship of mankind's basic needs—body, mind and spirit.

Theologically we hear much today about the importance of "the whole person." It is a term of convenience used by theologians and theorists to emphasize a dimension they might consider neglected. It is often used by those who contend that the Church attends to souls and forgets bodies. It may also be used by those who contend the opposite. The inconsistent part of our academic world today is that having sacrificed any cultural relativism at the level of technical advice and various "progress" programs, which are as paternalistic and ethnocentric as they could possibly be; it still persists in cultural relativism in the area of religion, and asks the question: why mission at all? Why not leave them in their state of happiness? This is probably one of the most common questions asked of missionaries by university undergraduates. Therefore, it is encouraging to find an eminent anthropologist like Goldschmidt committing himself in writing with the declaration that "we anthropologists must rid ourselves of the Rousseauean 'good savage.'" He was indeed discussing the dysfunction of societies and how to deal with the problem anthropologically, as he said: "There are enough instances on record of primitive peoples not being happy in their own customs, but not knowing how to escape them" (1966:138). The two things which impress me most about anthropology (as far as missiology is concerned) are (1) the number of basic concepts and models that speak to the situations with which we ourselves are trying to grapple, and (2) the number of significant shifts in the theory of anthropology in the post-war years that have made the discipline both more accessible and more acceptable to us. I believe the time has come for some vigorous thrusts in the redefinition of missiology in anthropological terms.

With respect to the relationship of history and missiology, again I feel we need a forward thrust and a bold rewriting, from a dynamic rather than a systematic point of view. With the passing of colonialism has come a terrific availability of documents, primary sources which were jealously guarded are now at hand. This will have to be ethnohistory. The new tools of history and anthropology, for data collecting, processing, copying and reporting, are available. The new day, or better, the new era of Christian mission is upon us. The continuity lies in the message; but the forms and approaches are certainly going to be quite different. The mission itself is an abiding thing—at least "until He comes," but the new missiology has yet to be worked out. The tools from history, anthropology and the other disciplines, we have beside us. We have to learn how to use them for our own purposes. As yet we are not quite certain what to expect; but the new discipline of missiology is beginning to materialize before our eyes.

BIBLIOGRAPHY

American Anthropologist

Allen, C. H.
1950　"The Marching Rule in the British Solomon Islands Protectorate: An Analytical Survey." Canberra: Microfilm, ANU.

Allen, Roland
1927　*The Spontaneous Expansion of the Church and the Causes Which Hinder It.* London: World Dominion Press.
1962　"Pentecost and the World." *The Ministry of the Spirit.* Ed., David M. Paton. Grand Rapids: Wm. B. Eerdmans Pub. Co.
1965　*Missionary Methods: St. Paul's or Ours?* Grand Rapids: Wm. B. Eerdmans Pub. Co.

Anonymous
1953　"Diognetus, Letter to" in Library of Christian Classics. Vol. I. *Early Christian Fathers.* Ed., C. S. Richardson.

Anthropological Quarterly

Arnesberg, C. M. and A. H. Niehoff
1964　*Introducing Social Change: A Manual for Americans Overseas.* Chicago: Aldine Publishing Co.

Attenborough, David
1960　*Quest in Paradise.* London: Lutterworth Press.

Ayer, J.C., Jr.
1952　*A Source Book for Ancient Church History.* New York: Charles Scribner's Sons.

Baeta, C.G.
1962　*Prophetism in Ghana.* London: S.C.M. Press, Ltd.

Bainton, Roland H.
1960　*Early Christianity.* Princeton: D. Van Nostrand Co., Inc.

Barbour, Ian
1974　*Myths, Models and Paradigms: A Comparative Study in Science and Religion.* New York: Harper and Row.

Barclay, William
1956　*A New Testament Wordbook.* London: S.C.M. Press.

Barnett, Homer G.
1940　"Cultural Processes." *American Anthropologist* 42:21-48.
1953　*Innovation: The Basis of Cultural Change.* New York: McGraw-Hill Book Co.
1956　*Anthropology and Administration.* Evanston: Row, Peterson Co.

Barrett, David B.
1968   *Schism and Renewal in Africa.* Nairobi: Oxford University Press.
1969   "Are Your Missions Big Enough?" *Church Growth Bulletin* V, 5:362-366.
1970   "A.D. 2000: 350 Million Christians in Africa." *International Review of Mission* X, 233:39-54.

Barzun, Jacques and H.F. Graff
1962   *The Modern Researcher.* New York: Harcourt, Brace & World, Inc.

Bavinck, Johan H.
1964   *An Introduction to the Science of Mission.* Philadelphia: Presbyterian and Reformed.

Beals, R.L. and H. Hoijer
1954   *An Introduction to Anthropology.* New York: The Macmillan Co.

Bede, The Venerable
1963   *Ecclesiastical History of the English Nation.* Giles' revision of translation. New York: Dutton.

Belshaw, Cyril S.
1950   "The Significance of Modern Cults in Melanesian Development." *The Australian Outlook* IV: 116-125.
1954   *Changing Melanesia. Melbourne: Oxford University Press.*

Benedict, Ruth
1934   *Patterns of Culture.* Boston: Houghton, Mifflin Co.

Benson
n/d   *The East and the West.*

Berkhofer, Robt. F., Jr.
1963   "Protestants, Pagans and Sequences among the North American Indians 1760-1860." *Ethnohistory* 10: 203-232.

Blaiklock, E.M.
1951   *The Christian in Pagan Society.* London: The Tyndale Press.

Bliss, E.M.
1897   *A Concise History of Missions.* New York: Fleming K. Revell Co.

Bloch, Mark
1964   *The Historian's Craft.* Trans. by Peter Putnam. New York: Vintage Books.

Boas, Franz
    1940   *Race, Language and Culture.* New York: The Macmillan
            Co.

Bowman, John W.
    1943   *The Intention of Jesus.* Philadelphia: Westminster.

Bradshaw, Malcolm R.
    1969   *Church Growth Through Evangelism-in-Depth.* Pasadena:
            William Carey Library.

Bready, J. Wesley
    1938   *England Before and After Wesley.* London: Hodder and
            Stoughton, Ltd.
    1942   *This Freedom Whence?.* New York: American Tract Society.

Buck, Peter H.
    1939   *Anthropology and Religion.* New Haven: Yale University.

Bunker, Robert and John Adair
    1959   *The First Look at Strangers.* New Brunswick, NJ: Rutgers
            University Press.

Burckhardt, Jacob
    1949   *The Age of Constantine the Great.* London: Routledge and
            Kegan Paul Ltd.

Carey, William
    1792   *An Enquiry into the Obligations of Christians to Use Means*
            for the Conversion of the Heathens. London: Hodder and
            Stoughton (1892 Facsimile).

Carr, E.H.
    1963   *What is History?* New York: Alfred A. Knopf.

Carrel, Alexis
    1938   *Man the Unknown.* New York: Cornwall Press.

Clark, Sidney J.W.
    1928   *The Indigenous Church.* London: World Dominion Press.
    1933   *Indigenous Fruits.* London: World Dominion Press.

Clemhout, Simone
    1964   "Typology of Nativistic Movements." *Man* 64: 14-15.

Codrington, R.H.
    1894   *Story of a Melanesian Deacon: Clement Maran.* Translated.
            Brighton: Society for Promoting Christian Knowledge.

Coulson, C.A.
1955   *Science and Christian Belief.* Chapel Hill: University of North Carolina Press.
1956   "Nuclear Power and Christian Responsibility." *Proceedings World Methodist Conference,* Lake Junaluska.

Cranfield, C.E.B.
1957   "Fellowship, Communion," *A Theological Word Book of the Bible.* Ed., Alan Richardson. London: S.C.M. Press, 81-83.

Crocombe, Ron
1954   "The Theological Student's Walkout, Raxoconga 1954." *Journal of the Polynesian Society* 79: 6-21.

Curriculum Committee on Missionary Training (C.C.M.T.)
1974   Report.

Davis, J.M.
1938   *The Batak Church: An Account of the Organization, Policies and Growth of the Christian Community of the Bataks of Northern Sumatra.* Dept. of Social and Industrial Research of the International Missionary Council.

Dearing, F.M., Sec.
1961   *Theological Education in the Pacific.* London: T.E.F. Committee of the International Missionary Council.

Deck, Norman
c1907 to 1927   *Dr. Deck's Letter.* A quarterly letter.

Deferrari, R.J. (Trans.)
1953   *Eusebius Pamphili: Ecclesiastical History Books.* Vol. 1-5. New York: Fathers of the Church, Inc.

De Quincey, Thomas
n/d   "On the Knocking at the Gate in *Macbeth." Masterworks of English Prose.* Eds., Bradley and Stevens. New York: Holt, Rinehart and Winston.

Derrick, R.A.
1936   *Course in Civics for Use in Fijian Schools.* Suva: Government Printer.

Durkheim, Emile
1961   *The Elementary Forms of Religious Life.* New York: Collier Books. Originally published 1912.
1962   *Rules of Sociological Method. New York: Free Press of Glencoe. Originally published 1938.*

Edman, V.R.
1949   *The Light in Dark Ages.* Wheaton: Van Kampen Press.

English, P.W.
1966   *City and Village in Iran.* Madison: University of Wisconsin Press.

Fichter, Joseph H.
1957   "The Marginal Catholic: An Institutional Approach." *Religion, Society and the Individual.* Ed., J. Milton Yinger. New York: The Macmillan Co., pp. 423-433.

Firth, Raymond
1963   *We, the Tikopia.* Boston: Beacon Press.

Foster, George M.
1962   *Traditional Cultures and the Impact of Technological Change.* New York: Harper and Row.
1969   *Applied Anthropology.* Boston: Little, Brown and Co.

Fox, Charles E.
1962   *Kakamora.* London: Hodder and Stoughton.

Frazer, Sir J.G.
1935   *The Golden Bough.* 12 vols. New York: Macmillan.

Frerichs, A.C.
1957   *Anutu Conquers in New Guinea.* Columbus: Wartburg Press.

Gardner-Smith, P. and F.J. Foakes-Jackson
1934   *The Expansion of the Christian Church.*   Cambridge: University Press.

(Ghana)
1958   *The Ghana Assembly of the International Missionary Council.* London: Edinburgh House Press.

Gieseler, J.C.L.
1854   *A Compendium of Ecclesiastical History,* trans. from German by S. Davidson. Vol. 1.

Gibbon, Edward
1923   *History of Christianity.* New York: Peter Eckler.

Gjessing, Gutorm
1968   "The Social Responsibility of the Social Scientist." *Current Anthropology* 9: 397-403.

Glazer, N. and D.P. Moynihan
1963   *Beyond the Melting Pot.* Cambridge, MA: MIT Press.

Glover, Robert Hall
1960   *The Progress of World-wide Missions.* Revised. New York: Harper.

Goldenweiser, A.
1937   *Anthropology: An Introduction to Primitive Culture.* 1946 ed. New York: F.S. Crofts & Co.

Goldie, John F.
   1917   *District Report.*

Goldschmidt, Walter
   1966   *Comparative Functionalism: An Essay in Anthropological Theory.* Berkeley: University of California Press.

Gottschalk, Louis
   1969   *Understanding of History.* New York: Alfred A. Knopf.

Gramberg, B.W.G.
   1942   "The Batak Church in Fiery Trails." *International Review of Missions* 31: 322-328.

Green, Brian
   1951   *The Practice of Evangelism.* London: Hodder and Stoughton.

Green, Michael
   1970   *Evangelism in the Early Church.* Grand Rapids: Wm. B. Eerdmans Pub. Co.

Green, Samuel G.
   1907   *A Handbook of Church History from the Apostolic Era to the Dawn of the Reformation.* London: The Religious Tract Society.

Guiart, Jean
   n/d   *Destin D'une Eglise Et D'un Peuple.* Paris: Directeur d'etude a l'Ecole Pratique des Hautes Etudes.
   1951   "John Frum Movement in Tanna." *Oceania* 22: 165-175.
   1956   *Un Siecle et Demi de Contacts Cultures a Tanna.* Paris: Musee de l'Homme.

Gustavson, Carl G.
   1955   *A Preface to History.* New York: McGraw-Hill Book Co.

Hancock, W.K.
   1968   *Attempting History.* Canberra: Australian National University Press.

Harnack, Adolf
   1962   *The Mission and Expansion of Christianity in the First Three Centuries,* trans. by Moffatt. Paperback. New York: Harper Bros.

Hauch, F.
   1965   "Koinonos, Koinoneo, Koinonia, etc." *Theological Dictionary of the New Testament.* Ed., Gerhard Kittel. Bromiley's translation. Grand Rapids: Wm. B. Eerdmans Pub. Co., III: 797-809.

Herskovits, M.J.
1951   *Man and His Works: The Science of Cultural Anthropology.*
New York: Alfred A. Knopf.

Heustis, E.
1963   "Bororo Spiritism as Revitalization." *Practical Anthropology*
10: 187-189.

Hiyane, Antei
1956   "Japan." Symposium on Non-Christian Religions, *Religion
in Life* xxv, 4: 519-531.

H.M.C.S.
1967   *Hawaii: Fact and Fiction.* Honolulu: H.M.C.S.

Hodgkins, L.M.
1903   *Via Christi: An Introduction to the Study of Missions.* New
York: The Macmillan Co.

Hoekendijk, J.C.
1964   *The Church Inside Out.* Eds., L.A. Hoedemaker and Pieter
Tijimes. Trans. by Isaac C. Rottenberg. Philadelphia: The
Westminster Press.

Hogbin, H. Ian
1939   *Experiments in Civilization: The Effects of European
Civilization on a Native Community of the Solomon Islands.*
London: George Routledge & Sons, Ltd.

Hole, Charles
n/d   *Early Missions to and within the British Islands. London:
S.P.C.K.*

Holland, William L., ed.
1955   *Selected Documents of the Bandung Conference.* New York:
Institute of Pacific Relations.

Horowitz, Irving Louis
1968   *Studies in the Life Cycle of Social Science.* Chicago: Aldine
Publishing Co.

Howe, Reuel L.
1963   *The Miracle of Dialogue.* Connecticut: The Seabury Press.

Howells, W.W.
1948   *The Heathens: Primitive Man and His Religions.* New York:
Doubleday.

Hunter, Archibald M.
1961   *Paul and His Predecessors.* Philadelphia: Westminster.

I.R.M.

    International Review of Missions. Annual surveys used:
    1938 (vol. 27), 1939 (vol. 28), 1941 (vol. 30), 1942 (vol. 31),
    1945 (vol. 34), 1946 (vol. 35), 1947 (vol. 36).

Jones, A.H.M.

    1962   *Constantine and the Conversion of Europe.* New York:
    Collier Books.

Judge, E.A.

    1960   *The Social Pattern of Christian Groups in the First Century.*
    London: The Tyndale Press.

Kahn, T.S.

    1962   *The Structure of Scientific Revolutions.* Chicago: University
    of Chicago Press.

Kamma, F. Ch.

    1972   *Koreri.* The Hague: Martinus Nyhoff.

Keesing, Felix M.

    1934   *Modern Samoa: Its Government and Changing Life.* London:
    George Allen & Unwin.

    1963   *Cultural Anthropology: The Science of Custom.* New York:
    Holt, Rinehart & Winston.

Keesing, Robert M. and Felix M. Keesing

    1968   *New Perspectives in Cultural Anthropology.* New York: Holt,
    Rinehart & Winston.

King, Arden R.

    1969   "The Old Ethnography: The Consciousness of Man."
    Concepts and Assumptions in Contemporary Anthropology.
    Athens, GA: Southern Anthropology Society, University of
    Georgia Press.

King, Joseph

    1902   "Oceania." *Christianity Anno Domini 1901. Vol. 1. Ed.,*
    William D. Grant. New York: Chauncey Holt.

Kluckhohn, Clyde

    1969   *Mirror for Man: A Survey of Human Behavior and Social*
    Attitudes. New York: Whittlesea House.

Kobben, A.J.F.

    1960   "Prophet Movements as an Expression of Social Protest."
    International Archives of Ethnography 49: 117-164.

Kraemer, H.

    1938   "The Netherland East Indies." *Interpretative Statistical*
    Survey of the World Mission of the Christian Church. New
    York: International Missionary Council.

    1953   "The Church in Non-Communist Muslim Asia." *Interna-*
    tional Review of Missions 42: 144-150.

Kroeber, A.L.
  1948   *Anthropology.* New York: Harcourt Brace & Co.

Lalive d'Epinay, Christian
  1969   *Haven of the Masses: A Study of the Pentecostal Movement
          in Chile.* London: Lutterworth Press.

Lanternari, Vittorio
  1963   *The Religions of the Oppressed.* New York: Alfred Knopf.

Latourette, K.S.
  1938a   *The First Five Centuries.* Vol. I of *A History of the Expansion
          of Christianity.* New York: Harper & Bros.
     b   *The Thousand Years of Uncertainty.* Vol. II of *A History of
          the Expansion of Christianity.* New York: Harper & Bros.
  1940   *Anno Domini: Jesus, History, and God.* New York: Harper
          & Bros.

Lausanne Committee on World Evangelization (L.C.W.E.)
  1978a   *The Pasadena Consultation—Homogeneous Unit,* Occa-
          sional Paper #1.
     b   *The Willowbank Report—Gospel and Culture.* Occasional
          Paper #2 .

Lavisse, Ernest
  1918   *Histoire de France.* 18 vols. Paris: A. Colin.

Law, Howard W.
  1968   *Winning a Hearing: An Introduction to Missionary Anthro-
          pology Linguistics.* Grand Rapids: Wm. B. Eerdmans Pub.
          Co.

Lawrence, Brother
  1958   *The Practice of the Presence of God.* Westwood, NJ: Fleming
          H. Revell Co.

Lawrence, Peter
  1964   *Road Belong Cargo.* Manchester: The University Press.

Leeson, I.
  1952   "Bibliography of Cargo Cults and Other Nativistic Move-
          ments in the South Pacific." Sydney: South Pacific Technical
          Paper No. 37.

Lessa, William A. and E.Z. Vogt, eds.
  1958   *Reader in Comparative Religion.* Evanston: Row, Peterson
          & Co.

Lindsell, Harold
  1968   "Missionary Imperatives: A Conservative Evangelical
          Exposition." *Protestant Cross-Currents in Mission.* Ed.
          Norman A. Horner. Nashville: Abingdon Press.

Linton, Ralph
1936   *The Study of Man.* New York: Appleton-Century-Crofts.
1943   "Nativistic Movements." *American Anthropologist* XLV: 230-240.

Linton, Ralph, ed.
1945   *Science of Man in the World Crisis.* New York: Columbia University Press.

Loomis, Albertine
1966   *Grapes of Cannan: Hawaii 1820.* Honolulu: Hawaiian Mission Children's Society.

Lovett, Richard
1879   *The History of the London Missionary Society: 1795-1895.* Vol. 1. London: Oxford University.

Lowie, R.H.
1920   *Primitive Society.* New York: Horace Liveright, 1961.
1952   *Primitive Religion.* London: Peter Owen.
1963   "Religion in Human Life." *American Anthropology* 65: 532-542.

Luzbetak, L.J.
1963   *The Church and Cultures.* Techny, IL: Divine Word Publishers.

Malinowski, Bronislaw
1931   Article in *Science and Religion.* London: Gerald Howe Ltd., 65-81.
1938a   "The Anthropology of Changing African Cultures." Editorial introductory essay in *Methods of Study of Culture Contact in Africa.* London: International African Institute (OUP).
  b   *Methods of Study of Culture Contact in Africa.* London: Oxford University Press.
1945   *The Dynamics of Cultural Change.* New Haven: Yale University Press.
1948   *Magic, Science and Religion.* New York: Doubleday & Co.

Mandelbaum, David
1958   *Selected Writings of Edward Sapir in Language, Culture and Personality.* Berkeley: University of California Press.

Marett, R.R.
1914   *The Threshold of Religion.* London: Macmillan.

Mariner, William
1827   *Account of the Natives of the Tonga Islands in the South Pacific Ocean.* Ed. J. Martin. 2 Vols. London: J. Constable.

Massie, J.
    n/d   *I & II Corinthians (Century Bible)*. Edinburgh: T.C. & E.C. Jack.

Maurier, Henri
    1968   *The Other Covenant: A Theology of Paganism*. New York: Newman Press.

McGavran, Donald A.
    1955a *The Church in a Revolutionary Age*. St. Louis: Christian Board of Publications (multigraphed).
       b *Bridges of God*. London: World Dominion Press.
    1959   *How Churches Grow*. London: World Dominion Press.
    1970   *Understanding Church Growth*. Grand Rapids: Wm. B. Eerdmans Pub. Co.

McGavran, Donald A., John Huegel and Jack Taylor
    1963   *Church Growth in Mexico*. Grand Rapids: Wm. B. Eerdmans Pub. Co.

McGlothlin, W.J.
    1914   *A Guide to the Study of Church History*. New York: G.H. Doran Co.

McLeish, Alexander
    1934   *Jesus Christ and World Evangelization*. London: Lutterworth Press.

McNairn, A.S.
    1934   *Native Church: Exotic or Indigenous*. London: World Dominion Press.

Mead, Margaret
    1955   *Cultural Patterns and Technological Change*. New York: The New American Library.
    1961   *New Lives for Old*. New York: Mentor Books.
    1969   *Culture and Commitment*. Garden City, NY: Doubleday.
    1970   *Culture and Commitment: A Study of the Generation Gap*. Garden City: Doubleday & Co., Inc.

Melanesian Institute of Pastoral and Socio-economic Service
    1974   *The Church and Adjustment Movements*. Ed., Theodor Ahrens. Point 1, 1974, "Forum For Melanesian Affairs."

Merivale, Charles
    1866   *The Conversion of the Northern Nations*. London: Longmans, Green & Co.

Metcalfe, John F.
    n/d   *Solomon Damusoe*. An unpublished manuscript.

Michener, James A.
1959   *Hawaii.* New York: Random House.

Miller, Donald G.
1966   *The Nature and Mission of the Church.* Richmond: John Knox Press.

Miller, F.S.
1939   *The Gospel in Korea.* New York: Fleming H. Revell.

Minear, Paul S.
1948   *Eyes of Faith: A Study in the Biblical Point of View.* London: Lutterworth Press.

Missionary Herald
1820-1 "Correspondence from Hawaii."

Mitchell, Howard E.
1969   "The Urban Crisis and Search for Identity." *Social Casework* 50, 1:10-15.

Myklebust, Olav Guttorm
1955   *The Study of Missions in Theological Education.* 2 Vols. Oslo: Egede Instituttet.

Nadel, S.F.
1958   *The Foundations of Social Anthropology.* London: Cohen & West.

Nida, Eugene
1954   *Customs and Cultures: Anthropology for Christian Missions.* New York: Harper & Row.

1960   *Message and Mission.* New York: Harper & Bros.

1962   "Initiation Rites and Culture Themes." *Practical Anthropology* 9, 4: 145-150.

Nock, Arthur Darby
1964   *Early Gentile Christianity and its Helenistic Background.* New York: Harper & Row.

O'Farrell, M.J.
n/d   *The Life of St. Patrick.* New York: P.J. Kennedy & Sons.

Oosthuizen, G.C.
1968   *Post-Christianity in Africa.* Grand Rapids: Wm. B. Eerdmans Pub. Co.

Opler, M.E.
1946   "Themes as Dynamic Forces in Culture." *American Journal of Sociology* 51: 198-206.

1948   "Some Recently Developed Concepts Relating to Culture." *Southwest Journal of Anthropology* 4: 120.

1959   "Components, Assemblage and Theme in Cultural Integration and Differentiation." *American Anthropology* 61: 955-962.

Orr, James
1899   *Neglected Factors in the Study of the Early Progress of Christianity.* London: Hodder & Stoughton.

Orr, J. Edwin
1975   *The Flaming Tongue: Evangelical Awakenings 1900–.* Second edition, revised. Chicago: Moody Press.

Pargellis, Stanley
1957   "The Problem of American Indian History." *Ethnohistory* 4: 111-124.

Parrinder, G.
1958   *Witchcraft.* London: Penguin Books.

Paton, David M.
1953   *Christian Missions and the Judgement of God.* London: S.C.M. Press.

Peill, S.G. and W.F. Rowlands
1930a   "Church Planting in Siachang, North China." *Church Planting.* London: World Dominion Press.
      b "Conditions of the Birth of a Living Church." *Church Planting.* London: World Dominion Press.

Penny, Alfred
1888   *Ten Years in Melanesia.* London: Wells Gardner, Darton & Co.

Pickett, J. Waskom
1963   *Dynamics of Church Growth.* New York: Abingdon Press.

Pozas, R.
1962   *Juan, the Chamula: An Ethnological Reconstruction of the Life of a Mexican Indian.* Berkeley: University of California Press.

Practical Anthropology

Radin, Paul
1927   *Primitive Man as a Philosopher.* New York: D. Appleton & Co. (Dover, 1957).
1957   *Primitive Religion.* New York: Dover Publications.

Read, William R.
1965   *New Patterns of Church Growth in Brazil.* Grand Rapids: Wm. B. Eerdmans Pub. Co.

Renier, G.J.
1965   *History: Its Purpose and Method.* New York: Harper & Row.

Rivers, W.H.R.
1922   *Depopulation of Melanesia.* Cambridge: The University Press.
1924   *Medicine, Magic, Religion.* London: Kegan Paul, Trench & Trubner.

Robinson, C.H.
  1917   *The Conversion of Europe.* London: Longmans, Green & Co.

Robinson, J.H.
  1904   *Readings in European History.* Vol. 1. Boston: Ginn & Co.

Rowlands, W.F.
  1931   *Indigenous Ideals in Practice.* London: World Dominion Press.

Sahlins, Marshall D.
  1962   *Moala: Culture and Nature on a Fijian Island.* Ann Arbor: University of Michigan Press.

Saltman, Paul D.
  1970   "The Village Agnostic Finds a Faith." *Los Angeles Times,* Sun., Sept. 13.

Sapir, Edward
  1924   "Culture, Genuine and Spurious." *American Journal of Sociology* 29: 401-429.
  1949a   *Language.* New York: Harcourt Brace & Co.
     b   *Selected Writings.* Ed. by D.G. Mandelbaum. Berkeley: University of California Press.

Scherer, James
  1964   *Missionary, Go Home! A Reappraisal of the Christian Mission.* Englewood Cliffs: Prentice-Hall, Inc.
  1970   "The Life and Growth of Churches in Mission." *International Review of Missions* LX: 125-35.

Schwartz, Theodore
  1962   *The Paliau Movement in the Admiralty Islands, 1946-1954.* New York: American Museum of Natural History, Anthropological Papers, Vol. 49.
  1971   "Cargo-Cult Frenzy in the South Seas." *Psychology Today* 51, 4: 102-03.

Selwyn, J.R.
  1897   *Pastoral Work in the Colonies and on the Mission Field.* Brighton: Assn. for Promoting Christian Knowledge.

Sevenster, A.
  1974   "Why Study Church History?" *The South East Asia Journal of Theology* 15: 80-83.

Shearer, Roy E.
  1967   "A Christian Functional Substitute for Ancestor Worship." *Church Growth Bulletin* IV, 2: 258-60.

Sherif, Muzafer
   1936   *The Psychology of Social Norms.* New York: Harper &
           Bros.
Shineberg, Dorothy
   1967   *They Came for Sandalwood.* Melbourne: Melbourne Univer-
           sity Press.
Smalley, William A., ed.
   1967   *Readings in Missionary Anthropology. New York: Practical
           Anthropology.*

Smith, A. H. and J. L. Fischer, eds.
   1970   *Anthropology.* Englewood Cliffs: Prentice Hall, Inc.
Smith, George
   1897   *Short History of Christian Missions.* Edinburgh: T. & T.
           Clark.
Smith, Gordon H.
   1945   *The Missionary and Anthropology.* Chicago: Moody Press.
Smith, Timothy L.
   1980   *Revivalism and Social Reform.* Originally published 1957.
           Baltimore: John Hopkins University Press.
Snaith, Norman F.
   1944   Distinctive Ideas of the Old Testament. London: Epworth
           Press.
Spicer, Ed. H., ed.
   1952   *Human Problems in Technological Change.* New York:
           John Wiley Sons.
Starkey, L.M., Jr.
   1965   *The Holy Spirit at Work in the Church.* Nashville: Abingdon.
Steenberghen, Pera Rombaut
   1959   "Neo-Paganism in Africa." Trans. from the French. *Frontier*
           2: 287-288.
Stern, Fritz. ed.
   1956   *The Varieties of History.* New York: World Publishing Co.
Stock, Eugene
   1899   *History of the Church Missionary Society.* 3 vols. London:
           Church Missionary Society.
Stavrianos, L.S.
   1966   *The Epic of Modern Man.* Englewood Cliffs: Prentice-Hall,
           Inc.

Stubbs, W.M.
1913   *How Europe was Won for Christianity.* New York: Fleming H. Revell Co.

Sturtevant, William C.
1966   "Anthropology, History and Ethnohistory." *Ethnohistory* 13: 1-51.

Sundkler, Bengt
1961   *Bantu Prophets in South Africa.* New York: Oxford University.

Taber, Charles and Tetsunao Yamamori, eds.
1975   *Christopaganism or Indigenous Christianity?* Pasadena: William Carey Library.

Tanner, R.E.W.
1967   *Transition in African Beliefs.* New York: Maryknoll Publications.

Taylor, John V. and Dorothea Lehmann
1961   *Christians of the Copper Belt: The Growth of the Church in Northern Rhodesia.* London: S.C.M. Press.

Tillich, Paul
1948   *The Shaking of the Foundations.* New York: Chas. Scribner's Sons.

Tippett, Alan R.
1947   "Fiji's Tomorrow." *The Link.* Also reprinted as a pamphlet.
1954   *The Christian: Fiji, 1835-67.* Auckland: Institute Printing & Publishing Society.
1956a   *The Nineteenth Century Labour Trade in the South Pacific.* M.A. Thesis, Washington, D.C.: American University.
      b "Methodism in the Southwest Pacific." *Proceedings World Methodist Conference.* Lake Junalusk, North Carolina.
1958   *The Integrating Gospel: Ethnological and Ethnolinguistic Study of the Communication of the Gospel.* Bound Volume. Pasadena: Fuller School of World Mission.
1960   *His Mission and Ours.* Bound Volume. Pasadena: Fuller School of World Mission.
1961   "A Historical Survey of the Character and Training of the Fijian Ministry." Davuilevu: Methodist Church in Fiji, (duplicated).
1963   "Initiation Rites and Functional Substitutes." *Practical Anthropology* 10: 66-70.

1964a "A Church Is Built." Fiji: Methodist Conference.

b *The Acceptance and Rejection of Christianity: Essays and Research 1962-1964.* Bound Volume. Pasadena: Fuller School of World Mission.

1965 "The Church's Cutting Edge." *The Spectator,* August 18.

1966 "Church Growth or Else!" *World Vision Magazine,* February.

1967a *Solomon Islands Christianity.* London: Lutterworth Press. Reprinted 1975 by William Carey Library, Pasadena.

b "The Growth of an Indigenous Church." Pasadena: Fuller School of World Mission (duplicated).

c "Religious Group Conversion in Non-Western Society." Research in Progress, Paper #11. Pasadena: Fuller School of World Mission.

1968 *Fijian Material Culture: A Study in Cultural Context, Function and Change.* Honolulu: Bishop Museum Press.

1969a "The Components of Missionary Theory." *Church Growth Bulletin* VI: 1-3.

b "From Awareness to Decision-Making." Research in Progress, Paper #12. Pasadena: Fuller School of World Mission.

1970a *Church Growth and the Word of God.* Grand Rapids: Wm. B. Eerdmans Pub. Co.

b *Peoples of Southwest Ethiopia.* Pasadena: William Carey Library.

1971 *People Movements in Southern Polynesia.* Chicago: Moody Press.

1972 *Adventures in Missiology.* Bound Volume. Pasadena: Fuller School of World Mission.

1973a *Verdict Theology in Missionary Theory.* Pasadena: William Carey Library (2nd edition).

b "The Phenomenology of Worship, Conversion and Brotherhood." *Religious Experience: Its Nature and Function in the Human Psyche.* Ed., Maloney. Springfield: Chas. C. Thomas.

c *Aspects of Pacific Ethnohistory.* Pasadena: William Carey Library.

1974a "Extension of the Cross-Cultural Conversion Model." Research in Progress, Paper #13. Pasadena: School of World Mission.

b "The Two-Dimensional Fellowship." *Missiology* II, 3: 275-278.

Turner, Harold W.
  1967   *African Independent Church.* London: Oxford.
  1974   "New Religious Movements." *World Survey Charts.* International Association for Mission Studies, Annual Meeting, Frankfurt.

Turner, Victor
  1967   *The Forest of Symbols: Aspects of Ndembu Ritual.* Ithaca: Cornell University Press.

Tylor, E.B.
  1871   Primitive Culture. 2 Vols. London: John Murray.

Van Gennep, A.
  1960   *Les Rites de Passage.* Paris: Nourry. English edition 1960, University of Chicago Press. Originally published 1909.

Vansina, Jan
  1970   "How the Kingdom of the Great Makoko and Certain Clapperless Bells Became Topics for Research." *The Historian's Workshop.* Trans. by L.P. Curtis, Jr. New York: Alfred A. Knopf.

Vatican II
  1966   "Decree on the Mission of the Church." *The Documents of Vatican II.* Ed., W. M. Abbott, 580-633.

Venn, Henry
  n/d   "Native Church Organization." Official Paper. London: Church Missionary Society.

Verwiebe, E.
  1938   "The Youth Problem in the Batak Church in Sumatra." *International Review of Missions* 27: 208-211.

Vicedom, George F.
  1961   *Church and People in New Guinea.* London: Lutterworth Press.
  1965   *The Mission of God: An Introduction to the Theology of Mission.* Translated by G. Thiele and D. Hilgendorf. St. Louis: Concordia Publishing House.

Visser't Hooft, W.A.
  1963   *No Other Name.* Philadelphia: The Westminster Press.

Vriens, Livinus et al
  1960   A Critical Bibliography of Missiology. Nijmegen: Bestelcentrale.

Walbourn, F.B.
  1961   *East African Rebels: Some African Independent Churches.* London: S.C.M. Press.

Walker, F.D.
  1930 *Romance of the Black River: The Story of the C.M.S. Nigeria Mission.* London: Church Missionary Society.

Wallace, Anthony F.C.
  1956a "Revitalization Movements." *American Anthropologist* 58: 264-281.
     b "New Religions Among the Delaware Indians, 1600-1900." *Southwestern Journal of Anthropology* 12: 1-21.
  1966 *Religion: An Anthropological View.* New York: Random House.

Wallis, W.D.
  1939 *Religion in Primitive Society.* New York: F.S. Crofts & Co.

Warneck, J.
  1911 "The Growth of the Church Among the Bataks." *International Review of Missions* 1: 20-43.
  1954 *The Living Christ and Dying Heathenism.* Trans. by N. Buchanan. Grand Rapids: Baker Book House.

Washburn, W.E.
  1961 "Ethnohistory: History 'in the Round.'" *Ethnohistory* 8: 31-48.

Webster, Douglas
  n/d *Should Our Image of Mission Go?* Prism Pamphlet No. 15. London: Blue Star House.

Welch, Adam C.
  1953 *Prophet and Priest in Old Israel.* Oxford: Basil Blackwood.

Wells, Charles L.
  1898 *The Age of Charlemagne.* New York: The Christian Literature Co.

Wesley, John
  1746 "The Means of Grace." *Forty-four Sermons.* London: Epworth Press, 1952, 134-51.
  n/d *Journal.*

Wesleyan Magazine, The

Westcott, B.F.
  1909 *The Two Empires: The Church and the World.* London: Macmillan and Co., Ltd.

White, Lynn T.
  1970 "History and Horseshoe Nails." *The Historian's Workshop.* Trans. by L.P. Curtis, Jr. New York: Alfred A. Knopf, pp. 47-64.

Whitelock, Dorothy
 1964   *The Beginnings of English Society.* England: Harmonds-
         worth. Penguin Books.

Wiant, Bliss
 1946   "Oecumenical Hymnology in China." *International Review
         of Missions* XXXV: 428-434.

Williams, C.
 1968   "The Fellowship," *New Dimensions in Theology Today.
         Vol. IV, The Church.* Philadelphia: The Westminster Press.

Williams, F.E.
 1951   *The Blending of Cultures: An Essay on the Aims of Native
         Education.* Port Moresby: W.A. Bock, Government Printer.

Wilson, Ellen
 1935   *Dr. Welchman of Bugota.* London: Society for Promoting
         Christian Knowledge.

Winter, Ralph W.
 1969   "Will the Extension Seminary Promote Church Growth?"
         Church Growth Bulletin 3: 339-42.
 1970   *The Twenty-Five Unbelievable Years: 1945-1969.* Pasadena:
         William Carey Library.

Wirth, Louis
 1945   "The Problem of Minority Groups." *Science of Man in the
         World Crisis* by Ralph Linton. New York: Columbia Univer-
         sity Press.

Wolf, Eric R.
 1964   *Anthropology.* Englewood Cliffs: Prentice-Hall Inc.

World Council of Churches
 1963   "Consultation on Church Growth." Meeting at Iberville,
         Quebec.
 1965   "On the Evangelization of West Africa Today." Meeting at
         Yaounde, Cameroun.

Worsley, Peter
 1957   *The Trumpet Shall Sound.* London: Macgibbon & Kee.

INDEX OF PERSONS

INDEX OF SUBJECTS

Recombination Theory, 400, 410
Reconciliation, Ministry of, 33, 34, 67, 70, 86
Reform, Capacity for, 232
Reformation, 93, 97, 118, 130, 151, 179, 235, 253
Rejection, xx, 48, 57, 72, 75, 76, 91, 105, 120, 135, 136, 138, 139, 143, 147, 153, 170, 175, 176, 184, 200, 206, 207, 230, 256, 270, 281, 286, 287, 289, 291, 293, 299, 307, 313, 317, 322, 328, 329, 354, 397, 408
Relativism, Cultural, 117, 146, 414, 415, 418
Relativistic Phase, 414
Religion(s), 6, 14, 24, 25, 48, 55, 66, 73, 74, 83, 95-97, 105, 111, 115, 119, 124, 129, 133, 138, 143, 148, 157-162, 166-172, 174, 175, 177-179, 181-183, 186, 188, 189, 192, 195-197, 199, 200, 206, 207, 211-213, 227, 230, 231, 233, 239-241, 248, 256, 260, 269, 274, 280, 292, 294, 296, 297, 313, 314, 316, 323, 324, 325, 329, 332, 339, 340, 369, 385, 396, 400, 409, 410, 414, 417, 418; Comparative, 14, 95, 105, 396; Function of, 160, 161, 166, 409; Great, 239; Integrative Function of, 409; Sieve of, 161; Traditional, 97, 129; Universality of, 410
Religious; Belief, Need for, 7; Change, 50, 60, 61, 87, 88, 91, 157, 162, 163, 168, 169, 171, 175, 178, 179, 185, 222, 223, 252, 255, 262, 274, 288, 354, 408, 412, 415, 418; Conversion, xv, 11, 25, 30, 34, 36, 37, 39, 46, 47, 51, 55-57, 61, 63, 64, 66, 73-77, 82, 83, 90, 91, 94, 105, 120, 123, 128, 129, 132, 133, 135-140, 142, 143, 160-162, 167, 169, 171, 175, 176-179, 182, 184, 185, 187, 191, 199, 200, 205, 210, 212, 223, 227, 237, 247, 252-254, 258-260, 262-269, 272, 286, 293,

309, 312, 313, 322, 327-330, 336, 338, 372, 399, 410, 412, 415, 418; Demoralization, 159, 162-168, 170, 171, 178, 182, 184; Experience, 13, 133, 178, 259, 397; Submersion, 162, 168, 172-174, 178, 182; Structures, 158; Types of, 163, 178
Renewal, 25, 88, 120, 134, 161, 179-182
Rennel Island, 193
Repentance, 54, 85, 232, 237
Research, xiii, xiv, xvi, 13, 14, 19, 26, 40, 47, 61, 76, 80, 87, 97, 117, 118, 121, 125, 129, 132, 133, 135-138, 141, 142, 145, 146, 154, 157, 173, 181, 186, 192, 204, 205, 213, 215, 225, 236, 238, 249, 250, 252, 253, 255, 258, 259, 262, 269, 270, 272, 282, 283, 285, 292, 354, 374, 384, 388, 397-406, 410, 412, 413, 415, 416
Resistance to Change, 228, 286
Responsibility, 14, 27, 28, 33, 49-51, 64, 67, 76, 90, 95, 96, 109, 118, 119, 120, 123, 124, 144, 145, 148-150, 161, 181, 187, 214, 232, 266, 279, 296, 297, 300, 320, 326, 330, 332, 338, 345, 355, 365, 374, 377, 383-385, 388, 390, 407, 414, 415; of the People of God, 14; to Society, 120, 161
Responsibility Enclosure, 67
Resurrection, 15, 23, 42, 52, 69, 82, 247, 249, 256
Revelation, 52, 148, 172, 180, 223, 231, 241, 249, 250, 360
Revitalization, 97, 120, 139, 140, 162, 179-182, 270, 300, 400, 410
Revival, 148, 179, 180, 212, 238, 266, 301, 353, 418
Rights, Human, 414
Rites of Passage, 82, 132, 136, 148, 186, 190, 191, 400, 410
Ritual, 41, 43, 82, 83, 136, 137, 157, 160, 174, 186-188, 190, 192, 193, 196, 259, 265, 276, 283, 325

266,001
T 59;